BLACK EMPIRE

Other titles in
The Northeastern Library of Black Literature,
edited by Richard Yarborough

WILLIAM DEMBY
The Catacombs

W.E.B. DU BOIS
The Quest of the Silver Fleece

JESSIE REDMON FAUSET
There Is Confusion

GAYL JONES
White Rat

JULIAN MAYFIELD
The Hit and *The Long Night*

CLAUDE MCKAY
Home to Harlem

ALBERT MURRAY
Train Whistle Guitar

J. SAUNDERS REDDING
Stranger and Alone

GEORGE S. SCHUYLER
Black No More

RICHARD WRIGHT
Lawd Today

BLACK

GEORGE S. SCHUYLER

COMPRISING

THE BLACK INTERNATIONALE
Story of Black Genius Against the World

AND

BLACK EMPIRE
*An Imaginative Story of a
Great New Civilization in Modern Africa*

EMPIRE

writing as SAMUEL I. BROOKS

Foreword by JOHN A. WILLIAMS

Edited, with an Afterword, by
ROBERT A. HILL & R. KENT RASMUSSEN

Northeastern University Press   BOSTON

Library of Congress Cataloging-in-Publication Data
Schuyler, George Samuel, 1895–
  [Black internationale]
  Black empire / George S. Schuyler ; foreword by John A. Williams ;
edited, with an afterword, by Robert A. Hill & R. Kent Rasmussen.
    p. cm. (The Northeastern library of Black literature)
    ISBN 1–55553–114–8—ISBN 1–55553–118–0 (pbk.)
    1. Adventure stories, American. 2. Afro-Americans—Fiction. 3. Blacks
—Fiction. I. Hill, Robert A., 1943– . II. Rasmussen, R. Kent. III.
Schuyler, George Samuel, 1895– , Black empire. 1991. IV. Title. V. Series
PS3537.C76B54   1991
813'.52—dc20   91–22499

Designed by Ann Twombly

Composed in Meridien by the Marcus Garvey and UNIA Papers Project,
University of California, Los Angeles, and Inprint, Hudson, Massachusetts.
Printed and bound by The Maple-Vail Book Manufacturing Group, Bing-
hamton, New York. The paper is Maple Antique Cream, an acid-free sheet.

MANUFACTURED IN THE UNITED STATES OF AMERICA
96 95 94 93 92 91   5 4 3 2 1

Contents

Foreword, by John A. Williams *ix*

Editorial Statement *xvii*

Black Empire

"The Black Internationale:
Story of Black Genius Against the World" *1*

"Black Empire: An Imaginative Story of
a Great New Civilization in Modern Africa" *143*

Afterword, by Robert A. Hill and R. Kent Rasmussen *259*

Appendixes

A. Schuyler's story notes (ca. 1936–1937) *325*

B. "The Rise of the Black Internationale" (1938) *328*

Bibliography: George S. Schuyler's *Pittsburgh Courier* fiction *337*

Acknowledgments *345*

Foreword

When I was a boy growing up in Syracuse, New York, one of the many jobs I had was delivering black weekly newspapers: the *Afro-American*, the *Chicago Defender*, the local *Progressive Herald*, and the *Pittsburgh Courier*. Occasionally, the daughter of a lieutenant of the local numbers king asked me if I had read a piece by a relative of hers named George Schuyler, who had grown up in town and left to join the army, among other things.

I did not meet him until many years later, although I had by then read much of his writing. At that time he was mainly doing book reviews for the *Courier*. When they were fiercely negative, he did not sign them. I fell victim to at least a couple of these attacks and confronted him personally about them. Schuyler did not deny he had written them; he simply shrugged off my charges of journalistic cowardice, turned his usually well-tailored back, and sidled off. This was during the period when he, and sometimes his daughter, the pianist Philippa (who died in an aircraft crash in Vietnam in 1969), seemed to favor— and quite publicly—any regressive move our government made anywhere in the Third World. For example, during the early 1960s, he was a member of the Katanga Freedom Fighters, which supported Moise Tshombe's secession from the Congo following Patrice Lumumba's assassination. (Schuyler was not the only black newsperson or former newsperson so involved abroad. And others supplied information to the FBI on domestic African-American "radicals" through the 1960s and 1970s.)

Schuyler once told me that he had "done everything and anything a man could do." And indeed, at one time or another he had managed, with A. Philip Randolph, the *Messenger;* served as business manager for the *Crisis* (1937–1944); and returned to the *Courier* to serve as a special correspondent (1944–1964), traveling to South Africa, the West Indies, "French" West Africa, and the Dominican Republic. He was additionally occupied as an editor for the *National News* and as a correspondent for the *New York Evening Post.* And as a correspondent for the North American Newspaper Alliance, he covered Nigeria, Portugal, and East Africa. All this was in addition to having served in the U.S. Army from 1912 to 1918, during which time he rose to the rank of first lieutenant. From 1918 to 1920 he worked as a civil service clerk in the quartermaster corps.

Schuyler was already an ultra-conservative when I met him about 1963. We did two radio shows together, one at the old WLIB studios in Harlem and the other with Barry Gray, downtown. I was amazed at how great a Red-baiter he was. He'd call anyone a communist, and even when I rebutted him with facts certifying the contrary, he never let up. He'd just sit back and smile. He was a charming, good-looking man with a little of the poppycock about him. He bore his age well. Invariably after these debates, in which he forced me to defend nearly everyone, we'd go have a drink, or two, or four. He loved gin martinis and, more important, he could hold them. I liked him, though he was irritating with his politics—which, with something like cool desperation, he never let me forget.

His work some thirty to forty years earlier was certainly memorable enough. Today, one can hardly pick up a book on the Harlem Renaissance or the post-Renaissance period without finding his name in the index. Schuyler was not, however, one of its "stars." His contributions to the literature came in short, often caustic bursts, published in magazines or newspaper columns and features. At a time when the major members of the Renaissance were publishing fiction and poetry, Schuyler's first book, *Racial Intermarriage in the United States* (1929), was nonfiction. His first novel, *Black No More,* was published in 1931, as the Renaissance began to wane.

During this time, Schuyler seemed to be looking in rather than out. Others would write about the world at large, but Schuyler would write about them and their work. In a piece he did for *Phylon* in 1950, "The Van Vechten Revolution," he cuffed those artists who had been upset by Carl Van Vechten's *Nigger Heaven* (1926), dismissing them by noting that they "had not read it but disliked the title," and commenting that Van Vechten "has done more than any single person in this country to create the atmosphere of acceptance of the Negro." He was variously a supporter and a critic of Langston Hughes. But Eugene Gordon, writing in Nancy Cunard's *Negro* (1934), characterized Schuyler as "an opportunist of the most odious sort."

In June 1926 Schuyler published the essay "The Negro-Art Hokum" in the *Nation,* espousing the view that "Aframerican" art should not be considered separate and distinct from American art, and that art, anyway, was something that did not interest the masses. Prior to the essay's publication, one of the *Nation'*s editors sent a copy to Langston Hughes, whose rebuttal, the classic "The Negro Artist and the Racial Mountain," argued that the art produced by black artists derived from, was for, and served the black masses. Clearly, Schuyler thought of himself as belonging to what W. E. B. Du Bois called the "Talented Tenth," a position that is reflected in much of his work.

Schuyler's style and language resembled a mixture of garlic and the tartest possible lemon (he was called the "Black Mencken"). The snakewhip wit and wordplay that laced such essays as "The Negro Art Hokum," and the perception and sardonicism that attend his novel *Black No More,* are not present in "The Black Internationale" and "Black Empire," which were written under the name Samuel I. Brooks (his middle name was Samuel) and serially published in the *Courier* between 1936 and 1938. They are here published together for the first time in book form, under the title *Black Empire.*

I don't know if Schuyler was writing to deadline for each chapter. "The Black Internationale" contains thirty-three chapters and "Black Empire," twenty-nine, for a total of sixty-two. If there were times when he was writing to deadline, then he would have produced about twenty-five hundred words each week, eight pages a chapter, more or less. Although he may have had periods when he did not have ready copy, nevertheless, his achievement over a two-year period exceeds, at least in quantity, even the writing of Charles Dickens. Dickens serialized in monthly publications; the *Courier* was a weekly.

The plots of these serials are "set-ups," with dei ex machina occurring at exactly the right times, and many displays of bravery and intelligence and romance that leap out of the popular imagination of the day. They are narrated in the first person, from the point of view of a former reporter for the *Harlem Blade,* Carl Slater. Slater is fascinated at first sight with Dr. Henry Belsidus, the ruthless, elegant genius who runs a vast, deadly, and secretive organization known to its members as the Black Internationale.

Slater, who is a Columbia University graduate, becomes the doctor's secretary; in this capacity, he is able to describe the doctor's organization and its members in detail. The Black Internationale, we discover, rids itself of spies by dumping them into tanks of acid; other kinds of murders are commonplace, but all are considered small revenges compared to what white civilization has done to black people. We encounter engineers and scientists who are easily able to plan and execute the revenge of a lynching in the South; accumulate wealth to fund farms and construction groups; build an air force; and, with the help of fifty international members, establish a network of religious temples around the world. Dr. Belsidus's companion is Martha Gaskin, a blonde intelligence operative who foments World War II (or something like it) and otherwise serves as Belsidus's conduit to the world's white power structure.

The second half of the novel finds the corps of brilliant African Americans established in Liberia, where they are setting out to liberate Africa from colonial rule. This section has far more action than the first, more tension and conflict; it shows rather than tells, though still from Carl Slater's point of view. It is as though Schuyler himself found detailing action more delightful than describing mere people, places, and things.

"I have led you to victory with your cooperation," Dr. Belsidus proclaims. "Now I shall lead you to a higher civilization than Europe has ever seen, with your consent." This would be the consent of the "Talented Tenth," for time and time again Belsidus summons these "great minds" to meetings, and Slater provides detailed descriptions of their genius, but we never see the masses, without whom the movement would not have been possible. The masses, therefore, it seems to me, are directed by a leadership trained by those in society who have heretofore oppressed both the masses and their leaders. For Schuyler, himself a military man, this leadership included those with training in the military arts.

The novels are a brief nod to the "Back-to-Africa" phase of the Garvey movement, but once that point has been made they become essentially a tribute to a black elite of brilliant men and women under the leadership of Dr. Belsidus, as it gathers its forces to shake off the all-smothering blanket of racism. There are no common people in the novels who are of any importance. Dr. Belsidus's chauffeur, significantly, is described as an "ugly" giant black man who has "bloodshot eyes and bulbous lips." And in "Black Empire," when the Black Internationale is established in Africa, "savages" and "cannibals" are discovered. I cannot say if these negative portraits were as potent to readers then as they may seem to many of us now, some fifty-odd years later, but I find them disturbing elements (somewhat like rooting for Tarzan in the movies instead of the indigenous people) in works that were seemingly designed to instill pride in African Americans of the time. And these elements reflected Schuyler's allegiances precisely; he approved of Van Vechten's "trickle down" theory of integration, in which one must "break the taboo on the highest levels" (i.e., the upper classes) and achieve a progress that will "seep down to the masses."

Schuyler himself said in his late essay on Van Vechten, "As one picture is worth 10,000 words, so one association with an *exceptional* Negro has the impact greater than a ton of pro-Negro propaganda" (italics added). Thus, I think that while Schuyler liked the idea of the Back-to-Africa movement, of black people gathering and making things happen on their own, he didn't think much of Garvey or those who constituted his legions. Schuyler, as did many prominent black persons of the time, believed himself to be an "exceptional" Negro on the "highest" level.

But let me set aside my carping on this aspect of the novels in order to detail some of Schulyer's virtuoso performances. As I read of black ingenuity in these novels, I had the sense that Schuyler must have been reading copiously, including, perhaps, the works of H. G. Wells and the popular science magazines of the day. His Black Internationale intellectuals develop hydroponic or aquicultural farming (growing vegetables in water) in the U.S. and transfer the process to Africa. I don't think this was recognized as a viable method to grow food until the Israelis began to use it, mainly through the drip process, after 1948.

We began to hear about underground aircraft facilities when the Gulf War began early in 1991. The Saudi Arabians had them and it was believed the Iraqis did, too. But we find them in *Black Empire* over half a century earlier. Schuyler's heroes *and* heroines (ahead of his time there, too) developed what we now call the fax machine, skipping over the telecopier that actually preceded the development of the fax. Television, in its swaddling clothes at the time Schuyler wrote the serials, is fully developed here and used in the closed-circuit mode. Undoubtedly, the conception of solar heat for energy had been considered for some time, if not used in rudimentary form. Schuyler's Black Internationale organization develops and uses solar collectors for the energy needed to run its buildings and machines. Once settled in Africa, its members dine on health foods—almost no meat, but plenty of vegetables produced artificially, and no coffee or tea, only natural juices.

On the grimmer side, Schuyler foreshadows the gas chambers the Germans used so prodigiously during World War II, when Martha Gaskin, having gathered the leaders of British industry into a concert hall in London, seals the door and turns on the gas. Similarly, allusions are made in the African scenes to mass euthanasia to rid the race of disease, practiced without benefit of any Nuremberg-like laws. Dr. Belsidus, in the final analysis, is a dictator, a fascist, though his goals are established as moral ones. Like Schuyler, Belsidus is also a soldier, disciplined and ruthless, with little or no use for folk with moderate intelligence or skills. A center pole of fascism is the sense of being superior to all who are not fascists; therefore, an anticommunist stand and a racist stand are vital components in the philosophy. If we substitute national origin for race in these works (for it is evident that Schuyler considered African *Americans* far superior to African *Africans*), their fascist assumptions become quite clear.

I believe Schuyler's conservatism came early on, shaping and reshaping itself until it could be accepted by white conservatives without extensive embarrassment. James Meredith, who integrated the University of Mississippi in 1962, held the opinion that if black Americans took over fifty cities in Africa they could run the continent; I was reminded of that when I read Schuyler's novels. I found myself disturbed by the thought that both Schuyler and Meredith could wind up as ultra-conservatives, Schuyler setting forth his case in his autobiography, *Black and Conservative* (1966), and Meredith turning up as an aide to Senator Jesse Helms of North Carolina for the 1990 election campaign. It was undoubtedly fortunate that Schuyler wrote these novels under a pen name; otherwise it could have been difficult for the white conservatives (assuming they had an interest in the black press) to have embraced him as heartily as they did. On the other hand, perhaps they would think that converts can be more fanatical than those who never undergo change.

Schuyler himself seems to have had little faith in the power of the black press; he says as much in his personal correspondence, but he also has Dr. Belsidus echo his opinion: "One of the greatest mistakes made by minority leaders in the past has been ballyhoo. Therefore we have established no newspapers or magazines, given no talks over the radio, staged no parades or demonstrations. Consequently the enemy has no inkling of what we are doing."

Revenge, racial redemption, and release from white oppression in all its forms seem to be almost mythic urges for several black writers. Chester Himes's unpublished novel, *Plan B,* which called for the destruction of white America through the most violent guerrilla means, is a later work with the same theme Schuyler used in his novels, but Himes isn't writing about a move to Africa or scientific breakthroughs. I like to think that my own novels *Sons of Darkness, Sons of Light* (1969) and, to a lesser extent, *Jacob's Ladder* (1987) are within this tradition.

Despite their "interior" faults, then, Schuyler's two "potboilers" clearly belong to a literary tradition and display a tremendous range of talent and imagination. In another time, he could easily have been one of the great journalists/novelists of the age. But my sense is that ultimately, at the time of his death in 1977, he was another victim of a society that was essentially closed to his talents.

John A. Williams
March 15, 1991
Teaneck, New Jersey

Editorial Statement

When George S. Schuyler wrote the stories that make up *Black Empire,* he had no thought that they would ever appear in book form. He was not attempting to write a carefully integrated, polished novel, but merely weekly installments of newspaper serials. So far as we know, he wrote and submitted each chapter just a week before publication. In all likelihood, as soon as he tossed off a chapter, he went back to work and forgot about the story until the next week's deadline caught up with him. It was inevitable that inconsistencies and crudities in content and style should slip in; however, they hardly mattered. Most of Schuyler's readers saw only one chapter at a time; they scarcely would have noticed minor lapses.

We have taken the title *Black Empire* from the second of Schuyler's two serials. The original chapter numbers of each serial are retained and the *Pittsburgh Courier's* headlines for each installment appear here as chapter titles. The two stories together total just under 95,000 words. The first part, "The Black Internationale," is the longer, with thirty-three chapters; "Black Empire" has twenty-nine. The first serial ran in the *Courier* from November 21, 1936, through July 3, 1937. The sequel ran from October 2, 1937, through April 16, 1938.

The text of the present edition was transcribed from microfilm copies of imperfect, often illegible, newspaper pages. The transcribed texts were later compared to the somewhat less damaged clippings in Schuyler's own scrapbooks at Syracuse University Library. Deciphering problems aside, transcription posed a number of editorial problems. Since Schuyler's original manuscripts have not survived, there is no way to compare what he submitted against what was actually published in the *Courier.* Nothing in his surviving papers indicates that he had any role in editing the published chapters, or that he even took any special interest in what became of his prose, once it left his typewriter.

Schuyler wrote these stories under the name "Samuel I. Brooks," one of several pseudonyms that he used during the 1930s, in order, as he told a colleague, "to avoid monotony." A bibliography at the end of this volume lists all the stories he is known to have published in the *Courier,* along with the various pen names he used.

Since Schuyler is not here to be consulted, we are left with the problem of how to present his work to modern readers. Wholesale copyediting and rewriting might very well achieve a smoother, easier-to-read book; however, it would not be *Schuyler's* book. Equally importantly, it would not be Schuyler's 1930s newspaper serial.

We have chosen to steer a middle course between a totally faithful historical text, such as we would normally publish in *The Marcus Garvey and Universal Negro Improvement Association Papers,* and a fully corrected and edited text. While we have worked to rectify the kinds of typos and grammatical errors that the original newspaper editors would have tried to avoid, we feel that modern readers, like readers of the original newspaper serial, must make allowances for textual imperfections.

In addition to the instances of typos that one finds in any newspaper, the original published texts contain numerous inconsistencies in capitalization, italicization, spelling, and punctuation. Since most such problems have little bearing on the flow of the narrative, we have tried to make usage and spelling consistent while minimizing our intervention. Thus, while we have corrected blatant spelling errors in most ordinary words, we have not changed archaic or eccentric spellings, such as "meagre," "okeh," "Mogadicio," and "Timbuctoo." We have silently supplied obviously missing characters as well as whole words, and we have restored to their clearly intended order lines printed out of sequence in the *Courier.* Schuyler's departures from accepted syntax and grammar, such as "I" for "me," are generally left unaltered if they do not detract from the narrative.

In instances where Schuyler rendered fictional names inconsistently, such as "Ezekiel"/"Ezekial," "Constant"/"Costant," "Delphane"/"Delhane," and "Gaskin"/"Gaskins," the more common forms are used throughout to avoid confusion. Likewise, we have standardized a few ordinary words, such as "gray" and "toward," to conform to the spellings that Schuyler himself most often employed in the actual serials.

More difficult to reconcile are the inconsistencies that do not suggest simple choices. Early in the story, to cite one example, the narrator is taken to a Black Internationale crime operation variously located at

"St. Nicholas Place" and "St. Nicholas Avenue." Both are real streets in Harlem; however, we have no way of knowing which Schuyler really intended. Much later, to cite another kind of problem, he gives a Brazilian character, Vincente Portabla, a thick, vaguely French accent that repeatedly breaks down, leaving his dialect an unintended polyglot. To avoid the massive intervention that regularizing Portabla's accent throughout the story would entail, we have merely standardized spellings of words that Schuyler himself rendered inconsistently, such as "ze" for "zee."

Capitalization in the original text is inconsistent. Schuyler often capitalized words for emphasis, particularly in dialogue. We have generally left original forms unaltered, except to capitalize all dialogue references to Belsidus as "the Chief" and "the Doctor" to reflect Schuyler's predominant usage. We have also added capitalization to a few proper names that would distract if left lowercased.

The *Courier* texts render numbers inconsistently, spelling out some and printing others as Arabic numerals. Such inconsistencies are left to stand, except within chapter titles, where we have spelled out numbers and words that were probably abbreviated to save headline space.

The *Courier* texts made sparse use of commas, at times making it difficult to identify subordinate clauses. After careful reflection and discussion, we have inserted commas and occasional semicolons wherever the clarity of passages clearly would suffer without alteration. Punctuation irregularities of a purely typographical nature, such as ellipses and dashes, have been regularized, and we have rendered all book and newspaper titles and ship names in italics. Some alterations in original line breaks between paragraphs have also been made

A fundamentally different and more difficult set of problems arises as a result of Schuyler's occasional lapses in narrative continuity. Considering the story's complexity and the conditions under which Schuyler worked—discussed in the afterword—such lapses are surprisingly few. In any case, while they may at times confuse readers, they should be regarded as part of the idiosyncrasies of serial fiction of that era. Black Internationale religious centers, for example, are variously called both "Temples" and "Churches of Love." At the end of "Black Internationale," Yakoba, Nigeria, is proclaimed the new capital; however, when "Black Empire" opens, Yakoba is forgotten and Liberia's Kakata is still the capital. "Black Empire" also opens with Carl Slater's alluding to five years' having passed since he joined the Black Internationale, even though the context suggests that only a single year could have passed. Schuyler also seems to forget how Slater and Pat Givens travel to Africa; he repeatedly alludes to a direct flight "from Texas to Sierra Leone" that they never made. Later in the narrative, he remembers Martha Gaskin's having done things early in the story that there is no record of her having done.

Perhaps the most jarring lapse occurs early in the first serial, where Schuyler repeatedly calls a character about to be liquidated a Gambian, then suddenly identifies him as "the Senegalese" at the climactic moment. Odd though this switch seems to be, it may simply reflect Schuyler's journalistic predilection in referring to black Americans as "Senegambians." It seems to us that something of Schuyler would be lost if the passage were altered for the sake of consistency.

In addition to the stories that constitute *Black Empire,* we have appended several documents to illustrate the development of Schuyler's thinking during the time that he was writing the two serials. Appendix A includes two versions of what appear to have been Schuyler's earliest notes for "The Black Internationale." The texts of the appendix documents are rendered according to the editorial principles used in the *Marcus Garvey Papers.* The few corrections and suppositional insertions that we have made are bracketed. Text that Schuyler himself crossed out is printed as canceled type (~~cancel~~). Additions and corrections that he made are incorporated into the printed text.

Finally, to support the historical apparatus of this volume, we have included an annotated bibliography of Schuyler's fiction published in the *Courier* from 1933 to 1939.

R.A.H. & R.K.R.

THE BLACK INTERNATIONALE

Story of Black Genius
Against the World

1

New York Reporter Sees a Murder,
Then Gets Taken for a "Ride"

They say curiosity killed a cat. Well, it certainly got me into something destined to shake the whole world. We had just put the *Harlem Blade* to bed. I was dog-tired and before turning in I stopped by the Pelican to have a drink and a bite to eat. As I gave my order to the waitress, the front door opened. A charming, young, blonde white girl swathed in a gorgeous fur coat entered the cafe, followed by a very tall, stern-visaged black man dressed entirely in dark gray and carrying a gold-handled cane in his gloved hand. The waitress showed them a table exactly across from me.

The girl was like dozens one sees in the better parts of New York City but seldom sees in Harlem. She was not an actress or entertainer, I gathered. Rather, someone of consequence. The man was something else again. His perfect white teeth contrasted sharply with his smooth, almost black skin. Although obviously a settled individual, there were no discernable lines on his face, no pouches or bags, those telltale marks of self-indulgence. He never smiled more than in a perfunctory manner nor revealed in any way the slightest interest in his mate. Instead, he sat almost impassive, looking thoughtfully out of the plate glass window as she animatedly talked.

I could not understand what she was saying because she spoke in undertones and was talking at a great rate. The black man continued impassively gazing across the street. She placed one bejeweled lily-like hand on his coat sleeve affectionately, almost reverently, as she changed to a begging, imploring mood. I could see the supplicant in her whole manner, could even see her lips quiver and tremble as she pleaded with him. He shook off her hand and, turning a stern and frowning face toward her, growled, "So you have failed. I cannot tolerate failure." His voice was cultured but deep and cruel. She recoiled, beaten, frightened.

"Who is that man?" I whispered to the waitress.

"I'm not sure but I think he's Dr. Belsidus. They say he lives downtown. He comes up here occasionally and he's always with some pretty white girl but I've never seen him with the same one twice. He's very refined and he tips out of this world."

This information merely quickened my interest. I wanted to know more about this mysterious doctor. As familiar as I am with Harlem and everybody who is anybody, I had neither seen nor heard of him before. When the couple finally rose, I was so consumed with curiosity that I decided to follow them. I wanted to know more about this majestic, handsome black man.

I watched him tip the waitress, then gallantly assist the pretty girl with her coat. It was after midnight when they left. They walked up Seventh Avenue to 144th Street. They were evidently engaged in deep conversation. Occasionally I could hear his booming negatives and the whimper of her pleading voice as I kept a respectable distance behind.

At 144th Street, they turned toward Lenox Avenue. I was following them on the downtown side, was indeed almost opposite them, keeping as much in the shadow as possible. Suddenly I saw the man glance up and down the street over the woman's head. Then he quickly stepped into a darkened doorway, yanking the woman with him. He placed his hand over her mouth but not before I heard a little agonized squeal. With his other hand he grabbed her throat. Then he held her tightly. Her struggles grew less and less violent. Finally, she sagged and he let her drop like a sack of oats.

Frozen to the spot by this drama, it had not occurred to me before to make any move or say anything. It had all been so sudden and unexpected. Now, as he deposited the limp body on the hall floor and turned to go, I impulsively shouted, "Hey, you. Stop! What are you doing to that girl?" I should have kept quiet and followed him, of course, but one doesn't think about such things until afterward.

He stopped in his tracks and whirled. Never have I seen such a look of trapped cruelty and sheer animal ferocity on a man's face. In his hand was clutched a wicked blue steel automatic, with a silencer on it.

"Come with me, young man," he commanded in a low gruff voice. "You have seen too much for your own good. Walk ahead of me now and walk very quickly. I shall not hesitate to kill you. You noticed, I imagine, that this gun is equipped with a silencer. The shot that kills you will make no sound."

I walked rapidly toward Lenox Avenue, cursing myself for getting into such a mess. As we got to the corner a Broadway-Columbus Avenue bus was approaching. "Hail it!!" my captor growled. "I'll pay the fare. No foolishness now or I'll kill you and everybody on the bus." I knew he meant it, too.

I got on ahead of him and sat down in the first seat. He sat behind me. One hand was in his gray overcoat pocket. I knew what was in that hand. I'm not kidding when I tell you I was frightened. Suppose the man were insane? Gooseflesh grew on me at that thought.

At 125th Street he pulled the cord, whispered a gruff "get out!" and we stepped down to the curb. The bus buzzed away, leaving us practically alone. Minutes passed, how many I don't know but certainly not more than 10. Occasionally I would steal a glance at my captor and was always confused to find those deep, stern eyes drilling me through.

At last a long black limousine, with curtains drawn, drew up to the curb. A giant black man in chauffeur's uniform was at the wheel. "Get in!" the doctor ordered, prodding me with the gun. I hastened to obey. He stepped in beside me and closed the door with a bang. In the second that the light flashed on I noticed that the car was luxurious in its appointments.

When we were seated, the limousine shot down Lenox Avenue. I tried to follow its direction. Dr. Belsidus must have noticed my preoccupation and in some uncanny way divined my purpose. He snapped on a light. "Open that cabinet," he commanded, pointing to a cleverly built-in cabinet in front of us. I obeyed with alacrity and saw before me an array of bottles and whiskey and wine glasses. Dr. Belsidus tapped with his fingers on the window in front of him. The car slowed up.

"You see that black bottle?" he asked. I nodded. "Well, fill one of those whiskey glasses half full, no more, and fill it the rest of the way with the contents of that brown bottle. Come, make haste!"

"What is it?" I asked, frightened anew at the suspicion of poison.

"Hush, and make haste!" he growled, glowering at me, irritation written in his tones.

There seemed no other alternative. With sinking heart I opened the black bottle and immediately my nostrils were struck by a strange, oriental odor of unusual pungency. With trembling hand, I poured a half glassful of the stuff. It was syrupy stuff, bright green in color. The limousine had almost stopped now.

I had a premonition of something terrible, some impending tragedy. I hesitated and then glanced appealingly at the stern, silent man, who was watching me intently.

"Well, go on," he growled, frowning.

Out of the three-sided little brown bottle I poured a jet-black watery liquid that smelled like good brandy. As it mixed with the half glass of green syrup it formed a strange coalescence, a weird agate-like pattern. I watched it hypnotically, wondering with fear and trembling what it might be.

"Drink it!" commanded Dr. Belsidus.

I took the glass in my right hand and brought it slowly to my lips.

What was this strange liquid? Was it a drug or was it a poison? Who was this cold-blooded, murderous Dr. Belsidus, who so impassively sent people to their death? Even as I felt that I might be breathing my last, my curiosity of a news hound was all-consuming.

"Will this kill me?" I asked, hesitating, before I drank.

"Drink!" commanded Dr. Belsidus.

With an unspoken prayer, I tossed down the concoction. It burned my throat like raw corn liquor. I was suddenly faint with nausea. My head whirled. The man beside me became a giant striding across the skyscrapers of Manhattan. And then, in a trice he was a gnome teetering on the edge of the whiskey glass. Then he assumed his natural shape. I noted just the trace of a malevolent smirk distorting his shiny black face.

Then there was a whirling of limbs. I felt my feet walking on the ceiling of the limousine. There was nothing left of my body but a humming feeling. The air seemed filled with vague perfume. The glass fell from my hand and seemed to take a century to reach the carpeted floor. When it struck, the sound seemed almost to burst my eardrums. I tried to fight my way back to consciousness but without avail. And yet it could hardly be said that I was unconscious. I could feel, see and experience, but what I saw was strange, uncanny, unthinkable, utterly mad.

I felt as if my head had been turned by 180 degrees. My abdomen became a soft, fluid mass, my face acquired giant dimensions, my lips swelled, my arms became wooden, my feet turned into spirals and scrolls, my jaw was like a hook and my chest seemed to melt away.

6

Suddenly, to my great surprise I found that I had no head but in its place a sheet of ground-glass like a camera-screen. Then my brain went dead and I remembered nothing more.

2

░░░░░░░░░░░░░░░░░░░░░░░░░░░░░░

Reporter Is Urged to Act as Secretary;
"Doctor" Bares Plans

Hours, days, weeks seemed to have passed. I felt a great weight on my eyes, a weight that pressed down upon the eyeballs. Slowly, very slowly, the weight lifted, to my infinite relief. It was my own arm!

The arm was stiff, almost paralyzed. I raised my heavy eyelids. All was blackness! Was I blind? I sat up panicky, yet, even though blind, thankful that I was at least alive. I looked hastily about. Everything was blackness, silent, awesome blackness. Horrible blackness.

I felt about me. There was the touch of linen. I sat up and felt further about me. I was in bed, a great, wide, soft bed. Gradually it seemed that once more I had legs and feet. I moved them almost gratefully and luxuriated in the soft caress of the bedclothing. I had on silk pajamas.

Where was I? What had happened? Then I remembered the drink and the strange, unbelievable phantasmagoria that had whirled through my brain before everything went blank. Again I asked myself, where was I?

I lay there for hours in that black silent room, or at least it seemed hours. Then very faintly and at great distance I heard the faint honk of an auto horn. It seemed like the embrace of a long-lost mistress. I sat up eagerly in bed and my heart sang. Then everything fell silent again and I drifted off into sleep.

How long I slept that second time I do not know. I was awakened by the feel of something cold and clammy on my forehead. I jumped with a shiver. I opened my eyes. A blaze of light blinded me. Now I rejoiced that I could see, after all. I looked up, then shrank back startled and frightened. The cold, clammy object on my forehead was the hand of the chauffeur of Dr. Belsidus. So I was still in their power, then? He was a very ugly black man with bloodshot eyes and bulbous lips. He was watching me intently. Looking about, I saw that I was in a large modernistic bedroom done entirely in aluminum and black. The bed was ebony inlaid with ivory, as were the other pieces of furniture. The walls were black and aluminum. The velvet drapes were dead white. The windows were closed with black shutters which I suspected to be steel. The lighting was indirect, shedding a soft glow. It was a rich but awesome boudoir, like the last resting place of some long-dead Egyptian Pharaoh.

"Where am I?" I asked.

The black giant shook his head solemnly and placed an index finger to his lips. He turned and pointed me to the long ebony and ivory bench in front of the dressing table. There, neatly folded, were my clothes. The black giant nodded his head as he pointed.

"What's the matter with you?" I asked. "Can't you talk?"

He shook his head sorrowfully. He pointed again to his mouth. Then he opened it. There was nothing but a great, red cavity surrounded by fine white teeth. His tongue was gone!

I shuddered and, rising from the white linen sheets and black pillow, I walked unsteadily, almost groggily, over to my clothing and began putting it on. When I had on my underwear, socks and trousers, the dumb chauffeur clapped his hands sharply together. I started at the sound. He grinned broadly. It was in such marked contrast to the mysterious solemnity of the whole procedure that I had to smile myself.

The door of the room opened silently. A colored maid, neatly uniformed in black dress and white apron and cap, entered with a wash basin full of water, a bar of soap and a fleecy white towel. She sat them down and without a word turned and disappeared the way she had come. The dummy pointed to them and grunted, indicating that I should perform my ablutions. I wondered if they didn't have a bathroom in the place.

Finally, I was ready. I was conscious of a great emptiness in my stomach and the pangs of hunger began to assail me. The chauffeur tapped me on the shoulder and pointed to the door. I went to it, opened it and walked out of the bedroom to find myself in a long corridor hung with heavy black velvet. The door was closed silently behind me. Down the indirectly lighted corridor I walked for perhaps fifteen paces followed closely by the dummy. At last there was break in the velvet drapes. My guard tapped me on my shoulder again and pointed to the door in the opening.

I turned the aluminum knob and pushed the door open to find my very breath taken away by the exotic magnificence of a stately dining room. The motif was green and rose and gold. The heavily piled rug was rose. The walls were a modernistic design of green and gold. Rose draperies hung from the steel-shuttered windows. Soft yellow lights from golden wall fixtures flooded the place with a gentle aura of illumination. On the walls were three beautiful murals invitingly showing all manner of exotic fruits and foods. In the center of the room was a great, long table spread with pea-green cloth. But most striking of all was the service with which the table was spread. The cutlery without exception was either golden or gold-plated. The great filigreed fruit dish, laden with huge oranges, apples, peaches and plums, was certainly golden. The cups, plates, the same precious material, eggshell thin.

I hesitated, nonplussed by such regal splendor. The door closed behind me. I turned around only to find myself again alone. I tiptoed over to the table and examined the marvelous service. Yes, it was indeed gold. Each piece carried the bold monogram "B" surmounted by a three-pointed crown. I stepped back with a little awe before such a treasure. Then I had a feeling that I was not alone; that someone was staring at me, studying me. I glanced up and down the room, puzzled. Then I turned around. There, standing silently and regarding me with a coldly amused intensity, stood tall, stern-visaged Dr. Belsidus.

"Good morning, Mr. Slater," he said. "I hope you slept well."

"Why, yes, I guess so. But where am I? What time is it? I've got to get back on the job."

"So you can write about what you saw last night and this morning?" he inquired sarcastically, with a slight sardonic smirk.

"Well, I'm a newspaper man," I said defiantly, "and you can't expect a newspaper man to keep quiet about murders in cold blood, drugging and all that sort of thing, can you?"

"But you will keep quiet, Carl Slater," he warned softly. "And you're not going back to that job. You are through working for the *Harlem Blade* or anybody else except Dr. Henry Belsidus."

"What do you mean?" I inquired, startled by his tone.

9

"You are working for me now, Slater, that's all," he said a little rough-ly in the tone of a man who must not be crossed. "I have spared your life because I need a competent young fellow like you as a secretary."

"How do you know I'm competent?" I countered.

"I know about every Negro intellectual in the world," he said calmly. "That is my vocation. Medicine is merely my avocation. I have been intending for some time to bring you into my organization. Now you come by accident. I need loyal race-conscious youngsters to help me. You are that type, Slater. You can do much to aid the cause of Negro liberation, not only in America, but throughout the world. White world supremacy must be destroyed, my lad, and it will be destroyed. I, Dr. Henry Belsidus, will destroy it with the aid of my loyal assistants in all parts of the world."

I couldn't help but smile at this grandiose scheme. He noted my amusement.

"It sounds mad, doesn't it?" he said.

"Yes, rather Garveyistic, I'd say."

"My son," he continued gravely, "all great schemes appear mad in the beginning. Christians, Communists, Fascists and Nazis were at first called scary. Success made them sane. With brains, courage and wealth even the most fantastic scheme can become a reality. I have dedicated my life, Slater, to destroying white world supremacy. My ideal and ob-jective is very frankly to cast down the Caucasians and elevate the col-ored people in their places. I plan to do this by every means within my power. I intend to stop at nothing, Slater, whether right or wrong. In-deed, in a plan such as this there can be no talk of right or wrong. Right is success. Wrong is failure. I will not fail because I am ruthless. Those who fail are the men who get sentimental, who weaken, who balk at a little bloodshed. Such vermin deserve to fail. Every great movement the world has ever seen has collapsed because it grew weak. I shall nev-er become weak, nor shall I ever tolerate weakness around me. Weak-ness means failure, Slater, and I do not intend to fail."

"But how can you succeed?" I asked, eager to learn as much as pos-sible. "Haven't white people got all the power, all the industry, all the money?"

"They have now," he admitted, "but they will not have it long. I and my comrades shall destroy them or make them destroy themselves. We have brains, the best brains in the Negro race. We have science of which the white man has not dreamed in our possession. We have courage. And we are absolutely ruthless."

"I noticed that last night," I said, significantly.

"You mean that white woman?" he asked. "Bah! I use their women to aid in their destruction. As long as they succeed in carrying out my mission, I spare them. When they fail, I destroy them. That girl failed to obtain a valuable secret I desired, so I destroyed her. Otherwise, she might have talked. You know, I do not trust white people. I just use them."

"But that's murder," I objected. "Cold-blooded murder."

"Of course it's murder," he said, smirking sardonically. "What of it? What are a few paltry lives compared to the goal we seek? Murder. Hah! Haven't they murdered millions of black people? If we murdered one of them everyday, it would take us several centuries to catch up, Slater."

"But come," he said, changing tone and gesturing toward the table, "let us have breakfast and then we can go into the details of your work."

"I haven't said yet that I want to have anything to do with this," I said boldly. "It sounds crazy to me. It sounds too much like jail."

I realized a moment after I had spoken that I should not have said what I did. Dr. Belsidus's face grew wooden and his deep-set eyes smoldered like twin volcanoes. He whirled and confronted me with upraised index finger, but when he spoke his voice was as soft as a purring leopard's. He half smiled.

"You remember the drink I had you take last night, Slater? That was Teyoth, a Hindu drug that induces temporary insanity. I did not want you to know where you were going. You knew nothing until you awoke this morning. No one saw you enter here. If I cannot persuade you to join me, young man, no one will see you leave. Indeed, in that case, you will never leave. Understand?"

I nodded slowly and with sinking heart. I had no alternative but to accept. I was in the power either of a madman or a genius.

"You are a sensible youngster," he said, smiling broadly for the first time. "After breakfast I shall tell you about The Black Internationale."

3

Dr. Belsidus Reveals Source of His Secret Wealth to Secretary

My first morning in the mysterious mansion of Dr. Belsidus was the most interesting and revealing I had ever spent. We dallied long over the breakfast table as he told me of his plans for Negro control of the world. As he spun out this strange, almost insane scheme, a malevolent, satanic smirk played about his stern mouth and his deep-set eyes glowed like coals in a cavern. With a golden spoon he traced geometric designs on the green linen cloth as he outlined the most amazing conspiracy in history. His voice was deep, alternately cruel and insinuating.

"Doubtless you wonder at all this," he said, a sardonic smile fastening down the corners of his determined mouth. He indicated with a wave the ornate dining room and let his glance linger on the dozens of solid gold dishes on the table. "Perhaps it seems rather garish and unnecessary, something like the extravagances of the newly rich. But I am no Trimalchio, my lad. There is method in what you might call my madness."

I said nothing, preferring to listen and learn.

"Take these golden dishes and cutlery," he continued. "These are not kept for purposes of ostentatious display, my boy. They are kept so that I may, in the oriental manner, always have a supply of wealth which the white man's government will not molest. Since no one is permitted to keep gold bars, gold coins or gold certificates, I have converted my gold into these articles and works of supposed art. I have millions of dollars worth of gold and jewels in this house and elsewhere in the world. Come, I'll show you." He rose and went over to a large red and gold and green closet whose sloping top almost reached the ceiling. He produced a small key, unlocked the doors and threw them open. What I saw left me breathless. There were eight shelves. On each shelf were stacked scores of large golden dinner plates, golden soup plates, golden candlesticks, and dozens of knives, forks and spoons made of that precious metal. They reflected in dull yellow beams the light from the room. He evidently enjoyed my amazement.

"Come," he said. "There is much more you must see, Slater. I want you to know everything. You are to be my secretary. I must have one with more than the ordinary intelligence whom I can trust. I think you fit the bill."

"But how do you KNOW, Doctor?"

"I'll show you," he said, striding ahead of me across the dining room to a wide door. He pressed a button in the wall. We waited for perhaps ten seconds. Then the door opened in the middle swiftly and silently and we were facing what appeared to be a small closet. We went in and then I realized that we were in a small residential elevator. My host pressed a button and we descended perhaps ten feet. When the door opened in obedience to the pressure on a button, we entered a room quite as large as the dining room but fitted out elaborately as an office.

Two large windows with panes of frosted glass were at each end of the room. Across from the elevator was another door which I surmised opened on a corridor similar to that on the upper floor. In the center of the floor between the windows were arranged about ten mahogany desks, each with a noiseless typewriter on a moveable shelf. Along the wall were filing cases of fireproof steel that reached almost to the ceiling.

"Look here," he directed, going to one of the files and pulling out a drawer. It was packed with hundreds of large cards. He fished out one and handed it to me.

To my astonishment it read:

SLATER, CARL, b. Richmond, Va., May 25, 1910. Father: Carl Slater. Mother: Thelma Slater. Came to New York with parents, April 19, 1916. Graduated from New York public schools, June, 1927. Valedictorian. Active in school sports. Outstanding in football and track. Editor-in-Chief of high school paper. Entered Columbia University, October, 1927, specializing in literature and journalism. Worked as a Pullman porter every summer. Graduated with high honors June, 1931. Unemployed that summer. Did reporting from 1931, for out-of-town Negro weeklies. Went to work for the *Harlem Blade*, January, 1932. Single. Parents liv-

13

ing. Does not gamble or dissipate. Drinks moderately. Sex life normal, but somewhat promiscuous. Apparently no steady girl. No political affiliation but seems to be intensely race conscious and familiar with the history of his people. Dark brown, 5 feet, 6 inches, 150 pounds.

"But how did you get all this?" Its amazing accuracy almost scared me.

"That is part of our work, Slater," he said nonchalantly, placing the card back in the file. "We keep track of every Negro of promise to our cause. Sooner or later I would have recruited you. As it is, you walked right into my hands at the right time."

"What do you mean—the right time?"

"Well, it's quite a story. You see, my last secretary was a rather clever man about your age. Yes, too clever." He smirked diabolically and stroked his smooth black cheek.

"What happened to him?" I asked, apprehensively.

"Oh, he was so indiscreet as to say things he should not have said. He discussed my business with others, and, of course, then we had to do away with all concerned. We can't have any talking out of turn, Slater. All of us understand that."

"Do you mean to say you murdered him?"

"A very ugly word, Slater, a very ugly word. We prefer euphemisms, but, if you choose, then, yes, we murdered him. Oh, nothing mussy, you understand. It is done quite quickly with a needle. In a minute it's over."

He must have noticed my revulsion because he smiled reassuringly.

"We must get used to bloodshed, Slater. We must be hard. We must be cruel. We must be unrelenting, neither giving nor asking quarter, until either we or the white race is definitely subjugated, or even exterminated. There is no other way. Softness is weakness. Compromise is disastrous. Tolerance is fatal."

His voice was cruel and bitter now, his face stern, his eyes smouldering with hatred.

"We must disobey all laws that hinder our plan, for all laws here are laws of the white man, designed to keep us in subjugation and perpetuate his rule. All the means of education and information, from nursery to college, from newspaper to book, are mobilized to perpetuate white supremacy; to enslave and degrade the darker peoples. No student of the race problem, Slater, can escape that conclusion. The problem cannot be solved by compromise, by cooperation, by tolerance. As well talk of cooperation and compromise between a hungry lion and a bleating lamb. As well talk of the fish tolerating the worm. No, we who have been on the bottom so long must now come to the top. We who have created the wealth of the world must now enjoy it."

"But how?" I asked, frankly puzzled. "You know very well that white people have all the wealth and all the power, and that our people are not only poor but in the main ignorant."

"Quite true, Slater, quite true," he agreed, beaming benevolently. "But white people haven't got all the brains. We are going to out-think and out-scheme the white people, my boy. I have the organization already, Slater, scattered all over the world; young Negroes like yourself: intellectuals, scientists, engineers. They are mentally the equal of the whites. They possess superior energy, superior vitality, they have superior, or perhaps I should say more intense, hatred and resentment, that fuel which operates the juggernaut of conquest. All they need is money, instruments, new weapons of science. I have the money, my boy. Yes, I have the wealth, and I am getting more daily. You will see in your time a great Negro nation in Africa, all-powerful, dictating to the white world."

"But how have you accumulated the money?" I inquired. "Has it come from your practice?"

"Partly, yes. Most of my patients are wealthy white women. I have great magnetism, great skill, Slater. I am unscrupulous. Whatever they want done, legal or otherwise, I do it if they have the money to pay me or can get it. I use them in many ways. When they are no longer useful, I either drop them or destroy them. Some I pretend to love. They are intrigued by the idea of a black lover, a man of culture and refinement superior to their husbands and orthodox sweethearts. I give them exotic surroundings, liquor, drugs. When I need them no longer I dismiss them."

"Or murder them," I added.

"Or murder them," he repeated calmly. "What difference does it make? They have murdered millions of black men, women and children, and indirectly destroyed millions more by impoverishment, discrimination, segregation, cruel and inhuman treatment. They haven't been very squeamish about it, have they, Slater? No, so why should I be? Well, my other wealth is derived in the following illegal manner.

Illegal, that is, from the dominant white man's point of view, my boy, not from mine. Sit down and keep silent." He waved me to a chair.

I obeyed. He clapped his hands twice. The office door flew open. The gigantic chauffeur stood at attention before us.

"Jim," commanded Dr. Belsidus, "tell Mr. Fortune to report on the night's work." The dummy disappeared. "A most trustworthy man," observed the Doctor. "He hates white people worse than I do, which is saying a whole lot. They burned off his tongue with a poker one day in Georgia about eight years ago. How he escaped is more than I can imagine but he outran the mob somehow or other. If I should command it, he would wring your neck without changing expression. You know, Slater, one must have loyal followers. Now I'll show you how we get much of our other wealth."

There came a tap on the door. "Come on in, Fortune," Dr. Belsidus called.

The door opened. A short, plump man, reddish brown with gray eyes, entered pushing a rubber-tired cart somewhat resembling a tea wagon. On it was heaped an amazing collection of jewelry: rings, earrings, necklaces, bracelets, necktie pins, watches, brooches and tiaras. The short man looked at me suspiciously.

"Fortune, this is a new brother, Carl Slater. He's on probation but I think he'll do all right. Slater, this is Alton Fortune, mechanical engineer, and a good one. Our good white folks won't let him work at his profession, so we're letting him work on them until we are ready to use his skill otherwise."

"Glad to know you, Slater," said Fortune, gripping my hand and pumping it energetically. I thought I detected in his eye something of the fanaticism that occasionally glowed in those of Dr. Belsidus. I mumbled something.

"So this is the night's haul, eh?" said the Doctor, fingering the hoard with satisfaction.

"Yes, the boys did some good work, Chief, and nobody caught."

"Is this stuff stolen?" I couldn't help but ask.

"A very ugly word, Slater," observed the physician, smiling sardonically, "a very ugly word. We don't use it here. This is wealth to finance the revolution. It is gathered by some of our nervy young men whom white civilization denies a chance, from wealthy men who have entirely too much."

"But the police," I objected, "suppose . . . "

"Ah, yes, I know what you are thinking. Follow me into the basement and I'll show you what we do with this stuff." Dr. Belsidus nodded to Fortune and led the way into the elevator.

4

⟁⟁⟁⟁⟁⟁⟁⟁⟁⟁⟁⟁⟁⟁⟁⟁⟁⟁⟁⟁⟁⟁⟁⟁

Slater Learns Secret Source of Belsidus's Fast-Growing Fortune

We went down two flights in the little elevator. Fortune opened the door and wheeled his jewel-laden wagon into the basement; I followed and Dr. Belsidus brought up the rear. We walked along a whitewashed corridor until we came to a steel door. The physician knocked twice in a peculiar manner. The door rolled upward. Beyond was a small room, whitewashed and prison-like. At the far end blazed an electric furnace. In front of it were several clay moulds. On a large oaken table nearby sat several golden vases, platinum vanity cases, golden plates and platters, goblets and chafing dishes of silver. Presiding over this chamber of Vulcan was a wavy-haired brown man who must either have had Hindu or Indian ancestry. He was dressed entirely in white with a pair of green goggles perched on his head.

"Hello, Chief," he said. "Got some more stuff there?"

"Yes, Sam, a very good haul this time," the Doctor replied. "By the way, Sam, I want you to meet my new secretary, Carl Slater. Carl, meet Sam Hamilton, one of the outstanding chemists in the United States. Sam's graduated from some of the best scientific schools in the country. The white people won't give him a break. But he'll show them a thing or two when we get our plant going, eh Sam?"

We shook hands. Then we all stood around while he went to work on the jewelry. Deftly, with delicate tools, he took jewels from their settings and after inspecting the baubles through an eye glass he would place them in a little silver box which stood at his elbow. The settings he would toss into three different fire clay containers, for gold, silver and aluminum. These he thrust into the orange glowing furnace. When reduced to molten form, he poured them into clay moulds: candlesticks, dinner plates, saucers, etc.

"You see," Belsidus boasted, "we have thought of everything."

"But what about the jewels? How do you get rid of them?"

"Ah," he wagged his head mysteriously, "there are ways."

It was nearly ten days before Dr. Belsidus would let me leave the house. During that period I supervised the office staff, consisting of 10 colored men, wrote his personal letters, which were numerous, and generally familiarized myself with the work. The ramifications of his organization were amazing, and as I learned more and more about it, my respect for the bloodthirsty, fanatical revolutionist grew.

Once outside the house I was surprised to find that it was a large private residence in the Seventies between Park and Madison Avenues. From the outside it seemed very austere and respectable. A simple brass plate on the door read "Dr. Henry Belsidus."

I hurried uptown to see my folks. Imagine my surprise when I learned that they had received letters every day signed with an excellent forgery of my signature saying that I was on an assignment and would be back shortly. At the *Harlem Blade* office I learned they had received a letter of resignation, also over my forged signature.

It impressed but at the same time depressed me. Suppose I should sometime want to get away from Dr. Belsidus? With such an organization of spies and agents as he undoubtedly had, how could I hope to escape?

Looking at the last number of the *Harlem Blade*, I noticed that the police had sought in vain to find out something concerning the murder of the young white woman on 144th Street. She had been killed by some deadly poison unknown to the police, killed instantaneously. How much I could have told them if I had dared!

With each successful haul, Al Fortune widened his operations. There were mornings when both shelves of the rubber-tired cart were loaded down with valuable baubles destined for the furnace and to assume an entirely different shape and form. He told me one morning that he had a corps of 40 young Negroes working on percentage, i.e., 25 percent of the value of all they stole. I was eager to learn more about the details of this lucrative business which the police seemed unable to stop.

Al finally consented to take me one night. We left the house afoot and boarded the Madison Avenue bus going uptown. At 110th Street we got off and caught a taxicab. He gave an address on St. Nicholas Place.

"I never call any taxis to the house," Al explained, "and I never leave that district twice in the same sort of conveyance. We've got everything down pretty fine but there's no use taking chances."

We stopped in front of a gray stone residence with stone balustrades that sat behind a tiny hedge and flower bed. Fortune led the way. In response to his ring a brown maid in uniform opened the door.

"Is Mrs. Harris in?" he asked, lowering the lid of one eye significantly. The maid quickly stood to one side.

"You'll find her in the sitting room," she said. Fortune walked in and I followed behind.

The curtains were drawn and there was no light. When our eyes got accustomed to the darkness, I noticed for the first time an enormous black woman, certainly all of 300 pounds, sitting in the center of a red plush sofa. She said nothing but studied us curiously like a great fat spider gloating over its prey. It was embarrassing to me. I glanced at Al Fortune questioningly. Then I looked more closely. Nothing seemed to move about the woman except her eyes and her mountainous breasts. She was garbed in a tent-like blue velvet dress edged with lace around the collar and sleeves. For one so large her shoes seemed incredibly tiny. Her little roaming, too-close-together eyes sparkled in the darkness like two beads on a black hat. A faint odor of perfumed perspiration rose from her.

Suddenly, she spoke in a voice that rumbled from some lower depth far in the recesses of the earth.

"Who's your friend, Mr. Fortune?"

"New secretary to the Chief, Mag. Come on, let's go."

"Well, okeh," she rumbled. She shifted one of her enormous hams and reached behind the back of the sofa. To my astonishment the red plush sofa began to move sidewise, slowly and noiselessly. Farther and farther it moved until it was some six feet to our left and where the grotesque woman had sat was only an empty expanse of parquet flooring. I looked at Al Fortune. He was watching the bare space as a bacteriologist might gaze through a microscope, alert, expectant.

Now a square of the bare flooring moved downward and away from us, disclosing a light collapsible steel staircase descending into a dimly lighted cellar. Without a word Fortune went down the steps with me close behind him. At the bottom I turned around and looked back. The collapsible staircase was already moving upward into a recess and the trap door was closed.

"Pretty neat," I observed.

"We take no chances," he observed gruffly. "Come on."

I followed him to the rear of the cellar. We stood facing the stone wall. There was no stairway, no door, nothing but the wall. I looked at him, puzzled by all these maneuvers. He was listening intently, his head inclined to one side. At last he stepped forward close to the wall. He touched the middle finger of his right hand against a small stone. It sank forward. At once a section of the wall, four feet wide and about six feet high, swung noiselessly on a pivot. Fortune stepped forward with me at his heels. We were in a wooden closet about six feet square. The wall behind us closed silently.

Now, whispering to me to keep absolutely silent, Fortune pushed aside an eyehole in the wooden wall in front of each of us. We were looking into a low room with cement floor, poured cement walls and whitewashed ceiling. About five feet in front of us an iron grill, through which one might reach, extended from floor to ceiling and surrounded the three sides of our closet. Otherwise, the room was completely bare. At the far end was a steel door.

Fortune pressed a button somewhere. The door at the far end opened. A flashily dressed Negro in spats, black form-fitting overcoat and pearl-gray fedora entered and walked briskly to the grill.

Fortune disguised his voice with a sepulchral tone. "What have you tonight, Sanderson?"

"This," said the man. He drew from his inside overcoat pocket a long, beautiful pearl necklace.

"Put it in the box." The man reached through the grill and deposited the necklace in a box on the floor in front of the closet.

"Is that all, Sanderson?"

"Yes, sir. That's pretty good, ain't it?"

"You are sure you were careful, Sanderson?" Fortune asked, ignoring the man's question.

20

"Oh, yes, sir. You know I'm th' cat."

"You may go, Sanderson." The man turned and hurried out. Man after man followed him. Yeggs, pickpockets, highwaymen, a motley file out of Harlem's criminals came one by one and deposited their loot in the box.

At intervals and while the room was empty Fortune would unlatch the little door at our feet and swing the treasure box inward. He would quickly empty its contents into a large velvet bag. Then, opening the wall into the cellar through which we had come, he would place it alongside the wall in there.

"That's just in case," he explained. "No telling what might happen."

He seemed highly elated with the evening's business. The box had to be emptied many times. I counted altogether 38 men. It appeared that two had been caught.

"We get them the best lawyer the town affords," he explained. "And if they can't beat the rap, well, most of them are the kind that can take it."

"Suppose one of them should squeal?" I asked.

"Well," he observed, "I don't know where he could go and stay alive. Our men and women are everywhere, and these rats all know it. But we only need a few more hauls and we'll be ready to get down to business in earnest."

I didn't know what he meant, but I found out the very next week.

5

⁂⁂⁂⁂⁂⁂⁂⁂⁂⁂⁂⁂⁂⁂⁂⁂⁂⁂⁂⁂⁂

Belsidus Bares His Plans for Conference
of Blacks of the World

No one coming to the office of Dr. Belsidus for treatment would have suspected what was going on above and below that main floor. His fashionable white patients saw only the well-appointed office of a wealthy physician, an immaculate office done in soft tones, with gleaming equipment, two smiling brownskin nurses and the handsome assistant of Dr. Belsidus, young Dr. Matson. The doors leading to the stairways going to the upper floors and the basement were always locked. They were camouflaged steel doors. Only Dr. Belsidus and Jim possessed keys.

I was struck by the number of Dr. Belsidus's patients. All day from 10 in the morning until 3 in the afternoon the gleaming limousines and town cars paused in front of our door. Mostly, the patients were female. Girls, young women, middle-aged women, old women, but always white women and always wealthy women. I learned from the nurse who kept the accounts that they paid fabulous fees.

The sinister physician was the very soul of courtesy and consideration. He bowed low, smiled occasionally, made witty remarks that kept his fair patients giggling, and worked with a swiftness and sureness that inspired confidence. At 3 o'clock sharp he retired to the upper floors.

It was the day following my trip with Alton Fortune to the mysterious basement under the house of Mag Harris on St. Nicholas Place that the little green light on top of my desk flashed twice and I knew that the Chief wanted me. I grabbed my stenographic pad and, taking the private elevator, went to the top floor.

The Doctor must have spent $25,000 furnishing that top floor apartment. It was strictly late Egyptian. As one left the elevator, one stepped immediately into a vast room at least 15 feet high and extending to the left and right the full length of the house. Directly in front of the elevator, but across the room from it, was the bed. It was 10 feet wide and slightly longer, not over a foot high and hung with a gorgeous canopy of royal purple edged with golden fringe. Inside the canopy was a great French mirror so arranged that it could be slightly tilted by the pressure on a small lever at whatever angle the occupant of the bed wished.

The walls were of sandstone. Extending all around the room were the most exotic murals in vivid greens and crimsons, rich chocolates and yellows depicting scenes of the wildest passionate abandon. Nymphs, Satyrs, cupids, angels and devils were depicted in the most suggestive and provocative poses. They poured red wine and lost themselves in nameless excesses of which common folk never dreamed in their wildest nightmares.

The dark red glass floor that clearly reflected every figure that crossed it was strewn with leopard and tiger skins. At intervals here and there were low Egyptian chairs and divans of dark red wood inlaid with gold. The four great windows, two at each end, were hung with royal purple drapes fringed with gold. Each window was equipped with a fine steel rolling curtain painted a deceptive green. These, with the steel doors, made the place impregnable.

Between the rear windows in a concave, softly lighted recess stood an amazingly life-like male phallic symbol made of translucent porcelain and fully six feet in height. In a similar recess between the two front windows stood a statue of three nude young women in the full bloom and vigor of life with their arms on each other's shoulders. They were obviously made of the same porcelain. One was a Caucasian, one an African and the other a Mongolian.

To the right and left of the elevator shaft were twin lavatories with sunken marble bathtubs, entered through embossed bronze doors. On the same side of the room and near the front was the door leading to the stairway to the third floor. The whole scene was suffused with a soft rose light from shielded fixtures imbedded at intervals in the sandstone walls. No one could long remain in the place without one's mind dwelling on soft flesh, rounded forms, perfumed breaths, libidinous movements and all the intimate lecheries the fertile mind of love has invented down through the countless ages of man's earthly sojourn.

In his usual position on the low upholstered bench at the foot of the bed lay Ben, the Doctor's trained leopard. As I entered, he opened his wicked eyes, frowned, and rose up threateningly. I stood still, a little frightened, as he moved toward me with a slinking crouch. I remembered what Al Fortune had told me about his daily diet of fresh raw meat and his almost insane ferocity. His yellow eyes glowed ominously.

"Ben!" At the sound of the Doctor's voice, the leopard returned sheepishly to his position, curling his tail about him as he closed his eyes. "Frightened you, didn't he?" said Dr. Belsidus, chuckling mirthlessly.

I turned to confront the physician, who, clad in grass-green silk pajamas and brocaded robe of the same color, was standing in the door leading to the front bathroom.

"Yes, he did frighten me," I admitted. "It's the first time I've ever faced one of those big cats."

"Never enter unless I am here," he cautioned, "or unless Jim is with you. Ben is friendly only with us. Others he promptly kills. I got him as a cub and trained him that way."

He strolled over to the bed, crawled between the pink linen sheets and lay back with his hands cupped under his head. I waited respectfully until he was settled, then I pulled one of the curved-back Egyptian chairs up close to him.

"I suppose you're wondering why I'm going to bed at four-thirty in the afternoon, aren't you, Slater?"

"Well, pardon me, but it does seem a little unusual."

"That's because you haven't been here very long, Slater. Whenever you see me retire at this hour, you know that I am not going to sleep." The corners of his mouth lowered in a sardonic smirk. "A middle-aged patient who has a million times more money than she has brains has succumbed to my wiles, Slater. Her check, which will be forthcoming in the course of time, will pay for our convention."

"What convention, Doctor?"

"That's right," he mused more to himself than to me, "I have not told you, have I? Well, take this message: 'Upon debarkation proceed immediately by taxicab to place designated.' Sign it 'World.' "

"To whom shall I send it, Doctor?"

"Look in File Number One in the office. There you will find a typewritten list of names. Send the same message to each of the 50 persons on the list. Some you will notice are en route on the *Queen Mary*. Others are coming on the *Normandie*. A few are coming in on West Indian

24

steamers. These men, 50 of them, will arrive tomorrow. They are delegates to our first convention of the Black Internationale, coming from wherever black men live, at my command and at my expense."

He paused a minute, eyeing me to see that the significance of what he was divulging was sinking in. "Now," he said, rising on one arm and frowning slightly as he concentrated, "you tell Al to tell Mag that as soon as they arrive at her place at St. Nicholas Avenue—that's where they're going from the dock—she is to send them downstairs, see that they have refreshments and everything. Al is to have two of our buses in front of the cabaret tomorrow night. He will ride in the second. Promptly at 8 o'clock he is to lead the delegates from Mag's cellars into the cabaret cellar and on out into the street."

"Then where are we going?"

"To a place where we may confer without interruption or interference," he snapped. "To my mountain place in Green County. Al knows the way. Remember, there must be no slip-up. Many of these men have taken their lives in their hands in making this journey. Most of them have been spotted as dangerous by colonial governments. They expect to be protected. They must and will be protected. Understand?"

"Yes, sir," I mumbled.

"Well, you may go then, Slater. Tell Jim to show the lady up when she arrives."

I followed directions exactly. The *Queen Mary* docked early the next morning, the Columbian Line boat came in round 11 o'clock. The *Normandie* got to the wharf at noon.

Following Dr. Belsidus's later instructions, I watched the passengers disembark. As each black or brown man went through customs, he promptly got his baggage together and hailed a taxicab. Each gave the same address. One hundred fifty-one St. Nicholas Place.

When the last man had gone uptown, I followed. Arrived at Mag's, I went down the steel steps into her basement. The fifty delegates from all over the world were sitting around talking, drinking and eating the buffet lunch Mag's cook had prepared. Although they came from all over the world, I was surprised to find all of them spoke English. Alton Fortune explained: "It was the Chief's orders, that they learn English. He says the Negroes can never be united as long as their leaders speak different languages and can't understand each other. After all, he has given them a year to prepare themselves."

Not long afterward Al gave the signal and we filed through the revolving stone door into the basement of the cabaret where Dr. Belsidus's thieves came to surrender their loot. Thence to the darkness of St. Nicholas Avenue. Two big buses were quickly filled. At another signal from Al, they lumbered forward up to the George Washington Bridge and through the night to the wilds of the Catskill Mountains.

6

⚞⚞⚞⚞⚞⚞⚞⚞⚞⚞⚞⚞⚞⚞⚞⚞⚞⚞⚞⚞⚞⚞⚞⚞

Delegates of Black Nations Go to Secret Rendezvous for Confab

It was well past midnight when the buses halted in a high wellwooded valley two or three miles off the road. The big headlights cut four holes in the black darkness. We were pulled up close to a large wooden building which had once been a country hotel or a sanitarium. Al Fortune got out and I followed suit. The 50 delegates piled out after us. The little plump fellow led the way up the steps to the broad verandah and we entered the building.

"Everybody sit down," Fortune invited, "and the waiters will serve you."

As he said it we were standing in a completely darkened hall which made his advice the more incongruous. Suddenly there was a click and the whole building was flooded with light. The broad entrance hall where we hung up our wraps opened into a large lobby beautifully carpeted and strewn with easy chairs, sofas and ottomans upholstered in red leather. At a large hotel desk stood two brownskin clerks waiting smilingly for our registration. Uniformed attendants stood rigidly by.

"Some dump, Al," I remarked, while the foreign Negroes looked about them in mingled amazement and growing respect. "Must have set the Doctor back something, didn't it?"

"Perhaps," he replied laconically. "I never asked him. We don't ask too many questions, Slater."

My curiosity rebuffed, I turned to study the strange group of Negroes Belsidus had summoned from the ends of the earth and who now sat around chatting in strongly accented English. Some were tall, hawk-faced and reddish brown. Others were short, stocky and black as midnight. Some were brawny, others were slight and scholarly in appearance. While a few showed little trace of racial admixture, others were obviously possessed of some Caucasian or Mongolian ancestry. All seemed just a little puzzled, a little uncertain, certainly somewhat awed by these efficient preparations. While they laughed and chatted in a normal fashion, I could detect in their tones some slight trace of uneasiness, outward evidence of inner preoccupation with the object for which they had traveled over jungle, desert, mountain and sea to this house hidden in the Catskills.

I noticed the ample rotund form of my gray-eyed friend, Al Fortune, moving among the delegates, dropping a word here and there, shaking hands as he introduced himself and was introduced. It was more talking than I had seen him do before. Yet his affability, I thought, was affected. There was a shiftiness in those deep gray eyes, a hard monotonous character to that voice that somehow always struck me unpleasantly, although our relations had been most cordial and friendly. What seemed singular was the light of recognition that illuminated the face of Momodu, the tall, slender, cadaverous black delegate from Gambia when Al approached him for a few words.

Supposedly, Al had never met nor corresponded with any of the delegates. Everyone present was a stranger, more or less, to everyone else. Only Dr. Belsidus knew them all. He alone had corresponded with them and had their photographs in his personal files. And yet here were Al Fortune and this Momodu meeting like people who had met before.

Now, I do not mean to say that their actions were obvious or sustained. Nothing of the sort. Indeed, Al talked no longer with Momodu than he did with the others. It was, rather, their manner that struck me as strange. Even though at the time I felt my suspicion to be foolish and was just a little ashamed of myself, I decided to keep my mouth shut and my eyes open. After all, I was the Doctor's secretary, and I felt that he trusted me and expected me to look after his interests during his absence.

We had been sitting in the lobby for upwards of an hour when one

27

of the uniformed attendants wended his way through the chattering throng and came up to me.

"Mister Slater?" he inquired, courteously.

"Yes, what is it?"

"The Doctor says the time has arrived. You are to follow me. The others are to follow you. You move up the stairway to the second floor, thence to the ballroom door. When it is thrown open, you are to move down the hall and stand behind the first chair alongside that of the Doctor. The others will form around the table in order. There must be absolute silence. You are to wait for any command before seating yourself. The others are to do as you do. Understand, Mister Slater? Those are the orders of Dr. Belsidus."

"Yes," I replied, "I understand." He stepped back. I clapped my hands to attract attention. When all was quiet and the delegates were eyeing me with expectation, I said, "Dr. Belsidus wishes us to assemble above. Please follow me in silence."

The attendant made for the stairway with slow and measured steps. I followed a few paces behind him. Up the stairs I went, followed by the sound of feet treading in unison. At the head of the stairs we turned to the right. I looked back down the stairs. The 50 delegates were ascending in single file, their faces grave and expectant.

The attendant stepped aside. I moved forward to the closed double doors which he indicated and halted. One minute, perhaps a minute and a half, I waited. I could hear the breathing of the others behind me. I could feel something of their suppressed excitement—the same excitement that was making my own heart beat loud.

Suddenly the doors opened inward as if by some mysterious force. The arrangement of the ballroom was certainly impressive, to say the least. Straight down the center of the highly polished floor ran a long, wide table covered with green baize cloth. Along each side were comfortable mahogany arm chairs. In front of each chair was a large blotter, a well-filled ink well, paper and pencils. At the head of the table stood a great, black, high-backed chair, elaborately carved and seemingly inlaid with silver. Behind this chair, but on the little stage, was a huge map of the world indirectly lighted. Otherwise the room was absolutely bare.

I walked in as I had been instructed, wondering where Dr. Belsidus might be. The others took places, each behind a chair, and stood in silence. We all turned as if by command to the empty chair.

"The gentlemen will please be seated," came the voice of the attendant from the doorway.

With less clatter than you would have imagined, the delegates seated themselves. The attendant stepped out into the hall. The double doors swung closed. The delegates looked questioningly at each other but none broke the silence. Looking down the table, I noted that Al Fortune and Momodu were seated side by side close to the door.

What was detaining the Doctor? The same thought must have been in other minds, for I noticed many a puzzled expression.

Somewhere a gong sounded. There was another sound of the gong and then every light in the ballroom was extinguished. I could hear the swift intake of breath that indicated everyone's surprise. The gong sounded a third time. The lights came on again as bright as before. There had been no sound beyond that of the gong, and yet, seated in the black high-backed chair at the head of the table was Dr. Henry Belsidus, garbed, as ever, in faultless and appropriate attire. The corners of his cruel mouth were drawn in a sardonic smile.

The fall of a feather would have been audible in that vast room as the delegates gaped wide-eyed at the tall black man who had appeared so mysteriously, so noiselessly from nowhere. He looked at each man in turn as though he were reading their minds in succession as one might read a succession of billboards. It was just a little awkward, being stared at in this manner. It was as if one were a guinea pig. He had not spoken a word and we were constrained to silence.

There was something awesome and eery about the whole thing. How had he got up here before us? How had he been able to enter the ballroom in the two seconds the lights were extinguished and seat himself without making a sound? Why didn't he start the proceedings? Yet, he sat there, tapping quietly on the blotter in front of him with his long, cruel, devilish fingers, his eyes half closed in sinister calculation.

The place was as still as death. Only the soft tap-tap of the physician's fingers broke the terrible silence or withdrew attention momentarily from his penetrating scrutiny. It was maddening. I thought I should scream. Then he lifted his head and in an even tone announced:

"Gentlemen, before we begin we must rid ourselves of spies. Three of you must not leave here alive!"

7

∧∧∧∧∧∧∧∧∧∧∧∧∧∧∧∧∧∧∧∧∧∧

Belsidus Does Away with the Three Spies
and the Meeting Proceeds

The announcement electrified the gathering. There was a swift intake of breath, a hasty glancing up and down the long table. I looked at Al Fortune and Momodu, the delegate from Gambia. The engineer was tapping silently on the green baize cloth, apparently lost in contemplation of his fingers' tips, his face an inscrutable mask. I thought I detected a small light of consternation in the narrow eyes of the Gambian. The room became as silent as the desert at midnight. All eyes studied the stern visage of the Chief. Fully a minute passed before Dr. Belsidus spoke again. Then in clear, measured tones he began:

"Gentlemen, I am Dr. Belsidus. Most of you have never seen me. Many of you will never see me again. But you will get my commands. You have sworn to carry them out. You will carry them out to the letter.

"I have brought you all here at great expense that you may receive your instructions personally and meet your colleagues. It is unnecessary for me to dwell at great length on our program. You know what it is. It can be summed up in a few words: For four hundred years our race has been in eclipse. For four hundred years we have been victims of superior forces. For four hundred years we have seen our civilizations crushed and controlled one after the other by the white man. We have suffered every degradation his fertile mind could invent. We have not only been enslaved in body, but in spirit and mind as well. We have been demoralized.

"Gentlemen, this must end. It is the business of the Black Internationale to end it. All revolutions are started by minorities who use majorities to do their bidding. All successful revolutions must be conducted along dictatorial lines by a minority obedient to one man. I am the man.

"I have the responsibility of directing this revolution. To direct it successfully I must be obeyed implicitly. Disobedience simply means death. Treason means death. Cowardice means death. Victory is certain if my directions are followed.

"We have been subdued by ruthlessness. Now we shall triumph by ruthlessness. The white man has not hesitated to use any and every means to degrade the Negro and keep him demoralized. We shall not hesitate to use any and every means at our disposal to degrade and demoralize the white man.

"We shall run him out of Africa, out of India, out of the West Indies, out of the South Seas. We shall elevate the Negro people to the proud estate they once occupied four hundred years ago. And those who help to bring about this revolution will not have reason to regret their allegiance to me."

His voice fell to silence and the vast room was still. Sitting close to the Doctor as I was, I could study his face. There was in it the sternness of fanaticism, the canniness of the fox, the savagery of the wolf. He tapped lightly upon his perfectly manicured fingers and looked about him, up and down the long table.

"Mr. Fortune," he said, and my heart almost stopped as I glanced quickly at my friend, the engineer, "please get rid of the three spies so that we may proceed. Our time is limited."

The wide-eyed delegates turned as if by command to see what was about to happen. If Al Fortune felt that his task was an unpleasant one, he gave no indication of it. His reddish brown face was a mask as he rose and swept the upturned faces with an all-inclusive glance.

"Every colonial government," said Dr. Belsidus, breaking in before Al could say or do anything, "is quite naturally opposed to any such organization as we have effected. Each one has a certain number of colored or Negro police agents to spy on such gatherings and conferences to find out what our people are doing or planning to do. In this way, and also by selling out, the Negro has been betrayed as often by his own people as by the white man. It is doubtful if we should have been degraded as we have if it had not been for certain of our own people.

"Hereafter all such Negroes must die wherever and whenever discovered. Such men and women cannot be reformed or reconditioned. Once a rat always a rat. I want every one here to watch closely what takes place and take it as a warning. Very well, Mr. Fortune, you may go on."

Al moved back his chair and then, turning, he walked almost to the end of the table. He stopped behind the chair of a very light Negro with Negroid features, half-closed eyes and a square British face. Al glanced significantly at Dr. Belsidus.

"Henry Pilkington," said the Chief, "you will have no opportunity to tell what you have seen and heard to the British Colonial Office. The English have an efficient spy service, Pilkington, but our service is just as efficient."

"It's a dirty lie!" cried the delegate from Jamaica, jumping up, red-faced and excited. Before he could say more, Al grabbed his head with his left arm and, bringing up his right hand in wide arc, he touched the struggling man's throat just as I had seen Dr. Belsidus touch the throat of the white girl some weeks before. With a hoarse cry, Pilkington's struggles grew weaker and weaker. Finally he collapsed back in his chair. It was only then that I noticed a black thorn sticking out of the neck of the unfortunate Jamaican. Like me, the horrified audience watched it with fascination.

Al walked around the end of the table and started down the other side. About three paces from me he halted again behind the chair of a slight brown man with mustache and goatee, pointed face and large, long-lashed eyes. Again he glanced at Dr. Belsidus. "Jules Constant," the Doctor began, "it is unfortunate that you will never see St. Louis, Senegal, again, but our plans and the lives of our revolutionaries are more important than your miserable existence. Mr. Fortune, please proceed."

The little man's eyes were filled with terror. He seemed helpless slumped there in his chair. Al reached for his head. Quickly and with great agility, Constant tipped his chair backward, throwing Al off balance. Then he sped toward the nearest heavily-draped window before Al could regain his feet, and yanking the drapes aside would doubtless have jumped to the ground. But instead of finding himself confronted with glass, he was faced with great steel shutters.

Al raced after him. Constant turned and whipped out a German Luger. I gasped. The others sat frozen to their seats. Constant's automatic came up, but before he could fire I heard a sound alongside me like the shaking of a spring from a window sash. The Senegalese dropped his

Luger and dropped on the floor, a neat red hole drilled in his skull. I turned to Dr. Belsidus. He was holding in his long slender hands an automatic equipped with a silencer. That was the swishing sound I had heard.

I watched the delegates. There was awe, horror and fear in their faces. Some of them shifted uneasily.

"The French Surete General will miss Jules Constant," observed the Doctor dryly. "He was a good operative. Very well, Mr. Fortune, you may proceed."

Quite unruffled, Al moved around the end of the table, passing behind the Chief's chair and moving back to his place. Who could the third man be? I wondered. The others must have been speculating about the same thing. Al was almost to his place now. The air was tense with expectancy. Al paused, then halted behind the chair of the delegate from Gambia with whom he had seemed to be on such good terms just a few minutes before. Momodu's cadaverous visage grew ashen.

"Hasha Momodu," said Dr. Belsidus, "you served the British Colonial office, so I suppose you are willing to die for it."

"But there must be some mistake, Doctor. There must be some mistake," cried Momodu. "You cannot do this. I am innocent."

"You are a liar, a fool, and a traitor, Momodu," the Doctor hissed. He looked at Fortune.

The engineer plunged a thorn deep into the neck of the Senegalese. There was a struggle, but it was soon over. The virulent poison with which the thorn was evidently smeared worked speedily as soon as it entered the blood stream. The Gambian collapsed like an empty sack.

Dr. Belsidus clapped his hands twice. Two uniformed attendants entered. One of them was the man who had led me to the conference hall. They were pushing a rubber-tired, three-tiered cart similar to the type used to transfer food in hospitals and army mess halls. Working swiftly, the two uniformed men lifted each corpse and placed it on a shelf of the cart. It was wheeled to a position two or three paces behind the Doctor and almost alongside the small stage.

Dr. Belsidus clapped his hands again. The room was plunged into darkness. Perhaps ten seconds passed. The Doctor clapped his hands again. The lights came on. The two attendants and the cart with its gruesome burden had disappeared.

I looked quickly and questioningly at the Chief. Just the suspicion of a smile pulled down the corners of his mouth. I knew he was amused by the amazement of the others.

"Now," he said with evident relief, "let us proceed. Afterward I shall show you our acid tank where we rid ourselves of the corpus delecti on certain occasions. Very handy to have. Before you return to your homes, Mr. Hamilton, our chemist, will show you how the acid bath is prepared. But now, let us consider our immediate plans."

The delegates leaned forward attentively to drink in every word.

8

▲▲▲▲▲▲▲▲▲▲▲▲▲▲▲▲▲▲▲▲▲▲▲▲

Dr. Belsidus Explains His Plan of Action to Redeem the Black Race

Speaking softly, but in a voice that carried his words clearly to each of the dusky delegates, Dr. Belsidus spoke.

"Previous efforts of the colored peoples to emancipate themselves from white supremacy have failed because we were not prepared to emancipate ourselves. Every nation of people is destroyed first from within. It must organize itself within if it is to triumph without.

"Why was Africa subjugated? Why were India and Malaysia subjugated? Why do the dark peoples in South America, the West Indies and the United States remain in bondage?

"You all know the answer. First, there was lack of unity. Secondly, there was lack of knowledge of the resources of the white man and of how to properly organize and exploit our own resources. Thirdly, we were spiritually enslaved, and still are. Our religion is that of the white man. Our so-called education is one long praise and glorification of the white man. Our sources of information are controlled by the white man. Therefore, we have the minds of white men. And so long as we have the minds of white men, we cannot free black men. In order to triumph it is necessary for us to believe that we are superior and invincible.

"Thus, it would be unwise to either challenge or attack the white man at this time. Embarrass the white man, disorganize the white man, disunite the white man, disturb the white man, but do not attack the white man except secretly and with skill and intelligence."

"But Doctor," objected the delegate from Sierra Leone, "what then shall we do? Why have a Black Internationale at all if we are not to strike blows for our freedom? I and my little group in Freetown are ready to die for the race. My comrades would not understand a policy that negatived attack."

Several of the delegates nodded in approval, especially Corda, the delegate from South Africa, and Monu, the delegate from Grand Bassam, Ivory Coast, who, I had learned, had suffered severe persecution for their efforts to bring about racial solidarity.

"It is your business, Joseph Kalanga," retorted Belsidus in a stern, hard voice, "to make your comrades understand my policy. Blows in plenty will be struck but we must first be prepared to strike them. Ignorance never won anything except poverty, disease and death. Still, I am glad you put the question because it will help to clarify our program in the minds of the delegates.

"Now," he continued, "who controls the Christian Church to which all the literate Negroes in Sierra Leone belong?"

"The white man."

"Very well," commented the Doctor, indulging a faint smile, "and who prints the books, magazines and newspapers you read?"

"Mostly the white man."

"And who dominates in the control of stores and trading stations?"

"The white man."

"And who are the engineers, chemists, architects, technicians and others of that type such as you have?"

"White men."

"If I am correctly informed," pursued the Doctor, apparently more amused, "your minority of educated Negroes are physicians and school teachers."

"That is true, Doctor."

"Then how can you hope to successfully attack a great mechanical civilization with great mills, mines, factories, fleets, and above all the thousands and thousands of skilled technicians necessary for the conduct of modern warfare as well as the perpetuation of machine civilization? It is quite impossible, is it not? Have you forgotten Abdel Krim, Haile Selassie and numerous other chieftains from Fuzzy Wuzzy to Cetawayo who threw themselves against the machines of white civilization and failed? We must never forget those facts, my men. We must always face them realistically. No, we are not yet ready for open attack. Today the white man is our superior in industry and commerce, and therefore is our superior in everything else because everything in our civilization is predicated upon industry and commerce.

"Our business is to prepare; to bring about unity among the colored peoples; to rid them of that deeply ingrained inferiority complex, especially those who have been most exposed to the white man's influence; to train technicians; and to obtain the money to do all this. We shall, wherever possible, use the resources and money of the white man to bring this about.

"It is easier to control and regiment literate than illiterate people. The latter usually believe only what they see or hear by word of mouth, while the former will believe anything they read. One of our first tasks for our 50 cells will be to teach the colored world how to read and write. It is easy, and any adult of normal intelligence can be taught to read and write in a week or more. Moreover, by the method we have perfected, it is possible to teach four or five hundred people at once. You will receive detailed instructions concerning this new method tomorrow. Before you leave, each of you will receive, in addition, a moving picture projector, several rolls of film, portable screen, and later you will be sent a gasoline engine, motor, and other accessories. With the aid of this equipment you will be able to show the people the white man's world and what Negroes are doing, you will be able to teach them something about the forces of nature and how to control them. You will be able to do it freely because there is nothing in any of the films with which white officials might quarrel. In fact, you will be commended for your zeal."

An expression of great craftiness came over his face as he said that. He stroked his smooth chin and then proceeded.

"But people cannot be held merely by education. Most people, white or black, really do not wish to learn. It is necessary to reach them through their emotions. Therefore we must have a new religion, a religion designed for suppressed colored people. We must have a church which will supersede the white churches and the colored church, which are based on the white man's religion. Tomorrow you will meet Rev. Samson Binks, the head of the Negro Church. It is something spectacular and colorful, with gorgeous raiment, pageantry and music, all based on Negro motifs and psychology. It is as religion is supposed to be. Nothing like it has been seen since the days of Egypt. One temple at least will immediately be erected by each cell. This will serve as a meeting place under the guise of religion, it will serve as a center for educational work just like the missionary schools. It will serve also as a center for propaganda. This much of the program will be completed before the end of 1937. In these temples of the Negro Church we shall gather the people, tell them what we want them to hear and show them what we want them to see. We shall have a first-class radio receiving set in each temple, and there shall be frequent distributions of free food, free shoes, free clothing and free tools to all those who join us. By this means we shall build up a fanatical loyalty."

"But Doctor," inquired Corda, the South African, "where shall we ever get the means to do all of this? How can we buy powerful radios, moving picture projectors and food, clothing, shoes and tools? How shall we build temples? All these things will cost millions. How can we get all that money and complete the program in just one year? I do not doubt your ability, for you have accomplished marvels, but I frankly cannot see how it can be done."

"You are all here at my expense, at the cost of $50,000. You haven't spent a penny and will not have to spend a penny. You follow my instructions. You will receive everything I say or the money with which to purchase it." There was a trace of irritation in the Doctor's voice but also great assurance. And certainly he had a right to be sure of himself. "Meantime, you will immediately select one young man and one young woman who have finished secondary school with honors and send them to America immediately for technical education. In July you will select 10 young women who have completed grammar school and send them here to be sent to American trade schools for six months."

There was absolute silence as the Doctor paused. All gazed at him, some in wonderment, others in awe, others with unsuppressed enthusiasm gleaming in their eyes.

As my pencil raced over that paper, taking down in shorthand his every word, a little doubt crept over me. How could he do what he said? Then I recalled his store of gold, Al Fortune's robber band and the hints of astonishing developments in other parts of the country which the Doctor had let drop from time to time. Yes, he might do it after all. Certainly he had thought the program out well.

"And now, gentlemen," said Dr. Belsidus, smiling and rising, followed quickly by the others, "we shall descend to the acid bath and see what has happened to our erstwhile visitors. And then, perhaps, to bed. There is much to do tomorrow."

9

The Secret Conference Disbands,
Then Carl Meets a Pretty Girl

Dr. Belsidus leaned down and pressed a button under the arm of his chair. Before our startled gaze a large section of the floor swung slowly downward, one end reaching to the floor below and constituting a ramp. I understood now how the cart of the three bodies of the three spies had disappeared so quickly.

At the physician's command we trooped down the ramp into a small room from which a similar ramp led into the basement. As we left each ramp, it moved slowly back into place.

In a six-foot pool at the far end, the nude bodies of the three spies lay in a heap. In the calm manner of a professor instructing a class, Dr. Belsidus explained the procedure followed in disposing of cadavers.

"Observe," he began, "that the pool is lined with black tile. Some such material is needed. The bodies are placed in the pool as you see them. Then they are covered with this corrosive acid made by our Mr. Hamilton. All right, boys." This last to two attendants who stood obediently at hand.

The two men rolled big carboys of the acid to the edge of the tank and emptied their contents. Other than the gurgling sound, the basement was as still as a tomb. A sharp, offensive odor pervaded the air. In the pool a rapid bubbling began.

"Watch closely, gentlemen," the doctor cautioned. The bubbling, hissing acid was omnivorously devouring the flesh before our eyes. Two more carboys were now emptied into the pool. The activity increased. Slowly the bodies began to disintegrate. The things that had once been living, breathing men were now reduced to lumps of flesh, to pulp. Bones liquified, hair merged and lost itself in the mass.

"Stir it!" commanded Dr. Belsidus. The two attendants seized long steel rods and aided the disintegration by stirring the bubbling, hissing, evil-smelling mess. It had now become a ghastly pudding which no one would ever have guessed had once been men. Gradually the devilish commotion died down. In ten minutes only an even scum, dark green and odiferous, remained.

"Get rid of it!" ordered the physician. One of the attendants walked to the stone wall and pulled a chain. Immediately the contents of the pool began to empty. Down, down it sank, while the awed delegates craned their necks to see. Soon there was a sucking, gurgling sound. In another fifteen seconds the pool was empty.

"In our work," observed Dr. Belsidus blandly, walking toward the other end of the basement surrounded by the others, "it frequently becomes advisable to kill. It is safer, in view of the acumen of the police, to leave no traces. Mr. Hamilton, our chemist, hit upon this very excellent method. You will all receive the formula for this acid before you leave. It will come in handy, I assure you."

He said all this in a calm, matter-of-fact tone that made the cold chills run down my back. Somehow or other he seemed not quite human. Rather, he was a cold, cruel, fanatically determined machine. Each day I realized more and more that the man would stop at nothing to gain his ends.

After three days of conferences and following receipt of detailed instructions, the delegates began to depart for their homes. I was rather glad to see them go, for the gathering had meant a lot of work for me. It had been part of my job to purchase motion picture projectors, films, portable screens, motors and gasoline engines. Dr. Belsidus had had special films made which in a very simple manner but quite effectively showed Negro progress in the United States. Others revealed the methods of producing various products such as plows, rifles, automobiles, and so forth. It was evident that he intended his followers to understand the background of the white man's supremacy. One set of films that particularly interested me was that used in teaching reading and writing. Exceedingly ingenuous it was, and I could readily understand how even the most stupid person might be taught in a few days to read and write simple words. Some of the sets were in English, others in French, Belgian, Dutch, Spanish and Portuguese, depending on the country to which they were destined.

While the routine at the mansion of Dr. Belsidus was unpredictable, I had thought things would go on much as they had before. But here I was mistaken. The very day following the departure of the Brazilian delegate, the last to leave, Dr. Belsidus summoned me to his suite. I promptly seized my pencil and pad and ascended in the automatic elevator.

When the doors flew open and I started to enter the exotic Egyptian setting, a sight met my eyes that made me gasp and stop short. Facing me, and talking to Dr. Belsidus across a small table on which two half-emptied cocktail glasses stood, sat the prettiest colored girl I've ever seen. She had the color of a pale Indian with the softness of feature of the Negro, and wore with trim and easy grace a modish dark green business suit. Perched on one side of her head was one of those cute modernistic hats.

Although she seemed perfectly proportioned, it was her face that held one spellbound. It was absolutely symmetrical, with lips not large but sensuously full, rather high cheekbones, and large, wide-spaced eyes like limpid pools under the moonlight on a tropic plain. Her general expression was one of unbelievable innocence and sweetness. It was this contrast between her and the sinister physician that so startled me.

I recovered my poise, finally. There was just a trace of tolerant amusement on the Doctor's face as he noted my perturbation.

"Slater," he said, rising. "I want you to know Miss Patricia Givens. Patricia, this is Carl Slater, my secretary, of whom I've been telling you."

"I'm so glad to know you, Mister Slater," she said, revealing two rows of glistening, white, even teeth in an infectious smile, and offering a tiny gloved hand. I stammered out the usual thing while trying vainly to keep my eyes away from her hypnotic orbs. "Henry has been telling me how shocked you've been since joining us."

Then she was in it, too! I didn't know just what to say. I was frankly ill at ease, for I did not yet know what her relations were to Dr. Belsidus and she seemed more desirable to me than any woman I had ever seen. I dropped my eyes with difficulty and waited for the Doctor's orders.

"Sit down, Slater," he said, "and have a cocktail." He clapped his hands. The colored maid in black dress and white apron and cap hurried across the gleaming floor, a cocktail for me on her golden tray.

"Now, Slater," the physician began, pursing his lips and stroking his smooth black jowls. "Miss Givens is making a tour of our various enterprises, going as far as Mississippi. I want you to go with her and learn all there is at first hand about our resources. None of our staff can hope to serve efficiently without a detailed understanding of our work. You can't get that sitting around here. I suppose it will take you about a week, won't it Patricia?"

"Just about," she said. She seemed to be just a little amused at my dazed expression. I've always been a sap for pretty girls, and I don't think there's ever been one to out-rank Patricia Givens.

"And when do we leave?" I managed to say. "What train?"

They both smiled at that. "Miss Givens travels everywhere by airplane," said Dr. Belsidus.

"We leave at daylight," she announced in a matter-of-fact tone. "Jim will drive us to the field."

"Just we two?" I asked, aquiver with excitement at the prospect of having this angel's company for an entire week.

"Just we two," she echoed, smiling mischievously. "You're not frightened are you, Mr. Slater?"

I passed it off with a confused laugh while a dozen questions tortured me. Who was she? What was her background? What interest did she have in this bloody movement? What was she to Belsidus?

10

△△△△△△△△△△△△△△△△△△△△△△△

Carl Slater Learns Patricia Givens
Is Head of Air Force

It was still dark when Jim awakened me. I shaved and dressed quickly, grabbed my travelling bag and ran down to the car, the mute giant in my wake. It was the long black limousine with which I was all too familiar. I stepped in. Miss Givens was already there. "All right, Jim!" she ordered. The long car cruised over to Fifth Avenue and turned north toward Harlem. Then she turned to me with that dazzling smile. "Well, we're on our way," she said. "You're going to see something, Mr. Slater, before you get back."

"Yes," I remarked dreamily. I was studying her at close range now, and the nearer one got to her, the prettier she seemed. This morning she was in green leather pilot's cap and jacket, green riding breeches and cordovan boots. It was a becoming costume.

We turned over to Seventh Avenue, sped to 155th Street, crossed the viaduct, followed the Harlem Speedway and so wended our way into the Bronx and Westchester County. Jim was losing no time. There was little traffic as yet and on some stretches we made great, if silent, speed. About eight-thirty we ran up a side road for a mile or two and stopped at what appeared at first to be a country club.

"Well, here we are, Mr. Slater," she said. "Let's get out."

"What place is this?"

"This is our air school. The boys live in this building. The hangars and workshops are away over there. You probably thought they were big greenhouses. They do look like greenhouses, don't they?"

"Yes," I answered, although I confess I was more interested in the girl than I was in the hangars. She was just perfect.

"We put in glass roofs so the boys would have more light," she explained. Then, turning to Jim, she said, "All right, Jim. You can go on back to town."

We walked into the long, low, rambling stone building with its wide verandah. A uniformed attendant, probably the steward, met us and showed us all through, although Miss Givens was apparently no stranger there. There were two beds to a room and about thirty rooms. A huge modern kitchen, an attractive dining hall and a well-equipped recreation room completed the picture.

"Come on," she said. "Our plane's waiting but I want you to see the workshops before we go."

We walked for about a half mile before we reached the hangars and workshops. The flying field was clear of weeds, well marked and lighted in accordance with government regulations. I have never seen a better-ordered place. In the two big machine shops, more than a score of young colored men and women were working over engines, doping wings and otherwise engaged in the making and repairing of aircraft. In the five big hangars I counted a total of twenty planes. Most of them were built for high speed but several were huge transport planes capable of long journeys or carrying huge payloads.

Miss Givens was studying my reactions, a little smile playing about her pretty mouth. In the air overhead two of the small speedy ships were performing the most hair-raising stunts, dipping, sliding, slipping, banking, spinning: every gyration I had ever seen. "Those are our two latest productions," she observed.

"But what's to be done with all these planes?" I asked, for I was frankly puzzled, yet impressed, by the place.

"Oh, we'll use them," she said, lowering her voice. "The time will come when we won't have nearly enough. We finish one every ten days or so. It's excellent training for our young mechanics and pilots. I have to keep them busy, you know?"

"YOU keep them busy?" I was really surprised by her remark. "What have you got to do with this?"

"Oh," she said, laughing a little proudly, "I guess I didn't tell you that I'm in charge of the Doctor's air force."

"You don't mean to say that you're in charge of the manufacture of these planes?"

"Of course. Why, don't you think a woman can do things like this?"

"Well . . . yes," I stumbled, awed now by her brains as well as her beauty, "but it's so unusual, you know. It sort of took my breath away. Let me congratulate you."

43

"Not me," she replied soberly. "Congratulate Dr. Belsidus. It was he who made it possible for me to study three years in France and learn the business from the ground up. He is the most brilliant man in the world today."

The tone of reverence with which she said this somehow irritated me, and then, ashamed, I realized for the first time that I was in love with this girl and jealous of the sinister physician, master of both of us. Afraid of betraying my emotion, I remained silent.

"Don't you think so?" she asked, gazing straight into my eyes.

"Of course he is a remarkable man," I managed. And then, anxious to change the subject, I asked: "Who is in charge when you are away? I mean, who heads the highly technical work on engines and instruments? Surely you don't leave that in the hands of students?"

"Certainly not." She turned and called back toward the largest shop: "Juan! Juan! Come here a minute."

A voice answered her from the building. Then in a minute a giant of a man, dull black, with powerful muscles and flashing white teeth, came striding toward us, grimy overalls flapping.

"Yes, Mees Geevens," he said. "What ees eet?"

"Juan, I want you to meet Mr. Carl Slater, the Doctor's new secretary. Mr. Slater, this is Juan Torlier, our chief aeronautical engineer." We smiled and shook hands heartily. After a pleasant exchange, he turned and went back to the workshop.

"There's a real story for you," she exclaimed. "I met him two years ago in Barcelona. He was working in an airplane factory there where they turned out some of the finest engines in Europe, and he was the foreman in charge of production. He comes originally from the Muni River Settlements, you know, Spanish Guinea. Some colonial official took a liking to him, sent him to Spain to be schooled, but he'd seen enough of their misrule in Africa for it to rankle in his heart. So it wasn't hard to get him into the organization."

What a group this Dr. Belsidus had assembled! The more I saw of it and its work, the more I began to lose my skepticism about the possibilities of success.

We walked out on the field where a small black and gold autogiro was standing, its engine running. The rotor blades were extended. All was ready for flight.

"Everything okeh, Sam?" she asked the mechanic.

"It's all right, Miss Givens," he said.

I got in beside her. She gave it the gun and after a very short run, much shorter than would been required for a regular airplane, we rose quickly and were off over the tree tops.

I couldn't get over this girl's sureness, her nonchalance. She handled the autogiro as I would an automobile. We followed the Hudson to a point past Poughkeepsie, then we turned slightly to the east and flew toward a cloud of gray dust that rose from behind a hill around which a railroad spur ran.

Miss Givens brought the machine down in a large open space before a huge gray building near the hill. Not far from it was a gang of men engaged in quarrying limestone which little cars carried to the nearby crusher.

"Well, here we are," she said, shutting off the engine. "This is our No. 1 cement mill. Come on, I want you to meet Bennie Simpson."

We walked over to the great building coated with cement. There the short, plump light mulatto with wavy hair, gray eyes and slightly freckled face who was in charge, took us through the place. We saw the hard limestone ground dry and mixed with the dried and ground clay. Then we saw the mixture dried and burned at a clinkering tempera-ture, and finally the light gray powder being bagged. In a nearby ware-house were thousands upon thousands of bags of cement piled to the roof. A considerable number of Negroes were employed. The little houses in which they lived were not far from the mill.

"We're turning out fifty tons of cement a week," Simpson boasted. "We've been running to capacity for almost a year now. If Doc don't start building pretty soon we won't have any room left to store this stuff."

"What building is he going to do?" I asked, puzzled, turning to Miss Givens. She smiled indulgently and her eyes sparkled.

"I'll tell you all about it when we get going," she said. "Come on. We've got to reach our Jersey farm before dark."

We bade Simpson and his cement mill adieu and were soon again aw-ing back down the Hudson. Frankly, my admiration and respect for Dr. Belsidus grew apace. The more I thought of him and his elaborate pre-parations, the more I wondered what, if anything, Patricia Givens was to him. She had spoken so worshipfully of him. Was she in love with him? If so, what chance had I? The thought was depressing, and I looked down idly as we passed over the Ramapo Hills. But inevitably my eyes came back to this brilliant, beautiful girl, and I wondered rather hopelessly whether and how I might win her affection. Then I laughed at myself when I realized that I had scarcely known her twenty-four hours.

11

Carl Sees Greatest Farm in World,
with Science at Controls

"Why all that cement?" I asked, as we tore through the dying afternoon toward our destination.

"You've heard of Rev. Samson Binks, haven't you?"

"Yes, I heard Belsidus mention him in connection with some new Negro religion."

"Correct. And that cement is for the temples. Oh, we're going about it thoroughly, make no mistake about that."

"You seem very sure about the success of this Black Internationale program," I observed. She turned toward me, eyes shining fanatically.

"Yes, I'm sure," she shouted above the hum of the motor.

"And what makes you so sure?"

"Because we're using the weapons and knowledge of the white man against him. In the past, subject peoples have tried to match primitive weapons against the latest instruments of warfare. Either that or they have been ill-prepared or unprepared with the industrial organization incident and necessary to the manufacture of such instruments. It is the skilled technician, the scientist, who wins modern wars, and we are mobilizing the black scientists of the world. Our professors, our orators, our politicians have failed us. Our technicians will not. Every day sees another trained young colored man or woman, sometimes both, added to our group."

"And the masses—what about them? Will they follow you as fanatically as your technicians?" I asked, chiefly to hear what she would say. "Can you depend upon their loyalty as you can that of Bennie Simpson, Juan Torlier, Ransom Just, Al Fortune and yourself?"

"We're not worried about the masses," she replied, airily, with a toss of her green helmet. "The masses always believe what they are told often and loud enough. We will recondition the Negro masses in accordance with the most approved behavioristic methods. The church will hold them spiritually. Our economic organization will keep control of those who shape their views. Our secret service will take care of dissenters. Our propaganda bureau will tell them what to think and believe. That's the way to build revolutions, Mr. Slater."

I loved the faint flush on her cheeks which the bright green helmet and jacket only accentuated, and I couldn't help but admire the expertness with which she piloted the plane. Would she be interested in love, I wondered—this beauty who superintended an aircraft factory, piloted planes across country and talked of conditioning the masses, world revolution and such things.

"Listen," I shouted, "don't call me Mr. Slater, call me Carl."

She turned quickly, and smiled. "It is silly, our being so formal, isn't it?" she said. And then, "I suppose you might as well call me Pat, too." The friendliness in her tone made my heart skip a little. Just like a young fellow, I began wondering about the future.

I noted in the distance what appeared to be a small swamp lake, yet it was perfectly square and was criss-crossed by what seemed to be paths. On one side of it were a number of barns and silos, a large farmhouse with a lawn of several acres in front of it.

"That's our New Jersey farm," she shouted, jerking her head toward it.

"I can't see any farm," I replied. "There's nothing but some farm buildings."

"You just wait and see," she said, smiling knowingly. "This is Sam Hamilton's first experiment."

We came on fast. Pat banked the plane. Our shoulders touched and I found myself thrilling like some school kid. Then we came down and, after a surprisingly short run, stopped almost directly in front of the farmhouse. It was colonial in style but quite new; so were the barns

47

and silos. The vast lawn on which we had landed was clipped short and looked like green velvet.

The sun was quite low now. I noticed that there were signal lights for night landing and a sleeve for wind direction on a nearby red and white steel-frame tower. We got out and approached the verandah. Pat rang the bell. Shortly, a uniformed servant admitted us.

"Come in and meet Sam," said Pat. "He'll show us something before dark."

"I thought he was in New York," I said, remembering that the day before I had seen him in the subterranean smeltery melting down precious ornaments and plates that had once graced the bodies and tables of rich white people.

"He always comes out once a day," she explained. "We're only about a hundred miles from New York, you know."

Sam strode out to meet us almost as soon as we had taken seats. Gone were the white clothing and green goggles he always wore in front of his furnace. Today he was dressed in a neat blue serge suit, a fitting contrast to his exotic, Hindu-like countenance.

"Glad to see you out here," he told me. "This is where the really big thing is going on. Of course we're not making any money yet, but pretty soon we'll knock 'em dead with our stuff."

"What are you doing out here on a farm?" I asked half seriously. "A chemist's place is in the laboratory."

"That's all you know about it," he laughed. "We chemists are soon going to put the farmers out of business. Come on out and I'll show you."

We followed him through the house and out the back door toward the lake. It was the most surprising, astounding lake I've ever seen. One can best describe it by calling it a mile-square rectangle of cement, gridironed by cement dikes a hundred yards apart. These gridirons converted the artificial lake or reservoir into contiguous pools, each about two acres in extent. Each pool was about four feet deep and half filled with greenish water in which plants were growing in serried rows. At intervals of about two feet, slender concrete posts were spaced across the pools and connected by ordinary fence wire. On to these the plants clung. The dikes were about ten feet wide, easily permitting a large car or truck to pass over them.

"This is our farm," announced Sam, a little proudly. "Only one of its kind in this country on a big scale. I understand there are some in Russia and Germany, though."

"Farm?" I echoed. "Where is it? Why, the whole place is under water."

Pat audibly snickered.

"Sure," explained Sam, "it's supposed to be. I had it built like this. We don't use any dirt at all, so soil erosion will never bother us. See those pipes down in the bottom of that pool? Well, they run along the bottom of every one of the 324 two-acre pools in this farm. When the water falls below a certain temperature, the steam is turned on to heat it up. In this time of year, the winter, it is on most of the time, although it doesn't stay so cold down here in south Jersey."

"But vegetables won't grow in clear water," I argued, although they manifestly WERE growing.

"That's what you think," he said, smiling, "but we supply each pool with liquid chemical food, the same elements vegetables extract from the soil. Sunshine does the rest. Not a thing is left to chance, my boy. There is no plant disease, no poor distribution of food elements, no excess or lack of light. Our plants grow quickly and the quality of the vegetables is better. Our tomato plants grow fifteen to twenty-five feet tall, and others in proportion. Soil culture produces about twelve tons of vegetables an acre. Our yield is 200 tons an acre. Each pool will produce 400 tons of produce, and it is ready for market long before products raised in the soil."

He reached down and pulled up a vine. It was loaded with strawberries, but such strawberries as I had never seen, nor anybody else for that matter. They were fully as large as full-grown plums, bright red and as luscious a sight as I've ever witnessed.

"White folks can't equal that," he boasted. "We're sending a crop to market in New York and Philadelphia tomorrow. They'll sell easily for fifteen cents a quart. Imagine the money we'll make! Why, the winter strawberries from the South and California won't be able to sell at all, except to the poor. We'll take all the quality trade, not only for strawberries but everything else."

"And the pretty part about it," added Pat, taking a big bite out of one of the strawberries with her strong white teeth, "is that they'll be carried to market throughout the East on B.I. trucks driven by Negroes."

"But isn't your overhead enormous?" I asked, a little weakly,

49

somewhat subdued by this miracle of modern chemistry. "It must cost a tremendous amount of money to steam-heat a mile of water two feet deep. Where is your powerhouse?"

"I can imagine you'll be surprised to learn," observed Sam, somewhat mysteriously, "that neither our steam or electric power costs us a cent. Tomorrow I'm going to show you a source of power, hitherto practically neglected, that is inexhaustible. Negro brains, in other words, your old friend Al Fortune, have harnessed it and put it to work to serve our ends." So Al worked here, too, eh?

He walked over to the pool to our left, reached well down and tugged at a vine. In the gathering dusk I could scarcely credit my vision. For there in his hand was a bright red tomato as big as a full-size grapefruit. It completely silenced me. I could only look on in unabashed awe.

"I told you so, didn't I?" gloated Pat, amused at my expression. "We're using the weapons and knowledge of the white man against him."

"Shucks," observed Sam, as we turned back toward the house. "We are way past white science already. Wait until you see our steam and electric plant tomorrow. We'll soon be able to turn every wheel in America."

12

▟▚▟▚▟▚▟▚▟▚▟▚▟▚▟▚▟▚▟▚▟▚▟▚▟▚▟▚

Carl Is Shown the Remarkable Powerhouse
in New Jersey

I had been amazed by the Black Internationale's airplane factory and cement factory; the liquid chemical farm frankly astounded me. I could now scarcely wait to see the steam and electric plant invented by Al Fortune and which cost nothing to operate. After a good dinner and a tour through the vast refrigerated storehouses where vegetables of astounding sizes were stored in bins from floor to ceiling, we turned in for the night, but I slept only fitfully.

I lay awake for a long time thinking about Dr. Belsidus and the Black Internationale, about the brilliant colored men and women he had assembled about him, about his spy system, his criminal acts, his fanatical plans for an international race war. But chiefly I thought about Pat. And with her face before me I fell to sleep.

It must have been two hours later when a noise of voices and coughing motors outside awakened me. I ran to the window, which looked out over the artificial lake. To my surprise the whole expanse was flood-lighted from above and also from below. Each pool of the 324 that comprised the "farm" was brilliantly lighted. In the chemically treated water hundreds of colored men swarmed gathering the miraculously grown crop. On the dikes between the pools scores of black and gold B.I. trucks and hundreds of crates awaited their loads. As the trucks were loaded they chugged off and disappeared into the darkness, either to the city markets or to the storehouses.

I stepped out on the back verandah to see better this remarkable sight destined to revolutionize truck gardening. So engrossed was I in the spectacle, that I had been watching for perhaps five minutes when I felt the presence of someone else, and, turning, confronted Pat gorgeously arrayed in flowing pink negligee.

"So it got you up too, eh?" she remarked, smiling. Then she exclaimed ecstatically, "Isn't it marvelous! Isn't it perfectly unbelievable?" My pounding heart sealed my lips as I feasted my eyes.

She was like a vision, something ethereal, a flimsy pink fairy out of the ages of folk imagination, an exotic shimmering flower. The faint scent of gardenia came from her rich robes and luxuriously titillated my nostrils.

"Don't you think so?" she asked, coming closer, a slight challenge in her tone, the light of enthusiasm in her large brown eyes.

"Why . . . why . . . yes," I stuttered. Then, unable to restrain myself or to longer conceal my emotion, I blurted out, "But not as marvelous as you are, Pat. Oh, forgive me, will you? But I can't help it. I had to say it because I feel it, feel it overpoweringly."

The flush deepened in her cheeks. She drew back and I thought some of the sparkle left her eyes to be replaced by a misty light. Instinctively she wrapped her negligee closer about her.

"I'm so sorry, Carl," she murmured, suppressing her emotion with difficulty. "We mustn't speak of such things. There's too much to be done . . . Please . . . please, excuse me." She turned quickly and hastened into her room.

I stood there unwitting of the spectacle before me, gazing straight ahead. Then, suddenly aware of the chill night air, I also repaired to my room, my thoughts dwelling not on Sam Hamilton's liquid chemical farm and the effect of flooding the markets of the East with huge fruits and vegetables, but on Patricia Givens, my sudden infatuation for her, and the possibility of her reciprocating my feeling.

The room telephone bell awakened me much sooner than I would have liked. The dull gray of daybreak had not been yet dispersed by the sun.

"It's Sam," came the voice on the phone. "We'll have to get out early because I've got to run back to town to work in the laboratory, and I want to show you our power plant before I leave. Hurry down and we'll have a bit to eat."

I hustled through my shower and shave, dressed and joined Sam and Pat at the breakfast table. I glanced at her and caught her eyes. She lowered them quickly and studied the piece of toast in her hand as her cheeks turned a dull red. It made my pulse leap. Then she had NOT forgotten last night! Perhaps . . . I wondered.

"I wish Al were here to show you this," said Sam as we strolled across the closely clipped lawn to the long line of buildings, "but I guess I can substitute for him. I'll have to. He'll probably be out this afternoon, but you'll be miles away by then."

He led the way to a long building about two stories high with a flat roof. We entered and climbed two flights of winding iron stairways to a penthouse opening on the roof which was about 300 feet long and all of a hundred feet wide. The roof was almost completely covered with some sort of machinery covered with canvas suspended by cable from tall steel poles placed at intervals at both sides of the roof.

Sam went around to the side of the building and immediately pulleys began to squeak, the steel cable grew taut and the great canvas began to roll away from the objects it covered. It was quite ingeniously arranged. The canvas ended up rolled tightly and lying along the edge of the roof. Now the sun had come out brightly from the East.

Disclosed were a great number of strange contraptions, possibly a hundred or more. At first glance they resembled a great battery of glass anti-aircraft guns or telescopes. They were glass- or aluminum-lined troughs set at an angle of 45 degrees on a steel framework. In back of the higher end was what appeared to be a cylindrical water pump, at the other end a small engine. From the engine, iron pipes ran down into the building.

"This is Al's famous sun engine," Sam explained, "probably the most revolutionary invention in the past thousand years. Men have been trying for a century to invent a cheap sun-harnesser which will cheapen sun power below the cost of coal power. Now, a Negro has done it. There have been other solar engines but this surpasses them all. It only costs $100 to make and it seems to last indefinitely. Of course, bigger units will cost more.

"It stores up electric power," he continued, "and also stores up power for other purposes. Our silos over there are insulated with the new 'glass wool' and are full of sand. They store up heat to extremely high temperatures and retain the heat virtually without loss for years. You see, we can only use these engines about nine hours a day at this time of the year and 12 or 14 hours a day in summer, but we need power all the time to keep our farm at an even temperature and to make electricity. Heat, of course, makes power.

"Now, here's the way it works," he went on, leading us over to the nearest machine. "The sunlight is caught on the surface of the highly polished aluminum mirrors, which are six feet long and two feet wide. You notice they're curved in such a way as to focus the rays on that long tube you see that looks like a thermos bottle resting in the bottom of the trough. It rests in a sort of cradle which can be turned to catch the full force of the sun's rays at any time of the day.

"The thermos bottle arrangement," he continued, "consists of three tubes, one inside the other. The outer tube is made of pyrex glass, six feet long, with an outside diameter of one and one-half inch and an inside diameter of one and one-quarter inch. This outer tube is known as the 'focus tube.' Within the focus tube is a miniature 'flash boiler' of the type used in the old-fashioned steam automobiles, like the old Stanley Steamer. This miniature flash boiler is a steel tube one-half inch in diameter, made of the latest high-grade steel, thin-walled, but strong enough to resist a pressure of steam up to 200 pounds per square inch. This steel tube slips into the pyrex glass focus tube, which is jacketed by a vacuum.

"The steel tube," Sam explained further, "is painted with lampblack, so as to absorb 85 percent of the sun's rays that fall upon it after passing through the focus tube.

"Within the steel tube," he went on, warming to the subject as he noted our intense interest, "is a third tube, known as the water tube. This is only one-eighth of an inch in diameter, and is joined along its entire length by four copper wings, well soldered with high-melting-point solder, to the inside of the steel tube. A supply of water automatically regulated by that meter you see in the rear passes through the inner tube at the proper rate to burst into steam at the desired pressure of 175 pounds to the square inch.

"As the four copper wings are such fine conductors of heat," Sam explained, "that heat produced by the absorption of solar rays in the lampblack on the outer surface of the steel tube penetrates with the utmost facility to vaporize the water. Thus, our heat and power here cost us nothing. The white man cannot successfully compete with any industry we may enter because he has no such machine as this. We have a distinct advantage of starting with something as far in advance of his industrial methods as steam was in advance of hand power."

Although Pat had seen it all before, she was trembling with excitement, her brown eyes sparkling like polished jewels. Involuntarily, quite unthinking, I know, her hand clasped mine and my heart jumped, although I knew her mind was only on the wonder before us. I forcibly banished thought of her and struggled to concentrate on Sam's scholarly explanation.

"Each of these units is only two horsepower," he was saying, "but there are 100 units on this roof alone. A similar battery is on the roof of every one of our 10 storage barns or warehouses. This engine is capable of converting the sunlight falling on an area of one square mile into 70,000 horsepower on a cloudless day. Imagine what that will mean when we set up these batteries in the tropics? Why, the sunshine falling on the State of New Mexico alone furnishes a hundred times as much energy per year as the total of all coal, oil and water power used per year in the United States."

Pat turned to me smiling, triumph in her eyes. "Now do you doubt that we can win?" she challenged. I smiled back and nodded a negative. "Well," she continued, "you haven't seen half."

54

13

Carl Returns to New York;
"Internationale" Moves into High Gear

The following week was like a dream, like traveling in some strange world. Down through Maryland, Virginia, the Carolinas and the lower South we sped, visiting truck farms, poultry farms, plantations and other enterprises until we were well into central Texas. Each establishment was equipped with its well-appointed private airfield and usually located some distance from a city. Each was headed by some bright young colored man or woman.

More marvelous than these economic enterprises, however, was the company of Patricia Givens. I hadn't summoned up the courage to tell her again what was uppermost in my thoughts. Her initial repulse had made me timid. So now I contented myself with feasting my eyes upon her beauty as she piloted the autogiro over the country with faultless precision. And although I had received no encouragement whatever, it was with considerable regret that I learned that we had reached the end of our journey and would now fly back to New York.

We walked through the plots of tomato plants fifteen and twenty feet high while the plane was being gassed. I wanted to touch her and to stroll arm in arm, but one glance at her face inhibited me. Whether or not she sensed my mood I do not know. We went on in silence save for a prosaic comment on the enormous vegetables that rose out of the chemically treated water and hung invitingly from the wire fencing.

"You're rather cold, aren't you?" I asked finally, with something of my suppressed feelings betrayed in my tone.

She turned suddenly, a dark flush under her clear skin. "Why do you say that?" she inquired. And by the way she asked it, I knew that she knew what I meant.

"Well," I said, a little confused by her abruptness, "you don't seem to think of anything except the Black Internationale. After all, you're a pretty girl . . . I'd . . . Well . . . I've told you how I feel . . ."

"Sorry, Carl, but there isn't much time for romance. There's too much to be done, and such a short time in which to do it. Romance can wait. Forget about it. There's plenty of time for that in the future."

"But you can't deny love," I insisted. "You can't dismiss it like that. After all, you are human just like I am."

"Yes," she said a little coldly, "and for that reason, I keep a good grip on myself."

"Do you love anyone?" I persisted, thinking of Dr. Belsidus. She smiled mysteriously. "Maybe," was all she said.

Jim was waiting for us at the Westchester airport when we came in and he drove us down to New York City. At dinner that evening in the green, gold and rose room, off the precious service, Dr. Belsidus, stern-visaged as usual, sat at the head of the table. Others present were Sam Hamilton, Patricia, Al Fortune, Ransom Just, Rev. Samson Binks, Dr. Andrew Matson, Bennie Simpson and myself. We were more than halfway through the meal when the door opened and the silent Jim admitted a tall, hatchet-faced brown man with long, acquisitive nose, deep-set, calculating eyes and gray hair and mustache. I had never seen him before.

"Carl," said Belsidus, "shake hands with Alex Fletcher. Fletcher, this is Carl Slater, my secretary. He's been looking over our enterprises. Sort of familiarizing himself with things."

"A good idea," observed the newcomer, eying me shrewdly.

"Sit down," commanded Belsidus. Then, turning to me, he explained, "Alex is our business expert, and a damned good one, too. But, like the rest of us, he soon discovered that race and color definitely limited him. He's handling our marketing and transportation now. How are things going, Alex?"

"Very good," he replied, clipping his words off short. "We're taking the strawberry and tomato market. The other dealers are squawking. There'll be even a bigger squawk when our crops from the South are sent into market. It'll take them a year or two to meet our competition."

"Suppose they use force?" suggested Sam. "You know these crackers won't take it lying down."

Dr. Belsidus's eyes glowed cruelly. "Just let them try," he said. "I know a few tricks, too. Don't forget that." Then he turned to Rev. Binks, a short, brown man with silver-rimmed spectacles, a head of graying hair that badly needed cutting, a scraggly mustache and a studious expression. He was a slovenly fellow, almost ill-kempt, but the wisdom that shone from his eyes compensated for all his shortcomings.

"How is your first temple going, Binks?" asked the Doctor.

"It will be completed in another month, Doctor." The clergyman spoke with deliberation.

"Everything?"

"Yes, everything."

"Good! We can't get started too soon. We want a temple in every Negro community before the end of six months. Our produce sales ought to swing that, don't you think, Alex?"

"Yes, Chief, if everything goes well."

"It's got to go well," grated Belsidus. "We must be in a position to strike by the end of this year. We can't have any delays. The international situation is ripe. We can capitalize on the present uncertainty, but first we must get the Negroes organized. That will be your job, Binks."

"I will do my part," said the preacher, quietly.

There was much to the same effect. The whole conspiracy was taking a definite head. The seriousness of the others, the earnestness of their expressions all conveyed that impression. I am sure we all walked away from that momentous conference quite a-tingle with expectancy.

In the next month, every effort was definitely speeded up. Cement and structural steel took form in a hundred cities and towns, and one by one the Rev. Binks's Temples of Love rose majestically out of disorder to architectural beauty.

Pat and I attended the opening of the first one in Harlem. It was a huge building closely resembling an Egyptian temple, and in the form of a truncated pyramid. It was a cement and steel shell, gray trimmed with blue and pink. A massive door was the only entrance and exit. Long and very narrow windows were spaced at intervals of fifteen or twenty feet down each side. Their panes were of colored glass, each window being guarded by a wrought-iron grill. Once one entered the front door, one crossed a wide flagged court to the temple proper. In the center of the court was an alabaster fountain. The temple proper was in semi-darkness, indirectly lighted by electricity, but along the tiled walls great candles flickered in huge candlesticks.

The most surprising thing about it, however, was the fact that there were no benches, chairs or other provisions for seating communicants, and that at the far end, its figure indirectly lighted and so standing out clearly from the semi-darkness, was a huge statue of a nude Negro standing with legs apart, gazing sardonically downward with arms crossed. It was all of 50 feet high and every part of the body was clearly depicted. In front of the idol was a great semi-circular platform. In front of that was a small altar, evidently for the priest. When our eyes got used to the semi-darkness, we noticed that there were a large number of camp chairs on the large platform.

"Rather awesome, eh?" I remarked to Pat. "Do you think the Negroes will fall for it?"

"Binks is no fool, Carl. He's going to give the masses of Negroes the sort of religion they want but haven't been able to get. Music and dancing, no collections, plenty of pageantry, keeping things down to earth with enough sex to make everything interesting. They can come here and get everything they need. Let's go downstairs."

We stepped out into the entrance court and, turning to one side, descended two flights of stairs to the basement. Here we noted in succession a restaurant, a grocery store, a drug store, a hair parlor, a gymnasium with a swimming pool, a clothing store and a bank, all opening off an arcade.

"Why, if this thing clicks," I observed, "the Black Internationale will virtually control the economic life of colored America."

"Yes, of course. That's our intention. Binks is making the church what it was to ancient times . . . a center of everyday life and activity, of amusement and instruction, conforming to, yet shaping, society."

58

14

Wherein a Session in the "Church of Love"
Is Described

I do not wish to burden you with uninteresting details, but so impressed was I with the first service at the Church of Love and so widespread did its influence finally become that I deem it necessary to describe it to you.

b ... the economic units in the
t ... y filling with Negroes, en-
g ... priestly robes of black and
i ... auditorium. As we passed
v ... ushion by a pretty girl. We
a ... black and gold uniform to
r ... dience was being seated in
F ... aisles leading down to the
... ut ten feet stood tall black
... olden ribbons about their
l ... et. They bore long, highly
... their shoulders from the
... ncing neither to the right

... . The many ushers hurried
... m, cautioning against the
... ingly at each other, plainly
... dings. Most of them were
... at it was all about. They
... shers discouraged them.

... ressive. Suddenly, strong
... ost blinding us. We could
... he lights went off. Looking

194 b

quickly, I noticed that the semi-circular platform had disappeared, leaving a great black void.

Now the trumpeters around the wall, as if by command, moved the mouthpieces of their trumpets to their lips. Somewhere a light flashed momentarily. The trumpets let out a throaty, musical blast. Now a thousand hidden lights illuminated the semi-darkness of the place with every color of the spectrum.

The far end of the church almost leaped out to meet us. The great platform began to rise from the void, silently, impressively. Seated on it in concentric circles facing us were at least 150 Negro musicians in black tailcoats faced with gold. The conductor, his back to us, stood with arms upraised. As the ascending platform stopped on a level slightly above us, he brought down his baton and a crash of majestic music filled the place. Its strong African theme was indeed stirring.

Now emerged from either side of the platform a single line of 50 brown girls, young, shapely, almost all of a cocoa brown tint and garbed in flowing, multi-colored tunics, many pointed and diaphanous, which fluttered as they walked. Gracefully they formed a single line in front of the platform, a line that stretched almost clear across the temple, undulating with the beat of the music.

Behind them on each side came 50 women in pale yellow tunics that reached to the floor. These grouped themselves in a knot near each end of the line of dancers and stood motionless.

The orchestra music died almost to a whisper. Now the two groups of yellow-gowned women began to chant, softly at first, then slowly, louder and louder until the great symphony orchestra was almost drowned out. Then the orchestra grew louder itself. The chorus and instruments seemed to vie with each other. Then the orchestra waned again. Soon only the powerful chanting of the women could be heard. Then toward the end the orchestra joined in. The trumpeters with muted instruments added their brassy tones.

I have never heard anything like it. The people sat tense, absorbed, transfixed. Pat's hand was gripping mine almost painfully. As the hymn ended we all relaxed as if by command, but I noticed that Pat's hand still held mine. Then suddenly she noticed it, colored, and removed it in confusion; a self-conscious grin was wreathing her pretty face.

Another blast from the encircling trumpets. Orchestra and chorus

14

◭◭◭◭◭◭◭◭◭◭◭◭◭◭◭◭◭◭◭◭◭◭◭◭◭

Wherein a Session in the "Church of Love"
Is Described

I do not wish to burden you with uninteresting details, but so impressed was I with the first service at the Church of Love and so widespread did its influence finally become that I deem it necessary to describe it to you.

When Pat and I came up from inspecting the economic units in the basement, we found the great temple slowly filling with Negroes, entering between a double rank of tall men in priestly robes of black and gold. We followed the crowd into the vast auditorium. As we passed inside we were each handed a round straw cushion by a pretty girl. We were directed by an equally comely usher in black and gold uniform to a place on the floor. We noticed that the audience was being seated in rows as in a theatre but with about a dozen aisles leading down to the platform. Around the hall at intervals of about ten feet stood tall black Negroes with flowing golden garments, golden ribbons about their heads and black and gold sandals on their feet. They bore long, highly polished brass trumpets that almost reached their shoulders from the floor. The trumpeters stood motionless, glancing neither to the right or left.

Soon the auditorium was completely filled. The many ushers hurried on soft-slippered feet to all parts of the room, cautioning against the slightest whisper. The people looked wonderingly at each other, plainly puzzled and no little awed by these proceedings. Most of them were obviously curiosity seekers wondering what it was all about. They wanted to chatter but the alert and pretty ushers discouraged them.

Five minutes passed. The silence was oppressive. Suddenly, strong lights blazed toward the seated audience, almost blinding us. We could see nothing at the other end of the temple. The lights went off. Looking quickly, I noticed that the semi-circular platform had disappeared, leaving a great black void.

Now the trumpeters around the wall, as if by command, moved the mouthpieces of their trumpets to their lips. Somewhere a light flashed momentarily. The trumpets let out a throaty, musical blast. Now a thousand hidden lights illuminated the semi-darkness of the place with every color of the spectrum.

The far end of the church almost leaped out to meet us. The great platform began to rise from the void, silently, impressively. Seated on it in concentric circles facing us were at least 150 Negro musicians in black tailcoats faced with gold. The conductor, his back to us, stood with arms upraised. As the ascending platform stopped on a level slightly above us, he brought down his baton and a crash of majestic music filled the place. Its strong African theme was indeed stirring.

Now emerged from either side of the platform a single line of 50 brown girls, young, shapely, almost all of a cocoa brown tint and garbed in flowing, multi-colored tunics, many pointed and diaphanous, which fluttered as they walked. Gracefully they formed a single line in front of the platform, a line that stretched almost clear across the temple, undulating with the beat of the music.

Behind them on each side came 50 women in pale yellow tunics that reached to the floor. These grouped themselves in a knot near each end of the line of dancers and stood motionless.

The orchestra music died almost to a whisper. Now the two groups of yellow-gowned women began to chant, softly at first, then slowly, louder and louder until the great symphony orchestra was almost drowned out. Then the orchestra grew louder itself. The chorus and instruments seemed to vie with each other. Then the orchestra waned again. Soon only the powerful chanting of the women could be heard. Then toward the end the orchestra joined in. The trumpeters with muted instruments added their brassy tones.

I have never heard anything like it. The people sat tense, absorbed, transfixed. Pat's hand was gripping mine almost painfully. As the hymn ended we all relaxed as if by command, but I noticed that Pat's hand still held mine. Then suddenly she noticed it, colored, and removed it in confusion; a self-conscious grin was wreathing her pretty face.

Another blast from the encircling trumpets. Orchestra and chorus took up the theme. The graceful dancing beauties moved like wisps, forming beautiful figures, leaping, pirouetting, swooping in perfect rhythm while varied colored lights from a cyclorama played upon them. No ballet could have been more perfectly trained.

Then an amazing thing happened. A great bell tolled from somewhere. A stentorian voice boomed, "Rise, All Ye Within! Rise, All Ye Within! Rise and worship the God of Love, Ruler of black men and women. Rise to greet Him!" The dancers stopped, transfixed.

All the lights seemed to die or concentrate themselves in one great spotlight, and this shone upon the huge 50-foot statue of the nude Negro.

"Rise!" boomed the voice again. The multitude scrambled to its collective feet, Pat and I along with them.

"Gaze upon Him!" boomed the voice again. We all looked upward.

The music had ceased now. Only the low chanting of the chorus relieved this awed silence.

Now the great arms which had been folded slowly unfolded and stretched out full length. The great breast began to rise and fall. The huge eyes became luminous and the great head began slowly to nod up and down. It was awesome indeed. The singing ended. The eyes continued to blaze. The great head moved up and down.

One could hear the hard breathing. I saw fear in many of those eyes that stared hypnotically at the great image moving like a living thing.

Suddenly, a woman screamed. Then another, and then another. They were piteous, agonizing screams, and a body fell to the tile floor.

"Cast down thy eyes!" boomed the voice. Obediently we looked toward the floor. I knew it was hokum. I knew Binks had rigged up this robot and I knew approximately just how it worked, and yet for the life of me I could not but enter into the spirit of the thing and obey the commands of the voice. I, too, looked downward.

A full minute passed. A great blast from the trumpeter startled us to attention. Two thousand pairs of eyes looked upward to the huge image. It stood cold and silent as before, the arms folded, the eyes dead, the chest still. Gone was every evidence of life that had so startled us.

"Be seated!" boomed the hidden voice. Like automatons, we returned to our cushions.

The great symphony orchestra, joined again by the chorus, produced blood-stirring music. The long line of girls danced like mad fairies. It was difficult to restrain one's self from participating.

Dozens of pretty ushers now passed between the rows, bearing large trays loaded with tiny glasses. "Take one and drink!" they commanded pleasantly. Pat and I obeyed along with the rest. It was a dark red, fiery liquor with a strong but pleasant odor. The usher paused until we had drained the tiny glasses and returned them to her tray. It was all done quickly and efficiently. In less than five minutes the vast assemblage had been served.

"Wonder what this is?" Pat whispered. "It tasted good."

Before I could answer, I felt a sharp pain in my chest. My head swam. Strange lights floated before my eyes. One moment the music was miles away. The next moment it almost burst my eardrums. The people about me were like hundreds of great corkscrews and Pat became a pane of brown glass. My hand weighed a ton. The top of my skull floated off into space.

As I fought against this strange drug, the music grew wilder and wilder. Bach and Sibelius gave way to evil, blood-stirring rhythms born in the steamy swamps of the Congo. From somewhere a crescendo of tom toms rent the air with their sizzling syncopation, and moaning minor chords tore the heartstrings.

"Dance! Dance! Move the Cushions to the walls, and Dance!" came again the command from somewhere.

Automatically, like zombies we obeyed, carrying the cushions to the sides of the temple, staggering under the effects of the drug, knowing nothing except to obey.

"Dance! Dance! Dance for Love!" commanded the voice. The eyes of the image again grew luminous. They held one with hypnotic intensity. As the music screamed louder, more insistently, I seized Pat and we whirled madly, insanely, drunkenly, like the others, in lunatic, erotic, passionate, frenzied embrace, as the women of the chorus and the beautiful ballet girls joined in the shameless orgy.

Gone was all restraint, gone all inhibitions as the throbbing drums and sensuous, pulsating music tore asunder and subjugated our conscious beings. The inner man, the subconscious mind, the primeval urges born in the Mesozoic ooze, completely controlled us, dominated us, motivated us.

62

And above the ordered din, the ecstatic screams and yells, boomed the hidden voice chanting, "Dance," while the luminous eyes of the gigantic God of Love looked down in hypnotic scrutiny.

Then my brain went completely blank, and I knew nothing.

15

Rev. Binks's Sermon in Church of Love
Sounds Keynote of Movement

I do not know how long a time elapsed or what we did. I only know that suddenly my reason returned and I was lying stretched out on the tile floor. I looked around. The temple was again in semi-darkness. Only a light here and there and the flickering candles relieved the blackness. But there was sufficient illumination for me to rise up on my elbow and scan the strange sight.

The entire surface of the floor was covered with sprawling bodies of men and women in every conceivable recumbent pose, as though all at the same time had been stricken down by some lethal gas. Beside me, her clothing disordered and her eyelids just flickering back to consciousness, lay Pat, more beautiful and inviting than I had ever seen her. The trumpeters all stood in their places along the wall, but the ballet and the chorus were gone. On the platform the men of the symphony orchestra sat at ease, the conductor leaning on his lectern. But, singularly enough, the great ebony image of the God of Love had disappeared.

I leaned over guiltily and kissed Pat, unable to resist the temptation of her beautiful lips. She opened her eyes with a start, looking wildly about like one awakening from a nightmare in a strange place. Then reason returned to her. Shamefacedly she arranged her clothing, permitting herself the while a sickly smile. Now all around us the others were stirring, rising, standing around, discussing in low tones what had happened.

"Well, Binks really put it on strong, didn't he?" Pat observed, putting her hair back into place. "If Harlem doesn't fall for this, I don't know my people at all."

"It's a solid sender, all right," I agreed. "That drink really takes away your will and about everything else. It acted just like that broth, the East Indian drug Belsidus gave me the night I got into this outfit. You know it induces temporary insanity. This was a lighter dose, though, or we'd be asleep for hours. As it is, we couldn't have been out of our heads more than ten or fifteen minutes."

"Well, I'd like to know what happened during that ten or fifteen minutes," she remarked, looking at me as if I might know. I could see a light of suspicion in her eyes.

"Whatever happened," I observed, reassuringly, "I'm feeling swell. Just as light as a feather. Really buoyant."

"So do I," she admitted. "That's why I have a dark suspicion in the back of my mind. The last thing I remember you and I were dancing wildly together."

There was no opportunity to pursue the matter further. The buzz of conversation all around us was rudely interrupted by a blast from the trumpets. The great voice boomed, "Get Your Cushions! Get Your Cushions! Good People, Get Your Cushions! Return and Be Seated! Return and Be Seated!" We all did as we were bidden and soon the vast assemblage was seated approximately as before.

There was a long quiet pause until the last rustle and whisper had died. Then the great orchestra came to light at the tap of the conductor's baton and soothing music swept through the vast auditorium. In about ten minutes it ended. The pretty ushers now cautioned everyone to maintain the utmost quiet.

Slowly the platform on which the orchestra sat sank out of sight below the level of the floor. The great orange-colored curtain that covered the back wall parted and a large silver screen was extended to view. From some hidden place rose the majestic peals of a pipe organ. Again the great hidden voice boomed out, "All Stand!"

Now down the central aisle from the great door at our backs moved a colorful procession. Marching four abreast came first a troop of twenty young boys dressed in long black and gold gowns and carrying three-foot black candles. As they proceeded down the aisle they shrilly chanted. Following them was a troop of tiny black dancing girls not one of whom could have been over eight years old. They wore ballet skirts of rose, purple and yellow. Behind them marched four giant trumpeters whose music accompanied that from the pipe organ. They in turn were followed by eight men bearing a golden throne on their shoulders. On each side of the throne strode a giant Negro in gold and black tunic bearing a huge ostrich feather fan which gently kept the air in motion. Seated on the throne, dressed in gold and black robes stiff with jewels, was Rev. Samson Binks, looking benign and papal.

The colorful procession moved down to the front of the temple. The platform had now been returned to its former position. The candle-bearers ranged themselves at equal intervals before it. The tiny dancing girls disappeared into the wings. The throne-bearers moved on to the platform and lowered their burden to the floor. Rev. Binks put out his hand. One of the bearers grasped it and helped him out. With the trum-peters ranged on each side, the clergyman walked to the small golden altar, the fan-bearers following close behind. Mounting the three or four steps to the canopied altar, he rested one hand on the lectern and lifting the other he blessed the vast assemblage. The singing of the youthful choristers died. The pipe organ was still.

"My people," he began, "today you have seen and experienced that of which there is no counterpart in the world. You have taken part in our services in honor of the God of Love. You will henceforward be ruled and commanded by love. You will realize that black people can only become great, black people can only become prosperous, black people can only become powerful by loving one another. It must be a wholehearted, unashamed, literal love which black people have from henceforth for one another. Loving each other, my people, we must therefore help each other. We must not quarrel or contend with each other. Our love must include all black people, all brown people, all yel-low people, for together these colored people are soon to rule the earth.

"That is the meaning of this church, that is the meaning of this reli-gion, that is the meaning of this God of Love which only a short time ago greeted you, that is the meaning of the great Black Internationale which dominates and will control all black people and will soon control world civilization.

"Follow the Black Internationale. Obey its commands and all the world will be given unto you. From an inferior you will become superi-or. Now despised, you will come to be honored and feared. From a people cursed by poverty, discrimination and segregation you will be great in the councils of nations.

"Those that oppose the Black Internationale will perish. The God of Love will strike down all those who sin against His injunction to black people to Love One Another.

"Leave your so-called Christian churches. Force them to close their doors. Christianity is a religion for slaves. You are no longer slaves. You are free men. You are warriors. You are rulers. You no longer serve the white man. You no longer bow down to the white man. You no longer take the white man's leavings. You no longer turn the other cheek when smitten. You no longer forgive your enemies. You no longer grin in the face of him who despises you. You stand with head high and shoulders square. A free man once more as were your ancestors in Africa.

"My people: This is the first temple. Hundreds are in course of construction. Thousands of young priests, choristers and dancers are being trained. We are making of organized religion something of color and beauty appealing to all the senses. This is religion as the temples of Egypt and Babylon knew it long ago. We have resurrected it so the church may again be the center of the people's lives and activities. So that the Negro may spiritually live again.

"All this, everything without exception, is the work of the Black Internationale. Through it you and yours will come to man's estate at last after centuries of servitude and inferiority.

"My people, I have spoken. Watch! See the power of the Black Internationale!"

Every light was extinguished. Only the line of candles flickered fitfully. Then a square of light leapt out of the darkness to the silver screen. In the half light Rev. Binks could be seen descending from the altar. Slowly the procession assembled, marched off to one side and disappeared.

Now followed an hour of talking from the altar. Slowly the reverend's lieutenants read propaganda charts and messages. Others showed factories, farms and powerhouses and all the far-flung enterprises presided over by Dr. Belsidus. But strangely enough the picture of that master plotter did not appear, nor were any of his able lieutenants like Sam Hamilton, Al Fortune, Pat and the others shown.

At the end, after a great world map depicting locations of the various

66

Black Internationale cells had been shown, the long services were ended. The pipe organ burst forth with peals of majestic music. The trumpeters joined in. Ushers showed the way to the several exits. These all led to corridors surrounding the auditorium which, in turn, led back to the great front foyer. There other ushers guided the people downstairs to the economic center where the restaurant, grocery store, drug store, clothing store, beauty parlor and gymnasium awaited them.

Pat and I went out and were about to hail a cab when I was tapped on the shoulder.

16

▲▲▲▲▲▲▲▲▲▲▲▲▲▲▲▲▲▲▲▲▲▲▲

Black Internationale Avenges Lynching
in Mississippi; Then . . .

I turned quickly. It was Jim, dark and grim as ever. He pointed to the familiar Belsidus limousine parked at the curb. Then he opened the door and bade us enter. I surmised that Dr. Belsidus wanted us. Jim got up front and soon we were moving as quickly as possible through the congested Harlem streets.

When we arrived at Dr. Belsidus's house, Jim pointed to the door and nodded insistently. "I wonder what's up," Pat murmured as we entered.

Dr. Belsidus met us in the foyer. I could see that he was unusually grim today. "I want to talk to you two," he said curtly. He led the way back to the elevator. In a few seconds we were seated around his desk in the office upstairs. What was he planning now? Why this sudden call? We didn't have long to wait. He produced a U.S. map.

"Yesterday," he began, "there was a burning of a Negro in Mississippi, in some little town called Newton. Our cell in Meridian has investigated the lynching and reports that the man was absolutely innocent of the rape with which he was charged. Innocent or not, the Black Internationale is going to put a stop to lynching. That's final."

"But what are we to do about it, Chief?"

"We're going to strike," he growled. "We're going to make them pay in the only way they understand. The South and those who rule it understand only one thing: force. That country lives and dies by violence. Therefore we shall repay violence with violence, burning with burning, death with death. Furthermore, we shall let them know why." His deep-set eyes glowed ominously, almost fanatically.

Pat looked somewhat uneasy and drummed on the table with her finger tips. I was wondering myself just what he had in mind. Then he spoke again.

"Of course," he began, a crafty smile playing around the corners of his stern mouth, "we shall neither say nor do anything that might imperil the Black Internationale program. We are not yet ready for open conflict with the whites."

"Then how is it to be done, Chief?" I asked, glancing hastily at Pat, who seemed to be as puzzled as I.

"You and Pat will do the job," he announced, challenge in his eyes. "You need the experience and Pat needs to test her skill. You leave the airport at ten o'clock sharp. You do your work at three o'clock sharp. Pat, you know what ship to take to get there in time. You should be back at the airport by eight o'clock without fail. Use the No. 1 thermite bombs. Here's your map, Pat, and here's a bundle of leaflets to toss overboard after the job is completed. That's all. Good luck. Remember, I want this done perfectly." He rose.

I confess that I was a little taken aback. I had not bargained for anything like this. To be associated with cold-blooded murder was bad enough; to commit it was worse. But here we were being ordered to murder human beings, many of whom were entirely innocent of any participation in the brutal burning of the Negro, Lester Peters, in Newton, Mississippi, the day before.

Dr. Belsidus must have detected my indecision. When he spoke again his voice was hard and threatening. "I need not remind you again," he grated, "that I will not tolerate failure. There'll be a lot more blood shed than this before we win our objectives. When you think of what the black people have endured and suffered at the hands of white people, Slater, a job like this must be a keen pleasure. I really envy you this opportunity to strike the first real mass blow for Negro freedom."

It was a beautifully clear March night. The ceiling was limitless. There was a slight breeze from the South, but not enough to make any difference in our speed. At nine-forty-five the great doors swung outward. Two mechanics and Juan Torlier, his white teeth flashing against his dull black skin, wheeled a huge, black, low-winged bomber out on the field and began warming up its motor. The engine was carefully gone over. Then the six 100-pound No. 1 thermite bombs were placed in their racks while Juan explained the method of releasing them.

At ten o'clock sharp, according to the chief's directions, we started the long run down the field and were soon winging our way west-southwest to our destination. Flying at six thousand feet and thundering along at 200 miles an hour, we passed in quick succession Newark, Philadelphia, Wilmington, and Baltimore. Shortly after eleven o'clock we passed over Washington.

Pat was flying with more than her usual care. It was not the first time we had flown at night, but the first time she had ever undertaken such a mission. She was grim and tense, and silent.

As we tore over Charlotte, I thought of the package of leaflets Dr. Belsidus had handed me. Curious, I tore open the package, extracted one of the sheets and perused it by the light from the instrument board. It read as follows:

PEOPLE OF NEWTON

This is Your Punishment By Command of
THE HOLY FATHER

You Burned to Death an Innocent Colored Man.
Now you, too, are Scourged by Flames.
Henceforth Live According to the Holy Scriptures and
Do Unto Others as You Would Have Others Do Unto You.
The Mother Church Will No Longer Tolerate
the Persecution of Black People
Contrary to the Teachings of Jesus Christ.
It Must Be An Eye for An Eye,
a Tooth for a Tooth, a Burning for a Burning.
The Catholic Church Stands with and for
the Oppressed and Persecuted Everywhere.

Signed: THE SONS OF CHRIST.

At the end was a large cross. Frankly, I was puzzled. What was the meaning of this jargon? What was the point in involving the Catholic

69

Church? What deep-dyed, villainous scheme was Dr. Belsidus now concocting?

I passed the leaflet over to Pat. She hastily scanned it, then grinned cruelly, that same half-maniacal grimace that almost all the Black Internationale staff seemed to have developed for occasions such as this.

"Pretty clever, eh?" she shouted above the roar of the motor.

"Maybe, but I don't exactly get the idea. What have the Catholics to do with it?"

"You'll see," she said, smiling knowingly. "It'll help bring things to a head. Doc is a wise egg."

Columbia, Augusta and Macon in succession leaped out of the darkness below glowing, with mazda phosphorescence only to disappear as we fled onward toward our goal. At last we swept over Montgomery and in a few minutes the lights of Meridian leaped over the horizon to meet us. In a short time we were over the dark hills of that city. It was exactly two-forty-five.

Pat and I exchanged significant glances. Nothing more was necessary. In ten minutes, I knew, we would be over our target. I opened the door in the floor of the plane. Pat shut off her wing lights and increased altitude until the thinness of the air was dizzying.

Now I could see the lights of Newton. Just a few there were. A water tower stood clear in the moonlight. Pat slowed down. I tossed out the bundle of leaflets and watched them flutter to the four winds. Pat nodded to me as she turned the nose of the ship down toward the courthouse roof. I grabbed the lever to release the deadly incendiary bombs.

Down, down, down we came, to 7,000, to 6,000, to 5,000, to 4,000. I released two of the gleaming metal cylinders. Almost side by side they sped to their mark. There was a resounding crash. Streams of blinding fire ran in all directions, igniting everything in their path. In quick succession I released the remaining four thermite bombs.

Flames swept everywhere. The town became a raging inferno. Pat grinned triumphantly and I wondered what sort of woman she was, for there was no compassion in her face. I closed the trap door. Pat swung the big ship around and climbing rapidly headed for home. Through my night glasses I could see the victims below running for their lives as dozens of blazes burned briskly. Then, suddenly and unexpectedly, the giant plane lurched sidewise and began to fall.

17

Pat in Forced Landing; Repairs the Plane;
Flies Back to Headquarters

Pat's face was as grim as death. She tugged at levers and turned wheels as the ship lurched sickeningly from side to side.

"What's the matter?"

She shook her head. We were losing altitude rapidly. I thought of our big load of gasoline. If we fell with that we'd be burned up even though the ship wasn't damaged very much.

"Why not jump?" I yelled, thinking of our parachutes on which we were sitting.

"No!" she shouted. "We stay with the ship!" There gleamed in her eyes that same fanatical light I had seen before as she tugged away grimly, watching the swiftly approaching ground with anxiety.

I was not to be outdone by the girl I loved. I killed my impulse to push open the door and jump to safety. Heroically she toiled away as I watched, helpless but fascinated.

We were down to 1500 feet. It wouldn't be long now. Just a matter of seconds. Only for Pat's consummate skill we would have struck before. I comforted myself with the knowledge that if we survived we would still be out of Mississippi, for we had again passed over Meridian just before something went wrong.

A million flashing thoughts. Discovery of the plane would connect the Black Internationale with the burning of Newton . . . Race war would result before the organization was ready . . . So much accomplished, perhaps all to be lost . . . How did it feel to crash? . . . How brave she was!

"We're landing!" she shouted. "Hold on!"

She cut the motor. We were wobbling sickeningly. With the most skillful piloting I've ever seen, she leveled the machine just before we struck.

I closed my eyes and gritted my teeth. There was a sharp bump and a lurch to one side. Pat was thrown against me. The shock had not been as great as I anticipated.

Then came peal after peal of hysterical laughter, wild, insane, maniacal laughter. I looked up in astonishment. With tears streaming down her pretty cheeks, Pat was sitting bolt upright in her seat, her hand still closed on the stick, her eyes staring forward and she was screaming with laughter. It was the strangest nervous reaction I've ever seen after a tense ordeal.

I placed one arm about her and drew her unprotesting form to me. As I held her in my arms she sobbed silently, the while she trembled as with the ague.

"Pat! Pat!" I called finally, "let's get out of here. We're not in New York, you know. We're in Alabama and mighty close to Mississippi."

"Yes, Carl, I know," she whispered, sobbing less violently. Despite the danger, I could not help but enjoy the exquisite pleasure of holding this gorgeous creature closely to me. At least five minutes passed. Then she must suddenly have realized where she was and what was going on. She straightened up a little shamedly, and gave her helmet an unconscious feminine pat.

It was bright moonlight. We were in a freshly plowed field. The nearest house loomed out of the shadows a half mile away. We bailed out. The big bomber towered over us as we walked around it to note the damage.

Singularly enough, the damage was slight, one wing tip being a trifle bent. Otherwise the plane was apparently as good as when we left the B.I. airport. Pat hustled around with her flashlight.

Soon I heard her curse softly from the rear compartment and she came out holding a curved wrench.

"That's the culprit," she announced, smiling with the joy she must have felt. "It got jammed back there. It's a miracle I didn't lose control. Boy, what a close shave! Come on, we've got to get out of here. These farmers rise early, you know."

"You telling me?" I Harlemed. "But how are we going to get a run in this muck?"

"Humph!" she exclaimed. "As bad as I feel after that narrow shave, I could get out of a teacup."

She walked over near the house across the field, looked around and then came running back.

"There's a wide dirt road just about 600 yards over there," she announced. "It's quite straight and will make a good runway once we get on it."

"Suppose we meet a car or a truck?"

"We'll just have to take that chance. And that's nothing compared to what we've just come through. Get in!" She jumped in and started the motor. Its roar must have carried for miles through the still moonlit early morning.

The big ship lurched over the newly broken ground toward the road. Luckily, the ground was not wet, or we should certainly have come a cropper. Slowly we approached the house and the road, wings dipping from side to side as we jogged across the deep black furrows. I noticed a light in one of the farmhouse windows. Pat saw it, too, but she could send us forward no faster in safety. The road was about fifty yards away now.

Then we both noticed the three-strand barbwire fence.

"Get the cutters and cut that fence," Pat cried. "Quick! Some of those damned farmers are coming!"

It was true. The door of the house had opened and two figures with shotguns stood silhouetted in the rectangle of yellow light.

I got the cutters, jumped to the ground and rushed for the fence. Moving swiftly, I made the six snips close to the two posts. This left sufficient space for our under-carriage to go between. Our wings were high enough to clear them.

The farmers, two men, were now running toward us, preceded by a hound. Pat sent the bomber through the space between the posts and gained the road.

"Hey! Hey! Hey tha!" yelled one of the men, now less than fifty feet behind us. "You gotta pay for that fence!"

Pat swung the ship around. There was a shot and fragments of glass from a broken window pane tinkled to the cabin floor.

Involuntarily I ducked. Pat shot the juice to the ship. We roared down the road, picking up speed at every yard. Up a gentle rise we tore, then down a hill which helped us off the ground. We were still flying low when a pine woods loomed straight ahead.

Pat cursed and bared her teeth. It was exasperating, coming just at

73

the time when our troubles were almost over. We were up fifty feet, now sixty, now seventy, but the trees were almost upon us.

With one last supreme effort, Pat shot the ship over the trees, the tops grazing our landing gear. It seemed as though I could have reached out and touched them.

Lighter now than we were on the trip down, we made remarkable time, doing always better than 220 miles an hour at an altitude of over a mile. At eight o'clock we sighted the Hudson River and shortly afterward Pat made a beautiful three-point landing on our field and taxied over to the hangar where Juan stood waiting. It was exactly eight-fifteen.

We ate breakfast with Juan and the boys in the attractive dining room and then took the train into New York.

Already the extras were on the streets, their screaming headlines telling of the catastrophe: "Flames Sweep Lynch Town; Equality Cult Blamed!" . . . "200 Die In Flames As Fire Guts City" . . . "Fire Lynch Town In Reprisal, 200 Perish" . . . One of the stories read:

> MERIDIAN, Miss., Mar. 5—Mysterious explosions followed by leaping flames wiped out the entire business section of Newton and many homes early this morning. The identified dead number 200, with many missing. Fire departments from this and neighboring cities finally subdued the flames but the town is a ruin. The Negro quarter was untouched.
>
> Officials are agreed that the fire was of incendiary origin, a view strengthened by the finding of numerous leaflets scattered around the immediate countryside warning of reprisals for the lynching of Ed Lovett, Negro farmhand, Wednesday afternoon, signed THE SONS OF CHRIST and claiming to be a Catholic organization.
>
> Catholic officials vigorously denied knowledge of any such organization and strongly denounced the outrage. Several Negro suspects are being held in the local jail for questioning.

Farther down was this item:

> INTERCOURSE, Ala. Mar. 5—A huge airplane landed on the farm of Jed Nixon about 3 a.m. today and left shortly afterward. Nixon claims occupants cut a section of his wire fence in order to get the big ship out on the nearby road, from which it flew off in the vicinity of Montgomery. Although fired upon by both Nixon and his son-in-law,

74

Alf Rackett, the plane refused to halt. It is believed the mysterious visitor might have had some connection with the incendiary fire at Newton, Miss., sixty miles west.

Dr. Belsidus turned the patient he was attending over to Dr. Matson as soon as we came in and joined us in the upper office.

"Well, Chief," I reported, "we succeeded."

"You only half succeeded," he growled. "I've read the extras. You bungled things by coming down on that farm. Then you bungled them again by not killing those damn farmers. Remember, Slater, dead men tell no tales. You're too squeamish. You must be hard. Understand? We don't want excuses, we want accomplishment. You can't have an omelet without breaking eggs . . . Now you two get some rest. I'll see you at four in my apartment. We've got to work fast now."

18

Belsidus Prepares to Wipe Out Two "Crackers"
Who Know Too Much

I don't know how long I had been sleeping when a heavy hand fell on my shoulder. I woke with difficulty. Jim was standing over me. As soon as I gathered my wits together I asked what was the matter. He silently pointed to the ceiling. Then he went out. I knew what he meant: Dr. Belsidus wanted me.

I dressed quickly and hurried to the ornate dining room of green and rose and gold. Places were set for 12. The goldenware gleamed dully, reflecting the green and rose of the furnishings.

But there was no time to ogle this magnificence. I hurried to the elevator. In a few seconds I stepped out in the Chief's apartment. Ben, the Doctor's leopard, rose up threateningly from his place at the foot of the bed. I hesitated. The apartment was empty and I knew that not even the Doctor's secretary dared enter under such circumstances. Ben would see to that. He was starting to walk slowly, suspiciously toward me, eyeing me all the time, making no sound on the polished, rug-strewn floor with his padded feet.

I was in a dilemma. What should I do? Ben would not permit me to stay. There was murderous menace in those narrow bloodshot eyes. Why wasn't Dr. Belsidus there? Was something wrong?

Well, better get in the elevator and go downstairs. I stepped backward, keeping my eyes on those of Ben. He was ready to leap, I knew. There was that tenseness of the rear leg muscles that signaled his intention. Well, one more step and I'd be inside the elevator. Then, pressing a button would close the door between me and the beast.

I moved my right foot back slowly for the last step into the elevator, my eyes still staring into those of the big cat. Then my heel struck the wall! I reached backward fearfully with my hand. The door was closed! Somebody had called the car. I was alone with Ben!

The big cat paused now, getting down closer to the floor, getting down until his belly almost touched. He spat ominously. Without any weapon, unable to move fast enough to avoid his leap, I was scared stiff. Cold sweat dampened my forehead and the palms of my hands. For some strange reason I took out my watch. Singular that Dr. Belsidus should have called me so early when he had announced the meeting for four o'clock. It was now only three. Ben came creeping ominously forward. I nervously dropped the watch but caught it by the chain on my vest. The movement probably saved my life. Ben's eyes rounded with astonishment. He gazed at the dangling watch in fascination, forgetting for the moment his mission. Lives and kingdoms, jobs and meals are lost, to say nothing of girls, by hesitation, by delay, by procrastination.

The door behind me flew open.

"Ben!" snapped Dr. Belsidus, coming out of the elevator past me. "Get back, boy!" The cat underwent an amazing metamorphosis. In a flash, the murder fled from his evil eyes to be replaced by the friendliness of the tame tabby. He turned about and ambled back to his place. I leaned weakly against the wall, struggling to regain my composure.

"You wanted me, Doctor?" I said feebly.

"Yes," he snapped. "Come here with your pad." He sat down in an easy chair by the table, pressing the buzzer at the same time. I sat across from him. He leaned back and closed his eyes. The stern face lost some of its hardness. I waited in silence.

"Did you ring, Doctor?" came a voice from the small screen in the center of the table.

"Yes, bring me a bottle of John Jameson and some club sodas, glasses for three, please." Why three glasses, I wondered.

"Yes, sir," came the voice of the maid.

Dr. Belsidus leaned back again and closed his eyes. Then, he suddenly straightened up, as if he had been pondering deeply and just that minute made up his mind. He looked sharply at me. Then a cunning expression came over his face and his deep-set eyes grew smaller.

"Take this telegram for the Montgomery, Alabama, cell," he dictated, grimly. "Eliminate Intercourse farmers immediately without fail. You know this code. Don't send it over the telephone. Carry it downtown yourself, probably to the office in the Grand Central terminal. After dinner will be ample time. Sign it Mr. Black."

I looked at him questioningly. A sardonic smile toyed with the corner of his mouth as he read my query in my eyes.

"Yes," he said, as though I had asked the question, "we've got to do away with those two cracker farmers. They've talked too much already. We're not ready for our identity to be known."

"But they didn't see us, Doctor," I protested. "They couldn't tell whether we were white or colored."

"They might have seen you better than you know," he replied quietly. "They certainly saw the plane in the moonlight. An error has been made, Slater. And when an error has been made it must be eliminated."

"But it seems like useless murder," I objected.

"Even so," he continued amiably, "I shall feel better with them out of the picture. It is the little things that wreck big movements. Come, let's not worry about two cracker farmers in Alabama who have probably helped in many a lynching. There's more wheels to be set going. Send this telegram in code to all State commanders: White Americans Heavy. Signed Mr. Black." Get that off after dinner, too. I want that distribution made by morning all over the country."

"But, I don't understand, Chief. What does it mean?"

"The White Americans," he explained slowly, "is an organization I have invented to oppose the Sons of Christ. It is anti-Catholic, anti-Jew and anti-Communist, composed of native white Protestants. We already have several thousand members, but I have been keeping them quiet until I was ready."

"It's too complicated for me," I admitted. "Here you have the Black Internationale, an organization working for black supremacy with a new religion, and at the same time you are sponsoring an anti-Negro and also a supposedly pro-Catholic organization. Just what is the point, Chief?"

"Slater," he said, smiling indulgently and passing a well-manicured hand over his smoothly shaven jaw, "have you ever heard of the British Imperialistic policy of 'Divide and Rule'?"

"Yes, of course. But what has that to do with all this?"

Before he could answer the elevator door flew open and the maid came in with the Irish whiskey and soda.

"Shall I pour them, Doctor?" she asked, putting down her golden tray and standing poised over the table.

"Pour two, please," he directed.

When she had retired again, he turned to answer my question.

"The Saxons conquered England," he said, "by dividing the Angles. They helped one king eliminate the others. The British did the same in India. The whites rule Africa because they used the same tactics. People are always more suspicious of each other, always hate each other more, when they are neighbors or kin. No war is as violent as civil war." He took a long drink, leaned back and then shortly resumed.

"I am using the same tactics against the whites. There are definite cleavages in the white population of which it would be foolish not to take advantage. Anti-Semitism is strong in the East where Jews are numerous and powerful. Anti-Catholicism is strong in the South, Middlewest and far West. There is almost everywhere a strong feeling against aliens, as one may gather from the anti-Communist propaganda. Where this hatred and prejudice is somnolent, we shall fan the smoldering embers into flames. We shall use force wherever it will further our ends. Our ends are to keep white people so busy fighting each other that we can carry out as much of our program as possible without their opposition, which, in the beginning, might well prove fatal. We're not yet ready to show our hand. We have generals and colonels aplenty, but too few competent captains and sergeants. Even when we come out openly against white imperialism, we can turn the rivalries and hatreds within the white race to good account. Today, it is generally believed among the ignorant white people in the Deep South that Newton, Miss., was burned by Catholics. Our White American Society's handbills will be distributed in 200 cities and towns, wherever we have a cell of the Black Internationale, before daybreak tomorrow by house-to-house distribution. I am particularly proud of those handbills." He paused and chuckled. "I designed them, you know, a long time ago."

"What will that accomplish?"

"It will bring in hundreds of thousands of new members into the White American Society," he replied, his deep eyes glowing. "Other things I have in mind will alarm and stiffen the opposition of the Catholics and Jews. The head of the White Americans will tell you all about it himself tonight."

"You don't mean to say he's coming here?

"Yes, of course. He'll be here for our staff dinner. He's done fine work. But his work has just started. He'll stir up plenty of trouble. And while the white folks are fighting each other, we'll be consolidating our position unnoticed."

19

△△△△△△△△△△△△△△△△△△△△△

Pretty White Woman Brings Belsidus "Tips"
as B.I. Idea Grows

"Send cables to all international units as follows," continued Dr. Belsidus. "Select twenty candidates immediately. Planes where feasible."

"That will cost a lot of money," I observed, "a thousand students."

"Naturally," he snapped. "But we must start their instruction at once. The situation is tightening. We've got to get them in technical schools NOW. We've got to have trained men and women. We mustn't make the mistake of Russia and try to work without brains and skill."

I did not pursue the subject further. I knew it would be futile. Besides, the Chief had demonstrated that he had thought out everything.

"Telephone Alex Fletcher to be sure and be at dinner this evening. We must know just how our businesses are progressing. Do that immediately. Then return at once. Tell Pat I won't see her now. It really isn't necessary. But she must be at dinner this evening. Tell Jim to bring the lady up when she comes. He'll know who."

I obeyed quickly and was back at the Doctor's exotic apartment in about five minutes.

"Take a record of all my visitor says, Carl," the physician commanded as I took my seat. "She will be here in a moment. Do not leave us alone unless I say to. I have no time for love."

He had scarcely stopped speaking when the elevator doors opened and a pretty white girl swathed in expensive furs hurried out toward us. I guessed she was in her early thirties and a real thoroughbred.

Dr. Belsidus rose with his usual courteous aloofness and kissed her beautifully manicured tapering fingers. He introduced her as Miss Gaskin and helped her with her queenly wrap. Then he offered her a drink. She swallowed it eagerly and promptly took another. She was obviously agitated.

"God, Henry," she exclaimed, "I certainly needed that. I'm worn out. My Lord! The things a woman will do for love." She looked at him softly and pushed back a fugitive hair that had escaped from the golden wealth upon her head.

"Did you get the information I told you to get?" asked Belsidus.

"Of course, darling," she exclaimed enthusiastically. "He was hard to track down but I finally made him. Talked like a phonograph after the fourth Scotch. Here, it's all written down here, just as he told me, dear."

"Good work," boomed the Doctor. "I'll take advantage of it."

There was an awkward silence. I knew she was anxious to be alone with him. I could see it in her eyes. I could also see that having got the information he desired, Dr. Belsidus did not want to be bothered with her. Smiling a little apologetically, she took a third drink. The color rose higher in her cheeks. She looked at him appealingly, as if to hypnotize him.

"Henry, can't we be alone?" she pleaded.

"Some other time," he replied abruptly. He rose to signify that the interview was concluded.

"Tomorrow? Oh, please, Henry!" There were eager tears in her blue eyes.

"Perhaps," he said, leading the way to the elevator. "I'm busy now."

At the door she cast aside her reserve and, throwing her arms about his neck, kissed him passionately, one foot kicked back in her excitement.

"An excellent worker," he exclaimed when she had gone, "but I suppose I'll have to get rid of her. You know, Slater, women work best for you when they are in love with you. They are most dangerous to you when they find that you are not in love with them. This woman, Martha Gaskin, knows Wall Street like a book and is thoroughly at home in the stock and bond market. She gets valuable tips that help us tremendously. She just brought in some inside stuff on the market. Last week through her tips we cleaned up over a half million dollars. But inevitably she will find out that I care nothing for her except to get this information. Then, Slater, she will be dangerous. And, of course, she will have to be removed."

"You mean killed?" I asked, amazed by his callousness.

"Dead women, Slater, are no more articulate than dead men. Miss Gaskin knows nothing about the Black Internationale nor our other activities, but there's no telling how much trouble a woman may cause when she feels that she's spurned."

Events happened so swiftly after that afternoon that I am able only to touch upon them briefly in order to give you some idea of the magnitude of the national crisis which the Black Internationale precipitated.

At dinner that evening were: Dr. Belsidus, Sam Hamilton, Rev. Samson Binks, Ransom Just, Bennie Simpson, Patricia Givens, Alex Fletcher, Juan Torlier, Gaston Nucklett, Sanford Mates and myself.

Each reported on the progress of his work. It was a meeting that would have gladdened the heart of any real Negro. Sanford Mates, the architect, told of the great progress in erecting Church of Love temples. Dr. Binks spoke briefly on the amazing reaction of black America to the new religion. Alex Fletcher related the manner in which our vegetables were capturing the public's fancy, and told how angry the farmers were becoming because of loss of markets. Sam Hamilton described how acre-production of potatoes had been jumped from 400 bushels to 2,000 bushels by cultivation in chemically treated water. Bennie Simpson was equally enthusiastic about increased production of cement and the manner in which Fletcher had cooperated with him in making deliveries of cement to Mates in B.I. trucks. Gaston Nucklett, a white Negro from Atlanta who looked exactly like a sandhill cracker, told with many a chuckle how he had organized the White American Society and was busy furthering strife within the white race in his publication *White America*, which attacked Jews, aliens and Catholics. Pat and Juan Torlier reported on the completion of additional bombers and pursuit ships and how ten more pilots had been licensed by the government.

But the most exciting things happened in the forty-eight hours after we had finished that memorable dinner.

First, about nine o'clock, I telephoned the Montgomery, Ala., cell in code, then I sent the second telegram in code to the 200 other cells of the Black Internationale in as many cities, and the cables to our half hundred national cells in Europe, Asia, Africa, South America and the West Indies.

Afterward I took a little run up to Mag's place with Al Fortune to watch his nightly collection. I was back at the headquarters looking over the midnight edition of the morning papers when a telegram came addressed to me. It read, "Please Thank the Doctor for His Double Invitation," and was signed, "Montgomery Black." I knew without consulting the code book that the two white farmers of Intercourse, Ala., who had seen too much were dead. It was deadly, uncanny efficiency.

Next morning the papers were full of it. Not only had the two men been killed, but everybody in the house, by a terrific explosion that had rocked the countryside. Nearby were found SONS OF CHRIST leaflets. During the night in over 200 cities, anti-Catholic leaflets had been thickly distributed through residential districts. It had been done quickly and efficiently.

The afternoon papers told of the mysterious explosions in Catholic churches in Boston, Buffalo, Baltimore, New Orleans, Cincinnati and Detroit. In each case leaflets had been distributed nearby preaching anti-Semitism and anti-Catholicism.

One incendiary act after another was reported hourly. They increased day after day. Newspapers were full of them. Editorials deplored the arson and murder, warning that civil war would be the result. Dr. Belsidus chuckled in demoniacal satisfaction.

Meantime, using the market tips secured by the white girl, Dr. Belsidus cleaned up over two million on the stock market. Taking advantage of the Bear movement which Miss Gaskin had accurately predicted and which had forced certain key stocks down from ten to fifteen points, he threw almost all his resources into a giant purchasing move. This, coupled with the even greater buying of the clique whose secrets the girls had learned, forced these stocks sky high. Just before they reached the point where he knew the others planned to get out from under and leave the "suckers" holding the bag, he sold everything.

The situation meanwhile grew more grim. Membership in Gaston Nucklett's White American Society grew by the thousands daily. Catholics were at the same time clamoring to join the militant Sons of Christ whose leaflets they had been reading but which only existed in the fertile mind of Dr. Henry Belsidus.

Within ten days there were clashes between Catholics and Protestants in over a dozen cities. Dead and wounded were reported hourly, Jewish synagogues were smeared with painted crosses or burned. Many beautiful Protestant and Catholic edifices were in ruins. Cells of the Black Internationale busied themselves further fomenting strife by acts of vandalism. In every part of the country each side was appealing to Negroes for their aid, but in the B.I. temples black people were being told to mind their own business.

By the time the 1,000 colored young men and women began to arrive in New York from various parts of the world and enroll in trade schools, civil strife was in full swing in America. Hatred having been stimulated through the Doctor's machinations, it was now rolling along under its own momentum. Business and finance felt the effect of the civil strife and the Black Internationale prospered. We were rapidly taking over the produce business with our giant tomatoes, potatoes, strawberries and other products. Our temples, now numbering a hundred or more, were filled every night. We had virtually captured the retail trade of sixty Negro districts through our temple basement stores and were rapidly monopolizing the amusement business. Alex Fletcher had purchased two cotton mills in Georgia and was negotiating for a shoe factory in Massachusetts.

Then, one evening at dinner, Dr. Belsidus announced dramatically but quietly, "Now we are going to have a REAL headquarters, a country of our own from which to direct our activities. Now is the time to get it while white people are fighting each other."

"And how are we to get it, Doctor?" asked Pat.

"We're going to take it," he announced grimly.

83

20

Belsidus Explains Details of His Plans
to Conquer Africa

Dr. Belsidus was a man of action, speedy action, but carefully thought-out action. All next day he pondered alone in his apartment, letting no one enter. Finally, around five o'clock he called for me.

"Notify all executives to be here for a dinner conference this evening," he ordered, "without fail. You'd better make it eight o'clock so as to give Nucklett time to get here. I understand he's addressing a big mass meeting of the White American Society in Richmond this afternoon. He's right on the job, Nucklett is. He's got these crackers steaming."

"Yes, sir," I agreed. "The morning papers were full of that bloody fight between white Catholics and Protestants in Indianapolis, and several of Nucklett's White Americans were jailed. And, of course, Chief, I know you've heard about those bombings of Jewish synagogues in Syracuse. Also, Nucklett's last report gave him three hundred fifty thousand members in his outfit."

"Good!" The Doctor rubbed his hands together in satisfaction and his deep eyes glowed. "By the way, tell Fletcher to bring Barton McNeel with him."

"But he's not an executive, Chief. He's just Fletcher's director of transportation."

"Send for him, I tell you," he snapped, frowning. "I know what I'm doing. McNeel distinguished himself in the Argonne during the World War. He was a captain in the 368th infantry, and was decorated by the American and French governments. He played a part, an important part, in the Chicago riot. I've kept track of him through the years. The Depression had him down and out when I put him under Fletcher to direct our transportation. He'll do a good job in Africa. Besides, we need an experienced military man to advise us."

84

"Then you were quite serious the other night about the conquest of Africa?"

"Of course I was serious, Slater; I'm always serious."

It was five minutes after eight when Gaston Nucklett walked into the dining room. The soup had not yet been served. The table was a symphony of green, rose and gold. Bowls of multi-colored blooms graced the center of the long gold-laden table, while a row of slender, tapering black candles in golden sticks shed a romantically flickering light. At the head of the table sat Dr. Belsidus. I sat next to him, my pad on my lap in readiness to take down what was said. Around the table were Ransom Just, Patricia Givens, Juan Torlier, Bennie Simpson, Sanford Mates, Alex Fletcher, Gaston Nucklett and Capt. Barton McNeel.

The dinner was the usual Belsidus culinary triumph, interspersed with rare wines: Rhine wine with the fish, sparkling burgundy with the fowl, champagne with the meat, Oporto port with the dessert and then with the demi tasse, a liqueur, half benedictine, half gin. The uniformed waiters moved noiselessly, efficiently, courteously. I found myself marvelling again at the remarkable discipline Dr. Belsidus had established.

At long last the dinner came to its inevitable end. Cigars and cigarettes were passed around and a blue haze soon hung over the heads of the executives. Dr. Belsidus leaned back in his chair and regarded them through partially closed eyelids. Finally he cleared his throat. At this signal conversation ceased. Silence ensued.

He clapped his well-manicured hands twice. The door flew open and the giant Jim hastened to the Doctor's side.

"Has Gustave Linke arrived yet, Jim?"

The dummy nodded his head in assent, then pointed downstairs.

"Bring him in as soon as he freshens up."

Jim saluted, turned and disappeared. The others looked at each other. I knew they were wondering who Gustave Linke might be. They were not to be kept wondering long.

"Gentlemen," said the Doctor, finally, "we are now about to enter the second phase of our program for the liberation of the black world. Our first objective was to get money and to organize the brains of the Negro race. We have succeeded in doing that. Since our international conference, each of our fifty foreign units has sent us a young man and a young woman, one hundred young Negroes in all, who are now enrolled at technological institutions in various parts of the country. Each unit has also sent us ten young men and ten young women, a total of one thousand in all, who are now in attendance at trade schools here in New York, in Pittsburgh, in Milwaukee, in Chicago and in Cleveland, taking six-month courses. In addition to these foreign students, we have two hundred American Negro men and women in institutes of technology and one thousand in trade schools.

"We have ten plantations from New Jersey to Texas, each with the latest equipment and methods of agricultural science. At each plantation we have an airfield. Our airport and airplane factory in Westchester County has trained five hundred colored pilots, men and women, and manufactured one hundred pursuit planes and fifty bombing planes since we started the work under the expert direction of Miss Givens and Juan Torlier.

"We have Sam Hamilton to thank for our agricultural progress, and Al Fortune to thank not only for his sun-power plants which have saved us so much money, but also for his able direction of our association of criminals which is responsible for bringing ten million dollars into our treasury in the past year.

"Rev. Binks has made his idea of a new religion for Negroes a reality. I had some misgivings about it at first. No one can have any now. Rev. Binks has brought in tens of thousands of fanatically loyal Negroes, the kind who are not afraid of being black and are willing to die for their beliefs. He has reported the erection of over one hundred Temples of Love in the United States and one hundred seventy-five under the jurisdiction of our foreign units in the West Indies and Africa. Alex Fletcher, who has done such a good job directing our business affairs and finances, reports that in each of the two hundred and seventy-five temples there are economic units: stores, beauty parlors, etc., just as in Harlem, which not only have the loyal patronage of our organization people but other Negroes as well, and doing a two-million-a-week business.

"Bennie Simpson," he continued, "has built and operated our cement plant most effectively, and established four more in various parts of the country. Our Gaston Nucklett, who is sacrificing much by living and working among white people, has done and is doing remarkable work in disrupting the white population, promoting civil strife and otherwise keeping attention focused away from us. It is a fine work and will continue on a larger scale. And, of course, excellent work has been done by Ransom Just in establishing powerful, secret radio stations; by Dr. Matson in the establishing of B.I. hospitals in Mississippi, Alabama, South Carolina, Georgia and Louisiana; by Sanford Mates in designing our various structures; and by Juan Torlier for his valuable work with Miss Givens as head of our aircraft factory. And, incidentally, I have made a couple million dollars myself on the stock market with the aid of my white girl friend good enough to bring me tips. Altogether, I should say that we have done our first job well."

The others nodded assent. It was an impressive record of things accomplished. I knew of many other things which he might have mentioned, such as the two-million membership which the Black Internationale now boasted.

"Now," continued the Chief, "as I told you the other evening, the period of conquest has begun. Listen carefully to your orders. I want no mistakes. We must not fail." His deep serious eyes ran over the group.

"McNeel," the tall distinguished man with gray hair looked up as his name was called, "you will be in charge of our expeditionary force of five thousand men. These men are to be physically fit, loyal and preferably with military experience because we haven't much time to spend on training. Fletcher has purchased fifteen thousand acres in South Texas. Mates has erected the barracks, six huge airplane hangars. The place will be used later as an airport. The whole thing is practically ready. Get the men from Rev. Binks. He has kept track of all his devotees with military training. The rest you can find in your motor transport division.

"There will be no uniforms. You will drill your men in the early morning just to be on the safe side, although you are forty miles from the railroad and five miles from the nearest road. However, Mates has constructed a good dirt road from the hangars to the main road. Fletcher is taking care of the food and equipment. You'll need plenty of small arms practice, bayonet exercise, grenade throwing and machine gunning. Mr. Just will supply you with radio equipment and instructors. Dr. Matson will send you doctors. Fletcher will arrange for truck and plane transportation to and from the camp. You must be ready to leave here in ninety days for West Africa."

21

⩘⩘⩘⩘⩘⩘⩘⩘⩘⩘⩘⩘⩘⩘⩘⩘⩘⩘⩘⩘⩘⩘

Belsidus Trains 5,000 Soldiers in Texas
and Sends Them to Africa

I confess that I was skeptical about the success of this latest venture. Dr. Belsidus had so far attained all his objectives with practically no opposition. Characteristically, he attributed this to his ruthlessness and to the fact that he had not advertised what he was doing.

"Slater," he said one afternoon while the expeditionary force was being secretly transported to the Texas coast, "one of the great mistakes made by minority leaders in the past has been ballyhoo. Therefore we have established no newspapers or magazines, given no talks over the radio, staged no parades or demonstrations. Consequently the enemy has no inkling of what we are doing. They associate our various enterprises with no central organization. Because they do not appreciate the magnitude of our work, Slater, they are unable to cope with it. What we do travels fast enough among Negroes without the aid of publication. If we had a newspaper and boasted in it about our far-flung efforts, white people would know all about it and crush us before we were ready."

"But, Chief," I objected, "you can't expect to train five thousand men in Texas and the white people not know about it. You can't expect to have Al Fortune's criminal corps keep on rifling the homes and stores of the country without white people eventually finding out. You can't expect to corner the produce business of the country and to corral all the Negroes in the Church of Love without white people knowing something about it."

He smiled indulgently and stroked his clean-shaven, militant chin. His deep-set eyes sparkled and glowed as he listened tolerantly.

"You are quite right, my boy," he agreed. "The white people will eventually find out what we have been up to, but by that time I'll not care because we shall have accomplished so much they'll not be able to stop us. Al Fortune's work is over so far as the criminal branch is concerned. We've stolen millions and gotten away with it. Now I'm going to use Al's engineering ability in Africa, where it will be needed. There will be stiffening opposition, of course, to our produce business and our other enterprises, but that opposition is being nullified by my policy of divide and conquer the white people. While they fight among themselves, they leave Negroes alone, and that's what we want. We have nothing to fear for a long time, my boy."

Later that day I drove down to our Jersey plantation with Sam Hamilton. On the way we passed fifteen or twenty truckloads of Negroes going in the same direction. When we arrived a little after dark, the place was a beehive of activity. Great flood-lights made the airfield as light as day. At one end were several rows of great bombing planes drawn up with propellers whirring. As each truck stopped, the men in it got down and, forming to a group of ten, marched over to one of the planes and piled aboard. Once loaded, the plane's door was closed, the portable step wheeled aside and, at a signal from a starter with a checkered flag, it would roar down the runway and soon disappear into the darkness.

"They'll be in Texas before daybreak," Sam observed, as he stopped his roadster in front of the farm headquarters. "Each plane carries ten men and enough gasoline and oil to get to our mobilization point. With fifty bombers we're sending five hundred men a day from here. Within ten days our entire force will be mobilized. It's good experience for the aviators. We've got a bunch of relief pilots at the other end. They bring these planes back tomorrow. The Chief chose this as a mobilization point because the presence of a whole lot of Negroes here arouses no comment. We're servicing the planes at the Westchester field when they return each trip."

We watched the proceedings for about fifteen minutes. Finally the field was empty. The last of the trucks had gone to the garages when a familiar black and gold autogiro dropped out of the sky and rolled to a stop on the lighted field.

I recognized Pat's familiar green garb as she stepped down out of the cockpit and spoke to a greasy mechanic who had run out on the field. She came over to where we were.

It was a happy culmination of a busy day. I always felt buoyant when

Pat was around, even though she gave me no encouragement. Since the day at the temple, though, she had seemed to be avoiding me, seemed self-conscious in my presence.

"What brings you down here?" I asked by way of saying something, although I knew she had to be there with all of her big planes hopping off with their human cargoes.

"You're coming back to New York with me," she announced. "Doctor's orders. An important conference, I believe."

"It'll be a pleasure to go back," I replied gallantly, "if you're going to fly me back." I put all that she meant to me in the glance that I gave her.

"That's why I came down," she replied indifferently. "We'd better go right back. The Chief is waiting."

We walked together over to the waiting autogiro. In a few moments we were soaring over the countryside toward the towers of Manhattan.

The twelve weeks of training and preparation were almost finished when Dr. Belsidus and I visited the Texas estate for the first time. Pat flew us down. A vast stretch of arid land facing the Gulf of Mexico about seventy miles above Brownsville, it was ideally suited for our purpose. The great hangars were camouflaged to make them almost invisible a mile away. The edge of the estate was five miles from the nearest road and almost forty miles from the railroad. The most prominent landmark was a water tower and twin radio towers. East of the estate was the Laguna de la Madre and the great barrier reef that barred the way to the Gulf of Mexico. A half mile off the reef, six freighters awaited their cargo.

McNeel drove up in his car as we landed. "Well, Mac, is everything ready?" Dr. Belsidus eyed him questioningly.

"Everything is ready, Doctor," he replied quietly. "Food, small arms, ammunition and field equipment are already aboard."

"Crackers give you any trouble?"

"No, sir. Those who have stopped by here think this is a big CCC camp laying out an airfield. But in the main we haven't had many visitors. This place is mighty far off the beaten path, you know."

"Yes, that's why we located here."

We got in McNeel's car. He drove us several miles across the estate until we came to the lagoon. A number of small wharves had been built and on these there was great activity, men moving goods of all kinds into barges towed by busy tugs across the lagoon. There, a channel just wide enough to accommodate the barges had been cut through the reef. They passed carefully through this channel out into the open sea and to the waiting ships. Altogether, the whole trip was seven miles.

"We embark tomorrow at daybreak," McNeel announced. Dr. Belsidus nodded approvingly.

We drove back to McNeel's quarters for dinner. There were the Doctor, McNeel, Pat, Hamilton, Just, Al Fortune and Juan Torlier gathered around the board. We were all in gay spirits. A difficult job was almost finished. We had trained five thousand Negroes and were embarking them for Africa, and white America knew nothing about it. Perhaps in the whole history of the Negro in America nothing had ever been accomplished so efficiently and so quietly. I observed as much to Pat just before we went in to eat.

"You're right, Carl," she replied, "but there's one little efficiency you don't know about. McNeel tells me that he had to remove about twenty of those Negroes who persisted in talking. You know Negroes, some Negroes, have just GOT to tell what they know. And of course that's against our rules."

I knew what that "remove" meant. I must have revealed something of my revulsion because she looked at me sharply, even a little disapprovingly. We joined the others without any further exchange. I kept thinking throughout the elaborate dinner what a cold-blooded young woman she was. And yet how much I wanted her.

Dr. Belsidus had purchased the six freighters in New York, loaded them very lightly with cement and cleared them for the West Coast of Africa. Secret instructions were for them to stop en route and pick up the B.I. expeditionary force. This was accomplished according to schedule and without incident or accident.

We stayed around all day until the last man was aboard the tossing freighters. The six captains met Dr. Belsidus, General Barton McNeel, Pat Givens and I in the cabin of the S.S. *Bessie Coleman* for final instructions. I had not previously met the black skippers whom the chief had secured from the West Indies, Venezuela and Senegal. They were fine, upstanding black fellows, serious and capable.

"Captain Jorre," said Dr. Belsidus, "I place you in charge of the fleet.

You will proceed in the S.S. *Samory* direct to the coast of Liberia. You'd better keep your ships about fifty or sixty miles apart. I don't want you to follow the usual shipping lanes, but I want you to be off Monrovia exactly three weeks from today. The others will take positions as follows: Capt. Campbell's S.S. *Nat Turner* off Robertsport, Capt. Williams's S.S. *Fred Douglass,* off Cape Palmas, Capt. Sinclair's S.S. *Sojourner Truth* off Sinoe, Capt. Sanchez's S.S. *Bessie Coleman* off Nanna Kru, while Capt. Bossona in the *Phyllis Wheatley* will stand off Monrovia with the S.S. *Samory.* You are to be ready at your stations on the afternoon of the twenty-second day. You will receive landing instructions from General McNeel who will be aboard the S.S. *Samory* with his staff. You will each associate yourself with the colonel in charge of the troops aboard your ship. The men will be absolutely under his charge.

"McNeel," he continued, turning to the gray-haired general, "you have my instructions. Kalanga, the head of our Sierra Leone cell, and Ralph Farley of our Liberian cell will supply the necessary guides. We confer with them about a week before your ships arrive."

He appeared amused at our expressions of surprise.

"Oh, yes," he said quietly, "I shall be there. Slater and Pat and I are flying to Freetown by way of Brazil. Well, that's all. Remember, men, there must be no failure. This is the greatest venture black men have embarked upon in centuries. There must be no failure."

22

▲▲▲▲▲▲▲▲▲▲▲▲▲▲▲▲▲▲▲▲▲▲▲▲▲▲▲

Dr. Belsidus Arrives in Africa to Start His Big Offensive

We fled up the Atlantic Coast with a helping wind behind us. The Chief sat brooding over a large map of Liberia as the black night hurried by. I was in front with Pat. She was intent on her task, watching her instruments, picking up radio weather reports. We cut across the Gulf to New Orleans and then made a bee line for New York. All through the night the silent man behind us marked up the map, made notes in his memorandum book, dictated into the machine, sometimes in succession, sometimes, it seemed, all at once. I have never seen anyone who could so lose himself in his work as Dr. Belsidus, and yet with no difficulty whatever take up consideration of any question submitted to him.

Pat and I exchanged a few, but very few, words. Somehow I had been imagining recently that she was becoming more distant. It wasn't anything she said, particularly, but certain little looks and movements that indicated a growing indifference. To be sure, she had never indicated that she cared anything for me beyond the comradeship of a man and a woman engaged in a hazardous, adventurous enterprise. She had even told me that there was too much to be done for the race for her to be bothered with love. And yet it somehow felt that she should be mine and I couldn't look at her radiant, intelligent brown beauty without my heart skipping a beat. I wanted to tell her of the passion that was consuming me, yet I quailed before the anticipation of her coolness, before the thought of rebuff.

Why was it, I wondered to myself, that courtship and romance often is so difficult these days and yet is more simple than in the past. The days of chaperons and "for men only" are gone. Men and women are on a plane of equality. Social and economic differences between the sexes have become a thing of the past. We vote and work and socialize and even go to war together these days. And yet this sexual democracy, this fraternization, this single standard has too often accentuated hidden irritations and antagonisms and clashing ambitions to the point where barriers arise between the sexes which sadly inhibit the normal urges and desires once so easily consummated.

Of course, I realized, it is largely psychological. We have to become conditioned to our changed environment almost over night, historically speaking. Physically, we live in the Twentieth Century; psychologically, we live many thousands of years ago. We come into this world made for a life as huntsman or herdsman and find ourselves in an environment of whirling machines, confusion upon confusion for the sake of order, complications and responsibilities and temptations that try the hardiest souls and often leave them balanced precariously on the precipice of insanity. Life has been made too complex, and man was intended to live a life of simplicity. Here I was, madly in love with Pat. Had I lived in another age, I could have taken her without delay or ado. Now, because of her career, because of what she wanted to do for the race, because of her probable desire not to settle down into wifely domesticity, I was held off.

Something of my disgruntled feeling must have communicated itself to her. She turned her eyes from the instrument board and the moon-kissed waters that tossed below us and looked at me with a half amused expression.

"What's the matter?" she shouted above the roar of the motors. "In love?"

I started and then sank back sheepishly as she enjoyed my confusion.

"You know darn well that I am," I shouted back.

"Well," she came back at me, "don't give up hope."

Her eyes were sparkling mischievously. Somehow that little exchange, which seems perhaps nothing at all to one reading in cold type what transpired, nevertheless made me buoyant. Perhaps, then, my love for her was not hopeless. Perhaps, in time, I could penetrate that reserve of career and independence into which she seemed to have retired, and make her acknowledge her love for me. At any rate, it was a hopeful thought.

I sank back with a pleasant feeling and fell gradually to sleep with, I believe, a smile on my face as large as that in my heart.

For the next week innumerable conferences with executives

followed mysterious meetings in Dr. Belsidus's apartment with impor-
tant-looking people. His entire store of gold vessels—dishes, vases, platters, knives, forks, spoons, umbrella stands and many other
articles—was turned in at the Assay Office at 36 dollars an ounce. This
act alone convinced me, if such had been necessary, that Dr. Belsidus
was planning operations of the first magnitude.

In two days the transaction was completed and the money amount-
ing to two and a half million dollars added to the millions already
standing to the Doctor's account in the American National Bank.

On the sixth day after the sailing of the expeditionary forces, the
Chief held his final conference with Alex Fletcher, Gaston Nucklett,
who flew up from Atlanta, Juan Torlier, Pat and, of course, myself. Rev.
Binks was delayed but dropped in just as we had reached the cognac
and coffee. It was midnight before full instructions for the conduct of
operations had been given and discussed, and the meeting adjourned.
We were all a little excited throughout. The Doctor was the coolest of
the lot, but even in his expression one could see some of that sense of
expectation that pervades the beings of all humans on the eve of great
adventure.

It didn't seem that I had slept more than fifteen or twenty minutes
when faithful old Jim shook my shoulder until I grumblingly awoke.
It was five-thirty. I showered, shaved and dressed quickly. Dr. Belsidus
and Pat were already in the big limousine when I got down to the curb.
Dr. Matson stood at the window and waved farewell to us as the car
pulled away toward Fifth Avenue.

It was seven o'clock when we reached our airport. A huge black and
gold transport plane stood in the field near the quarters. It glistened in
the rising sun like some huge prehistoric bird with wings spread, pulling a worm from the earth. Jim drove the limousine within about fifty
feet of the air cruiser. We got out of the car. Juan Torlier, seemingly a
little sleepy, was taking a final look over the engine.

"How much gas, Juan?" Pat asked as she crawled into the cabin.

"Six hundred," he replied. "Everything's ready, Miss Givens."

Dr. Belsidus greeted the airplane expert with a cordial nod. Two mechanics stood ready to kick the chocks from under each wheel. In back
of us the entire group of pilots and mechanicians, designers and engineers stood silhouetted against the rising sun, bidding us adieu.

The Chief paused on the steps of the plane and, turning toward them, he spoke slowly and deliberately, a certain note of tenseness in his voice.

"Boys and girls, we are on our way to the supreme test: that for which we have striven all these months and years. We have everything we need to succeed. The physical means are in our hands. We have learned how not only to use the instruments the white man uses but also how to make them, and that is of most importance. So long as the Negro did not make the machinery of modern civilization, so long as there were inner secrets to which he was not privy, just so long was the Negro doomed to remain a slave of the white man. We never lacked courage, we never lacked willingness; what we lacked was knowledge. Now we have acquired knowledge. Now we have accumulated wealth, a point for the spear of knowledge. We are not only the equal of the white man now, we are his superior. I say we are his superior because we know that which he does not know. We know what we are going to do. The white man does NOT know what we are going to do.

"We are leaving now, my comrades, on our great adventure. A week from today we shall be on the shores of Africa. Two weeks from today a new note will be sounded in international affairs. Young men and women, be ready! I shall call upon you. Be sure you are ready to do my bidding."

A great cheer arose from the crowd. The young men and women rushed forward, as he shook the hand of each. Then he went inside and sat by the table that had been installed for him and began to pore over his map and notes as if there were no cheering crowd outside.

I got in and seated myself alongside Pat. In the rear of the compartment a tall black fellow in jaunty blue uniform sat at a table with headphones clamped on and a sending and receiving set before him. I knew he was the navigator.

The engine started with a roar. Pat sent the big plane down the runway for almost a mile before we left the ground and shot over the Hudson River southward. This was no leisurely autogiro. In a half hour we were thundering down to Havana at two hundred and thirty-five miles an hour and cruising at five thousand feet.

We spent six hours at Havana and then flew on to Port-au-Prince, where Dr. Belsidus talked quietly with a slender black man for upwards of an hour. Then we hopped over to Jamaica for a few hours' stay. The second evening found us in Port of Spain. There, a Negro, part East Indian, drove us through steep, palm-lined avenues to his white house amid a bower of tropical blooms.

The next day, after a brief stop at Georgetown, British Guiana, we hopped off for Recife, where the commandant of the Brazilian cell flew up from Rio de Janeiro for a conference. On the morning of the fourth day, bright and early, Pat sent the giant plane down the runway and leaped off to Africa.

Hudginson, the navigator and radio man, plotted our course with uncanny accuracy. After an uneventful and monotonous nine hours over the south Atlantic, the young man tapped the snoozing Dr. Belsidus on the shoulder and pointing straight ahead said, "Africa, sir!"

23

△△△△△△△△△△△△△△△△△△△△△△

Belsidus Completes Plans for Surprise Attack on Monrovia

In a few minutes, the cloud-wreathed mountains in back of Freetown, Sierra Leone, loomed straight ahead of us and shortly we were above the pretentious white government buildings from which the Union Jack fluttered. Pat circled until we located the large private field made ready by the Freetown cell of the Black Internationale and described in our reports from Joseph Kalanga. Pat sent the ship over the field and then, turning, came upwind to a perfect three-point landing.

As the plane came to a halt, a little crowd of white-clad black men ran out on the field. I immediately recognized Joseph Kalanga. The others were officials of the organization in Sierra Leone. In accordance with the Doctor's orders, there was no demonstration. We merely shook hands all around. Then the black customs officials and the white British health officer came to do their duty. After a few whispered words between Dr. Belsidus and Kalanga, we all left in several automobiles for the nearby city. In fifteen minutes we were closeted in the library of Kalanga's pretty tropical home. Shortly afterward, Ralph Farley, commander of the Liberian cell, arrived.

"Doctor," began Kalanga, "we have carried out your orders to the letter. A month ago we received the empty grenades and, following the instructions of Sam Hamilton and Rev. Binks, we have filled them with the incendiary chemicals in our workshops underneath our Temples of Love."

"You have made the distribution?" asked the Doctor.

"Yes, sir. Two weeks later—that's a fortnight ago—we sent them by fast couriers. Night before last the drums notified us that the distribution was completed. At a given signal every European shop and home, and every white man, woman and child inside them, will be destroyed. That takes in French Guinea, Portuguese Guinea, Sierra Leone and the French West African hinterland." He was obviously proud of his accomplishment.

"Very good, Kalanga, very good. I have received similar reports from Dakar, Bathurst, Bingerville, Accra, Abomey, Lagos, Libreville, Stanleyville, the Portuguese Angola and South Africa," Dr. Belsidus announced. Then, turning to the Liberian commander, he inquired, "Mr. Farley, how is the picture in Liberia?"

"Everything is ready, sir," the Monrovian replied. "I have carried out your instructions to the letter. The hinterland chiefs are ready to march to the coast when the signal is given. Most of the Liberian Frontier Force has been concentrated in Monrovia through our machinations. Our men on the Coast, the Krus and Greboes, but not the Vais, are ready with their boats and canoes at the various ports."

"Why not the Vais?" asked the Doctor, obviously somewhat surprised.

"They are not to be trusted, sir. We could take no chances. The incendiary grenades are ready in our Temples of Love. Distribution will be made if and when you give the orders."

"Has everyone been well paid?" inquired the Chief.

"We have distributed the entire cargo of leaf tobacco, salt, rice, canned goods, salt fish and liquor which you sent a fortnight ago. We have also given out over a thousand pounds in 'dash' to the Paramount Chiefs."

"And the airport," continued Dr. Belsidus, "has that been prepared?"

"Yes, sir," replied Farley, smiling, "just as you directed. It is five miles back of Monrovia and not far from the road to the Firestone plantation. The government thinks the land has been cleared for an athletic field for one of our Temples of Love nearby."

The Liberian commander then produced a recent map of Liberia and a smaller one of Monrovia and vicinity on which were indicated the locations of the ten Temples of Love, the airport and various towns from Robertsport to Harper.

"You have done well, comrades," said the physician. "You may go. I counsel you to silence on pain of death. Assemble here tomorrow evening. By that time Miss Givens, Slater, Mr. Hudginson and I will be refreshed and we can complete our arrangements."

In another week the troopships would be off Monrovia. We were far from idle in the meantime. Pat and Hudginson flew over Liberia, familiarizing themselves with the location of the airports outside Monrovia and in the vicinity of Robertsport, Harper, Sinoe and Nanna Kru. Dr. Belsidus conferred with numerous close-mouthed Negroes, some in European clothes, others in native robes betokening their rank, met with various steamship agents and otherwise prepared for the momentous campaign.

Freetown is a pretty little city of glistening white buildings that start from the waterfront and march up the green hills. Everywhere black officials were evident, on the streets, in government buildings, in the customs house and in the post office. Kalanga informed us that these black officials were generally more loyal to the British imperialists than King George VI. The only opposition he had encountered had been from them. How little they knew of the changes in store.

When I was not attending the numerous conferences Dr. Belsidus held or getting acquainted with the cell commanders who came in from all over West Africa to meet Dr. Belsidus, I was busy decoding messages. On the last two days these messages came in batches. The evening of the twentieth day following the departure of expeditionary forces from Texas, I closeted myself with Dr. Belsidus and Patricia in Kalanga's library, the day's messages spread out before me. The Chief, in that gay mood he always affected when work had been well done, ordered me to proceed.

"Doctor," I began, "we have the following reports: Gaston Nucklett wires that Jews and Christians staged a pitched battle in Chicago last night, while Catholics and Protestants clashed in Baltimore, Cincinnati,

99

Louisville, Boston and Los Angeles. The White Americans now has a membership of four million and the circulation of *White America* jumped two hundred thousand last week to an all-time high of five million."

"Nucklett is doing fine work. He'll keep the white people so busy fighting themselves that they'll have no time to bother us," observed the Chief.

"Here's a brief dispatch from Alex Fletcher. He says the B.I. farms are showing a profit of one million monthly and the economic enterprises of the Church of Love are running well over three million this month. He says our newest freighter, the S.S. *Kelly Miller*, left day before yesterday with complete machine shop, foundry equipment, smelting plant, saw mills, construction machinery and mining equipment. All technical students left America this week on various steamers following the completion of their courses. Juan Torlier and his entire mechanical staff have flown in to our Texas estate and dismantled the Westchester plant."

"You see," Dr. Belsidus interrupted, "how essential it is that we win."

I continued: "Rev. Binks reports the completion of one hundred more temples in the United States this week and one hundred and fifty by our foreign units in the West Indies and Africa. Negroes are leaving the established churches in droves."

"Well," commented the Doctor, sipping his Scotch and soda, "it is as I expected. The established churches, as they call themselves, have nothing to offer the Negroes except prayers and collection plates. We are giving them an economic foundation and a better show in the bargain. That makes two hundred temples in the United States and three hundred and twenty-five elsewhere. And that means an equal number of grocery stores, meat markets, beauty parlors, recreation halls and other economic units bringing money into the treasury."

I went on with reading the messages. "Bennie Simpson has dispatched a shipload of cement and mixers on a chartered West African–American freighter to Monrovia, consigned to Farley. It should arrive about the same time as the S.S. *Kelly Miller*."

"And from Capt. Jorre," I continued, "comes word that the entire fleet of troopships arrives off Monrovia at midnight tomorrow. General McNeel merely says that the health of the troops is well except for one case of fever, which is not serious."

"Good," he commented. "And now, Miss Givens," turning to the charming brown aviatrix, "what have you to report?"

"We checked the five airports on the Liberian coast and those established in the hinterland of Pandame, Zor Zor, Naama and Sanoquilly. They seem to be adequate. Here are the aerial photos taken by Tom Hudginson."

"Then," observed Dr. Belsidus, "we are all ready for the conquest. Tell Kalanga to get that motorboat ready for tomorrow evening. Tell Ralph Farley to give final instructions to his Kru and Grebo boatmen and guides. Wire Martha Gaskin at the Regal Hotel in London that the time has come."

"What will that mean?" I asked, wondering what tricks he had the beautiful white girl up to now.

"The whole world will hear tomorrow," he remarked, a look of cunning secrecy coming over his handsome black face. "As we have stirred strife among the white people of America, so must we do in Europe, Slater."

The twenty-first day came with the sun burning the earth and men panting helplessly in the African heat. During midday we talked over a long luncheon, but when at three o'clock the heat began to abate, Kalanga drove us down to the waterfront, where we boarded a long, fast, rakish motorboat for our trip to meet the ships off Monrovia at midnight. Pat and Hudginson stayed behind with the big bombing plane until the word should come that we had won. Quickly we stepped aboard and rounding the neck of land that shields the harbor from the outer arm, Kalanga's mechanic opened the throttle wide and we tore down the coast for our epochal rendezvous with General McNeel and Captain Jorre off Monrovia.

"Tomorrow night," shouted Dr. Belsidus over the roar of the motor, "Monrovia should be in our hands. Indeed," he added grimly, almost to himself, "it MUST be."

24

▲▲▲▲▲▲▲▲▲▲▲▲▲▲▲▲▲▲▲▲▲▲▲▲▲

Dr. Belsidus Gets Secret Message
as Offensive Starts

As the sun dipped into the ocean we passed Cape Mount and glimpsed the white residences of Robertsport. The sea was smooth as a lake and the waves from our speeding boat eddied far to right and left. It was so hot even at this hour that we welcomed with relief the coming of darkness.

Until it was too dark to see, Dr. Belsidus sat silently poring over two maps, one of Liberia and another of Monrovia and environs. I don't believe he spoke once during the entire journey.

Pitch darkness came with characteristic tropical suddenness. Kalanga's mechanic pulled farther out to sea to avoid the sandbars that fringe the Liberian coast. He proceeded more slowly and carefully now, guiding himself by the light on top of distant Cape Mesurado.

At ten o'clock we were three miles off Monrovia. The few lights in the capital clearly indicated our whereabouts even if the big lamp in the lighthouse had not shone so brightly.

Dr. Belsidus got out his night glasses and scanned the horizon. I did likewise. There, off to the right, looming like a ghost and about a half mile away was the freighter. The mechanic turned the nose of our boat toward her and pulled up close to within a few feet.

"Africa!" yelled Kalanga through the megaphone.

"Africa!" came back a voice from the deck. "This is the S.S. *Samory*, Captain Jorre speaking."

"This is Dr. Belsidus," said the Chief, rising. "Let down your ladder, captain, we're coming aboard."

"Aye, aye, sir," replied the captain. Then to his men: "Lower away."

With a screeching that carried far in the still night, the ladder came down. Our boat pulled close. A sailor stood at attention on the bottom step with a lantern. Dr. Belsidus ran lightly up to the deck. Kalanga and

I followed him. Captain Jorre and General McNeel greeted us and led the way to the skipper's cabin. The Chief immediately got down to business.

"We'll just have a sandwich and a bottle of beer," he said, when Captain Jorre asked him if he wanted to dine. "There's too much to do to bother with dinner. Now, General, are you all ready?"

"All ready, sir. I have carried out your instructions to the letter."

"And how about the other ships, Captain?" turning to the skipper.

"I have just heard from all of them, sir. The *Nat Turner* is two miles off Robertsport, the *Fred Douglass* will be off Cape Palmas in a short while, the *Sojourner Truth* is riding off Sinoe and the *Bessie Coleman* is just outside Nanna Kru."

"Very well. Now, Captain Jorre, signal Ralph Farley to go ahead."

The French Negro stuck his head out the cabin door and shouted an order.

Five minutes passed. A sailor tapped on the side of the open door. He saluted the captain and reported, "We have received the signal from the shore, sir, that all is in readiness. The *Phyllis Wheatley* is almost alongside and Captain Botsona reports all's well."

"All right, John, you may go," said Captain Jorre. "In another hour, Doctor, the native boats will be alongside. Perhaps even before that."

Dr. Belsidus grunted his approval and munched a sandwich from the pile a steward had brought from the galley. He was the calmest man I've ever seen to be embarking upon such a momentous adventure. Immaculately dressed in tropical whites with neatly manicured fingers and faultless white shoes and socks, he might well have been preparing to attend some festivity. I felt that he was expecting some word from somewhere. Every time a sailor reported to Captain Jorre, the chief was at once alert. When the chatter of many strange voices and the bumping against the side of the freighter informed us that the fleet of native boats had arrived, I caught him listening intently for a second, only to as quickly relax. We all sat quietly drinking our beer, waiting for the next word from him.

On the deck below the soldiers were lining up at the low-voiced command of their officers. Squad by squad they descended the ladders and entered the bobbing Kru boats.

At last a tall black officer, a major, entered and saluted McNeel. "Sir," he said, "I have the honor to report that the native boats are loaded and awaiting the command to pull away. Similar word comes from the others."

"Very good, major. Wait for the command. The officers all know their objectives." Then General McNeel turned to the Chief inquiringly.

"No, not yet, McNeel," sad Dr. Belsidus. "I'm waiting word from London."

Tense minutes succeeded each other. I consulted my watch. It was eleven-forty. The chief looked at his watch and frowned for the first time since we had left Freetown. General McNeel calmly sipped his beer. Captain Jorre, snapping his fingers and nervously whistling a monotonous little French ditty, kept running out of the cabin to give an order and then bouncing back again.

Midnight! We all consulted our watches again as eight bells sounded on the two ships. Dr. Belsidus scowled more darkly and banged his glass impatiently on the table. He muttered something that I could not understand. But I gathered that his patience was rapidly running out. Outside on the water below and on the deck there was a buzz of subdued voices. Only the command of Dr. Belsidus was awaited and the attack would begin.

Minutes passed and no command came. Twelve-ten. We all furtively consulted our watches. Dr. Belsidus was looking grimmer.

There was a knock at the cabin door. Before anyone could say "enter," the radioman, a young slender mulatto, hurried in and handed Dr. Belsidus a message. It contained but two words, "Yes. Martha."

A broad smile, one of the few I'd ever seen, wreathed the Chief's countenance. He stroked his chin and a light of cruel satisfaction came into his deep-set eyes.

"All right, McNeel," he commanded. "Let's go. Remember, the cable station first. Then the telephone exchange. And whatever you do, be sure and take charge of the Firestone radio station at Duside before morning. There must be no looting of shops. Sparks," he turned to the radio man, "tell the other ships the time has come."

I was consumed with curiosity about the message and what it meant. When Dr. Belsidus, Kalanga and I were again in the motor boat and following the fleet of war canoes toward the channel in the sandbar, I got up courage to ask him.

"What does it mean?" he boomed good-naturedly. "It means that Martha has succeeded. Before the white world knows of our action here, we shall be established. They will be too busy with their own affairs to bother with us. That message meant that our plans in London have gone well. Prime Minister Baldwin was assassinated this evening by a bomb tossed into 10 Downing Street, where he was holding a conference."

"How do you know the details, sir?"

"Hah, why my lad, the details were worked out long ago," he said. "That will crowd everything off tomorrow's newspapers. By the time they hear of our conquest, it will be a fait accompli."

We approached closer and closer to the sandbar. On express orders from General McNeel, there was no sound save the cough of our motor and the squeaking of the oars in their locks as scores of oarsmen bent their bare backs to their tasks. One by one the boats shot through the narrow channel into the placid waters of the shallow harbor. Scarcely ten feet apart now, the long line of craft stealthily approached the shore while helmsmen strained their eyes. It was quite dark with only a few stars overhead. Now the boats took positions several feet apart all along the shore from Kru town to the last warehouse. There was much splashing as the men jumped over the sides and waded ashore in the darkness. Here and there I caught the glint of a rifle or machine gun. Our motor was silenced when we were about one hundred yards from the dark shore. Dr. Belsidus wanted to be in a position where he could command the entire scene. In the native boat next to us, General McNeel sat close to a field radio set getting messages from the shore.

It was positively uncanny. No sound of warfare, no struggle apparently. Not a shot had been fired. It was one-thirty.

"The cable station and the telephone exchange are in our hands, Doctor," McNeel shouted gleefully over from his boat. "The city is surrounded. No one will be able to get through . . . They have just taken the police station and jail . . . The police have surrendered their arms, sir . . . The First Battalion of the First Regiment has left on the double for the Frontier Force barracks."

"It was easier than I thought it would be," commented the Chief. "We'd better go ashore, Kalanga. Tell the boats and the ships to turn on their searchlights, McNeel."

In a few moments scores of searchlights from the bobbing boats augmented by the huge shafts of light from the ships lighted up the entire struggling little city. Black Internationale bayonets were everywhere. The mechanic ran our boat to the customs house wharf and we went ashore with the general. Once on land McNeel was busy receiving reports from messenger after messenger.

"There was nothing to it, Doctor," he exclaimed enthusiastically.

Suddenly, the crack of rifles drowned out his voice and the whiz and whistle of bullets forced us to fall flat. There were cries and screams in the darkness beyond the reach of the searchlights and the clash of steel on steel. Had something miscarried? Was there resistance after all?

25

▰▰▰▰▰▰▰▰▰▰▰▰▰▰▰▰▰▰▰▰▰▰▰

Liberia Is Captured without Opposition;
President a Prisoner

You can always tell the calibre of a leader by the manner in which he acts. Dr. Belsidus might have been resting comfortably in his ornate apartment in New York, considering the calmness with which he deported himself.

"Where is that firing, McNeel?" he asked.

"A messenger has just reported, Doctor, that a number of soldiers evidently armed with sub-machine guns are defending President Barclay's residence. We shall silence them, sir. I am going forward now."

"We'll go with you," Dr. Belsidus calmly announced.

"But it's dangerous, sir," General McNeel objected. "We don't know how many there are. It is a surprise even to Farley."

"Come on, let's go," the Chief insisted, a little roughly. "Farley should have known about those special guards."

Motorcycles with sidecars had now arrived from the ships. We jumped in them and, led by McNeel, we raced up the rocky hill; the numerous searchlights from the ships and from the native boats were pretty well lighting up the scene. From the President's private residence came bursts of rifle and machine-gun fire. There must have been 20 or

30 men defending the place. As we stopped to watch the operations from a concealed position, Ralph Farley came up and saluted.

"I'm sorry, sir," he said apologetically. "We tried to find out everything. This must have been a secret guard known only to the President. I know he feared assassination."

"All right, all right," growled the Chief, a bit irritably. "Next time don't make any mistakes."

Meantime, a hot fire was coming from the house, to which our men were answering spiritedly. But it was soon all over. A volley of tear gas bombs brought out the defenders. The last man to emerge with hands over his head and tears streaming from his eyes was the President of Liberia.

It was only three o'clock. Word came that the two companies of the Frontier Force had surrendered at the barracks. Monrovia and environs were completely in our hands.

We went immediately to the Executive Mansion on Ashmun Street, where Dr. Belsidus set up headquarters. He occupied the President's office and I was installed in the adjoining office customarily occupied by Barclay's aide de camp.

Messages were coming in thick and fast. At four o'clock came the word that our troops had taken over Robertsport, Harper, Sinoa and Nanna Kru. At 4:15 our motorcycle detachment reported that it had taken over the wireless station on the Firestone plantation at Duside.

At 4:30 Dr. Belsidus called me. He was sitting at the President's flat-top, glass-covered desk sipping a cup of black coffee and poring over some papers.

"Now, Slater," he began, "from now on we must be careful. It is at the time of success that we must be most careful. There is much to be done but I think we can get some sleep by ten o'clock at least. First, tell Farley to send a message to the Paramount Chiefs by the drums to assemble at Kakata for a conference three days from now."

"At Kakata, sir?" I asked, rather surprised. "Why, that's nearly 50 miles back in the bush, sir."

"Exactly, Slater, exactly. That's where the new capital is to be. Monrovia is too close to the sea, too close to the white man. We must get back where we'll have time to prepare in case we are attacked, where we can only be attacked by an expeditionary force and not blasted out by the big guns of battleships."

107

I immediately saw his point. As usual, he seemed to have thought out every eventuality.

"Wireless Miss Givens to come here immediately," he continued. "Cable Alex Fletcher to charter a fast freighter and send over a shipload of cement. It must be here in 15 days. That's imperative . . . Cable Hamilton and Fortune to fly immediately to Texas and leave there with the air fleet . . . Wireless Juan Torlier to hop off with the entire fleet as soon as Hamilton and Fortune arrive. They are to follow instructions and refuel at the secret airport in Venezuela . . . Cable Martha Gaskin the following message: "Success. Follow schedule."

"What does that mean, sir?" I asked.

"It means that she is to strike the second blow. The first blow was the assassination of the Prime Minister of Great Britain. That will drive everything else off the front pages of the world's newspapers for a couple of days. Now we shall blow up the French Chamber of Deputies." He said it all quite calmly, as though it were the most ordinary thing in the world. I must have revealed my surprise. The corners of his mouth went down in a cynical smirk.

"We need plenty of diversions," he said. "We must keep the white world in pandemonium while we are solidifying our position. We must spread terror, secretly of course, until we are strong enough to come out in the open . . . Take this message to Gaston Nucklett: 'Now is the time.' . . . Nucklett's done good work but there's not yet enough dissension in America. That message will start a series of floggings and killings of prominent Catholic and foreign-born business men and public officials . . . There! With all that going on I believe the white world will be so busy it won't have time to think about what we're doing here. You know, Slater, we shall succeed as long as we are bold. Failure comes only when one hesitates. A little bloodshed, a little destruction, why, that's nothing at all compared to what Negroes have suffered for centuries at the hands of white people. Now, go and get those messages off immediately. And by the way, tell McNeel that as soon as the cement mixers get ashore to start all available men to working on that Kakata road. That's all."

The next week saw more changes in Liberia than there had ever been in its history, ancient or modern. In three days' time our motorcycle corps had established outposts along the entire boundary. The S.S. *Kelly*

108

Miller had arrived with a machine shop, a foundry, smelting plant, construction machinery, saw mills and mining equipment; all the leading politicians had been arrested and jailed. Pat flew in the morning we captured Monrovia, arriving about nine o'clock from Freetown. Two days later the entire Black Internationale air force was parked on the Monrovia airfield while hundreds of men toiled to erect the temporary hangars.

The most auspicious occasion, of course, was the conference with the Paramount Chiefs at Kakata, on the fourth day following the fall of Monrovia. It was well carried out. In accordance with Farley's directions, each chief had brought a colorful retinue of warriors, wives, court attendants and other functionaries. Some of the warriors had old flintlocks but most of them were armed with spears, bows and arrows.

The conference was held in one of the great palaver kitchens erected for the 1928 conference assembled by former President C. D. B. King. In the adjoining palaver kitchen there were long tables which groaned under the weight of venison, beef, mutton, strong liquors and good wines. It must have cost a pretty sum.

Dr. Belsidus was determined to make a good impression on these native kings and their warriors because he realized that their allegiance was essential. His huge throne was at the far end of the palaver kitchen on a dais. Comfortable chairs were supplied for the chiefs, chairs which recently had graced the drawing rooms of Liberian aristocrats. At intervals big electric fans on high standards whirled fresh currents of air over the perspiring nobility. The power came from a portable electric light plant. Most of these men had never seen ice or consumed an iced drink, but on this day they were served Tom Collinses and rickeys. Expensive cigars were freely passed around by the box.

New rifles and a hundred rounds of ammunition were distributed to each warrior. All the day previous motor trucks had come up from Monrovia with these small arms. Each chief had received upon arrival at the conference several bolts of cotton cloth, brass kettles, a case of good gin and a hundred pounds of leaf tobacco, along with a complete shaving set including soap, brush and safety razor. Big multi-colored tents had been erected for the chiefs, with smaller surrounding tents for their wives.

It was three o'clock in the afternoon when Farley assembled them in the big palaver kitchens. Of course, by this time they had received something from the government instead of giving everything to the government. They conversed among themselves with bright eyes and much head-wagging as they waited for the man whom they considered their benefactor.

It was exactly 3:30 when our trumpeters blew a great blast and the saluting pieces rolled up in front of the conference place were fired 21 times, as Dr. Belsidus in the black limousine with which I was so familiar drove up to the entrance. He was immaculate as usual in spotless tropical clothes.

Paying no attention whatever to the awed chiefs, he walked to his throne, with General McNeel on one side and I on the other.

26

Native Chiefs Bow before Dr. Belsidus
after Great Speech

Ralph Farley served as interpreter, since he was well versed in Kpwessi, the lingua franca of Liberia.

Dr. Belsidus spoke without rising from his throne. I have kept a copy of his brief talk, not because it frankly outlined his grandiose plans for the future of Liberia, but because it was cleverly phrased in the idiom of the jungle. He must have given much time and thought to its construction, perhaps being assisted by Farley.

"Great Kings," he began, "today you are greater than you have been in countless moons. Great Kings, today you have the power of the white man in your hands. Great Kings! No longer must you bear oppression and fear the floggers. For you are the brothers and comrades of one who is greater than the white man. White man makes guns, I make guns. White man makes bullets, I make bullets. White man makes hut that runs along the road, I make hut that runs along the road. White man has big palaver kitchen that floats across the sea. I also have big floating palaver kitchen. White man rich, I am also rich.

"A great log has been removed from your path and now you and your warriors will march as you did in the days of the Kumbwa people. I am the great leopard come not to destroy you but to give you life. I am the great elephant that breaks down the trees and jungle in my path. I am the great crocodile that snaps off legs and arms and leaves the body helpless. I am the thunder that strikes the huts in darkness, I am the rain that brings good crops. I am swift as the goat that jumps on the hillside, swift as the pepper bird that calls at dawn. Strong as the ocean that breaks through the sandbar. I am the King of Kings.

"I do not know fear because I am the great leopard. Liberian people would not let you have guns, but I give them to you. Is it not so? Liberian people would not let you have bullets, but I give them to you. Is it not so? Liberian people take food and wine from you, but I give you food and wine. Is it not so?

"When you are strong, I am strong. When you are weak, I am weak. I must be strong and you must be strong. I will send wise men to train your men to shoot the guns that buzz like great bees. I will send to your towns canoes that go by themselves. I will give your warriors clothes like the white man and huts to sleep in at night. I will give your warriors great pans of rice and fish, much chicken and goat, plenty sheep and foufou gourds of palm oil and palm wine. Good will I be to you while you serve me. Like the angry leopard shall I be if you deceive me.

"I am the King of Kings. I have thousands of warriors. I have iron birds that fly across the sea. I have power greater than the white man. You are my comrades. You will have big stone houses like the white man. You will talk over wires. You will eat and grow fat and have rich cloth and many young wives shall occupy your compound.

"You will follow me into the English country and into the French country. Together we shall run the white man into the sea. All the land for six months' journey to the north, east and south shall be ours. We shall not fight, kill and enslave black men. We shall free black men and make them great. But those who oppose us shall die. All Africa will worship in our temples and live in peace and plenty as our people did in the great long ago.

"Eat, drink, laugh, dream of the future because it belongs to you. Today you have nothing to fear, for today, I, the King of Kings, rule.

"You have guns. You have rich cloth. You have boxes of bullets. You have food and hot wine. Is it not so? You have seen how easily I have put the Liberians in stick. So I shall do the white man.

"Return to your homes. Make the drums talk all over Africa. Tell strangers far away what has come to pass. And when I call you and your warriors, you will come running as does the baby elephant to its mother. I have spoken."

Spontaneously, these grave, sedate chiefs jumped up shouting and singing with enthusiasm as Ralph Farley translated the last of the speech of Dr. Belsidus. Then something happened that gave me a queer turn, because it was my first time to witness it. One by one these venerable rulers came forward to the throne, fell flat upon the ground and, grasping the Doctor's highly polished shoe, kissed the toe. Then, rising, each one backed away worshipfully.

On the fourth day Pat flew us down to Sinoe, where Dr. Belsidus addressed another bevy of chiefs. The following day we flew to Harper for the same purpose. Then we returned to Monrovia.

It was two weeks before Dr. Belsidus permitted any of the white people, even consular officials, to communicate with the outside. In those two weeks not one word of the conquest of Liberia had gone out, and even if it had, there were so many other seemingly more important items in the news that no one would have bothered reading about what was happening in Liberia. As I have written, the assassination of Prime Minister Baldwin was a sensation. It was only surpassed in the news by the blowing up of the French Chamber of Deputies the following night. These atrocities were followed by increasing anti-Catholic and anti-Semitic riots in the United States, the mysterious sinking of an Italian cruiser following an explosion in her magazine, an attempt to shoot Herr Joseph Goebbels, the German Minister of Propaganda, and similar acts of terror all over the white world. Martha Gaskin had been doing her work well, aided by our cells in various European capitals.

When the news first broke, the report went out that there had been an insurrection of tribesmen, well-armed and well-led. There was no intimation that the expedition had come from abroad. It was not until a month had transpired that the real story leaked out. Dr. Belsidus had remained much in the background. Pat and I, McNeel, Torlier, Farley and a few others were the only ones who saw him.

It came as a tremendous surprise to the white world that a well-trained army of American Negroes had crossed the Atlantic in their own ships without the knowledge of the white man, landed and conquered a country the size of Kentucky or Ohio.

In that month Dr. Belsidus worked swiftly to consolidate his gains. The road from Monrovia to Kakata was completed and a journey that had taken four hours by automobile before could now be accomplished in a little over an hour. Airfields to the number of nineteen were scattered over the Republic. Motorcycle outposts were established every 20 miles along the boundaries between Liberia and Sierra Leone, French Guinea and the Ivory Coast. Non-commissioned officers sent to the headquarters of every Paramount Chief had been busily training native soldiers in the small arms and European military formations. For the first time in its history Liberia had its coast well policed. A fleet of swift motorboats armed with machine guns patrolled from Cape Mount to Cape Palmas, effectively preventing smuggling, through which the previous government had lost much revenue. Twenty saw mills had been flown to as many parts of the land and set up under the management of a young technician trained in America. Two gold mines were already in operation. By flying cement in large quantities to the various districts, the concrete troughs for the chemical farms had been quickly made and some were already in operation. Batteries of sun engines were in operation at Kakata, Naama, Sanoquilly and Harper, where concrete buildings for small arms and ammunition factories had been erected and the machinery was already in place. Gustave Linke, a little black French metallurgist, had already arrived to supervise the making of arms. Under the direction of Ransom Just and with the co-operation of Pat's air fleet, radio towers had been transported and set up in several parts of the country. By this means and the placing of a large radio in every town in Liberia, it was possible for Dr. Belsidus to address the entire population any time he wished.

The Black Internationale freighters had returned to the United States for more machinery, cement and supplies. Al Fortune, at last doing the thing he so wanted to do, was superintending the building of a coastal road running the length of Liberia from Robertsport to Harper with a thousand workers in five divisions. He swore that it would be completed in three months. In the meantime, dynamite squads were blowing the rocks out of the St. Paul and Loffa rivers to make them navigable by barges far into the inland.

113

Dr. Belsidus, who was working 19 hours a day and almost wearing me out, had already moved into the new government building at Kakata. Thousands of cement blocks were being turned out for the other building in course of erection.

As Provisional President, Dr. Belsidus had assured the various foreign governments that merchants, missionaries and foreign planters would not be molested, and he told the fiscal agent of the Firestone Company that he would respect the agreement of 1926 drawn up between it and the Liberian government. Two weeks afterward Dr. Belsidus paid off the $2,500,000 Firestone loan in full.

We then held a conference and laid out plans for bringing a million Negroes from the United States. It was at this juncture that trouble arose with the French.

27

Pat Admits Her Love for Carl;
Trouble with French Government Looms

The new capitol of Liberia was a two-story, mission-style building of concrete blocks with stucco finish, built around a huge central garden in the center of which was a large cement and tile swimming pool with the latest equipment. Green and yellow chairs and tables shaded by colorful parasols surrounded the pool. And at the end of the garden was a small bandstand, screened by palms. Gorgeous tropical flowers, freshly transplanted, fringed the garden with a riot of color and filled it with exotic perfume. Certainly Kakata had never seen its like before.

As one entered the building, corridors ran to the right and left with offices on each side. Immediately in front was a double staircase curving up to the second floor. Here were the great dining hall where moving pictures could also be shown, the conference room where the staff met, the ballroom and an elaborate apartment for Dr. Belsidus. Around the entire building on both floors extended a wide balcony. On the roof were cleverly concealed water tanks. It was strictly utilitarian, that capitol building.

Nearby, four- and six-room one-story bungalows were going up in rapid order, as fast, indeed, as concrete blocks could be turned out.

I stood at the window of my office, which adjoined that of Dr. Belsidus, and watched the feverish building activities in all directions. Over there, big lumbering trucks loaded with cement, reinforcing iron and factory equipment were coming in on the new improved road from Monrovia, where our freighters were unloading. Over to my right the new airfield, with its concrete runways, control tower and vast expanse cleared in a week by 2,000 native workers, was in full operation. Some of the trucks loaded with cement and tools were delivering their loads to big bombing planes, which promptly took off to all parts of the Republic.

Then my heart almost stopped. Reacting to a loud sound, I looked out my office window and saw an old autogiro flutter to the field, skid a few feet and stop. The cowl was pushed back and out jumped Pat. She was dressed as I remembered her on that morning ages ago when we took off from the Westchester County airfield. The same green pilot's cap and jacket, green riding breeches and cordovan boots. She looked my way, saw me standing at the window and waved cheerily. Worn as I was with the terrific grind, the slave-driving of the tireless Dr. Belsidus and the countless details to which, as his secretary, I had to attend, the coming of Pat was a tremendous lift.

We had scarcely seen each other since that afternoon six weeks before when we parted on the dock in Freetown. I waited impatiently for her to come up, fearing that any moment I might be summoned by Dr. Belsidus. I did not have long to wait before she burst in, radiant, but seemingly just a little tired.

"Hello, Carl," she said, coming quite close. "It seems ages since we met, doesn't it?"

"Yes, a new world has started, Pat. We have attained our first goal but it's an awful grind. Aren't you worked out?"

"You said it! Why, I don't know how we've managed to do what we have. Do you know that, since I flew down from Freetown, we've been going every minute? Every day parachuting cement, gasoline and equipment all over the country, trying to keep airfields in shape with native labor you can't understand, scattering pictures of the Chief all over the jungle."

She paused, breathless, and then grinned broadly, revealing her perfect white teeth.

"But I love it!" she exclaimed. "I love it, Carl. Oh, what a privilege to be doing what we are doing. Think what it will mean!"

"Well, what about us?" I interrupted, placing my hands on her shoulders. "What about OUR love? You know I'm mad about you, Pat? Darling, I want you SO badly, more than I've ever wanted anything in the world. And now, dear, we've attained those things you said must be attained before we could speak of ourselves. We've both given ourselves unselfishly, Sweet. Can't we go on from here together?"

I saw the softness of love mist her eyes and her beautiful lips part invitingly. They were so close to me. Her faint perfume intoxicated me—the familiar gardenia that had intrigued me that night long ago on the balcony at the New Jersey chemical truck farm. In another moment I had embraced her and pressed those precious lips to mine. Wordless, we clung to each other. There was nothing to say. We knew each other's thoughts, knew what we meant to each other, knew what we wanted.

"I just felt this would happen today," she said softly. "I knew it when I looked up and saw you standing at the window. I started not to come in for that reason. I knew I couldn't trust myself once more with you, Prince Charming."

"And I think I should have died if you HADN'T come in," I whispered, drawing her again to me. "It didn't seem I could stand to see you another time and keep my equilibrium. Busy as I've been in this tremendous undertaking, I've been terribly lonely for you. Just starved. You know what I mean."

"Yes," she said, some of the old mischief returning to her eyes, "I know what you mean."

"I'd be delighted to marry you this minute, Patricia Givens, if you'd have me," I whispered into her ear.

"Well, Carl Slater," she said, grinning, "that's a little sudden. I must exercise the feminine prerogative and think it over."

Dr. Belsidus summoned me over the communicating telephone and, tearing myself from Pat's passionate embrace, I hurried in. The Chief was seated at a huge desk in one corner of the vast room whose only other furnishing was a large easy chair alongside his desk. On the wall over his head was a huge map of Liberia. Otherwise there was only the highly polished parquet floor and the great French windows that lighted the office from three sides. He was immaculate, as usual, in cream-colored tropical suit, cream-colored shoes, cream-colored socks with purple clocks, purple shirt and handkerchief, and a purple and cream striped cravat. He looked up as I entered.

"Ah, yes, Slater. Sit down. I've ordered other chairs. I'm expecting the French consul and his assistant. It looks as though we're going to have trouble with them. I have learned some interesting things about their plans. They feel it necessary to strike now before it is too late."

This gave me quite a start. I knew that the French had long had designs on Liberia and at various times had been on the verge of taking over the country but were prevented by American diplomatic intervention. Now that they saw a real threat developing, it was probable they were ready to make another stab at us. What chance had we against the might of France? They could take the coast at once, and in a week they could have their Senegalese army at our gates.

"That sounds serious, Chief."

"It is serious," he admitted, without showing emotion, "but I anticipated it."

The door at the far end of the office was swung open and the uniformed doorman announced, "Monsieur Rapport, Consul of the Republic of France," and stood aside. The tall, blond, anemic Parisian whom we had met in Monrovia the day after the conquest strode in, followed by the Vice Consul Constaint. Uniformed flunkies brought chairs for the two men. It did not take long for Consul Rapport to get to the reason for his visit.

"Excellency," he said, "my government has viewed the events of the past six weeks not without certain misgivings. Your former government always maintained cordial relations with France, and my government never had occasion to be perturbed over the course of events in Liberia. Today, however, my government feels that the unnecessary military display and activity on your boundaries may conceivably disturb the peace of the tribes in French Guinea and Ivory Coast. Several of your planes have been observed flying over French territory in violation of international law. Incendiary propaganda probably distributed by plane and obviously coming from Liberia has been scattered over the Ivory Coast districts bordering Liberia. This inflammatory material is contributing to the unrest of the natives.

"My government is also alarmed by the speedy construction of concrete machine-gun nests all along your boundary, the erection of arms factories and the general evidences of military activity which must obviously be aimed at neighbors. My government also has reason to believe that the so-called Temples of Love which have been widely established throughout our territories have some connection with your movement.

"In view of these facts, my government must view any further such manifestations with alarm and take proper precautionary steps, although it is not, of course, our desire to impair Liberia's sovereignty."

I glanced swiftly at Dr. Belsidus. Consul Rapport meant in plain words that unless we halted our program France would strike swiftly and surely. It was a crucial moment. I wondered how Dr. Belsidus would meet the challenge. Could he defy mighty France?

28

⋏⋏⋏⋏⋏⋏⋏⋏⋏⋏⋏⋏⋏⋏⋏⋏⋏⋏⋏⋏⋏⋏⋏⋏⋏⋏

Belsidus Parries French While He Prepares Armies

Dr. Belsidus listened gravely to Consul Rapport, occasionally shooting a significant glance at me. When the Frenchman had finished, the Chief spread his manicured fingers on the edge of his glass-topped desk and leaned forward slightly, an expression of great affected sincerity on his finely chiseled face.

"Mr. Rapport," he began, the cordiality in his tone masking the hatred I knew was in his heart, "the government of Liberia is regretful of any action on its part which your government might consider in the slightest degree unfriendly. Some of its aviators in their zeal may have flown over French territory. These young men and women will be warned at once that there must be no repetition of such violations if it is found that any have been guilty. I shall immediately issue strict orders to that effect.

"However," he continued with his snake-like suavity, "we must disdain responsibility for any incendiary literature which may have appeared in your territories. Our desire is to live at peace with all our neighbors. We are much too busy trying to build Liberia to interfere with your natives, and we disavow and condemn the distribution of any propaganda which might disturb the peace of your colonies. We have no connection whatever with the so-called Temples of Love to which you refer. The sect has representatives in Liberia just like the Catholics, Episcopalians, Baptists, Methodists, Moslems, and these representatives are welcome. This particular sect has given us no trouble whatever and we regret to hear that the missionaries in your territories are accused of indiscretions. I shall immediately issue a warning to all missionaries against political activities. We wish to do nothing or seem to countenance anything which might give offense to the French Republic, the friend of all black people."

His voice was soft and soothing. He ended with a smile of pretended friendliness and goodwill and leaned back in his chair. I could see that M. Rapport was reassured, that he felt he had frightened Dr. Belsidus by his threat of "proper precautionary steps." He was not quite satisfied, it developed.

"In the name of the French government," he replied, "I am extremely pleased to find the Executive reasonable and conciliatory and shall notify my chief. However, Doctor, there is one more matter, which my government views with misgivings, and that is the military development in Liberia. Your boundary is being fortified, your arms factories are nearing completion, your airplane factory, I understand, is finished, and the natives have been given arms. My government finds it difficult to perceive why such preparations are necessary in view of the notorious peacefulness of West Africa, and indeed all Africa."

Dr. Belsidus beamed upon him in a more ingratiating manner than I had ever seen him affect.

"Permit me to reassure the French government. My government is concerned only with making Liberia impregnable as near as possible. My country, as you know, has suffered in the past because of its military weakness and the division that has existed among our people. We are trying now to initiate a sense of unity and nationalism and we find that military training does this most effectively. Since we have the trained technicians we find it less expensive to make our airplanes and train our aviators here than abroad. Any move of hostility toward our neighbors is farthest from our minds. We want the love and friendship of our neighbors, and we want them to understand that."

Consul Rapport seemed reassured, although I had a suspicion that he was not completely satisfied. However, he affected joviality when he departed. As the great doors were closed behind him I turned to Dr. Belsidus.

He was glowering with rage. I could almost feel his indignation. "White fools!" he hissed. "Do they think they can frighten us? Do they think they can stop us now? Notify everyone of the staff, Slater. There is to be a meeting at once. I don't care where they are or what they are doing, they must come at once. Shoot a wire to Martha Gaskin in code to bear down on the French. Giving us orders! Threatening us! I'll show them what black men can do."

"You were very conciliatory," I reminded.

"Of course, I was," he snapped. "I am playing for time. In another month or two I'll talk differently. France is powerful, my boy. It will take the best black brains to beat her. And after her there is an even worse enemy of black people: the British."

I hastened out to radio Martha Gaskin and to send out the call for the conference. By sundown speedy planes were bringing in staff members from all parts of Liberia. After dinner we all met in the conference room around the great oval table. Dr. Belsidus lost no time in getting down to business.

"I had long been expecting some action on the part of the imperialist powers. France is the first that has decided to strike. The French consul was here today. Slater, read them what he said."

Taking out my notebook, I read M. Rapport's words. The others listened attentively. When I had finished Dr. Belsidus spoke again.

"We have come far in the past two months. We are going farther. Al Fortune, how is that road coming from Robertsport to Harper?"

"About seventy-five miles more and we'll be finished, Chief. Everything is working fine. We've got five thousand good men on it, and we're finishing it at the rate of five miles a day. We ought to be completely finished at the latest in three weeks, and perhaps in two weeks. It's flat, sea-level work."

"Get it finished in two weeks," ordered the chief, "even if you have to use a thousand more men. Give them double-time for overtime, give them more food, give them anything but finish in two weeks. Meantime, I want you to get to work on roads from here to Naama, from Naama to Kolahun, and from Naama to Sanoquilly, that will carry trucks. Mr. Farley will get the additional men from the Paramount Chiefs. And now, General McNeel, how goes the training?"

"We've got ten thousand men under arms in each of the five districts, or fifty thousand native troops altogether. They've had six weeks of intensive drill. In another six weeks they'll be ready. What we need is more rifles and ammunition, more equipment of all kinds. There is a shortage of machine guns and we only have two batteries of light artillery. There are no anti-aircraft guns and only one tank. I hardly think we are prepared for an important war, Doctor."

"Well, we'll have to GET prepared," said Dr. Belsidus, frowning. He turned to the little black metallurgist with the long sweeping mustache. "Mr. Linke, how soon will you be ready to turn out small arms and ammunition? What are the prospects for the artillery General McNeel needs?"

"We start," said the French Negro, "to turning out small arms next week. By that time we'll be getting iron from the native mines. In the meantime, however, I am using a boatload of scrap iron we bought from the Belgians. The sun-ray engines are doing their work well. However, it will be another month before we'll be able to turn out artillery. Some of the equipment is still en route from the States."

Dr. Belsidus then turned to slender, octoroon Alfred Hartman, assistant to Alex Fletcher on financial affairs, who reported steadily mounting revenue from the farms and business enterprises in America, purchase of two more freighters, a fleet of motor trucks and a fast submarine chaser. Encouraging reports came also from Sanford Mates, the architect, who was busy erecting the industrial plants; from Dr. Matson, who was about to move in a big new hospital at Naama; from Bennie Simpson, whose cement plant and stone crushers were feverishly working to supply the materials for roads and buildings; from Patricia Givens and Juan Torlier, whose plants were at work turning out new planes. But most significant of all, from Rev. Samson Binks, who gave a lengthy report on the 500 Temples of Love already established throughout Africa and their economic and educational departments.

It was an impressive report of work done, monumental work done in so short a span of time, a brilliant testimonial to the careful preparations made and carried out according to schedule, the start of a new era in Negro progress.

"Two more months," observed Dr. Belsidus, "and we shall be ready for a real showdown with the imperialists. Go back to your respective tasks. Work hard to get through on time. Use every man in Liberia, if you must, but get through on time."

"And at the end of two months?" inquired General McNeel.

"Then," declared Dr. Belsidus gravely, "we shall strike for the conquest of Africa."

29

▲▲▲▲▲▲▲▲▲▲▲▲▲▲▲▲▲▲▲▲▲▲

Ladies and Gentlemen,
The Hour for Which We Prepared Is Here

It was around the first of June when we got the ultimatum from the French. Dr. Belsidus, as I have said, had decreed that the conquest of Africa should start in two months, or around the first of August. The ensuing eight or nine weeks were the most hectic Africa has ever seen.

Al Fortune completed the motor truck roads. The great sun-power plants, more huge than any we ever had in the United States, were now completed and functioning. A brand-new cotton mill was turning out cloth in thousands of bales on a 24-hour shift, using cotton imported from America until our Liberian plantations could produce. The great chemical vegetable farms which now dotted Liberia were turning out an incredible volume of food. Not only were the Liberian natives better fed than ever before in history, but great truckloads of yams, tobacco and salt fish were sent to our 500 Temples of Love throughout Africa for free distribution to congregations. Gustave Linke, the little French armament man, was turning out first-class rifles, machine guns and small cannon from the three great factories that drew their power from the sun. Another factory turned out rifle and machine-gun bullets, hand grenades and shells. Our fleet of freighters numbered twenty.

But even then it was apparent by the second week in June that it would be physically impossible to get all we needed in the way of airplanes and munitions in time for the great push.

On the 15th of June, after our secret agents in Europe under Martha Gaskin had blown up several key buildings and drydocks at the French naval station at Toulon, Dr. Belsidus sent word to her to arrange for immediate purchase of fifty bombing planes according to Patricia's specifications, several thousand rifles and machine guns and millions of rounds of ammunition. In order to effect immediate delivery, he paid cash.

Meantime, young men and women from America, some of the cream of the Negro race, were pouring into Monrovia and immediately being dispatched to key places in Liberia. On the 5th of July and every week thereafter a thousand arrived, close-packed on freighters chartered for the purpose. It was these youngsters who, as foremen and forewomen, helped to keep production at a peak. Coming in the midst of the rainy season, they found living conditions most unpleasant. Several died from malaria and yellow fever. But most of them adjusted themselves to the new life. In every case they had paid their own money for passage to the new land of opportunity. At that time we were offering the low fare of $50 for passage from America.

By the first of August everything was as near readiness as possible considering the hectic pace. Working 18 hours a day, Dr. Belsidus was watching every development. He grew increasingly irritable as the zero hour approached, so great was the nervous strain to which he and the rest of us worked. He snapped and snarled now, where before he had been suave.

Consequently, you can imagine our surprise when at his call we assembled that evening in the huge dining room in the capitol building at Kakata. He was smooth-shaven and immaculate as ever, faultlessly dressed in cream-colored tropical evening clothes. He didn't seem to have a care on his mind.

There was a short table across the width of the dining hall at which sat the entire staff of the Black Internationale, with the exception of Alex Fletcher and Gaston Nucklett, who were in America, and Martha Gaskin, who was in Europe. Down from the cross table ran two long parallel tables the entire length of the hall, which seated nearly 500 diners. These included all industrial heads, all foremen and superintendents, all field officers of the new Liberian Army, and every important native chieftain in the country.

Outside, a hundred-piece symphony orchestra sent ethereal music up to us, while white-clad, bare-foot native workers brought in the heaping bounty of food and drink. It was the first time such a gathering had sat down together and perhaps it would be the last.

It was eleven o'clock when, after several preliminary speakers had their say, Dr. Belsidus rose to speak.

"Ladies and gentlemen," he said, "the hour for which we have prepared is at hand. Whether Africa shall remain slave or free depends upon us. I need not tell you more but I warn you that death shall be the portion of any man or woman who falters. The white man can and will be run out of Africa or exterminated. You all have your orders in detail. Go, and carry them out."

The zero hour was set for midnight, August 1st. The heavy tropical rain was falling in torrents, thundering on the roofs and against the window panes, sloshing into the gutters, almost making the airfield a lake. On that airfield in serried rows of glistening wings and bodies stood the Black Internationale air force. Would they be able to fly tonight? I doubted it. On the well-lighted field I could see Pat in her familiar green gear making her final inspection. I wanted to see her so badly before she took off. It suddenly came to me with a sharp pang that I might not ever see her again. Anything could happen over those trackless jungle wastes. Although we had a long lovers' talk before she went out to the airfield, I was eager for one more word, for one more caress.

But just then came a ring from Dr. Belsidus. I rushed into his office. It had been completely transformed. One wall was completely taken up by a huge map of Africa fifteen feet high and equally as broad. On it every important African town was marked in electric lights set to turn green if in our hands and red if remaining in the hands of the whites. Underneath this map sat a row of telephone operators ready to talk to all parts of Liberia or to transmit messages from the aerial fleet. At the end of the office Dr. Belsidus sat in his accustomed place, garbed in black and gold pajamas, sipping a cup of black coffee.

"Well, Slater," he said, calmly. "I guess you'd better get yourself into something comfortable because we're going to be right here for a long time. Come right back now, I'll be needing you. Be sure and get things going on the drop of midnight."

"Very good, sir." I turned and left his office and entered mine. There I telephoned downstairs and ordered the beating of the huge tom tom which was to command all Africa to strike.

Boom! Boom-Boom-Boom! Boom! Boom-Boom-Boom! The great drum roared its message through the slackening rain. Over hill and dale, across swamps and deserts sped the word to strike. To 500 Temples of Love went the word to exterminate all white people and their black allies. As fast as sound can travel, the message of murder sped.

Dr. Belsidus and I sat at his desk, sipping coffee and smoking as the booming signal went to millions of waiting black men and women, waiting with revenge in their hearts and the joy that comes from striking back at persecutors.

The rain suddenly stopped. Shortly afterwards the roar of a hundred airplane motors split the darkness. My heart sank a little. Pat was going up. I might never see her again. A great realization of my deep love for her swept over me and I wished that I might be with her in the cockpit of her plane. But that was impossible. My post was with the Chief.

One by one the bombers and pursuit ships took off. In 15 minutes they were all winging their way to various destinations within a radius of a thousand miles.

At 12:15 came a laconic but tremendously significant message from Martha Gaskin. Decoded, it informed Dr. Belsidus that in accordance with his instructions the giant British battle cruiser *Hood* had been sunk by a time bomb with a loss of 900 sailors in Italian waters.

The Chief rubbed his palms together and chuckled softly. "That ought to start things going," he said. "Nations have gone to war for less. By God, that white girl is doing swell work for us."

"You place great trust in one of another race," I observed.

"I place trust in no one," he growled. "I have arrangements to crush those who deceive me. However, Martha has been faithful and deserves credit."

I was tempted to ask him more about this clever white girl who served him so well, when telephone and radio messages began to pour in. Most of them were laconic but no less encouraging:

Dakar, Senegal: Warehouses, railroad shops and barracks destroyed. Two French hangars burned.

Freetown, Sierra Leone: Third squadron successfully bombed white hotels, government building. Trading posts, missions and government buildings in interior fired.

Grand Bassam, Ivory Coast: Railroad shops, barracks and warehouses bombed and destroyed.

Nairobi, Kenya: Docks, warehouses, railroad shops burning. Whites fleeing massacre.

So it went, hour after hour. Green lights jumped out all over the huge map. The campaign had been well planned and was being well executed. For weeks and weeks Temples of Love scattered over the Dark Continent had been storing up thermite grenades and bombs for incendiary work. In each colony secret chemical laboratories had been preparing these incendiary bombs. In each community Dr. Binks's followers had been secretly supplied with revolvers, ammunition and long sharp knives. Now the slaughter was proceeding with clocklike precision while the investments of Europeans went up in smoke.

30

♦♦♦♦♦♦♦♦♦♦♦♦♦♦♦♦♦♦♦♦♦

Fires Flare and Swords Clash
as Big Conquest of Africa Nears Climax

With increasing rapidity as the night wore on the green lights on the great map of Africa increased in number while the red lights decreased. It was exciting in the extreme because we knew that each change from red to green meant another community had changed from white control to black.

Reports by wireless and radio telephone continued to pour in. The distribution of incendiary grenades in the 500 Temples of Love throughout Africa was proving to have been a wise move on the part of Dr. Belsidus. From every part of the continent came shocking reports as mobs of frenzied natives burned churches, warehouses, residences, stores—everything that belonged to the hated white man who had held them down for four hundred years.

By five o'clock, when the first faint suggestion of dawn came out of the east, the swift night of horror was coming to a close and only a few white strongholds held out. A summary made at that time for Dr. Belsidus showed that every white habitation or business from Morocco to Cape Town had been destroyed and the white people without exception exterminated.

South Africa, Cape Town and Algeria still held out, while white control remained in Nairobi, Asmara, Cairo and the north coast, but everywhere else the blacks were firmly in control.

Taken completely by surprise, the 40,000 or 50,000 whites in West Africa had been exterminated as quickly by the infuriated natives as had the whites in East Africa and the million whites in South Africa.

Unless the garrisons in Italian East Africa, at Nairobi, Cape Town and Pretoria received reinforcements from abroad, they would be unable to hold out.

But it was evident by noon that there would be no reinforcements from abroad, for Europe itself promised hourly to become a seething cauldron.

The British, with a great empire at stake, had been striving ever since the Italian rape of Ethiopia in defiance of the League of Nations to preserve the peace of the world: a peace based on the subjugation of colored people. The sinking of the battle cruiser *Hood* in Italian waters now made it almost impossible for war to be avoided.

The news of the sinking shocked the white world. The Italians disavowed the act, laying it to Communist sabotage, but it was clear from summaries of press opinion relayed to us by our European agents that the British and French believed the Italians, backed by the Germans, were responsible for the outrage. Martha Gaskin had done her work well. The time bomb placed by her agents had sunk the world's greatest battleship without a trace. In the absence of absolute proof of the cause of the sinking, the finger of suspicion pointed to Italy.

The British cabinet met hurriedly with Premier Chamberlain at 10 Downing Street, while a similar meeting was called by Premier Blum at Quai d'Orsay. Masters of conciliation and recognizing the possibility of losing both their empires, the general staffs of these two master imperialist nations sat throughout the hot August afternoon trying to find out what do. The chances are they would have patched up some sort of truce with the Fascist powers in a few days, but all their efforts were in vain against the clever scheming of a black man and the bravery and skill of a black woman.

Dr. Belsidus had anticipated the fright into which the great imperialists would be thrown by the threat of European war and the frantic efforts by the various chancellories to prevent a break. He realized then that an apparent British reprisal for the sinking of the *Hood* would have to be made upon the Italians. It would have to appear that the British were punishing the Italians for sinking their great battle cruiser.

But Dr. Belsidus and Liberia were both a long way from Italy and any of the Italian possessions. While the Black Internationale's secret agents were everywhere in Europe and particularly in Italy and Italian possessions, Dr. Belsidus did not believe they could make the sort of shocking reprisal he wanted.

This was where Pat and her air force came in. Immediately upon completing the conquest of Liberia, arrangements were made for caches of gasoline, oil and parts to be established with as great secrecy as possible at Salaka, in the Gold Coast; Yakoba, in Northern Nigeria; Yagusi, in the Ubangui country; and near Gore, in western Ethiopia. These caches were approximately 700 miles apart, and were in close proximity to Temples of Love. Some of the gas had been transported by truck, some by camel, some by porter and a considerable amount had been parachuted by airplane. A very large consignment had been shipped down the Nile and then transported by motor truck and camel to Gore.

Whatever the means of transportation, by the evening of July 31st, the priests of the Temples concerned reported that all was in readiness. Pat was jubilant because of the successful working out of a plan for whose details she was responsible.

So when the zero hour arrived, 100 planes took off under Pat's command, loaded down with high explosive and incendiary bombs.

Following the West Coast eastward, twenty of the remaining planes bombed in turn Bingerville and Grand Bassam, Sekondi, Accra, Takoradi and Lagos. At the same time a fleet of the same size flew up the coast from Monrovia and bombed Freetown, Konakry, Bathurst and Dakar.

These operations were completed without accident or interruption before daylight. Long before dawn a dozen towns and cities between Morocco and the Cameroons were in flames.

But it was the brief messages from Pat with her main fleet of 100 planes that claimed our main attention. Leaving sharply at midnight, she had brought them down on the field ringed with flaming torches at Salaka at 3 o'clock. There they replenished their supply of gas and oil. Taking off again at 3:30, they arrived at Yakoba, Northern Nigeria, at 6:30. Refueling again, they made for Yagusi, in the Ubangui country, where the same operation was completed. At 10 o'clock they left again with full tanks for the airfield not far from Gore, Ethiopia, where they radioed back at one o'clock that they had arrived.

At the end of each message was the laconic comment, "All whites killed." We knew that meant there was no opposition whatever through the whole section of the continent they had crossed.

At 1:20 Dr. Belsidus radioed Pat to leave at midnight for her objective. By that time the pilots would be completely rested.

About 7:30 on August 2nd, the terrible reports began to trickle in from the Congo. The wing section under Juan Torlier, which had spread fire and devastation and death from Monrovia to Lagos, refueled at the latter place from British supplies of gasoline which natives had taken over, and proceeded further south, bombing as they went. Reaching the Belgian Congo, they bombed Banana, Leopoldville, Stanleyville and other settlements. But it was the natives who did the most destructive work.

Not only did they in a few hours destroy what the Belgians had laboriously and cruelly erected in almost fifty years of colonial exploitation, but they slaughtered white men, women and children with great ferocity. You have no idea of the blood-chilling effect of the laconic report from the head of the Black Internationale cell there which read: "Belgian Congo belongs to us. No white person is alive." Later in the day we learned that in many of the principal cities the whites had been beheaded, their hands and feet cut off to be dried as charms, and their bodies thrown to crocodiles. The Belgian Congo was a shambles, indeed, but nothing else could be expected in view of the long series of Belgian atrocities.

At noon we received the report that Cape Town was in flames, fired by the Zulus and other oppressed tribesmen. Surrounded, the white soldiers and native police had fought until lack of ammunition and great clouds of smoke forced them to surrender and plead for their lives. They were promptly murdered, in accordance with Dr. Belsidus's orders that no prisoners were to be taken. At 3 o'clock came the report that the Boer farmers at Pretoria had been slaughtered.

Sleepless and haggard, Dr. Belsidus was finally induced to retire for a few hours. He took one last look at the great wall map which indicated that only Ethiopia, Eritrea, and French, British and Italian Somaliland remained. He turned and smiled that old enigmatic smile, then walked unsteadily to the door.

"Slater, take care of things," he said, "while I snatch forty winks. Order the air forces to remain where they are at Dakar, Stanleyville and Gore until I order them to move."

Just then a message came in from Europe. It was from Martha. It read: "Mussolini conciliatory, realizing he is not prepared. British and French may postpone war. We must strike now."

Dr. Belsidus handed the message to me. "Well," he remarked as he passed out the door to his room, "I think Miss Givens will take care of that."

31

▲▲▲▲▲▲▲▲▲▲▲▲▲▲▲▲▲▲▲▲▲▲▲▲

European Nations Plunge into War
as Africa Is Redeemed

A horrified white world got word of the great African uprising about five o'clock on the morning of August 2nd. Cables and radiograms from our agents conveyed something of the awful shock with which the news was received. From noon onwards we got report after report.

At four o'clock Martha Gaskin radioed in code: "Italians and British about to patch up differences in view of African uprising. Must act swiftly if peace is to be averted."

I hated to awaken Dr. Belsidus although I realized the gravity of the situation. Confronted with the loss of all their colonies, the white imperialist powers would stop at nothing to avert war and send punitive expeditions to Africa. Something had to be done at once.

Rather than disturb the Chief, I decided to act for the first time on my own initiative. At 4:30 I radioed in code: "Pat moves at midnight. Cannot get away before. You do what you can." I signed my name. I figured she would understand that Dr. Belsidus was asleep.

At seven o'clock, as I dozed over my umpteenth cup of black coffee, an orderly brought a cable in code from London signed by Martha. It was brief but terrible in its import: "Italian embassy blown up here at 4:15." I rushed with the message to Dr. Belsidus's room and after some difficulty awakened him.

"What is it, Slater?" he said irritably, lifting himself on one elbow. I handed him the cablegram. He read it, pursed his lips and whistled softly.

"Smart move," he murmured more to himself than to me. "Smart move. That girl really earns her money."

I explained a little hesitatingly how I had taken the authority upon myself to advise her to act.

"Well," he said, "I left you in charge, didn't I?"

I nodded acquiescence. He pondered a moment, gently scratching his head. Then he looked up, scanning my face.

"You must be dead, my boy," he said in a softer tone than was his wont. "Go get some sleep. I'll take over."

And that's how I slept for the first time in almost 24 hours.

I felt as if I was in a Turkish bath. I opened my eyes and the brilliant African sun almost blinded me. I was soaking with perspiration, lying across the bed just as I had fallen, fully clothed. My watch informed me that it was 8:15. I had slept 12 hours.

Feeling refreshed but guilty to have slept so long in the midst of momentous events, I hurriedly disrobed, took a lukewarm shower, shaved and was soon striding into the Doctor's office.

He was sitting at his desk, immaculate as usual in freshly laundered tropicals, eating a breakfast of papaya, goat's milk, a slice of smoked meat and scrambled eggs.

"Get a good rest?" he asked cheerfully, flashing his white teeth. He seemed to be in rare good humor.

"I'm afraid I overslept, sir." I apologized. "You see, I'd been up for almost 24 hours."

"Quite all right, my boy," he went on, lolling back in his chair and sipping the goat's milk. "Everything has gone as I wanted it to go."

"What happened while I've been asleep?"

"Plenty. Around 11 o'clock our agents in Rome bombed the British embassy, and by a clever ruse got a crowd of those fanatical Fascists to cheer around the building. Of course, it was immediately dispersed by the police but the damage was done. It appeared to be a clear act of reprisal. It was the next to the last straw needed to break the back of white imperialist peace.

"Then," he continued, "came the last straw. Pat took off from Gore at midnight. In accordance with our instructions to Ras Kaner, the signal fires lit by the Ethiopians in the hills directed part of our squadron to Addis Ababa, Diretawa and Djibuti, part to Asmara and the rest to Mogadicio."

"Yes, and what happened?" I interrupted.

"Nothing that surprised me," he said quietly, balancing a forkful of eggs. "They bombed every Italian barracks and supply station. At the same time the Ethiopians attacked. It was a massacre. They didn't have time to make any effective resistance whatever. Those incendiary bombs wreaked havoc. Those that we didn't kill in their beds, the Ethiopians did. With the arms and ammunition they've got, the Italians will never reconquer them."

"How did that affect the conference at 10 Downing Street?"

"Very badly," he replied, grinning with ill-suppressed satisfaction. "The diplomats reflected the rising tempers of the two peoples. On both there were charges, counter-charges, all sorts of accusations. The Italians charged that British planes from Aden had raided their colonies, spreading fire and death. Before the British government could formulate a reply, we bombed Westminster Abbey and planted a dead Italian inside as 'incriminating' evidence."

I must have visibly recoiled at his cold ruthlessness. He smiled and went on.

"Coming so soon after the loss of their African colonies, the sinking of their biggest warship and the slaying of their ambassador, it was more than the stolid British could stand. The conferences flopped at 7 o'clock. Just before you came in I received a radiogram that the Italians had bombed Malta and Gibraltar. The French, acting with England, bombed Genoa and Venice. The war is on, my boy."

War had been terrible in 1914–1918. It was nothing compared to what the world witnessed now. Europe's numerous thickly populated cities were blown to bits as swarms of opposing airplanes dropped their deadly wares. Tanks rumbled to meet tanks and the thunder of big guns made night and day horrible. Nothing like this swift, ruthless, unremittent bloodshed had ever been conceived.

Dr. Belsidus was in high glee. Forgetting that he had not slept for 12 hours or more, he lost himself in his inevitable maps, planning and scheming.

At noon the Germans turned the noses of their planes toward their old enemy, France, and in support of their ally, Italy, and raided Paris. By nightfall every European country was involved and thousands of trucks, tanks and cannons were rumbling toward their respective frontiers.

Dr. Belsidus retired sometime before 5 o'clock. Every few minutes a new laconic message from our own forces told of the progress of our conquest. It had made all Africa once more the possession of black men. The Near East was seething and watchful India was prepared to strike once more for freedom.

Through inquiries I learned that Pat's fleet was waiting at Asmara, Adowa and Mogadicio. I shot through a message to her. I wanted to see her, now that all objectives had been attained, and get firsthand accounts of what had happened on our eastern front.

As I waited for a reply, reports came in from every part of Africa telling of the insane joy of the people at being at last released from the white man's yoke. I could close my eyes and see the happy groups dancing in hot village streets while drums boomed and pulsated. I felt like dancing myself.

Hour after hour dragged by and still no word from Pat. Could she have cracked up after that memorable flight across Africa? It was not like her to remain silent so long when on such an important mission.

At 4 o'clock Dr. Belsidus emerged fresh as a daisy. I immediately told him of the lack of communication with Pat. He frowned deeply as his eyes ran quickly over the sheaf of radiograms and cablegrams.

In the next three hours he radioed three times. To each message there was no reply.

Where could she be? What had happened? Was there anything wrong? Why her silence?

32

Pat Breaks Silence as European Nations
Fight to Bitter End

It was very strange. Pat had always been so punctual, it appeared certain something must be wrong; she had let hours go by without communicating with us. I wondered what Dr. Belsidus would do. Even though the World War we had stimulated was now under way and the attention of the entire white world was diverted from us, it would be a severe blow, nevertheless, to lose 100 of our planes.

"We've got to find out what's going on, Slater," he said finally, "and I guess you would be interested in doing the finding, wouldn't you?"

"Why . . . Well . . . yes, of course," I stammered, my cheeks red.

"Oh, I know how you and Pat stand," he said, smiling. "I've known for a long time. Fine girl, Pat. She's the sort of girl I'd like to marry if I was the marrying sort."

"Thank you, Chief. I appreciate that. But tell me, don't you ever intend to marry? You have practically gained all of your objectives now and I should think you would turn to domesticity, if I might be so bold as to suggest it."

The doctor again smiled faintly. "Marriage is for the incomplete," he said disdainfully. "I am complete. Years ago I married myself to the ideal of a free Africa, Slater. That ideal has stayed with and nurtured me, sustained me, and given me the courage to go on. It has done everything that a wife is supposed to do and so seldom does. I need women,

134

Slater, and I've taken them wherever and whenever I wanted them. I have used them to serve my ends, to give me pleasure, to help me accomplish what I set out to do. I need no woman to share my defeats or victories. I shall go on alone, Slater, taking my pleasure where I wish without being tied down by female pettiness and possessiveness."

"Aren't you a little harsh, Doctor?"

"Of course, I am harsh. I am always harsh, always have been harsh, always will be harsh," he replied with evident relish. "I am harsh because I tell the truth and act the truth, and do not let scruple or sentimentality interfere with my desires and ambitions. There was a time I might have married had I been able to find a really civilized woman. But even the best of them are incurably sentimental, essentially petty and lacking in true idealism.

"A woman," he proceeded, warming to the subject, "invariably tries to devour her mate as does the female spider. In this she is industrious and persistent. Ultimately she succeeds because of her concentration on that objective. In the end she always has her way. And in the process the man loses much of his individuality and takes on some of the color and characteristics of his wife. That is why civilizations where there is continuous and uninterrupted monogamy inevitably become feminine. And such civilizations finally succumb to newer, cruder ones in which the male is dominant."

This was a Dr. Belsidus I had not known. Perhaps because we never before had discussed women, I could see his point but could not share it. I could not be complete without the woman I loved, without Pat; I knew I should be completely miserable if I had to go through life without her. I had never felt that one could completely enjoy a woman unless she was one's very own and she shared in ownership. After all, there is much more to the man and wife status than the physical intimacy that seemed to be the extent of the Doctor's interest in women, aside from his use of them to further his diabolical ends.

"Yes, we are quite different, my boy," he said, reading my mind. "There are very few men like me. I spoke in a matter-of-fact tone without boasting or bragging. If I were not unique, I should have been unable to accomplish what I have."

Dr. Belsidus called in Captain Thomas Hudginson, who had been navigator on Pat's plane when we flew from Texas to Sierra Leone.

"Captain," he said, "I want you to fly Mr. Slater to Ethiopia as quickly as possible. We must find out what has happened to General Givens and the First Air Fleet. Our last message came several hours ago from Asmara. How soon can you make it?"

"By using Colonel Torlier's new stratosphere plane, sir, I can do it in eight hours. I can average 400 miles an hour with that. But the colonel gave strict orders that it was not to be touched. With one of our fast pursuit planes I can reach there in twelve hours."

"Use the stratosphere plane," commanded the Doctor, "by my orders. We must know what is going on. I can't stand this silence from Pat. She has never done this before. Are you ready, Slater?"

"Quite ready, sir."

"Well, get going, then, and whatever you do, keep me advised."

"Very good, Doctor."

The Captain and I turned to go. I was wondering about the stratosphere plane, wondering whether it would be entirely safe up in those rarefied spaces where one's life depends entirely on the oxygen tank, when Dr. Belsidus's telephone rang insistently. He grabbed the instrument and listened eagerly to whoever was talking. I saw his eyes brighten and the smile return to his face.

"Good!" he shouted, hanging up the receiver. He turned beaming toward us. "Never mind that trip. We've heard from Pat at last!"

A great load lifted from my heart because I had been worried a great deal by her silence. Now she was safe.

"They'll be in tomorrow morning. Then we'll get the details. You may go, Captain. Slater, we'll read over the latest dispatches."

So Pat was on her way back! I was quite buoyant over it, although I wondered about her long silence that had so upset us. But there were other matters to occupy my mind.

The war was growing more devastating by the hour. Every principal city in Europe had been bombed by one or the other of the belligerents, and in every case incendiary and gas bombs had been used. All restrictions were off and human brutality was revealed at its worst. Hospitals, churches, homes of non-combatants, all were blown to bits by the terribly destructive aerial attacks. Millions of armed men hurled themselves against the artillery, machine guns, liquid fire, tanks and bayonets of opposing armies. And as each report came in the grin of Dr. Belsidus grew more diabolical. He actually revelled in news of the collapse and destruction of white civilization.

"Magnificent!" he shouted when German bombers blasted a hundred buildings in Brussels.

"Never heard anything better!" he exclaimed when Italian submarines sank four British cruisers outside the harbor of Alexandria. "At this rate, there soon won't be any white people left. Oh, how I've longed for this day!"

The new mechanized warfare was taking a tremendous toll of lives, according to radio and cable advices from our European agents. All through the night Dr. Belsidus gloated over the reports. Between times he issued cryptic orders to his subordinates spread over Africa from Timbuctoo to Cape Town. There was certainly a lot to straighten out, with looting in some places and utter disorganization in others. But thanks to the Temples of Love and their disciplined followers, some semblance of order was beginning to appear.

At daybreak a great roar of motors overhead told us that Pat and her planes had returned. A heavy rain was falling, making the landing field soggy and slippery, but one by one the great ships came down and taxied to their hangars.

Shortly afterward I heard light footsteps on the stairs. The door flew open and there was my Pat, face smeared with grease, but smiling triumphantly, and as pretty as ever.

33

∧∧∧∧∧∧∧∧∧∧∧∧∧∧∧∧∧∧∧∧∧∧∧∧

Dr. Belsidus Finally Establishes African Empire as Story Ends

It was September and the Second World War had been proceeding devastatingly for a little over a month. After the first major
battles in which white people both on the fronts and behind them had
died like flies, the conflict settled down to a stalemate similar to that of
1914–1918, while pitiless and persistent air attacks reduced the civilian
populations further into bestial fear and terror.

Following the swift and terrible conquest of Africa, the Black Internationale had been busily consolidating its gains, restoring order, gaining the allegiance of chiefs and kings in its far-flung empire. Europe
was too busy to lift a finger to regain the vast territories from which it
had drained so much wealth. Europe had made its death bed and was
doomed. We felt safe and jubilant. The longer this new world war
lasted, the more time we would have to strengthen our position and
bring Africa's diverse peoples securely and definitely under our rule.

Of course, we had to use ruthless methods in some places. There
were miseducated Negroes who still favored the rule of white men to
the rule of black men. There were still Negroes who had been given a
few crumbs from the tables of the exploiters, who now tried to help
them by stirring counter-revolution against us. These Dr. Belsidus
ruthlessly purged and executed.

The ruthless and expeditious manner in which white rule had been
brought to an end had electrified the entire world. Europe had too
much on its hands to do anything about it. Australia, New Zealand,
Canada and other British dominions and allies were deeply involved in
the European mess and likewise could do nothing to save Africa for the
whites. A powerful faction in America had talked of intervening to save
the prestige of the white race, but Gaston Nucklett's "White Americans," with its constant instigation of civic strife, had so entirely dis-

rupted the country that it was unable to "compose" its internal affairs, let alone composing those of Africa. An uprising in India instigated by our agents there made it exceedingly unlikely that the British would be able to send the expeditionary force to Africa, composed of Indian soldiers.

We were all naturally quite jubilant. We had gained an empire at small cost, an empire rich in everything, and were rapidly on the way to unifying it. It was then that our Second World Conference was announced.

By the first of October delegates were assembled from all parts of the world: every part of Africa, Australia, India, the West Indies, South America and the United States. But this time they were not sneaking to a hidden retreat in the New York State hills. This time they were not using the white man's transportation. This time they were being brought from all over the world by our airplanes to the two-story building of concrete blocks at Kakata, Liberia, that in so short a time had grown from a wayside settlement to the capital of the new Empire of Africa.

I shall never forget that great imperial conference, the largest and most significant ever held by black men. There were nearly a thousand delegates present. These included all the heads of Black Internationale cells in the various dark sections of the world, all the chief technical officers responsible for industrial development, all the high military officers and the bishops of the Church of Love from all parts of the earth.

Forming just before dinner outside the capitol building, we marched in twos through the entrance, up the double staircase and into the great dining hall. Uniformed ushers guided the delegates to their respective places. Across the end of the vast hall was a table which crossed the two long ones at which the delegates were sitting. At that head table were the familiar faces of the Black Internationale staff, the Brain Trust, the wise and courageous men and women who had made all this possible. There were Sam Hamilton, Al Fortune, Gustave Linke, Dr. Matson, Rev. Samson Binks, Ransom Just, Pat, Juan Torlier, Bennie Simpson, Alex Fletcher, Sanford Mates, Gaston Nucklett, Martha Gaskin, General McNeel, myself and many whom I knew through our files and correspondence but had never seen because of their occupation in Europe.

One chair, in the center, was empty. That was the chair of Dr. Belsidus. As I gazed around at the excellent decorations, the gold and black banners, the gorgeously uniformed guards and attendants, I wondered where the Doctor could be.

Then, somewhere a trumpet sounded, to be joined by a chorus of trumpets. The lights in the hall lost their brilliance and grew dimmer and dimmer. Finally, the place was in darkness. There was awed whispering. Then the chorus of trumpets flourished again and the lights came on slowly. We all instinctively looked toward the chair of Dr. Belsidus. He was seated there, expressionless. I recognized the stunt as excellent theater, a characteristic Belsidus gesture.

At a wave of his hand to the major domo, the 100-piece band below in the sunken garden burst into a new selection, *Caprice Africaine*, written expressly for this occasion. The serving of the dinner began.

It was a little past nine o'clock and the coffee and cordial had just been served when three loud taps from the major domo's staff brought the delegates to attention. Dr. Belsidus, still the stern immaculate figure in faultless tropicals, rose in his place and quietly began to speak:

"Africa belongs once more to the Africans. Africa will remain in the hands of the Africans. Never again shall the white man set his foot in our land, steal our wealth and enslave our sons and daughters.

"Africa is rich. Those riches will remain in Africa. Africa is populous. That populace will remain here and the products of its toil will remain here. From henceforward black men will labor to advance the interests only of black men.

"Africa does not need and does not want the white man. Africa will not have the white man. We will have our own culture, our own religion, our own education, our own army, navy and air fleet. We have the natural resources, the will and the ability to create the greatest civilization the world has seen. While the white man destroys himself with the infernal machines of his invention, we shall prosper and expand.

"This conquest proves that white men are not our superiors. This conquest proves that the white men are definitely our inferiors. They had all the power, all the money, all the machinery of information and communication. We had nothing but our wits. And what happened? How well you know what happened! With nothing but our wits we got money, we assembled men and women of brains, we trained hundreds of technicians, we disrupted white society and under the cover of that disruption we trained and transported a fully equipped army to these shores and fired the shots that have been heard wherever men breathe.

"The white men are tearing at each other's guts. Why? Not because they really want to do it but because we forced them to it. We did it. We brought about suspicion, strife and conflict because we had an objective and we could not attain that objective as long as white men were united.

"But remember this. As we gained an empire through our unity and intelligence, we must maintain it the same way. Negroes for 400 years were the slaves of white men because they had not learned the lesson of unity, of solidarity, of a common cause. Too often they aided the white man in his nefarious schemes to partition Africa, and always he succeeded because some Negroes, consciously or unconsciously, failed us.

"Let us continue to be alert. Let us continue to relentlessly pursue our selfish interests. Let us utilize every ounce of intelligence and knowledge we possess to make Africa impregnable.

"Now that we have ousted the white man from Africa, let us not waste time hating the white man. Let us keep an observant eye on him and profit from his mistakes. Let us stay out of his lands and be sure that he stays out of ours. The world is plenty large enough for both of us. If we properly take care of our part, we shall maintain our independence forever and forever.

"And now, my dear friends and associates," he said, and more emotion crept into his voice, "I would fain give up my leadership. For twenty years I have struggled and striven to free Africa, and I am tired, very tired. But I am not going to quit now. No, there is still much to be done. There is still need of consolidating our power, of making Africa a political and industrial entity while the white nations bleed themselves to death. Until this is accomplished, you need a strong, a ruthless, an intelligent leader. Negroes are not yet used to freedom, and so for a time we must have dictatorship, but that will depend upon you and the manner in which you carry out my orders. For, as you know, I will not tolerate disobedience or inefficiency or laziness.

"So, I am not going to give up my leadership. To be completely safe from white attacks and nearer the center of the continent, we are going to build a new capital at Yakoba, in Northern Nigeria. We are going to build roads. We are going to build factories, operate giant collective farms, ranches, mines, mills, become self-sufficient.

"Oh, yes, my friends, there is much to do because Africa is still far behind. But as we have succeeded in this task, so shall we succeed in the others. I shall serve you as I have served you, and you must serve me as you have served me. Together we can build here on this, the second largest continent, an empire of black men and women working toward a cooperative civilization unexcelled in this world. And to that task, my friends, the Black Internationale rededicates itself. Brains and organization triumphed once. They shall do it again."

There were wet eyes and damp cheeks when Dr. Belsidus ended. I saw Martha Gaskin look longingly at him. She realized she would never possess this black man for whom she had risked so much, and I felt sorry for her.

Pat was almost overcome with emotion. She squeezed my hand tightly and dabbed at the tears on her cheeks. Then she leaned toward me with that softness of the eternal feminine in her brown eyes. I wanted to kiss those pointing lips right there before a thousand pairs of eyes, but I contented myself with one whispered word: "Tomorrow."

She smiled and whispered back: "Yes, love. Tomorrow we, like Africa, shall be united, after so long. United forever."

"Forever!" I repeated reverently. And how I meant it!

BLACK EMPIRE

*An Imaginative Story of a
Great New Civilization
in Modern Africa*

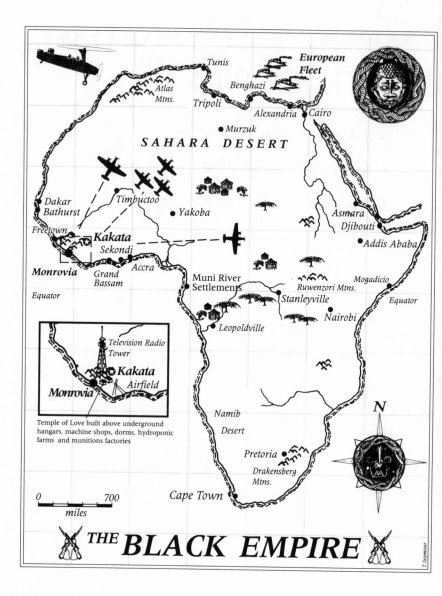

European Fleet

Tunis

Benghazi

Atlas Mtns.

Tripoli

Alexandria • Cairo

• *Murzuk*

SAHARA DESERT

• *Dakar Bathurst*

Timbuctoo

• *Yakoba*

Freetown

Kakata

Sekondi

Accra

Monrovia *Grand Bassam*

Equator

Muni River Settlements

Asmara Djibouti

• *Addis Ababa*

Ruwenzori Mtns.

Mogadicio

Stanleyville

Nairobi

Equator

• *Leopoldville*

Television Radio Tower

Kakata *Airfield*

Monrovia

Temple of Love built above underground
hangars, machine shops, dorms, hydroponic
farms and munitions factories

Namib Desert

Pretoria

Drakensberg Mtns.

N

0   700
miles

Cape Town

THE BLACK EMPIRE

T. Seymour

1

≜≜≜≜≜≜≜≜≜≜≜≜≜≜≜≜≜≜≜≜≜≜

Dr. Henry Belsidus Starts Developing
an Empire in Africa

The conquest of Africa was history. Moving with a swiftness that amazed the world, Dr. Henry Belsidus, the sinister, suave, inscrutable black man who had once ministered to New York's sick white aristocracy, now sat in his large, almost-bare office in the capitol at Kakata, Liberia, complete master of the second largest continent in the world. Starting with a handful of loyal, brilliant Negroes, he had carefully built up the greatest revolutionary organization the world had ever seen: an organization which in its rise to power had known no law save that of expediency, no mercy except to people of color: an organization so ruthless in attaining its objectives that even I, Carl Slater, who, as the doctor's secretary, knew more about this ruthlessness than anyone except the doctor . . . sometimes even I shivered at the memory of the past.

When the delegates from 50 countries had secretly assembled in rural New York for the First World Conference of the Black Internationale, there had been elaborate preparations to conceal the meeting from the police and the agents of colonial countries. That had been five years ago. Now, a thousand delegates from every country where dark men and women dwelt were assembled at the new African capital at Kakata, Liberia, to listen to the reports of the technical and military officers. Last night they had heard Dr. Belsidus conclude his memorable address with the long-remembered words:

"There is much to do because Africa is still far behind. But as we have succeeded in this task, so shall we succeed in the others. I SHALL serve you as I HAVE served you, and you MUST serve me as you HAVE served me. Together we can build here on this the black continent, an empire of black men and women working toward a co-operative civilization unexcelled in this world. And to that task, my friends, the Black Internationale re-dedicates itself. Brains and organization triumphed once. They shall do so again."

It seemed a tremendous program, almost an impossible one. Here was a continent, almost wholly agricultural, with several hundred diverse nations speaking a half thousand languages. The European nations, whose colonies we had taken in the recent short campaign of blood and terror, were now locked in a fight to the death which our agents had instigated. But how long would that war last? And when it was over, would the victors ignore Africa? Would they let us go ahead and grow powerful before they attacked us? If they attacked, how could we hope to hold off their mighty battle fleets and their swarms of airplanes? Our technical staff was driving ahead feverishly to prepare for the inevitable struggle, but our progress was maddeningly slow. Here in a few months we had conquered a whole world and in a few short months we might lose it.

I dismissed the gloomy thoughts and concentrated on our honeymoon. Patricia Givens, whom I had loved from the first moment I met her in Dr. Belsidus's office in New York, was now Mrs. Carl Slater. In a few moments we would be winging our way to Ziggeta, high in the Liberian mountains where the Black Internationale's chief architect, Sanford Mates, had built a beautiful resort for staff members.

The door opened and she came striding in, brown, slender and beautiful, looking trim as usual in her green helmet, green jacket and riding breeches of the same shade which disappeared into highly polished cordovan boots.

"Ready, Sweet?"

"Sure, I have gassed the plane and all our luggage is packed inside. The Doctor has given us a month off. Isn't that swell? He said he guessed airplane production could continue without me for a month."

"I guess it can, too," I said, "but let's get away from here. You know, I'm jealous. I want you all to myself."

"For how long?" She was holding her head on one side, smiling with a twinkle in her eyes.

"Forever, Pat," I replied, drawing her to me. The look in her eyes told me better than words that she knew how much I meant it.

A few minutes later we climbed into one of the Black Internationale's black and gold pursuit planes, and were soon hurtling through the cloudless sky on the happiest trip of our lives.

It brought back memories of the first time I had gone aloft with Pat, a time that seemed ages ago but which only was really a little over four short years. Then we were flying from the Black Internationale's private airfield and factory in Westchester County, New York, with its big hangars and machine shops presided over by Juan Torlier, the dull-black giant airplane designer from Spanish Guinea who had received his training in the airplane factory in Barcelona. I recalled how we had flown first to the Black Internationale's great cement factory near Poughkeepsie, where Bennie Simpson, the freckled mulatto, superintended production and supplied the material for the hundreds of Temples of Love where Rev. Samson Binks schooled Negroes in the new black man's religion. And then had come the amazing chemical farm in New Jersey where gigantic vegetables grew in giant trays filled with chemical solutions that made soil unnecessary. But no less wonderful had been the batteries of steam engines operated by sunshine and efficiently maintained by their inventor, short, reddish brown engineer Alton Fortune, just as tall, studious chemist Sam Hamilton operated the amazing farm.

Today all these marvelous technical innovations and inventions of black scientists had been multiplied a hundred-fold in little Liberia. They would soon be multiplied a thousand-fold throughout all Africa.

Three-quarters of an hour later, Pat brought the little fighting plane down in a perfect three-point landing on the spacious field at Ziggeta. A staff car was waiting to drive us to the hotel, perched high on the side of a verdure-clad mountain whose summit was crowned with mist.

There was quite a number of the staff week-ending at the hotel. On our way to our suite we met Gustave Linke, the black French metallurgist in charge of our armament factories; Ransom Just, the short fat mulatto radio engineer; Martha Gaskin, the slender blonde in charge of our espionage in Europe; and General Barton McNeel, the burly, gray-haired World War veteran who had led our expeditionary force to Liberia, after training it in a remote section of Texas, and conducted the recent conquest of Africa. It seemed as though all the important officials had decided to come to Ziggeta to rest up after the strenuous round of activities at the Second World Conference.

We dined that evening with Dr. Andrew Matson, the handsome young Howard graduate, once Dr. Belsidus's medical assistant, but now

Surgeon General of Africa. He was a striking figure in his white tuxedo and black trousers, as impeccable but not as sardonic as his boss.

"A mighty fine-looking couple, I'll say," he remarked, making no effort to conceal his admiration for Pat. I didn't blame him. She was indeed lovely in her tight-fitting, rose-colored evening dress.

He said a number of other nice things, and then the talk inevitably got around to shop.

"How long do you think it will take to build enough hospitals for all Africa?" I asked. "About ten years?"

"We shall have very few hospitals," he said calmly, then smiled at our visible surprise. "We are going to do new things in medicine in this country," he went on. "We are going to abandon Christian ethics and deal with the problem of health and sickness rationally."

Pat leaned forward, intrigued. "What do you propose to do?"

"Yes," I added, "there's a lot of disease in Africa: sleeping sickness, yellow fever, yaws, elephantiasis, malaria, syphilis, blindness . . . how can you treat all this disease without hospitals?"

"Before the white man came to Africa," he said, unperturbed, a smile twitching at the corners of his mouth, "there were no hospitals, and yet the Bantu peoples had lived here for 50,000 years. How do you suppose they managed to flourish and develop such fine physical types? I'll tell you: In one way or the other they eliminated the unfit. That's what we shall do. That's what we ARE doing."

"You mean you are killing the sick!?" I was shocked in spite of myself. It seemed so monstrous.

He threw back his head and exposed his fine teeth in a hearty laugh when he saw the revulsion in our faces.

"I see you are still soft in spite of everything," he jeered. "Meet me tomorrow morning at ten o'clock on the verandah and I'll show you what the Black Internationale health service is doing for the health of Africa."

148

2

▲▲▲▲▲▲▲▲▲▲▲▲▲▲▲▲▲▲▲▲▲▲▲▲▲

Surgeon General of Africa Reveals How Sickness Is Handled

We arose early for newlyweds, but the brilliant African sun was well above the eastern hills when we came down to breakfast. The dining room was already filled with uniformed officials. Dr. Matson, immaculate as usual in his white uniform with gold buttons and epaulets, had already breakfasted and was engaged in earnest conversation with Ransom Just, a short, fat, light-brown man who had accomplished wonders as the radio technician of the Black Internationale. At Pat's suggestion we joined them. The two men rose, greeted us pleasantly and resumed their seats.

"We were just talking about the new installations," said Just, his round face reflecting his enthusiasm.

"What installations!" It was becoming bewildering, this matter of installations. Since the day we had taken control of Liberia there had been a continuous and feverish succession of installations: tray farms, sun-power plants, airplane factories, new roads, lumber mills, mines, cotton mills, temples, steel mills and the thousand and one technical assets needed for the building of a great empire. Now Dr. Belsidus and his Black Brain Trust were driving ahead with the same program for all Africa.

"Better to show you than to tell you," said Rannie. "When you finish, we'll go over to the temple. You've got to go there anyway to see Andy's clinic."

"Who ever heard of a clinic in a church?" asked Pat, incredulous.

"Well, you know," I reminded her, "we're following the same system here that we did in America. The Temples of Love are the center of everything—schools, stores, recreation halls, beauty parlors, radio stations, and now, clinics. It's the Doctor's idea that religion being the most basic thing in life, the church should be the center of all activities."

"Let's go," said Andy. "I don't think you two have seen our temple here. I know you didn't get up in time for mass this morning."

"Mass? When did that start?" I hadn't heard about that.

"It's another one of Binks's ideas," he explained. "Sort of taking a leaf from the ancient Egyptians. Every temple now has services at sunrise and sunset, to greet the rising and sinking of the sun. Quite impressive ceremonies, too. Atheist that I am, I was really moved by the first mass I attended. It beats the Catholic ceremony all hollow. . . . Well, let's get going."

We rose and walked out of the high-ceilinged room to the tiled corridor.

"We'll go this way," said Andy, pointing to a stairway by the underground passage. "I understand that every temple and surrounding buildings are connected by a labyrinth of underground passages. This one goes deep underground."

"What for, I can't see," Rannie remarked.

"You'll see quickly enough if there's ever an air raid," said Pat. "It's protection for our people in case of war. And you know we're likely to have to use them any time."

We walked down the cement stairway two flights and found ourselves in another corridor which led to an elevator door. Andy pressed the button and the car came up. The door slid open and we entered. The car descended perhaps fifty feet, the door slid open and we found ourselves in a musty-smelling cement passageway, brilliantly lighted and scrupulously clean. We walked along this for about a thousand feet until we came to a heavy wooden door. Rannie pushed it open and we found ourselves in an immense room no less than six hundred feet square. The ceiling was about twenty feet high with a row of cement pillars every two hundred feet on which rested big long teakwood beams supporting the ceiling. The floor was smooth cement and the place was indirectly lighted. On the floor were six or eight pursuit planes and a big bombing plane, among them Pat's little black and gold pursuit plane in which we had flown up from Kakata. In the rear of the vast room was a well-appointed machine shop and several gasoline and oil pumps. In the front was a series of steel doors that rolled upward, permitting the planes to be rolled out to the big elevators that carried them to the airfield above. Several young men and women in overalls were busily at work on two big engines.

150

We walked across the room to a small elevator which automatically lifted us about forty feet.

"You see," said Pat a little proudly, for the underground hangars were her idea to protect our planes from bombing in case of air raids, "it will be almost impossible to destroy our ships from the air. The temples are always built immediately above the underground hangars. If a bomb strikes the temple it will of course collapse, but that will only further protect the hanger underneath."

"That's a clever wife you've got, Carl," said Andy.

"Humph! You telling me?"

The elevator came to a stop, the door slid open and we found ourselves in the retail service department unit, immediately under the temple and just above. Corridors ran in two directions with shops and offices opening on each. The whole place being air-conditioned was as cool as if it had been in Canada. Tropical clothing such as we wore made us positively chilly. The corridors were crowded with natives: Buzis, G'Bandes and Mandingoes wrapped in their striped cloths and gowns, waiting amid much jabbering to get into the big clinic that ran along one side of the main corridor next to the Turkish bath and tonsorial parlor.

"Come right on in folks," Andy invited. A stalwart black policeman opened the door of his office and we entered. It was plain, efficient, clean, with not a superfluous article. We sat down on a modernistic cream leather sofa while Dr. Matson changed to his surgeon's white duck uniform.

"This clinic," he explained, "is almost exactly like the thousands we are building throughout Africa. We have a staff of four or five specialists and six or eight nurses. Every person in the district is given a rigid physical examination. No one can refuse. They bathe in the shower room there before examination. If examination shows them to be incurable we give them something to end their sufferings."

Pat gasped audibly. Andy smiled. "It seems so brutal," she complained.

"No, on the contrary, it's quite sensible and altogether humane. Incurable people are not only a drain on our all-too-meagre resources but they are a worry and strain on their relatives, and besides, they are often in constant pain. It is better to end it all and devote our time to those whom we can help."

151

He was ready now. An attendant gave each of us a long white apron. Andy led the way first into a long chamber lined on both sides with booths seven feet square, each with a small window.

"Here is where we permanently cure arthritis, malaria, asthma, St. Vitus' dance, gonorrhea and syphilis. We are also getting pretty good results with certain mental diseases. I worked it out. We call it the fever box. Take a look inside."

We looked in the first booth. A young girl was lying completely nude on a low operating table sweating profusely.

"What's the idea?"

"Well, we blow in humid air, increasing its temperature until the patient's body is raised to fever heat, where we sustain it for a given period. We repeat it as long as necessary but after a few treatments the patient is cured. As you can see, we can handle fifty people at a time. Formerly we used short-wave radiation, but we found this method more effective and economical."

We walked through the long room peering here and there through the window of a booth. The nurses were hurrying about consulting thermometers. Doctors were busy in one end of the room with their examinations.

"We're working on an entirely new theory of medicine," Andy explained. "We never use drugs of any kind except when necessary, and that is seldom. Most physical disabilities are due to the inability of the body to throw off poisons or to combat deleterious germs because it has been improperly nourished and accordingly weakened. This is true of most dental, eye, lung and stomach trouble. Patients suffering from pellagra or other nutritional deficiency diseases are placed on a rigid diet of fresh, raw food tastily prepared. We permit no liquors; we have outlawed flour, rice, hominy and white sugar. Our dieticians have discovered ways of preparing uncooked foods quite as attractive and palatable as the old methods of preparation. Nothing that we ate at the hotel was cooked, and you notice that neither tea, coffee, liquor nor beer was served. This is now the rule in every district in the empire and is incorporated into the tenets of our religion. Of course, it is too soon to be able to say what the effect of this will be throughout Africa, but here in Liberia, where we've had much longer to work, we have virtually done away with sickness, with the result that the people are happier, more industrious and more productive, as our Department of Labor will testify."

"Well," said Pat, a little wistfully, "I like my pork chops occasionally. What harm does a good stew or baked ham do?"

"Application of fire to the delicate membrane and cell structure of plant and animal life destroys most if not all its nutritional value," the physician explained, "reducing its nutritional value from fifty to eighty-five percent. Introduction of this dead matter into the system imposes a burden upon the body which it is unable to perform, deprives the human cells of needed material for replacement, with the result that what we call sickness results. The weakened organism is then unable to resist malignant germs and we have all the maladies with which we are familiar. Dr. Belsidus is in agreement that disease must be banished from Africa and that this drastic means is the best. Now come into the model diet kitchen and I'll show you how food is prepared by the new method."

We passed through an opaque glass door and entered the strangest kitchen I had ever seen.

3

Model Diet Kitchen Explained;
Dr. Matson Tells of Advantages

There was not a stove in the kitchen. Along one side was a long row of heavy wooden tables, each equipped with a number of electrical appliances. Along the other side were glass cases with coils of frost pipes inside, keeping the great pans of prepared food chilled. Men and women in spotless white were busily engaged preparing vegetables, meats and fruits for the next meal. The place was perfectly air-conditioned, with figured linoleum on the floor and occasional chairs and settees down the center of the room.

"We do not call these people cooks," Andy explained with a smile, "because they don't cook. We call them dietitians. As you know, this is where the students get their initial training before being assigned to other kitchens. Eventually we are hoping to have one of these kitchens in every district in Africa, utilizing the available supply of food."

We walked over to the nearest work table. A young, dark girl was cleaning and slicing some large fish. As she cut each slice she placed it in a large enamel pan where it was just covered with some liquid. Then she would dip into a big yellow bowl near at hand, take out a couple of slices of onion and place them on top of the fish. Then she would cut another slice.

"This is our method of preparing fish," Andy explained, nodding to the girl. "It is soaked overnight in lemon juice and onion. In the morning it will flake apart as if it had been cooked because the sharp acid of the lemon has that effect on the ligaments. In the morning she will take it out of the refrigerating room, place it in a squeezer to remove all the lemon juice, mix it with mayonnaise dressing and serve it on lettuce leaf. The soaking takes out the sharp fishy taste. We prepare most of our fish that way, although some is preserved in honey."

We moved on down the room. Next was a young man preparing fresh beef. We watched him with much interest. He put the meat in an electric grinder along with an occasional onion and green pepper. Then he poured into it a large cup of sauce made of lemon juice, honey, black pepper, chile powder, olive oil, cinnamon, nutmeg and sage in definite proportions, mixed it in a nearby electric dough mixer and then turned it into an oblong white enamel pan. It was pressed down securely with the hand until the pan was full. It was then turned upside down on a very large platter. Slices of tomato were placed along the side, with a row across the top lengthwise. Then he poured mayonnaise dressing into a canvas bag with a spout and made geometric designs across the dish of meat, the yellow contrasting pleasantly with the red and the occasional bits of green pepper. Chopped parsley was sprinkled over the top and the whole was ready for the chilling table.

"A dish like that is allowed to set for three or four hours," said Andy, "while the rich sauce permeates it. Then, as you will see at lunch, it is delicious."

At the next table was a young woman making layer cakes. She dumped raw cashew nuts into a grinder and they came out as a fine flour. This was mixed with honey, spices, cherry juice and flaked coconut to form a dough. It was rolled out to a thickness of a half inch, placed on a wooden platter and set in a nearby electric dryer which removed the excess moisture.

154

"Sometimes it is dried in the sun," the Surgeon General explained. "We use whichever method is most convenient, although sunshine is obviously superior since it adds to the nutritional value of the dish."

The young woman now ran washed raisins through a peanut butter machine and they came out as a paste. Whole wheat flour was added until a workable dough was secured. This was sprinkled with various spices and grated lemon peel and thoroughly mixed with powdered dried olive. It was rolled out and also put to dry. This operation was soon completed. She took the two layers out of the dryer and placed them one on the other with a layer of finely sliced mango alternating between slices until the whole was about five inches high. Then whipped cream was spread on top and the girl deftly placed halves of large sliced strawberries in an attractive design. She bore the cake away proudly to the pantry in the rear.

"Well, Doc," I said, after we had inspected a number of tables and watched preparation of salads, ice cream, desserts, fowl and refreshing drinks, "this is all very interesting, but you know very well that, efficacious as all this may be, you cannot expect people to change the dietary habits of a lifetime."

"Ah, but they will, Carl," he replied. "It is always much easier to eat food that is prepared for you than to prepare it yourself. The whole plan of African life of the future will center around the temple. Here will not only be the recreation of the community but the dining hall as well. This will relieve women from the drudgery of cookery and free them to take up other pursuits if they wish. Then, too, we are giving the people something unknown in modern civilization."

"What's that?" asked Pat, suddenly breaking a long silence.

"Through our educational system which also centers in the temples we are disseminating the truth about disease. You know that in the past, doctors have made the matter of life and death rather more mysterious than it really is. We are simplifying the whole thing by telling the truth as we see and know it, and showing them the relation of diet to health. This is something new. We can do it because we have no cliques with a vested interest in selling injurious food and drugs to the people. We can do it because we who have Africa's health in our care find it more profitable to keep people well than sick. We are building here a rational society."

"Well," said Ransom Just, "the folks down at Kakata are eating pretty much as they please."

"The officials, yes," Andy admitted, "but that won't be for long. Dr. Belsidus is in agreement with me on this program. As we establish our setups in each locality and erect a temple, there we shall have a clinic, a kitchen and all the things you see here. And we shall feed the people in our communal kitchens. The marvelous physique of the Africans where they have not come into contact with white people is due largely to their superior nutrition. Even where and when they cooked their food, it was fresh food, not preserved food. We in the Western world have preserved food. We in the Western world have been reared on dead food, embalmed food. Here we are going to feed our population on fresh food."

"But, Doctor," said my wife, "how are you going to keep food without canning it or something?"

"Canning is really old fashioned and unnecessary today. Let's go in the rear. I'll show you what we do." He led the way out of the stoveless kitchen. We entered a corridor which we crossed with the doctor in the van and came to an elevator which dropped us perhaps five or six stories farther under the ground.

We stepped out into a small room. Dr. Matson pointed to a window in a door opposite the elevator. We walked over and looked in. It was an extensive warehouse. In crates, bins and boxes were a profusion of the fruits, vegetables and meats of Liberia. A gray haze seemed to hang over the place. I mentioned it to Andy.

"You see," he explained, "it has been recently discovered that by quickly freezing food seventy-five or one hundred degrees below zero, it can be kept fresh indefinitely. Under the circumstances, it is unnecessary to rid it of three-quarters of its value by canning or otherwise preserving it. There will soon be one of these storehouses far beneath every temple. And as you've probably guessed, we're even down beneath the underground hangar. Our food supply is well protected. With one of these in every district and the natural fertility of the soil, we shall have sufficient food to withstand any drought or siege. We're building for the centuries here, Slater."

"Yes, so I see and I'm mighty glad, Doc, to get this close-up of what you are doing. Down there at Kakata we've been so busy we haven't had much time to keep track of your achievements. But tell me, what are these installations you and Just were talking about before we came out of the dining room?"

"It's about time I had a chance to show you what I'm doing," said Just, the radio engineer. "Get back on this car. I want to show you something up above that is making educational systems as we have known them unnecessary and ditto for the newspapers. We're not catching up with the white man any more, we're surpassing him. Come on!"

We piled into the elevator again. The Surgeon General pressed a button and we were on our way to the Ziggeta radio and television station designed to make Africa a cultural unit.

4

Black Empire Has Radio and Television Station
Which Is Finest in the World

We got out of the elevator on the clinic level and, with Rannie Just in the lead, we walked down the broad corridor to a small door. The radio engineer unlocked it and we entered. Dr. Matson switched on the light. We were on the platform at the beginning of a small tunnel in which was laid a narrow-gauge track. Nearby was a small electric car with four rows of seats but no top.

"Get in," said Rannie, waving to the vehicle. "We're going to give you something to lift your eyebrows about."

"Where are we going?"

"Right under the mountain," said Dr. Matson, seating himself in the front seat alongside the engineer. When we were all placed comfortably in the upholstered seats, Rannie Just pulled the lever and the little car sped straight ahead into the well-lighted tunnel which was only about eight feet in diameter. At intervals there were recesses in the cement wall where, Dr. Matson explained, workmen could stand out of the way of the car when they heard it approaching.

When we had gone about a half mile, we came to the end of the line and piled out on a cement platform. Rannie Just pressed a button alongside a heavy wooden door. In about 15 seconds the door slid aside and we entered a small cage. The door closed, a button was pressed and we shot upward for about three minutes without a pause. Then the elevator stopped, the door slid open and we walked out into bright sunlight. We were standing on a curved balcony of cement work with broad windows through which the hot Liberian sun poured relentlessly, and yet we immediately noted that it was much cooler here than it had been at the hotel.

"Where in the world are we?" asked Pat, as we walked over to the windows. For answer Dr. Matson merely pointed out and down.

It was a magnificent view. We could see for the more than 150 miles to the ocean across the great expanse of hills and jungles, a vast carpet of tropic green. Here and there a column of smoke issuing from the verdure marked a village. Far below us on the side of the mountain stood the trim little hotel and to one side and at the foot of the mountain stood the great Temple of Love with its gray domed roof with a broad balustraded ledge. In front of it a great expanse had been cleared as an airfield, and even as we watched a little black and gold pursuit plane came zooming out of a yawning opening in the ground, catapulted from the platform above the subterranean hangar, and flew off in the direction of the sea.

Near the temple we noted many other buildings we had not yet visited and about ten miles away we could see the gray roof of our new electric steel plant which Al Fortune, our engineer, Sanford Mates, our architect, and Gustave Linke, our metallurgist, had rushed to completion just the week previously.

"We're nine thousand feet up," said Dr. Matson, lighting up a cigarette, "and approximately 4,000 feet above the temple."

"Well, what's the idea? Observation post?" I was curious. It seemed a waste of valuable material to go to the trouble and expense of building a tunnel, an elevator shaft and this formidable structure on the peak of the mountain merely for such a purpose.

Little Rannie Just's rotund face took on a look of outraged astonishment. "Why, this is our radio and television station!" he almost shouted. "We get excellent results here because we're so high. This is probably the highest station in the world. We can send and receive to and from the ends of the earth by short wave. Come on, I'll show you a thing or two."

We followed him down the balcony, enjoying his enthusiasm and consumed by curiosity also. Television to us was but a name. We knew nothing about it, had never seen it, but we knew that even in England and America it was in its swaddling clothes. My respect for Rannie Just's knowledge rose higher than ever when I realized that this Negro was doubtless in advance of all the white radio engineers in the world.

Finally we walked off the balcony to a flat yard leveled right on the very top of the mountain next to the concrete radio station, whose two lofty steel towers pointed like gaunt fingers into the blue. The level space covered about three acres. An acre was taken up with a small powerhouse, in which dynamos hummed. This place had a flat roof on which were scores of Al Fortune's unique sun-power machines. They covered the entire roof of perhaps fifty by one hundred feet, and re-sembled futuristic anti-aircraft guns or Brobdingnagian mosquitoes. They were troughs about five inches deep and ten feet long, lined with polished aluminum and set on legs so that they inclined at an angle of 45 degrees. In back of the higher end was a cylindrical water pump, and at the lower end, a small engine. From the engines steam pipes ran down into the powerhouse, where the steam power was converted into electricity. Two young black engineers in faded overalls were moving among the machines, checking their performance.

"You're probably more familiar with how these things work than I am, Carl," said Rannie, "and if you don't know everything, ask those boys over there. They're Al's proteges."

They were almost exactly like the machines I had studied at the chemical farm in New Jersey. The sunlight was caught on the highly polished surface of the aluminum, which was so curved as to focus the rays on a long tube resembling a thermos bottle, made of Pyrex glass with an inside diameter of one-half inch and an outside diameter of one and one-quarter inches, and called the "focus" tube. Within the focus tube was a miniature flash boiler of the type used in old-fash-ioned steam automobiles. It was a steel tube one-half inch in diameter made of the highest-grade steel, thin-walled but strong enough to resist a pressure of steam up to 200 pounds per square inch. The steel tube slipped into the Pyrex glass tube, which was jacketed by vacuum and was painted with lampblack so as to absorb 95 percent of the sun's rays that fell upon it after passing the focus tube. Inside the steel tube was a third tube known as the water tube, only an eighth of an inch in di-

159

ameter, and joined along its entire length by four copper wings, fastened with high-melting-point solder to the inside of the steel tube. The supply of water to the tube was automatically regulated by the meter in the rear.

The four copper wings were fine conductors of heat, enabling the heat produced by the absorption of solar rays in the lampblack on the outer surface of the steel tube to penetrate with the utmost facility to vaporize the water. In this way it was possible to get power for nothing beyond the cost of manufacturing the engines. Each produced steam at the desired pressure of 175 pounds to the square inch. Each machine produced four horsepower and there were 100 machines on the roof.

Next to the powerhouse stood three big silos insulated with "glass wool" and filled with sand. As the sun machine could only function while the sun was shining, these silos were used to store up heat at extremely high temperatures and could retain it almost without loss for years. Thus, whether some days were short or cloudy did not matter. Steam was always available, and thus electricity was always available. I noticed there were a score of the machines on top of the radio station. "The sun is our greatest asset," observed Dr. Matson, pointing to the burning disk in the cloudless blue sky.

"Yes," I agreed, "it frees us from dependence upon coal and oil, and without those two products no modern nation can become great. There's no place in the world that has more sunshine than Africa and the supply is inexhaustible and eternal."

The remaining space atop the mountain was laid out with lawn, shrubbery and benches, but two canvas-covered anti-aircraft guns added a grim note which quickly brought one's mind back to hard reality.

We followed Rannie and Andy to the balcony from whence we had issued and entered a room of strange, gleaming, futuristic camera-like machines. The place was hung with black velvet draperies and was powerfully lighted from every direction.

"Sit over there, all of you," Just directed, bustling with importance. We went over to a long sofa on a slightly raised platform. Just went over and spoke to his three assistants manning the apparatus. Then he took his position nearby at an instrument board.

"Now," he said, "we'll get in touch with the Chief. Watch that mirror." He pointed to a glass screen four feet square which was set in the wall about four yards from us.

Switches were turned and machinery began to hum. The powerful point of cold light played over us like sunshine pouring through the lattice work of forest leaves. Just's voice droned, "Calling ZXQ2R, calling ZXQ2R, Dr. Belsidus, please. Calling ZXQ2R, Dr. Belsidus, please. Yes, MXQ2R calling. Ransom Just. Yes, yes. Come in, ZXQ2R. All right. Go ahead!"

5

▲▲▲▲▲▲▲▲▲▲▲▲▲▲▲▲▲▲▲▲▲▲▲▲

It's War Again! Italy and France Strike
to Destroy Black Empire

There was a click and a hum. An image began to take form on the glass screen in front of us. Gradually it grew more distinct.

"More juice," yelled Rannie, frowning and waving his hand at his assistants, who leaped to obey.

Now we could plainly see Dr. Belsidus, in spotless white, seated at his broad flat desk in the capitol at Kakata. He looked up and gave one of his rare smiles.

"Well, are you newlyweds enjoying your honeymoon?" he asked. His voice came to us as clearly as if he had been sitting in the room.

"Oh, yes," said Pat, pressing my hand as she spoke.

"That's good," he remarked. "Have a good time because I'm likely to be calling you back any day."

"Is that so?" The news gave me a sinking feeling. I had hoped to get a long and happy rest. "What's wrong, Chief?"

"The white nations have patched up their differences," he said, gravely. "We may expect an attack at any time. I know we'll lose North Africa and probably Egypt, but we must hold the rest. At any rate they haven't attacked yet. There is still a breathing spell to get ready. I don't need you two now, but maybe pretty soon. I know you'll come when I call."

"We'll come right now, Doctor," said Pat, "if you want us."

"No, have your fun," he insisted with a faint preoccupied smile. "It's probably the last you'll have in a long time. Goodbye."

"Goodbye, Chief."

There was another click. The current died and the image vanished.

"Well, what do you think of it?" asked Rannie, eager for compliments.

We both assured him it was wonderful, and we weren't being untruthful.

"The best they can do in America," he boasted, "is to send about twenty miles. We can send and receive from any point between Cairo and the Cape. Boy, we're teaching the white folks something. We've got twenty of these machines placed already. All I've got to do is turn the knob and I can talk to our men in Dakar, Takoradi, Lourenco Marques, Tananarive, Cairo, Casablanca, Zanzibar, Stanleyville, Addis Ababa, Nairobi and a number of other points. Later we're going to send over plays and concerts and lectures. All Africa will soon be able to not only hear but see us."

"How did you get it set up so quickly?"

"Why don't you ask your wife?" he chided. "Her boys flew the parts and the mechanics to the various points. The stuff was delivered inside of two days."

"Yes," Pat interrupted, "and it would have been delivered in one day if you'd had all of it at the airfield like you promised."

"All right. All right," he said. "I'll do better next time."

"You're making pretty good progress on these communications, Rannie," I said.

"Pretty good?" he echoed. "Say, brother, there's nothing like this been done before. And what you saw isn't all. We have a sending and receiving station in every one of our 500 temples, and it's some job keeping them in running order, especially when we're working often with green hands. But just give us another month and we'll be delivering newspapers every morning to every part of the continent."

"How? With airplanes?"

"No, by wireless," he said, enjoying my incredulity. "Let's show him something, boys."

He walked over to the other side of the studio and we followed him, wondering what was up. He stopped in front of a large cabinet radio on top of which sat a large box with a slit in it like a mail box.

"This is the receiver," he explained, "through which we receive the facsimile newspaper. Inside is a photoelectric cell. The basis of the system is the impulses similar to those that make possible the sending of dots and dashes of the Morse code. The receiver is connected to the wires of the loud-speaker. The attachment is set in operation by the electrical energy supplied by the receiver and is connected to the wires that change that energy into mechanical energy, which prints the reproduction of the picture or reading matter broadcast. Watch closely, now, and you'll see. All right, boys. Call Kakata."

Switches were thrown and again the machinery hummed. Rannie stood in front of the glass screen, the points of light playing over his figure. The assistant's voice droned out the call letters. A figure on the screen took form. It was one of the radio engineers I had seen about the capitol building at Kakata.

"Hello, Jake," said Rannie.

"Good morning, Mr. Just. Do you want something?"

"Yes, I wish you'd send over the first page of some pamphlet. I'm showing Mr. Slater how the machine works."

"Yes, sir. Right away, sir,"

The image faded. Rannie came over to the radio set again.

"Now, watch that slit," he directed.

A light flashed on the inside of the box and wheels began to turn. Suddenly the edge of a piece of white paper protruded from the slit. Then more and more came out, seemingly a sixteenth of an inch at a time. There was printing on it. In five minutes a large nine-by-twelve-inch section was torn off and presented to us, as Rannie stopped the machine. It was one of the propaganda pamphlets we had scattered over Africa, an exact facsimile.

"We've just started experimenting on this," he explained, "and it's working perfectly. I'm already arranging for mass production of these sets, and as soon as they come out of the factory we'll fly them to the various temples. You know the Chief is nuts about communication."

"Yes, and about everything else, if you ask me," Andy added, speaking for the first time. "But let's get going. I've got to fly down to Kakata."

He led the way out of the radio-television station to the balcony. After one look at the magnificent panorama from the 9,000-foot level, we entered the elevator, descended to the tunnel, boarded the electric car and were soon back under the temple. From there we walked back through the underground passage to the hotel. As we strode along, Dr. Matson talked.

"You know," he said, "our aim is to have a duplicate of this setup in each one of the five hundred departments into which Dr. Belsidus is dividing the continent. Each department will just be about the right size: twenty thousand square miles, twice the size of the American state of Maryland."

"They won't all have the same number of people, though, will they?" asked Pat, who had flown over so much of Africa during the recent campaign.

"No, of course not," Andy continued. "Some of them will almost be without population, especially in the desert areas, but Alton Fortune and Sanford Mates were telling me of a plan they're working out to place surplus population in the Sahara."

"But that would be suicidal," I objected. "There's absolutely nothing up there but sand."

"Nevertheless, they've already established one artificial oasis, as they call it. Al is at the hotel now. Why don't you have him show you what they're doing up there. It's right near Timbuctoo. You can get there in five hours in Pat's plane."

"Maybe we shall."

We entered an elevator and a minute later stepped out in the corridor of the hotel. We had gone a mile from the place and a mile up in the air, yet had only been above ground once, when we visited with Al Fortune.

We had lunch, as Andy suggested, with Al Fortune. Power and authority hadn't changed the short, plump, reddish brown engineer very much. He was still the bitter anti-white fellow he'd been when he was directing Dr. Belsidus's robber band at night and experimenting with chemical farming in New Jersey by day.

"Sure, I'll be glad to have you come up tomorrow," he said, as we sat down to the meal of strange but tasty and nutritious dishes, "but we haven't any suitable quarters yet. Sam Hamilton spends a lot of time up there puttering around. It's going to be a bigger farm than we had in New Jersey. We struck plenty of water when we got down 2,000 feet."

"Water in the desert? Come, come, Al." It seemed incredible.

A gong sounded insistently. A hundred conversations died. Then the familiar voice of Dr. Belsidus came over the loudspeaker.

"I want all executives to return to Kakata this evening. Conference at five o'clock. Europe has started its war to recapture Africa. The Italians bombed and took Tripoli an hour ago. A French air squadron has flown over Tunis demanding surrender and we may expect the British to strike at any time. Patricia Givens, General McNeel and Carl Slater will return immediately. That is all."

We sat in stunned silence for a full half minute before chairs scraped and the buzz of voices filled the dining room.

"Well," said Pat, rising, her face grim, "let's go."

6

▲▲▲▲▲▲▲▲▲▲▲▲▲▲▲▲▲▲▲▲▲▲

Dr. Belsidus Undisturbed as White Nations Sweep Forward to Recapture Black Empire; Has Plan to Make Enemy Fight His Way!

There was a rush for the door. Pat and I hurried to our suite, threw our clothing into our bags and ran downstairs to the underground corridor that led to the hangar. Close behind us was General Barton McNeel, tall, gray-haired and very dark, a distinguished, thoughtful man, veteran of two American wars who had led our forces to victory in the recent campaign which cleared the white people out of Africa. I had never seen him excited, even under fire that night when we landed in Monrovia. But now it seemed that he had lost just a little of his calm. He was more grim and tense than I had ever seen him.

The motor was already roaring as we entered the subterranean hangar, and hurriedly climbed in. I sat next to Pat while General McNeel took the remaining seat in the rear. Pat gave the mechanic the signal, the blocks were taken from under the wheels, and the ground men pushed the little fighter slowly forward until it was clear of the hangar and on the catapult outside. The door of the hangar rolled shut and the steel cover over the catapult was rolled swiftly aside. Then, with the motor making a deafening noise, we were suddenly flung upward like a jack-in-the-box, out into the sunshine and sent tearing through the hot afternoon to Kakata.

I glanced back at General McNeel. He was looking thoughtfully at the gray roof of the new electric steel plant, operated by sun power, which had only last week been completed. I knew exactly how he felt because I felt the same way. We had schemed, sacrificed, risked our lives to free Africa and build a powerful empire that would make black men and women forever honored and respected. We had tasted the cup of victory. We had seen the white men run off the continent and black men triumphant from Cairo to the Cape. We had hope for peace, for time to build here on the bosom of Mother Africa a great united land—one people, one soul, one destiny. We had hoped to build here a haven for all those wearing the burnished livery of the sun, who wearied of battling discrimination and segregation, disfranchisement and perpetual insult in alien lands and yearned for a place of rest. We had hoped, now that we were able to hold up our heads with the free people of the earth, to be able to demonstrate here the genius of the black people in the pursuits of peace.

But we all knew now that it had been but a dream, an ambitious hope, an idle fancy. Yes, we all knew it. I could see it in the look of tired resignation in McNeel's face, in the grim intensity of Pat, as she strained her eyes for the towers and smoking chimneys of the new capital at Kakata.

I looked below me at the verdant land glistening with numerous little square patches of water that indicated the chemical farms already feeding half of Africa. All this might be destroyed, I thought. And then, strangely enough, I thought of Dr. Belsidus. What would he do now?

Pat brought us down without a jar in a perfect three-point landing on the great airfield at Kakata. The three of us hurried over to the two-story, mission-style concrete block with stucco finish where the business of the African empire was transacted. We went up the wide double staircase that curved to the second floor and made our way hastily to the Doctor's spacious office. A uniformed attendant halted us respectfully, bowing.

"The Doctor says to come to his apartment, sir," the man told us.

That in itself was unusual. In New York Dr. Belsidus had almost always received those of us who were very close to him in the privacy of his apartment to talk over matters of state. But since establishing the Kakata capital, he had taken to meeting with us in the conference room, due to the vast increase in the number of executives.

Another uniformed attendant stood outside the apartment door. He bowed low as we approached, then saluted General McNeel. Turning to one side, he spoke into the mouthpiece of the communicating telephone at his side.

"Pardon me, sir," he said, "but General McNeel, Mr. Slater, and Commander Givens have arrived."

"Let them in," said a familiar voice.

The man swung the door open and we entered the Doctor's black and gold apartment. The floor was of red glass. The walls and ceiling were dull black. A great chandelier of gold and cut glass and ornamental wall lamps fashioned into exotic gold figures shed illumination upon the scene of sombre magnificence.

In the exact center of the long wall opposite the door was the spacious regal bed. It was around 18 inches high with a gorgeous cloth of gold spread on it. At the head a startling canopy of highly polished mahogany fringed with gold curved over the bed like a protective shell. In the ceiling of this canopy were mirrors that showed the bed below. At intervals along the walls were fragile-looking gilded chairs with yellow satin seats. On the wall on each side of the bed were life-size paintings of beautifully formed nude girls. The picture to the right depicted a dark reddish brown African girl, an incomparable figure against a background of exotic green jungle. On the left was a young white girl reclining invitingly on a large red couch. On the wall opposite were three other life-size paintings showing Chinese, Navajo and Hawaiian beauties. The five beautiful paintings were illuminated by indirect flood-lights. There were no windows in the apartment. It was air-conditioned like the entire building and Dr. Belsidus considered windows distracting and unnecessary in a chamber to which he repaired only when he was through temporarily with the outside world and sought absolute privacy.

We saw him as soon as we entered, lying high up in the bed, dressed in purple and white pajamas and nonchalantly smoking one of his special cigarettes six inches in length in a holder equally as long. He didn't seem at all perturbed.

"You made good time," he said, waving us to the chairs an attendant had brought and ordering refreshments. As the man walked away on his errand, the Doctor shouted after him, "Tell Portabla to come in." The attendant bowed assent.

I looked at Pat, frankly puzzled. I knew of no one by that name with whom Dr. Belsidus was intimate enough to call to his private apartment. I could see that she knew nothing about him either. Nor did General McNeel, from the looks of his face.

We didn't have long to wait. In a few moments the door opened and the flunky bowed and brought in a skinny black man with an ungainly stride, long arms and eyes that seemed sunk far into his head but which glowed like those of a person possessed.

"You call for me, Doktor?" he asked with heavy Latin pronunciation.

"Yes, Vincente, I want you to meet Commander Patricia Givens, head of our air force, General McNeel, Commander-in-Chief of our armed forces, and Carl Slater, my secretary. Friends, this is Vincente Portabla, formerly professor of physics at the University of Rio de Janeiro and exchange professor at the Lenin Institute in Moscow. He has come down to help us."

Prof. Portabla bowed low. It made him seem comical because of his awkwardness. He mumbled a few words and then lapsed into silence, brooding with a vacant stare like some zombie. I wondered what on earth Dr. Belsidus was going to do with this fellow. It wasn't professors we needed now, it was munitions of war.

We all sipped our drinks in silence. Once or twice I stole a glance at the Doctor. He was resting as easily as though he hadn't a care in the whole world. Although I knew his inactivity belied his inner feelings, personally I couldn't help but fume within. Precious moments, minutes, hours were being lost while he dawdled.

Tripoli had fallen. French war planes had demanded the surrender of Tunis. Doubtless the British fleet was even now plowing the sea to its African colonies and protectorates. And what did we have to combat such a mighty force? Four or five hundred planes, a hundred pieces of field artillery, a few score anti-aircraft guns, a few thousand veterans and millions of black men and women who were willing enough to fight for Africa but for whom we had not nearly enough firearms. We had done our best but we hadn't had time to prepare properly. The whites knew this, I supposed, which was why they were attacking now, before we became strong.

"We can only be defeated," said Dr. Belsidus, "if we fight the white people their way, and with all the advantages on their side. I intend to make them fight my way, with all the advantages on my side."

"And may I ask, Doctor," I inquired, "how that is to be done?"

"In just a few moments," he said, "you will see, my boy, you will see."

7

Dr. Belsidus Prepares to Meet Invading Forces
of England, France, Germany and Italy
with a Strange and Deadly Army

"Pat," he asked turning to my wife, "how many of those new stratosphere planes have we now?"

"Torlier had fifteen just before I left for Ziggeta, Chief."

"What is their non-stop range?"

"Six thousand miles. You see, once we get to the ten-mile level, our consumption of gasoline is cut almost in half. But of course we'd need almost all our space for gas, Chief. We wouldn't be able to carry any bombs."

He smiled that cruel, sardonic smile that I had seen so many times before when some devilish idea intrigued him.

"I do not want you to carry any bombs," he said. "I want you to carry something much lighter but much more dangerous."

"More dangerous than a bomb?" she asked, surprise in her tone.

"Much more dangerous," he said. "After all, air bombs do not win wars. Look at the examples of Madrid and Shanghai. They continued to be held even after repeated heavy attacks from the air. No, my dear, what I have in mind is far more dangerous than bombs."

The Doctor sat up and spread out on the table a large map of Africa which had been rolled up alongside his bed.

"The effective enemies of Africa," he said, "are England, Italy, France and Germany. Our job is to prevent them from taking Africa. McNeel, what have you mapped out to combat this invasion?"

The General's solemn face grew sterner. He looked down into his drink, then turned the glass around two or three times in his large capable hands.

Finally he spoke in his usual slow measured tones. "We have our strategy for such an eventuality as this, of course, but frankly I doubt that it can be very effective. At the moment I cannot see how we can prevent them from taking the entire coast. We have less than 500 planes. And any one of the airplane carriers of England, France, Italy or Germany carries that many. We have an insufficient supply of gasoline to last through a long war, and our South African plant for extracting gasoline out of coal will not be completed for a few months. We have only a hundred field guns of various sizes, and that is nothing to use against even a second-rate power. We have a million rifles, ample stores of small arms ammunition and thousands of machine guns. That's a wonderful showing for the short time we have had our plants in operation. But frankly, Chief, it couldn't last long in the face of such opposition as we have now. We can bomb battleships, troopships, and landing parties, but we can only do it as long as we have control of the air."

"And that won't be long," added Pat. "I'm afraid we couldn't take it long, Chief."

All the time Dr. Belsidus was poring over the map, using an architect's compass to measure distances. It was plain that he was paying very little attention to General Barton McNeel. Finally he looked up with the same sardonic smirk on his handsome face.

"So you think we're washed up, eh?" he inquired, cutting his eye at the General.

"Well . . . " McNeel hesitated, "of course, Africa's a big place. We have the advantage of tremendous distances. They could only take the coast. We could really last for years in the interior, especially now that we've armed the masses. But we are woefully deficient, sir, in the things with which war is made, and while we are acquiring rapidly the means of supplying them, we just haven't got time, what with the enemy already in possession of Tripoli and on his way to take the rest."

"Yes, I understand. It's not your fault or anybody's fault. We just didn't have time. But in spite of that we have a good chance to stop them."

The three of us could not conceal our surprise, but Prof. Portabla remained imperturbable, as if nothing in the world mattered.

"Stop them how, Chief?" I asked, eager to learn what he had in mind.

"By the same means that we conquered this continent, Carl," he replied grimly, "by using our brains. No matter what the white man's got, black men have the brains to duplicate it, improve upon it or originate something entirely different. The latter, my friends, must be our course."

"Yes," objected the General, "but we haven't time to originate anything now, Chief. The enemy is upon us."

"That's all right," he scoffed. "They'll soon get off us. I have not been idle. I anticipated this move of the white powers. That is why I sent for Professor Portabla."

He clapped his hands and a flunky hurried to the bedside. "Bring my clothes, boy," he ordered. Then, turning to Pat, "Commander, I want you to prepare your 15 stratosphere planes at once with your best pilots, navigators and radio men. We cannot have any mistake. McNeel, you and Slater and Portabla come with me."

Pat hurried out to get ready. We lingered while Dr. Belsidus dressed.

Finally he was ready. We all went down to the entrance of the building, where we got into an official car and were whirled to an obscure concrete building about a mile away. The building was not over 12 feet high. It was completely surrounded by a ten-foot moat filled with water, and around the moat was a 15-foot, close-mesh wire fence. A sign on it read, "Danger. Charged wire." I had never had much curiosity about the building. There were hundreds of such structures scattered around Kakata. One couldn't keep track of all of them. Yet it struck me that I remembered seeing Dr. Belsidus entering the place once or twice.

We got out of the car. Dr. Belsidus warned the uniformed chauffeur to wait. We walked to the gate. An attendant admitted us. He pressed a button and a drawbridge lowered from in front of the door of the concrete building. With Dr. Belsidus in the lead, we walked across. He pressed a button alongside the door. It creaked open slowly and a pair of inquisitive eyes studied us from the dark interior. Then the door was swung open and we all entered as the uniformed attendant stood to one side.

171

"This is my experiment room," the Chief explained, turning to the right and walking up a flight of six steps. We went through a short hallway to a thick glass door that looked over the entire floor below, with the exception of one corner which was partitioned off with shatter-proof glass. Around the sides of the long room ran a balcony about six feet below the low ceiling.

"Come on out," the Doctor invited. We followed him and there below us on the floor of the vast room were at least 50 large cages about ten feet square and two feet high. Each cage was swarming with rats. We gazed at the scene amazed, incredulous.

What new madness was this? Here with the enemy upon us, Dr. Belsidus was taking us to see his rats. Was the man mad?

"There are close to a thousand in each cage. They shall serve us well, the little dears." He chuckled diabolically. Then he stepped back, turned and shouted to the attendant at the door. "Hey, Kandie! Telephone the garage for 15 open trucks at once, a derrick and about ten men."

For the first time now Prof. Portabla opened his mouth. "What ees thees rats for? Why do you keep them?"

"For an emergency like this," said the Chief. "I knew this would be forthcoming. I prepared. I told no one, not even you, Carl. You will observe that each cage has a large sign attached to it. It seems meaningless because the letters don't seem to make sense. But don't be fooled. I have been preparing for this for a long time. That sign marked C means cholera. The one marked ST means spotted typhus. The one marked BP means bubonic plague, and so on. It has taken hard work, doing this in spare time with almost no assistance, but now we are practically ready."

"I don't follow you, Chief," I said.

"Ah, but you will, my boy, you will." Then, hearing the sound of the trucks outside the moat, he roared, "Good," and began to direct the men.

"Open that front door wide enough to get those cages out, hear? And be sure and don't let one of those rats bite you or it will be your finish."

We went downstairs and out front to watch the operations. The front door had been swung back until the doorway was about 12 feet wide. Soon the laborers were bringing the cages out and placing them on the trucks with much growling and cursing. One by one they came out until the 15 trucks were loaded and the last had chugged away. Then Dr. Belsidus led us back to our limousine and we were sped to the airfield.

Already lined up on the field were the torpedo-like stratosphere planes. Piled on one side of each plane were a score of wire cages about two feet square. Alongside each pile of cages stood one of the trucks from the laboratory with its strange squealing burden.

The attendants grouped around each plane stood at attention as the Doctor hurried over, shouting orders. "Get those rats in those smaller cages. Be careful now. Don't let any get away and don't let any of them bite you."

It took about an hour to get the rats from the huge cages to the little ones, and then to transfer the little cages to the airplanes. We all watched the operation with great curiosity. We didn't yet know what Dr. Belsidus had up his sleeve. Then he called to Pat.

"While you were gone," he told her, "I increased the supply of gasoline at Fez 100 percent. You will fly your planes there at once, as soon as those cages of rats have been loaded on, and refuel. Here are sealed instructions. Get going. I expect you to succeed. It means everything."

8

Black Empire's New Stratosphere Planes Take Off on Epochal Flight, Set to Invade European Countries

Pat paused a moment as if undecided, looking first at me and then at Dr. Belsidus.

"Well, what's the matter?" he snapped, frowning. "Hadn't you better get going?"

"Chief," she began, her eyes softening, "I know it's a silly request when there is so much to be done and so few of us to direct it, but cannot Carl go along with me as . . . er . . . well, as a sort of observer. We haven't been together much you know, and . . ."

"It's no time for sentiment," he snapped, "but I suppose I'll have to let you do it. Go ahead, Slater, if you want to go, but hurry up. Every minute counts. Return immediately to Fez when you have completed your task. I'll wire you special instructions to Fez, Slater."

Pat was radiant. As for me, I was much surprised because I had not dreamed of accompanying the raiders. She took her place at the controls and I got in beside her. I looked back in the cabin and there was young Tom Hudginson, black and handsome as ever, who had been our navigator on the flight from Texas to Sierra Leone. I felt sure we would reach whatever destination we were directed to with him doing the navigating.

We closed our cowling, sealed all openings and were ready for the flight. It was a magnificent sight to see the fifteen bullet-like tri-motor planes lined up with their propellers whirring for the getaway. It was three-fifteen exactly.

"All right, Number One," Pat shouted into her mouthpiece.

The huge black and gold ship on the extreme right streaked down the field, climbing rapidly into the blue. The other ships followed one by one until we were all aloft. Although I had been in many planes, I had never seen any climb so rapidly and at such a steep angle. Our altitude meter registered in succession: 1,000, 2,000, 3,000 and 4,000 feet. But this seemed only a beginning. We went on and on. At 20,000 feet we were far above the clouds in a lonely, spaceless world accompanied only by our fourteen companions now in perfect "V" formation. Hudginson was kept busy correcting our course.

"Turn on your oxygen," commanded Pat. "The air's getting thin." She turned from her mouthpiece and glanced at me, then she pointed at the valve she had previously indicated. I turned it.

A hiss of air penetrated the thunder of the motors. I immediately began to feel better, more refreshed, more buoyant as the precious air filled the cabin. I had begun to feel dull and sleepy as the air became thinner.

We continued to climb. We were up 50,000 feet before Pat gave the command to flatten out. Our speed in this rarefied atmosphere was 325 miles an hour, but because of the thinness of the air, gasoline consumption was far less than an uninformed person would have imagined. The rareness of the atmosphere made the air resistance negligible.

I looked at the clock in the instrument board. It was exactly 6:45. We had gone 1,000 of the 1,600 miles from Kakata to Fez. Tom Hudginson corrected our course again and Pat shouted orders for the dive for Fez when she gave the signal.

On we went, literally flashing through the air now, ten miles above the earth. The sun had disappeared; it was almost black dark. Pat watched carefully now for the wing lights of neighboring planes, while she shouted cryptic orders over the radio. It was ticklish business, this blind flying ten miles aloft with no earth in view, but the first brilliant stars were appearing out of the void above.

In another hour we had covered nearly 400 miles. Pat called to the other ships. We had 200 miles to go. "Down to forty thousand," she commanded. We could see the lights of the other ships dip as they dove for the new level. Ten minutes later she cried, "Down to thirty thousand." After a similar interval, she gave the command "Down to twenty." Then, turning to the intercommunicating telephone, she called Hudginson: "How are we doing, Tom?"

The navigator paused and consulted his instruments for a moment; I listened in to the conversation with my head set.

"We're due to be about ten miles due south of the Fez airfield," he said.

"Prepare to land," she commanded the others, switching to the radio mouthpiece. "In order: Number One first on the extreme right of the field."

In a second or two she began calling the airport. "Hello, Fez! Hello, Fez! B.I. Stratosphere Squadron landing. Yes, all right, Fez. Coming down."

We dipped sharply. Below, a square of brilliant light shone where floodlights played on the airfield. It shot up to meet us. We were landing fast. There were already four of our planes on the ground with another descending. We crossed the field twice before it was our turn, then came down to a perfect three-point landing. The other planes followed suit.

The field was surrounded by mounted troops keeping the Moorish populace back. A black official drove up with eight limousines to take us to headquarters. He and the others saluted admiringly as Pat stepped down from the cockpit. Negro mechanics swarmed over the giant machines while great gasoline trucks drew up alongside them to fill up the tanks and replenish the supply of oil.

At the airport headquarters a half mile away where the black, green and gold of the New Africa had displaced the tri-color of France, we gathered around a long table in an inner room with Pat at the head and the airport commander at the foot. There were 46 of us in all.

We had rare steak, salad, tomato juice and fruit. Pat permitted each man a small glass of wine. When we had finished, the commander of the airport switched on the television machine. There was a hum, a cloudiness on the mirror and then the image of Dr. Belsidus at his desk in Kakata appeared. His voice was clear and firm.

"Hello, Sandu," he said. "So the squadron has arrived safely! Well, Pat, you've done a good job. Follow your instructions to the best of your ability. Slater, instructions in code have been sent to you. Do not open them until you are aloft again. That is all."

The image faded and in a moment was gone.

Pat drew out the heavy manila envelope containing her instructions:

> Attention, everyone. Commander Sandu will issue you at once as many small parachutes as you have cages of rats. I think you will each need about twenty. Attach them immediately to your cages but be sure none of the rats bite you.
>
> Ships Numbers 1, 2, 3, 4 and 5 will constitute the First Flight. Ship No. 1 will fly immediately to Rome, Italy. There you will drop half of your cages. You will then proceed to Naples and Palermo, dropping half of the remainder over each city. You will then return here and await further orders.
>
> Ship No. 2 will proceed to Genoa and Turin, dropping half your cages on each city, and then promptly return to Fez.
>
> Ship No. 3 will deal similarly with Milan and Venice, Ship No. 4 will take as its targets Munich and Vienna, while Ship No. 5 will take Budapest and Trieste.
>
> Ships Numbers 6, 7, 8, 9 and 10 will constitute the Second Flight. No. 6 will proceed directly to Glasgow to drop half its load and then will drop the other cages at Liverpool. No. 7 will proceed to London and Plymouth, dropping 15 cages on the former and five on the latter, thence returning to Fez. No. 8 will go to Lisbon and Cardiff, dropping half its cages over each city, and returning here. No. 9 will drop its cages at Bordeaux and Brest, while No. 10 will proceed for the same purpose to Birmingham and Manchester, returning to Fez.
>
> Ships Numbers 11, 12, 13, 14, 15 will constitute the Third Flight. No. 11 will go to Marseilles and Lyons, No. 12 to Paris and Lisle, No.

13 to Brussels and Amsterdam, No. 14 to Antwerp and Hamburg and No. 15 to Berlin and Leipzig, all returning to Fez.

The dropping of the cages should be completed before daybreak and all planes should be back in Fez as soon as possible. This whole operation is be conducted in the utmost secrecy. In case of forced landing, the plane is to be immediately destroyed.

It is now 9 o'clock. Our farthest objectives are Berlin and Glasgow, only 1,500 miles. That, at most, is a five-hour trip unless you run into a storm, which is unlikely at the altitude at which you will travel. You should be back here by 7:30 tomorrow morning at the latest. If you all understand, let's get going.

The pilots and navigators filed out of the room, each pilot telling Commander Sandu the number of small parachutes he wanted. Sandu noted this on a piece of paper which he handed to a sergeant orderly. We piled into the limousines and were whisked back to our ships. Another great adventure was about to begin.

9

△△△△△△△△△△△△△△△△△△△△△△△△△

Carl Accompanies Pat on Stratosphere Flight to London; Dr. Belsidus Orders Him to "Bail Out"; Follows Orders and Is Attacked

I was about to follow Pat into the ship when a lanky black soldier hurried up on a motorcycle. He saluted, handed me a sealed envelope and saluted again. I knew what it was and could scarcely contain myself until we were in the ship and had finished tying the parachutes to the cages of the rats, a job that required about ten minutes.

One by one the big planes left the ground and disappeared into the blackness of the Moroccan night. At last it was the turn of our No. 7. Pat gave her the gun, we raced down the field like a shot and then began climbing steeply. Every so often Hudginson corrected the course.

This was blind flying with a vengeance. We seemed to be soaring aloft into nothingness. I looked at Pat, so cool and calm at the controls, and I felt more proud of her than ever.

When we were beyond the 3,000-foot level and still climbing steeply, I pulled out the envelope and tore it open. Then, turning on a nearby light, I got out my code book to decipher the message. In a few minutes I had it. It was from Dr. Belsidus and read:

> After London errand proceed north twenty miles until you see four red lights going on and off simultaneously. Bail out. You will be picked up by friends. The word is "Kakata." Go to London headquarters. Further instructions there.
>
> THE CHIEF

I re-read it and silently passed it to Pat. She was apparently as puzzled as I.

There was no plumbing the mind of Dr. Belsidus. Schemes of the most amazing complexity and subtlety sprang from his mind like corn from a popper. He had said nothing to me previously about going to London. Why could he not have told me before? Why all the secrecy? And why should I go to London when Martha Gaskin, his chief white European agent, had been doing such a swell job there disrupting the international picture?

I slowly tore up the message and tossed it out of the window. We were now four miles up. We sealed the cabin and turned on the oxygen. Higher and higher we went until we flattened out at fifty thousand feet to a speed of close to 350 miles an hour.

Eleven o'clock. Hudginson gave Pat our position. We were not far from Plymouth. The big ship dipped for the dive toward our first target. I went back to aid Hudginson. We both hung on desperately as Pat sent the plane down at an angle of 45 degrees. We strained our eyes for the first glimpse of the English city.

We hadn't long to wait. When we broke through the last belt of clouds, there a few miles ahead were the myriad lights of the ancient shipping center. In a few moments we would be above it. Pat dropped down to about 3,000 feet.

Hudginson opened the trap door in the floor of the plane. Pat throttled her motor and we idled over the city. I handed Hudginson the first cage of rats, taking care that my hands were not bitten. He tossed it out, pulling the string of the small parachute, which immediately opened. Swaying from side to side, the parachute and its sinister burden floated slowly to the roof tops below. Four more cages followed it within the next minute. The navigator closed the trap door, Pat gave the motor the gun and we were off to London.

London from the air! A spectacle not easily forgotten: a faery tracery of light against a background of black velvet! The metropolis, the brain, the heart and soul of the world's greatest empire!

After all, what could we hope to accomplish against the might of Britain? And how much less than that could we accomplish against Britain combined with the rest of the white world? Still, Britain hadn't always been big, and had there not been a time when Africa was powerful and looked down upon puny European countries? If this had happened before, could it not happen now? And yet how inadequate were our resources compared to those of England, France, Italy, Belgium, Portugal and Holland.

We were high above the British metropolis now. Pat circled over the densely populated poorer sections as indicated on her map. Again we opened the trap door and one by one sent the fifteen remaining cages floating with sinister leisureliness toward the earth.

I went back to my seat while Hudginson returned to his instruments.

Pat looked at me and I looked at her. We were both thinking of being separated again when only a couple of days before we had been wed. But Pat was a good trouper. Not a sign of her real feeling appeared on her face. She just looked at me and her eyes told everything.

We were moving off toward the north now. We both watched for the four mysterious red lights. The thickening fog made observation difficult. We were over the place now, cruising at 3,000 feet.

"I can't see anything," Pat shouted, "and I'm afraid to go any lower. This soup is awful." She looked over and smiled through her annoyance, one of those heartening smiles that sends men away to high adventure with singing hearts.

At last there they were: four tiny red dots just below us. Pat looked at me again with eyes that said, "Be careful." I got up, adjusted my parachute, and then leaning over gave my wife a parting kiss.

Hudginson opened the side door. We shook hands and I dived out head first. When I was clear of the ship, I pulled the cord and in a few seconds was floating gently earthward. The four red lights were a little to my left now and the breeze was carrying me still farther away. But there was nothing I could do about it.

Suppose I should miss them? Suppose something should happen before they could reach me? It was certainly not a pleasing prospect. England was spy crazy after the ruthless activities of our espionage. Every stranger was suspect.

I was only three or four hundred feet up now. The pattern of things below me was quite plain. Evidently, I was coming down on a golf links or an estate just outside of London, for not far away was a row of houses. I could see nothing of the four red dots. Would they be able to see me?

The damp earth rushed up to meet me and I was dragged several feet before I could get out my knife and cut myself loose. A little stunned, I stood up, stretched and looked about me. I was definitely and absolutely alone in a field as still as a grave at midnight.

It was a little more than I had bargained for. After all, I had no relish for a firing squad, and how could I explain my presence in England without a passport or landing permit?

I decided finally to walk toward the row of houses and get on a main road where it might be easier for our men to find me. To think was to act. At one o'clock in the morning in a spy-mad country one is apt to get the jitters.

I had walked not more than a hundred feet toward the row of houses, feeling my way through the thick grass, when I heard a sudden movement just a few feet to my right. I stopped dead still, my heart thumping like a trip hammer, my automatic pistol gripped in my hand.

There was no sound. Again I proceeded, more cautiously this time, trying to peer through the Stygian darkness. Again came the sound, closer now. It was unmistakable.

I could feel my hair rising. Here I was in a strange country, one o'clock in the morning, ignorant of my whereabouts except in a very general way, and being stalked by someone.

I decided to wait and watch. Accustomed now to the blackness, I was able to discern objects a few feet away. I turned around and around, pistol gripped tensely, awaiting attack, from what direction I did not know.

In the distance to the south I could see the glow of the myriad lights of London. Although I knew that in that direction lay grave danger if unaccompanied by one of our agents, it seemed eminently inviting in comparison to this desolate heath.

Another sound. More definite: closer. I waited tensely, peering fearfully into the blackness. I thought I saw something blacker than the night moving along the ground. My heart leaped as I whirled and leveled my pistol.

Suddenly I was leaped upon from behind and knocked down by a heavy body, my pistol lost in the scuffle. Dazed by the impact, I threw up one arm. There was a low snarl, a guttural blood-curdling snarl that chilled the blood and conjured fearful emotions. The arm I had lifted to ward off a blow was seized by a gigantic mouth with terrible teeth. I felt a huge paw at the back of my neck. Surely no dog in the world was so large or strong. What manner of beast could it be?

10

*Slater Arrives in London on Special Mission
for Belsidus*

I struggled but in vain; and yet the beast made no effort to touch me beyond holding me down to the ground. Then out of the Stygian darkness came a peculiar two-toned whistle, repeated twice. The beast stiffened to attention at the first sound. At the second he released my arm, jumped off my back and stood to one side. Again the peculiar whistle sounded, nearer this time. The strange animal now emitted a crying sound similar to that of a small woman in distress. I stood rooted to the ground, fascinated by this singular experience, but not without the foresight to get out my pistol for use in case the beast decided to attack again.

Once more the peculiar whistle sounded. It was quite near now. I looked expectantly, pistol ready, in the direction from which it came. Again the beast cried in reply, and a moment later two figures emerged from the gloom to my left and were immediately beside me. I pointed my gun and stepped backward. "Get away or I'll shoot," I threatened.

"Kakata," muttered the other.

"Kakata!" I replied joyfully, as I recognized the password. "I was looking for you fellows. I didn't know what happened."

"We saw you come down," said the taller of the two, "but then lost you in the darkness. We had to send Mira to find you." His voice was definitely English.

"Mira? Who is Mira?"

"Mira is our leopard over there," he said, turning toward the beast now standing at a respectful distance. "Come here, Mira."

The big beast padded over close to where we were standing. The man turned a flashlight on her. She was a magnificent animal, entirely black and with as wicked an expression as I've ever seen on a beast.

"Let's get on," growled the smaller of the two men.

"Righto," said the other.

He snapped on his flashlight, turned its beam toward the row of houses, made several mysterious signals, and shut it off.

"Come on, we'll go this way." With one of my strange companions on either side and the black beast following close behind, we strode along over the field toward the houses.

Finally we reached a paved road. The tall man signaled a halt. We had not long to wait. Two headlights leapt out of the darkness and raced toward us. In another moment a huge black limousine jerked to a stop beside us.

"Get in, Mr. Slater," the short man invited.

I stepped in and they followed me. The black leopard jumped in the seat next to the chauffeur. The big car started and moved with high speed toward the metropolis. As we entered the city we slowed down considerably and were soon barely creeping through the crooked old streets of a miserable tenement section. Billows of fog shrouded the sorry buildings bordering the stinking streets while bleary lamps blinked feebly through the murk.

I could see my two companions now for the first time. One was tall, raw-boned and grim. The shorter man had a little more flesh on him but also had the thin bony features of the London Cockney. Both were very light mulattoes and were well dressed. As we lurched past a flickering street lamp again, the little fellow caught me studying him. He smiled faintly.

182

"Aye, Mister Slater," he said, "I guess you find all this rather mysterious: parachuting, trained leopards and the like."

"It's a bit out of the ordinary," I conceded, "but I've got to the point where nothing the Black Internationale does is very surprising."

"My name's Stradford," he said, and then gesturing toward his associate, "and this lad's Wilbern. We've heard a lot about you, Mister Slater, and all the other great men surrounding Dr. Belsidus. Miss Gaskin has told us much."

Martha Gaskin! The mention of the name conjured up the vision of the pretty blonde, hopelessly in love with Dr. Belsidus, who headed his European espionage corps. It was she who had been responsible for the terroristic acts that had precipitated the short-lived European war. What was she planning now? And what part was I supposed to play?

We were getting downtown. More people, more lights, more traffic. The big car rounded a sharp corner into a side street and after proceeding a few yards turned into a driveway leading to a warehouse. The limousine kept on toward the closed door. As we neared it, the door suddenly opened from top and bottom like a mouth and we crept inside. The door closed with a thud behind us. Lights turned on, brilliantly illuminating a large garage. There were four other cars in the place and equipment for all sorts of emergency repairs.

Stradford and Wilbern got out and I followed. The leopard jumped down from the front seat. Then for the first time I noticed the chauffeur was a black giant close to seven feet tall, a powerful man strong enough to fell an ox with his fist. Cut into his forehead just above the bridge of his long cruel nose were three vertical African caste marks. He reminded me very much of Jim, the gigantic, dumb chauffeur-valet of Dr. Belsidus.

Wilbern, as tall as he was, just came to the chauffeur's shoulder. He and Stradford grinned when they noticed the awe with which I was looking at the giant.

"That's K'bamgi, Mister Slater. K'bamgi, shake hands with Mister Carl Slater."

The giant extended his ham-like paw, which enveloped mine like a blanket. His wicked little eyes were dancing with pleasure.

"K'bamgi is glad. K'bamgi has heard all," he boomed. "K'bamgi is glad, indeed." He bowed low and then straightened like a ramrod.

"Come on," growled Wilbern, his eyelids half drooping over hazel eyes. "She's waiting for us."

183

He led the way to the back of the garage where a brick wall barred the way. He walked to the wall and pressed against it. The brick touched by his hand sank inward about an inch. To our left a square section of the floor turned upright, revealing a flight of metal stairs. The short man motioned to me to descend. They followed: Wilbern, Stradford, Mira and K'bamgi, in that order behind me. As I reached the floor below I looked back in time to see the trap door above fall into place.

"We've always got to take the utmost precautions," said Stradford, noticing my glance. "London is a nest of spies, informers and police. We take nothing for granted."

The giant Negro nodded his head affirmatively. Wilbern simply grunted, and handed me the key to a small iron door. I walked to it and turned the key. The door opened easily enough but there was another door beyond it, a door of armor steel, shining dull gray in the dim light of the lone electric light bulb. I pulled the knob but the door wouldn't budge.

I looked back at the others. With the exception of the big slinky black cat, they all were enjoying my discomfiture.

"You see, Mister Slater," said Stradford proudly, "we have taken the utmost precautions." Then he brought a little pipe about four inches long out of his inside coat pocket. It would be better to describe it as a twin pipe because there were really two pipes fastened together but with a single mouthpiece. He put it to his mouth and blew. Again I heard the peculiar two-toned whistle that had called Mira away from me out in the suburbs. And again Mira emitted that crying sound similar to a small woman in distress.

There was a rattle of bolts from the other side of the door and in a moment it opened slowly outward. One by one we stepped inside a narrow, dimly lighted hall carpeted with a heavy-pile runner. Black velvet drapes hung from ceiling to floor, killing every superfluous sound. The hall was all of 15 feet long and about five feet wide. Halfway was a small table at which sat a tow-headed little man: a hunchbacked mulatto sitting before a wide instrument board with radio earphones clamped over his misshapen head.

As we entered the hallway, I saw him press a button. The steel door behind us closed with a bang. He then inserted a plug in a hole. A light sprang up.

"They have come," I heard him mumble into the receiver on his chest. He listened to the voice on the other end, nodding his head up and down, then pulled out the plug. Now he turned his narrow yellow face to us and grinned an expanse of discolored fangs.

"You may enter," he said, bowing to me. "The others are waiting."

He pressed a button. The black velvet drapes at the other end of the hall parted and a heavy vault-like steel door slowly opened outward.

11

▲▲▲▲▲▲▲▲▲▲▲▲▲▲▲▲▲▲▲▲

Martha Gaskin Demonstrates How Spies
Are Dealt with as Carl Attends Secret Meeting;
Dr. Belsidus Speaks from Africa

"Wait," ordered Wilbern, pulling me back. "Put this on."

He thrust a black mask into my hand. I fastened it on, and then was permitted to enter the chamber beyond. I noticed that Stradford and K'bamgi were also masked. Mira, the leopard, brought up the rear.

The long rectangular chamber was completely hung with black velvet drapes and the same material obscured the ceiling. At the far end was a life-size painting of Dr. Belsidus in surgeon's uniform with scalpel in hand. Down the center of the room was a long mahogany table at which sat 20 masked men, 10 on each side. At the far end sat Martha Gaskin, pretty as ever and without a mask, her golden hair in sharp contrast to the black background.

"Hello, Carl," she said, smiling. "Just sit anywhere. We've been waiting for you."

"Yes, Martha, I know. We got here as soon as we could. The boys had a time finding me out there in that miserable blackness. I don't suppose you people in London ever see either the sun or the stars."

"The fog is a great help sometimes, Carl," she replied, a significant tone in her voice. "I just don't know what we would do without the fog to help some of our operations."

All the time the others sitting around the long table looked in my direction but said nothing. Some toyed with pencils or fountain pens. Others sat with folded hands, waiting.

"Comrades," said Martha. "Carl Slater is now here and we can proceed." She picked up a communicating telephone and spoke into the receiver: "Ezekiel! We are almost ready."

She hung up the receiver and turned again to us. "Sit down," she said, indicating the vacant chairs. We took seats, all except K'bamgi, who took his post behind Martha's chair. I sat at the foot of the table.

She clapped her hands twice. From behind the drapes to the rear of her came a dark brownskin girl with a small box and a sheaf of papers. She was a tall, handsome girl with delicate features that spoke of royal blood and an air that betokened acquaintance with refinement and leisure.

"All right, Della," Martha directed.

The colored girl opened the box, which was revealed as a fingerprinting plate. She went to the first masked figure, sat the box before him and laid one of the sheets of paper on the edge of the table.

"Who are you?" she asked.

"I am Number One," he replied.

"And the password is . . . ?"

"Kakata."

"Very well. Place the fingers of your right hand on the inked surface and then place it here." She indicated the square on the paper. The masked figure obeyed her. She picked up the sheet and handed him the towel on her arm with which to wipe his hand. Then she passed on to the next person and so on around the table. Martha Gaskin was the only one she did not fingerprint.

In about ten minutes she was finished, departing as quietly as she came, and in the same direction.

Ten minutes more passed, during which the utmost silence obtained, except for the tap-tap of occasional pencils, pens and finger tips on the polished surface of the rich mahogany table.

At last Della returned, an implacably grim expression on her face. She handed a slip of paper to Martha Gaskin and then retired.

Martha read the slip in the midst of almost painful silence. Not even a pencil tapped now. She patted her blonde hair with one slender, delicately manicured hand. K'bamgi moved nonchalantly from behind her chair and sauntered along behind the masked figures on that side until he was about halfway. He was taut, as if about to spring. I saw Martha's right hand slip under the edge of the table. I watched the scene fascinated, curious, terrified.

Martha's right hand came back to rest on the edge of the table. She looked up now for the first time and smiled sweetly.

"Number Eighteen," she purred, her voice and expression suspiciously soft, "even I cannot leave this place unless permitted by Ezekiel, the little hunchback in the corridor. What chance, then, have you? Will you talk willingly and tell us what your masters know about us, or must we make you?"

At the mention of "Number Eighteen," K'bamgi had moved as stealthily as a cat to a position immediately behind the masked figure that had boldly called out his number to the beautiful Della a few minutes before.

The accused moved suddenly and his hand shot to his mouth, but K'bamgi was faster. His great hands closed about the man's wrist and twisted it cruelly until the small vial the hand held fell with a tinkle to the table.

The masked figure next to the culprit reached over and snatched off the black mask of the accused. Before us was revealed a young white man, ghostly pale. K'bamgi held the man's hands behind him with one of his tremendous paws and looked toward Martha for further instructions.

"Search him, Number Seventeen," she ordered.

Deft fingers expertly frisked the man, bringing forth a small pistol cleverly concealed in a secret pocket and three vials of poison.

"Are you ready to talk freely?" asked Martha.

"I have nothing to say," he muttered, and then closed up like a clam.

"Take him away, K'bamgi," she directed, "and make him talk."

"Ah, yes," chuckled K'bamgi, "I make him talk."

He yanked the young man out of his chair and hustled him through the drapes behind Martha in the direction the girl Della had gone.

"Now you may unmask," she said.

The unmasking revealed such an assortment of humanity as it would be difficult to find gathered in a chamber anywhere in the world. Some were black, others were varying shades from brown to white, and some were white. Again Martha telephoned to the hunchback in the hall: "We're ready now, Ezekiel."

187

There was a crackling of radio static, a buzzing and blurring. Then distinctly we heard the sound of a distant voice: "This is Kakata, Super–Short Wave. You may go ahead, London." Martha picked up a microphone from the table in front of her and began speaking.

"Gaskin talking. All well for Slater. Cargo safe everywhere. No planes reported down. We await the voice."

"Attention, London," came over the air through the concealed radio set. "The Voice talking. This is the Chief. Carl, remain with friends. More later. That is all."

"Well, that's once the Doctor had no orders," said Martha. "He must be in mighty good spirits in spite of the invasion."

"But what's the idea of dropping the rats over London?" asked Sam Wilbern. "What help will that be?"

Martha smiled grimly. "Dr. Belsidus is carrying the war to the white man and he is doing it in a new way. More people are killed during wars by cholera, spotted typhus and bubonic plague than are destroyed by bullets. Is that not so?"

"Sure, but I . . ." Wilbern wrinkled his brow.

"Remember," Martha went on, "each of those diseases is best transmitted by rats. Each one of those rats our planes dropped tonight is infested with one or the other of these dread diseases. Each plane, I am informed, carried 20 crates of rats with 160 odd to a crate. Eight hundred in Plymouth. 2,500 in London. How long do you think it will be before the plague sweeps all England? And mind, 50,000 of these agents of death roam European cities tonight."

There were swift intakes of breath as she spoke so calmly of the devilish warfare of Dr. Belsidus.

"But what about us?" asked Wilbern. "Won't we get it, too?"

"When it gets bad, we'll leave," she said, fixing him with her cold blue eyes, "but we'll not leave until our work is done. Do you understand, Sam Wilbern?"

12

▲▲▲▲▲▲▲▲▲▲▲▲▲▲▲▲▲▲▲▲▲▲▲▲

Martha Gaskin Reveals the First Step Black
Internationale's Espionage Group Will Make
to Attack Enemy by Way of "Back Door"

K'bamgi returned to his place behind Martha's chair. Della Crambull, the pretty brownskin girl, came out and took a seat near me.

"Who was he?" asked Martha without turning her head.

"Him Reginald Duncanson, British secret service."

"Did he talk?"

"Oh, yes," the black giant grinned cruelly and the vertical caste marks in his forehead came together. "Him talk plenty when we make."

"What do they know?"

Now the colored girl, Della, spoke up. "Very little, Martha. He was working on a personal hunch. He trailed Number Six here, he said."

Martha's blue eyes grew hard. "He must know more. How did he come into possession of the whistle? How did he know the password? He must tell us that. We must know at once. Use the acid. We must know. Too much is involved. It means our lives."

Della rose and disappeared beyond the velvet drapes. K'bamgi followed her.

"What is this about acid?" I whispered to the rat-faced Stradford, who sat next to me.

He grimaced faintly, then whispered: "A very corrosive acid is dropped on various tender parts of the body and permitted to eat its way to vital organs. If the man talks, the drops cease. If not, well . . ." He shrugged his shoulders and tapped gently on the smooth surface of the mahogany table, just the suggestion of a sardonic smile twisting one side of his face. My shudder must have been perceptible.

Was there no end to this cruelty, this ruthlessness, this cold and calculating killing? But then what omelet was ever made without breaking eggs? How had Africa been enslaved except through murder? Even at the moment this clean-cut Englishman was being tortured to death, countless thousands of black men and women in Africa were nursing the wounds inflicted upon them by ruthless white masters before the genius of Dr. Belsidus had freed our race.

"Now," said Martha, "let's get down to business. Our plan to involve Europe in war was a success, as you all only too well know, but self-interest, the fear of mutual destruction, brought on an early armistice, and now, with white ships and armies converging on Africa, our whole program is imperiled.

"Dr. Belsidus is depending on us to attack from the rear, to demoralize and disorganize the enemy so that his whole program will be undermined and destroyed. He has approved our Plan Number One for England. You see, we cannot depend upon the plague alone. Some means of combatting it successfully may be found. Besides, it will take some weeks for it to get going to epidemic proportions. In the meantime we must strike an effective blow.

"That effective blow is Plan Number One." Her voice fell to a whisper.

"What is Plan Number One?" asked a handsome brownskin man in evening dress.

"It is without a doubt the most effective we could use," she said, "and is characteristic of Dr. Belsidus."

What new scheme was this from the brain of the Chief, I wondered? The man seemed to fairly sweat devilishness.

"In a way," continued Martha, "our civilization is like an inverted pyramid standing on its small end. The swarming billions get their goods from several million stores, but these stores get their goods from only about a half million factories. Of this half million factories scattered over the modern industrial world, less than 40,000 make industrial machinery which the other factories use. Of these 40,000 machine shops, less than 1,200 make the machine tools, the machines which make all other machines, including their own.

"Now imagine what would happen if some superhuman power were to destroy all the machine tools in the modern industrial world? And suppose we were prevented from making any more? We could not make automobiles, electrical devices, household conveniences, plumbing fixtures, railroad equipment, airplanes, steel ships, movies, no more machinery of any kind."

"And," interjected Stradford, "no more cannons, machine guns, rifles, pistols, nothing."

Martha nodded her blonde head. "Exactly, Jake. Now, of those 1,200 tool factories, 350 are in the United States, 150 are in Asia, 50 are in Australia, 25 in South America, 20 in Canada and the rest are in Europe. Of these 605 European tool factories, 300 are here in England."

"And all we got to do is destroy them?" a light brown man eagerly asked.

"Yes,"she continued, "if possible, but Dr. Belsidus's idea is that tool factories can be rather rapidly rebuilt, although it will naturally take time to build hundreds. But that would only be a matter of a few months in an emergency where the fate of the British Empire was at stake."

The velvet drapes parted behind her and Della and K'bamgi came out. The black giant took his position behind Martha while Della went to her seat. I saw K'bamgi lean down and whisper at length in the white woman's ear. Then he sauntered down the room. When he reached Number Six, a real black, evil-looking fellow, he suddenly grabbed the man's arms and, whipping out a pair of handcuffs, snapped them on the Negro's wrists.

It all happened so suddenly that the swift execution left us breathless.

"You see, Fancher," said Martha, looking straight at the man who cowered in his seat with the giant K'bamgi towering above him, "the young Englishman did talk. He told us everything. Understand? You let a pretty white woman get information from you that might mean the death of all of us, and you never got a cent for it. Now you are in for it, my man. Britain with all its might cannot save you. You must die, Fancher, a victim of your lust, but before you die you will talk. K'bamgi, see that Fancher talks, for we must know everything."

The giant grinned cruelly. "He will talk," he boomed, yanking the ashen-faced Negro from his chair and hustling him out of the room. This time Della did not go with K'bamgi.

"Now," said Martha, as if dismissing an unpleasant but not very important subject, "let us go on. Oh yes, I was saying that these 300 tool factories in England, these 300 key factories of British industrialism, could be rebuilt in a few months in an emergency. The World War showed us what can be done in speedy construction. Dr. Belsidus

191

realizes this. But he realizes also that it takes many years to produce a tool maker. There are 65,000 of these tool makers in Great Britain. At least 6,000 of these are key men. Remove them and the industry is severely handicapped. Remove the entire 65,000 and British industry is destroyed for a generation."

"And that means forever," growled hazel-eyed Sam Wilbern.

"Exactly, Sam," Martha went on. "We know the location of every single one of these key tool factories. Moreover, we know the name and address of every foreman, superintendent and manager. We must act at once. Our first job is to remove them. This must be accomplished before the week is out. We shall start with the men in direct charge of operations. There are only a few hundred of them. Della will give you whatever you need in the way of money and supplies. Wherever possible for safety's sake use only white assistants. You are to proceed carefully. Remember, the whole future of the African Empire depends upon it. Della, the lists, please."

The dark girl got up and disappeared into the other room. Almost immediately she returned with a big pile of typewritten sheets and began handing batches of 40 or 50 sheets to each operative. I looked at one of Sam Wilbern's sheets. On it was typed a long list of names with street address and city typed alongside each one. Opposite some few names were red stars.

"You will notice," Della explained, "that several names in your group are marked with red stars. They are to be removed first. K'bamgi will give you additional pistols with silencers and as many boxes of poisoned darts as you wish."

All eyes now turned to Martha for final word. "I have nothing to add," she said. "You know that if you fail, Africa may be lost. All over the white world our operatives are working on similar projects. See that you do your part. Dr. Belsidus will countenance no less."

As she finished speaking the steel door to the hallway opened and little hunchbacked Ezekiel shambled in like some grotesque nightmare, propelling his dwarfed and twisted body toward me, a yellow sheet of paper in his outstretched hand. "For you, Mister Slater," he said, "From the Chief."

I read the few words on the paper that made my heart skip a beat.

13

⧊⧊⧊⧊⧊⧊⧊⧊⧊⧊⧊⧊⧊⧊⧊⧊⧊⧊⧊⧊⧊⧊

Carl Ordered to Remain in London
and Expedite Execution of "Plan No. 1";
Martha Gaskin's Identity Revealed

"Remain as a personal representative," the message from Dr. Belsidus read, "and work with Gaskin. Your newspaper experience will come in handy. Expedite execution of Plan No. 1. Time is short. Situation critical. Speed absolutely essential. Ample funds transferred to Bank of England from New York. All planes safe."

What could I do here in London, unacquainted as I was with the city? Martha Gaskin knew far more than I about it. How could I help this woman who was an expert in espionage and terroristic tactics? I had not thought that I would have to remain in London. What of the plague which would soon be sweeping the city unless the calculations of Dr. Belsidus were all wrong? Would I ever see Pat again? I frowned involuntarily. Certainly the prospect was not a pleasing one. And yet, dead or alive, one had to go ahead. There was no backing down now even if I had wanted to do so.

I glanced up and caught Martha's keen gaze. I knew she was curious about the note, so I carried it to her. The others waited in silence.

The white woman looked up from the message, a thoughtful expression on her face.

"We shall have to change our plans somewhat," she announced to the gathering. "Mr. Slater, please come with me. You, too, Della, Jake and Sam. The others will wait here until we return."

She rose, and we followed her behind the black velvet drapes, through a door and into a small sitting room like thousands of others in apartment houses throughout the world. There were etchings on the walls, a radio, two easy chairs, a library table, an overstuffed couch and two small Chinese rugs. Martha waved us to seats.

Somewhere near at hand I could hear low groans. Suddenly there was a pitiful shriek. Then silence. I looked around uneasily. Martha, noting my perturbation, smiled indulgently.

"K'bamgi is making our friend Fancher do some talking," she observed, a sinister mocking in her tone. She lit a long Russian cigarette and leaned back on the couch, eyes half closed.

"We can't get rid of them quick enough by the usual methods," she snapped. "We've got to think of something else. These key men of British industry must die immediately."

"You can't eliminate six thousand people in a flash," I objected, "unless you're going to get them all in one place and gas them. Otherwise we'll have to do it through assassinations, as you originally planned."

The other three nodded their heads in agreement and waited for the white woman to speak.

"Well," she said finally, "why not get them all in one place?"

"That's impossible," snorted little Jake Stradford, contorting his little rat face.

"I thought we had agreed to drop that word," she rebuked. "Listen—"

For upwards of an hour she talked rapidly, outlining the most devilishly ingenious plan I have ever heard. We went over it in every detail, checking and re-checking, changing and altering until we had polished the scheme to what seemed perfection.

"It will cost an awful lot of money," observed Della.

"Yes," observed Martha enthusiastically, "but think of the results!"

When we returned to the conference room, Martha dismissed the agents with a warning to do nothing until further orders. As they were filing out of the room into the corridor beyond, K'bamgi came in.

"Well, what did Fancher have to say?" asked Martha looking up at the solemn black giant.

"Him talk when K'bamgi ask him," guffawed the savage, rubbing his sardonic countenance with a huge paw, evidently well satisfied with the results of his efforts. Then he leaned over and whispered to her earnestly. She nodded her golden head and the blood drained from her face.

"Number Six and Number Seventeen, wait," she cried, running out into the corridor to get the two men.

They came back hurriedly and she whispered to each one in turn. They nodded and hastened out.

194

When we were alone at last, except for Della, Jake, Sam, K'bamgi and the hunchback Ezekiel, I asked her what Fancher had revealed.

"He was crazy about a white girl," she explained. "I don't think he was really disloyal but he got to boasting as men will when they are drinking and with a girl who fascinates them. He cannot remember all he told her but admits he was indiscreet."

"What will you do with him?" I asked.

"K'bamgi done take care of him," said the giant. "He gone."

"Gone? Gone where?"

"Do you remember the acid bath we used at our first conference?" asked Martha, smiling sweetly.

"Oh, yes . . ." My memory flitted back to that horrible scene years before when a traitor had been dumped in a vat of acid that consumed him like paper in a flame.

"Well, we have one here, too," she observed, archly.

The others snickered diabolically.

I don't know how many hours I had been sleeping in one of the spacious underground bed chambers when I felt the tap of a clammy hand on my bare arm. I woke with a start and recoiled from the gnome-like face of Ezekiel.

"Day has broken," he announced. "Your tub and breakfast await you, sir."

Struck by the efficiency with which everything seemed to be run, I hurried through bath and a light breakfast. K'bamgi came in with underwear, a tweed suit, shirt, socks, cravat, shoes and overcoat, and while I dressed, he brought in a small trunk and a suitcase which he informed me were packed with other clothes.

"How did you get these things so quickly?" I asked.

"Ha! Black Internationale have everything. Tailor, laundry, everything . . ."

"In this building?"

"In many buildings. Black Internationale have great organization. Change face, change nose, change hair, change finger tips, do everything necessary."

He grinned broadly at my wonder and the vertical caste marks in his massive forehead came close together.

It was now around 10 o'clock in the morning. I went out into the little sitting room. Della and Martha, fully dressed, were awaiting me.

We made our way upstairs to the garage, K'bamgi in his chauffeur's uniform preceding us and blowing one of the peculiar whistles whose blast opened the way through steel doors.

He opened the door of the big black limousine and we piled in. Sam and Jake, looking very genteel in morning clothes, were already seated inside.

K'bamgi started the big car and drove toward the closed garage door. When we had almost reached it, the door flew open and we passed through. I looked about to see who had opened it, remembering a similar occurrence the night before, but we were the only persons in sight. Martha noted my puzzled expression and laughed.

"It's the photoelectric eye," she explained. "Whenever the tiny stream of light is broken either inside or outside, the door opens, but not otherwise. It is most important when you are being pursued. We have to be prepared for every eventuality."

"Where, Miss Gaskin?" asked K'bamgi.

"To the town house."

"Town house?!" I echoed.

"I neglected to tell you, Carl," she explained, "that socially in London I am the Countess Maritza Jerzi. It is very convenient when you want to hobnob with the British nobility and perhaps pick up some useful information. It will be helpful in carrying out Plan Number One, too."

"But how did you manage it?"

"Well," she said, "the Count was of an excellent Polish family but he didn't have a shilling to his name. He was fortune hunting and was glad to marry into what he thought was wealth. We had quite an elaborate wedding, really. Dukes, Barons, Counts, Princesses . . . Oh, everybody was there . . . But, alas, three weeks later he died!"

"How?" I asked, curious.

"Oh, he just died suddenly," she said, as the others guffawed.

14

∧∧∧∧∧∧∧∧∧∧∧∧∧∧∧∧∧∧∧∧∧∧∧∧

Martha, as Countess Jerzi, Completes Details for Completion of Black Internationale's "Plan No. 1"; Dread Disease Strikes in London

That day and the next two days were hectic, indeed. Martha, as Countess Jerzi, flitted around town, contacting the best people for the sponsorship of a great dance recital by Della Crambull, who had gained flattering notices for her dancing at the Palm Leaf Club. This was an exclusive Mayfair cabaret, owned by Martha, where the beautiful dark girl appeared twice nightly, at nine and eleven o'clock, supported by a troupe of African dancers, all in the pay of the Black Internationale.

In the meantime, I was kept busy as the press representative of the Countess, sending out numerous news releases to the metropolitan and provincial press accompanied by photographs and mats. On the second day we began mailing out the invitations to the 6,000 key technicians. These read as follows:

> The Countess Maritza Jerzi has the rare privilege of announcing an elaborate and exclusive dance recital by DELLA CRAMBULL, the incomparable African dancer of the Palm Leaf Club, supported by her native African dancers, in honor of the Master Technicians of Great Britain, whose genius and efficiency assure British world supremacy, Friday, January 7, at 8:30 p.m. The Great Delphane Hall, the London Symphony Orchestra. Please present invitation at door.
> CHAIRMAN: H.R.H. LORD DESBOROUGH.

Then followed a long list of distinguished sponsors, the cream of British nobility, several of whom were listed as speakers.

Coming at a time when British industrial, political, and military supremacy was threatened by ambitious rival powers, there was a generous response from those who realized all too well their debt to British technical genius. Names that loomed big in *Who's Who* lent the project its support. The gay Countess Jerzi was promising a series of such performances as a token of appreciation of the part played by science in British world supremacy.

What particularly amused us was the willingness of many wealthy persons to contribute substantial sums toward meeting the expense of bringing the technicians from all parts of England and Scotland to London free of charge. We had planned to bear the entire expense.

It was well that we had decided to launch our No. 1 immediately. On the morning of the third day after my arrival, the London papers reported:

RARE DISEASES STRIKE DOWN MANY

London physicians are puzzled and disturbed by the number of deaths from rare diseases in the past two days. Almost every hospital in the city is reporting a sudden increase in the number of cases of spotted typhus, cholera, yellow fever and smallpox in most virulent stages. There have been several deaths, and the medical profession has launched an investigation to determine the source of this alarming visitation. If the incidence of these diseases continues to increase, it will, say some doctors, be necessary to institute a quarantine in affected areas. At present, however, such a step is not considered necessary but medical authorities are not relaxing their vigilance.

We were just sitting down to breakfast in the stately dining room of the mansion on Berkeley Square at which Martha, as the Countess Jerzi, had had so many social triumphs.

K'bamgi entered the room dressed in his chauffeur's uniform. We nodded to the big black. He hurried to Martha's side, leaned over and whispered into her ear.

"Was it clean?" she asked aloud.

"It was as you wished," he replied, straightening up.

"Good," she exclaimed, visibly pleased. "There'll be no more interference with our plans now."

Della, Jake, Sam and I looked up curiously, expecting an explanation. K'bamgi left the room.

"What was it?" asked Della.

Martha leaned forward and lowered her voice to a whisper. "Six and Seventeen have reported. Sir Robert Von Humpstead is dead."

"The head of Scotland Yard?" asked Jake, awe and satisfaction struggling for supremacy.

"Exactly," said Martha, firmly. "Fancher talked to the English girl and she talked to Duncanson, who communicated his suspicions to Sir Robert Von Humpstead. He had little to go on but it is certain that he would have followed up Duncanson's absence. Nothing must interfere with our plans now. We're working against time as it is, what with the plague spreading."

"From them damn rats?" asked Sam, in a voice indicating that he knew the affirmative answer.

"Yes," observed Della, "and it's going to spread like everything. They may quarantine the town in a couple of days when they get real panicky."

"Aye, that they will," agreed Jake, "and then what a time we'd have getting away."

"Shut up," snapped Martha. "We'll all be cleared out before then. I hope." She was irritable under the terrific strain as, indeed, were all of us. There were a thousand and one angles to Plan No. 1.

The rest of the day I stayed close to the telephone in Martha's town house receiving reports from all parts of England, giving directions for the smashing conclusion of Plan No. 1.

By three o'clock the entire group of Black Internationale operatives had received their final instructions and were at their stations wherever there was a key machine shop in England and Scotland. It was white men who were to do the actual work of destruction. It was our black agents who directed them.

At four o'clock Ezekiel, the hunchback, telephoned that the stratosphere planes had left Fez.

Shortly afterward I heard from Jake and Sam that all preparations had been completed for the dance recital at Great Delphane Hall.

I met with the gentlemen of the press for the Countess Jerzi in her drawing room. Martha was too busy checking on final arrangements to see them.

When we all gathered at the dinner that evening, an air of suppressed excitement was in the atmosphere. I am sure none of us ate very much. Della seemed the most composed of all. The white woman was the most jittery. This surprised me because Martha had always been so calm. But then, when before had we launched upon such an ambitious project?

She looked at her wrist watch at 7:30, and then glanced around the table. There were Della, Jake, Sam, K'bamgi and me.

"K'bamgi," she began, "you will drive us to the hall immediately. That will take 15 minutes on the outside. You will immediately come back here and burn everything that might be incriminating in the fireplace. You will then go to the rendezvous and get Ezekiel. He has his instructions to destroy the place when he leaves.

"Jake, have you and Sam attended to everything? There mustn't be any mistakes tonight, you know."

"It's perfect," he assured her. "If we can keep the doors closed five minutes we'll be successful."

"Good," she exclaimed. "Now, remember, when the signal is given, Jake and Sam will let loose with everything they have, then immediately go to the roof. I will leave my box exactly five minutes before and go to the roof to await. Della, when your buzzer sounds, you join me. They've already taken your clothing to the roof and you can change in a minute. Carl, you will stay at the periscope as long as you safely can do so.

"K'bamgi, you and Ezekiel motor immediately to our country place as soon as the rendezvous is destroyed."

"And what of our operatives?" I interposed. Were they to be left to their fate?

"They have their orders to assemble at the country place at midnight."

"And their white assistants . . . ?"

"They'll have to do the best they can," she snapped. "We can't save everybody."

She rose and along with the rest of us went out to the long black limousine. In a moment we were away and threading through the fog-bound traffic, to carry out the most astonishing and diabolical plot man has yet conceived.

15

▲◣▲◣▲◣▲◣▲◣▲◣▲◣▲◣▲◣▲◣▲◣▲◣▲◣▲◣▲◣

Plan No. 1 Works as 15,000 People Die in Delphane
Hall; London Fog Closes Down to Trap Martha
and Carl as Plane Crashes

K'bamgi let us out at the stage entrance of the Great Delphane Hall and immediately sped away. We went immediately to Della's dressing room. It was exactly seven-forty-five.

"Now," Martha reminded Jake and Sam, "as soon as I leave my box you are to go to work. Have you arranged for the front doors?"

Sam nodded. "Yes, we'll have them barred right after the bell for the second act."

"Good," she said, "the police have been instructed to let no one in or out after that time. We've got clear sailing."

"And I've told my troupe," said Della, "to go immediately to the roof as soon as the curtain falls on the first act."

"Then we understand everything perfectly," Martha remarked. "Take your posts."

Jake, Sam and I left and went downstairs. In the basement was the giant fan that blew fresh warm air into the vast auditorium. Nearby were several huge steel drums attached to a pipe which ended in front of the fan and could be turned on and off. Sam demonstrated how it worked while we stood by. Then I went to another part of the basement nearby, from where I could view the audience through a periscope.

It was exactly 8 o'clock but already the auditorium was half filled. White shirt fronts and studs gleamed out of the semi-darkness. Martha was in a front box with Lord Desborough, Lady Desborough and several other nobles. She was fascinating in shimmering white, nodding and smiling graciously, an accomplished coquette. It was a marvel how she could appear so nonchalant at the verge of such a terrible crime.

At 8:15, the London Symphony Orchestra filed in. At 8:25 Roberto Cacceli, the conductor walked in hurriedly, bowed gracefully to the deafening applause. At 8:30 he raised his baton for the opening bars of the Congo Ballet overture. The lights dimmed and the house was in darkness. At 8:35 the curtain was raised on the West African village scene and the great ballet began.

I could see nothing of this from my periscopic outpost, but the generous applause indicated that it was being well received.

Finally, after almost an hour the final curtain dropped on the first act and the last strains of the exotic music died. The lights sprang up, followed by a great buzzing of voices as the multitude rose to stretch legs and go to the salon.

The 15-minute intermission was scarcely half over when the seats began filling again with the talkative audience. Having a good opportunity to count them now, I estimated the crowd at no less than 15,000. There was no doubt that the technical brains of England were assembled and that everybody was pleased with what they had seen.

How little they knew about their immediate future! Not a soul there suspected he was catching his last glimpse of earthly joys.

Three more minutes and the orchestra would begin the overture for the second and last act. The musicians were already taking their places.

Suddenly I heard in the distance a dull boom. I knew the hunchback Ezekiel had destroyed the secret underground chambers of the Black Internationale. How much had been plotted there beneath the streets of London: bombings, arson, assassinations, espionage, every fiendish scheme for the overthrow of white supremacy had been mapped there with devilish cunning and carried out with consummate skill. Only one more plot awaited completion before our work would be done. . . .

I kept my eyes glued to the periscope. At 9:30 Conductor Cacceli tapped with his baton and the lights dimmed. I saw Martha gracefully rise and excuse herself, and hurry backstage. In the pause before the crash of music I heard very faintly the hiss of escaping gas. I hurriedly donned my gas mask. This was not a gas to take chances with. Studious brown Sam Hamilton, the Black Internationale chemist-in-chief, had invented it. Odorless and colorless, heavy and lethal, it surpassed anything the white chemists had been able to produce for speedy asphyxiation. One died from it with never a suspicion that anything was amiss.

The overture was scheduled for five minutes. One minute passed and I noticed several people wiping their faces. Two minutes passed and during a pause in the music I could hear the hum of the great fan as it speeded the vapor of death. Three minutes passed. A number of people slumped forward in their seats. As Conductor Cacceli lifted his baton he fell forward, prostrate. The musicians rose panic-stricken, but one by one they fell back into their seats or to the floor. One or two gained the door under the stage but that was securely barred, in accordance with our plan. There was screaming and running about.

Four minutes passed. There were a few faint shouts, mostly from the balconies, but the majority of the audience sat lifeless. The place was still in the darkness. It was all too tragically evident that Plan No. 1 had been a success.

It was time for me to go. I noticed that Jake and Sam had preceded me. I raced up the iron staircase and tapped on the penthouse door, which was immediately pulled open. I stepped out on the roof and took off my mask. The fresh air smelled mighty good.

In the center of the roof stood an autogiro, or windmill plane, into which the dancing troupe was piling. Soon the door slammed shut and with a short run the autogiro rose almost straight up and disappeared in the fog.

It had scarcely gone when another autogiro landed and took off with Della and the remainder of the dancers. This plane also threshed away into the foggy darkness.

We waited five minutes. I was getting nervous. Suppose someone should break into the hall and discover that vast concourse of people asleep for eternity. The police would search the roof as a matter of course. The others were as nervous as I.

"Why doesn't he come?" Martha complained. "I told him to be here at 9:40 sharp and to cruise overhead until the other planes had cleared."

"I hope nothing's happened, lady," said Jake, apprehensively, "or we'll be in the soup, sure."

"Aye," said Sam, "that we will, but I fancy we've at least an hour. If nobody breaks in and finds the mess."

The four of us paced back and forth. Down below in the streets we could hear the motor horns and see the lights of the long line of parked cars. Several times the whistle of the traffic policeman at the intersection floated up to us through the thick fog. I thought about Pat and wondered would I ever see her again; thought about Harlem and the good times I'd had there; thought about Dr. Belsidus and the future of Africa. It was Martha's voice that brought me back to the present.

"I hear it!" she cried, in ecstatic relief.

Sure enough, there was the sound of an airplane motor in the distance. It came nearer every second, but we could see nothing through the opaque fog. The plane circled around and around.

"He can't see the roof," cried Jake. "That's the trouble. I'll get in the center and turn on my flashlight."

Suiting action to word, Jake ran to the center of the broad roof and turned the beam of the flashlight into the sky. The autogiro was still circling around. The pilot still could not see where to land. Every second the fog was getting thicker.

"We're done for, mates, if he can't land," mumbled Sam. "It's 9:45 now. Somebody'll smell a rat pretty soon and then we'll be done for, I'm tellin' you."

The autogiro settled again, lower this time, yet we were unable to see it as, doubtless, he was unable to see us. Lower and lower he came, circling around and around in our vicinity.

We felt once more buoyant as rescue seemed near. Yet the inexorable minutes ticked their way into eternity and still we remained on that broad roof. The autogiro came lower. It was sure to land now. The sound of the motor was almost deafening.

It came lower. We could see it at last! It was scarcely 20 yards above our heads and settling rapidly. As it neared, my spirits rose. After all, we were going to get away with it. We moved over to the edge of the roof so as not to be struck by the plane in landing. The motor died.

Suddenly a gust of air from the street cavern below shot up and caught the plane at the edge of the roof. It side-slipped, dipped drunkenly and plunged into the street below where it struck with a resounding crash.

I looked at my watch and I noticed that my hand was shaking. It was 9:50. Rescue was now out the question, it seemed. We all looked at each other wondering what we should do next.

16

▲▲▲▲▲▲▲▲▲▲▲▲▲▲▲▲▲▲▲▲▲▲▲

Martha and Aides Escape from London after
Asphyxiation of Vast Assemblage, But Are
Stopped, Arrested on Highway

We looked at each other hopelessly. We had told the other autogiro pilots NOT to return. Would they disobey our orders when we
didn't show up? And if they returned, would they return soon
enough? At any time now the terrible tragedy in the great hall below
might be discovered. There are always slips like that. Once discovered,
how could we hope to escape from London? We no longer had a secret
place in which to hide, either, even if we got off the roof.

"Let's get out of this!" snapped Martha. "They won't get back in time,
even if they do return. We can't stay here and be caught like rats in a
trap. Come on!"

"Aye," Sam agreed, "let's get out of this."

"But how?"

"Down the fire escape," Martha directed. "Quick!"

Jake led the way. Fortunately, the fog remained dense. That was our
protection from prying eyes. Down we climbed, one, two, three, four
flights of slippery iron steps, until we were on the last platform above
the alley. We would have to reach ground by a weighted ladder. Scarcely twenty paces away stood a stalwart London bobby, his broad back
turned to us. Could we get down without detection?

Again Jake led the way. He stepped gingerly upon the rounds of the
ladder. It slowly began to swing to the ground. He began climbing
down. Martha followed him, gathering up the train of her evening
dress with her left hand. I came behind her and Sam brought up the
rear.

The end of the ladder was now not more than two feet from the
slimy cobblestones of the alley. Fortunately for us it had been well oiled
and not a squeak had come out of it. The big bobby still stood with his

back to us, with his hands clasped behind him looking out at the passing traffic.

One by one we stepped off the iron ladder and moved into the shadow. Sam was the last to step off. As he did so, the ladder, free of his weight, swung easily upward and struck against the lower platform of the fire escape with a resounding bang.

We shrank against the wall in the deep shadows, but Sam wasn't fast enough. The bobby turned around as if on a pivot and saw him.

" 'Oo's there!" he challenged, walking back in our direction. "Come out of there. Hi saw ye."

We stood perfectly still as he approached us. A chill of apprehension possessed me. Had we fulfilled so much of our mission only to be caught now? I saw Sam and Jake pull out their silencer-equipped pistols, but Martha restrained them with a gesture. She stepped out into the light.

"Officer," she called sweetly, "I wonder, would you help us."

He hesitated, looking past her at the three of us standing in the shadow, and then returning his gaze to her smiling countenance.

"Wot is it, Ma'am?" He was frankly suspicious, but with masculine chivalry ready to serve a lady in distress.

"We've got to get some costumes from the warehouse very quickly. These fellows are part of the troupe who are going with me to get them. In the rush of getting ready we forgot them. Will you get us a taxi and go with us to clear the traffic? We're in a terrific hurry."

"But Hi cawn't leave my post, Ma'am," he objected.

"Oh, please," she pleaded. "We must have those costumes for the last act. It won't take long." Then lowering her voice to almost a whisper, "There's five pounds in it for you, sergeant."

"Five quid?" He gasped in awe and avarice. " 'Ow long will hit take, Ma'am?" He looked behind him to see if he was observed.

"Just about fifteen minutes if we hurry. Just call a cab and tell the chauffeur to speed!"

"And 'oo are you, Ma'am?" There was still just a trace of suspicion in his voice.

"I am the Countess Maritza Jerzi!"

"O! Well, ma'am, w'y didn't ye tell me before? W'y yore givin' th' bloomin' affair, ain't ye?"

"Of course, officer."

206

"Come on!" he hurried out of the alley to the curb and whistled for a taxicab. Martha stayed close beside him. We followed, proud of the manner in which she had saved the situation but wondering how we would get rid of the fellow once we were out of the neighborhood.

We hurried into the old-fashioned taxi that trundled up to the curb. The four of us sat in the rear seat while the bobby stood on the running board. Martha gave an address about a half mile away. We pulled out from the curb and roared down the street, making traffic lights and traffic signs with ease.

Out of the bright-lights district, we turned down a side street and entered a mean quarter. Martha motioned for Sam's pistol, a gleaming black, stubby weapon with a silencer attached. We three Negroes watched her, fascinated. Then we turned a corner into a shabby, dimly lighted, crooked street and as the dense fog rolled about us, she brought up the pistol.

"Schicck! Schicck! Schicck!" Three shots that sounded like the breaking of the mainspring of a watch. The big officer plunged forward into the gutter with three holes drilled in the back of his head.

The chauffeur, surprised by the officer's fall and ignorant of its cause, stopped the taxicab with a lurch, got out and ran to the sprawling body. As he bent over, Martha's pistol rose again.

"Schicck! Schicck! Schicck!" Three lead bullets buried themselves in his back and he fell across the body of the bobby.

"Get out, Jake," she ordered, "and be sure they're dead. Sam, you drive. Take that fellow's cap."

The two men did as ordered. Sam took the chauffeur's cap and got in the front seat. Jake carefully but swiftly examined the bodies, then jumped back into the cab.

"They're stone dead," he reported.

"All right. Now drive to the estate."

The tall mulatto nodded and, starting the motor, tore through the narrow street. Rat-faced Jake Stradford leaned back in the seat, a diabolical smirk on his reddish yellow face.

"That was mighty neat, lass," he complimented Martha. "I thought we'd have to drill that bobby right in the alley. We'd probably not have got away with it, what with all them other flatfoots away."

"Well, we made it anyway," she sighed with relief. "Now if we can only get to the plane everything will be fine."

"How far is it?" I asked.

"About a hundred miles. We can make it in three hours at the outside, counting all stops for traffic. We ought to be there now."

"Righto," said Jake, lighting a cigarette, "because they'll sure send out the alarm when they discover what's happened at Delphane Hall. England will damn well be too small for us."

We were rushing through the suburbs now, making fifty miles an hour. Traffic was scarce and we were outstripping all there was. The miles reeled off and as we put more and more distance behind us, our hope rose high. Just a little farther and we'd be safe. I looked at my watch.

"What time is it?" Jake growled.

"Eleven o'clock exactly."

"Well, the dirt's out by now," he exclaimed. Then he shouted to Sam, "Speed her up, old man." Sam nodded.

We were going down a straight black stretch through the black and silent countryside, making about sixty miles an hour. Suddenly we spied a waving red light ahead and coming closer we noticed three constables standing in the middle of the road. They were pointing rifles. Sam slowed down upon Martha's advice.

"What's the matter, sergeant?" asked Martha in her most sugary tone. "We're in a dreadful hurry."

"I'll bet ye are," the sergeant growled grimly. And then, "Come on, pile out of there."

"What for, officer?"

"Ye're under arrest!"

17

Martha and Her Group Shoot Their Way Out
of Police Trap and Arrive at Rendezvous;
London Bombed as Return Air Trip Begins

"What do you mean . . . under arrest?" asked Martha, summoning her most haughty tone. "Are you mad? Come, stand aside, constable, I'm in a terrible hurry."

"Ye're under arrest, I tell ye," insisted the beefy police sergeant.

"For what?" she asked aloud, but under her breath she said, "shoot out!" Jake Stradford looked at me, his evil eyes almost closed.

"Orders, ma'am," boomed the officer. "We've got orders to let no cars pass, especially not this taxicab."

"But why not? I hired this cab in London to take me to my estate."

"Aye, but the driver of this cab, the man who owns it, was murdered a little while ago in London, and a policeman along with him. Ye're in the taxicab, so we'll have to hold ye 'til the Hinspector comes. Besides, there's been somethin' terrible happened in London."

"Oh, what happened?" asked Martha, seemingly all excited. At the same time she nudged both Jake and me.

"Lottsa people killed at Delphane Hall, ma'am. They think hit's spies done it. So we gotta arrest everyone on th' road that can't prove who they are. We gotta be sure. So you'll have to get out and come inside an' let th' Hinspector take a look at ye."

"Very well, Sergeant, if you insist, but it's a great nuisance." Then, turning to us, she said very loudly, "All right, gentlemen, I suppose we'll have to get out," then, softly, she told us, "Now!"

Martha opened the door of the taxi and held out her hand. The police sergeant took his rifle in one hand and extended the other to help her. At the same instant, Jake and I lifted our pistols simultaneously and drilled the other two constables. They yelled and sprawled forward. The sergeant turned in alarm. As he did so Jake, who was closest to him, reached his pistol past Martha and shot him in the side of his head.

At the hissing sound of the silencers, Sam Wilbern, who had kept his motor running, started the car and we went forward with a lurch, soon attaining a high speed. We breathed freer as we left the site of our narrow escape behind, but we were all visibly shaken by the ordeal. My respect for Martha grew. It was only her casual manner that had thrown the constables off their guard and enabled us to drop them.

Twenty minutes later we gratefully left the road and turned into the gate of an estate. For a couple of miles, we drove through dark and silent woods, and then we came into open country, a great closely cut meadow, elaborately flood-lighted like an airfield. Four huge planes stood in the center.

"Well, here we are," said Martha. "Drive up close to the planes, Sam."

The mulatto followed her directions. I immediately recognized the ships as our stratosphere planes. We piled out of the cab. The first person to meet us was K'bamgi. He nodded his huge head and grinned. Around us were the assembled Black Internationale secret agents, Della Crambull and her troupe of African dancers, and several other Negroes from the Liverpool and Glasgow offices.

Hunchbacked little Ezekiel Maxton shambled his way through the group, carrying a sheaf of papers in his yellow claw.

"Are we all here?" asked Martha.

"All except No. 4," reported the hunchback. "He got caught in the explosion in Manchester."

"What are the reports on the working of the plan?"

"Of the 300 key factories," continued Ezekiel, "we completely destroyed 243 by explosion, 32 were partially destroyed, and fires are still burning in 25."

"Very good, although not as good as it might have been," she commented. "Now what about London? Have you picked up anything out of the air?"

"They discovered the bodies in Delphane Hall just before eleven o'clock. A wireless was immediately broadcast to stop all cars coming from London. And then a second warning to especially watch for a taxicab with three men and a woman. I don't see how you got through, Miss Martha."

"We had to shoot our way out of a trap," said Martha, casually. "It was a narrow squeak. Now, what's the latest report of the plague?"

"Cases increased five-fold during the night. The same story from Plymouth, too. Reports from Europe also tell of the spread of the epidemic. Paris, Marseilles, Rome and Vienna have the most alarming conditions."

"Good! Another week and they'll be too busy to think about Africa." Then, turning to K'bamgi she asked, "K'bamgi, what about our headquarters and the town house?"

"K'bamgi and Ezekiel do good, good, very good job. Nothing left." He revealed his beautiful white teeth.

"Fine! Now we've got to get going. This place is too hot for us. Scotland Yard may be here any minute. Who's commanding those planes?"

People moved aside for the flight commander to come through for his orders. Since I knew most of the important officers in the air service, I looked with no little curiosity to see who had directed the flight of the squadron from Fez. As he came closer, my heart leaped as I recognized that it was not a man, but my Patricia.

I snatched her to me and we embraced hungrily while the others looked on, all smiles.

"You didn't expect me, did you?" she asked, laughing mischievously.

"No, darling," and I pressed her to my heart again.

"Hello, Martha," she said, recognizing the others at last.

"Hello, Pat. It's good to see you. Is everything ready to go?"

"We're all ready to take to the air. We filled our tanks while we were waiting for you to come. Another hour and we'd have been gone. We didn't know what had happened to you."

"We'd better go on, then."

"Okeh!"

I followed Pat to her plane and hopped in beside her. Martha, Della, Jake, Sam, Ezekiel, K'bamgi and two others piled into the big ship with us. Where on my last flight there had been crates of rats piled high, there were now ten seats fastened to the floor. In the back of the compartment were piled up a dozen heavy opaque glass cylinders about a foot in diameter and four feet long on a special rack. It was not until we were on our way that I found out what they were for.

We left the ground quickly. I was sitting next to Pat. Right in back of us, with his instruments on a small metal table, sat Tom Hudginson, the big, black, handsome fellow who had been navigator on the memorable flight from our secret Texas training camp to Freetown, Sierra Leone, on the evening of our conquest of Liberia.

The powerful engines sent us up fast. We circled high above the fog and the clouds until we were above the sprawling metropolis of London. The altimeter read 7,000 feet. The other three planes were to the right and left rear and straight behind to form a spearhead.

Pat turned around and signalled to Hudginson. He leaned down and turned a small wheel. The narrow trap door in the floor of the plane opened downward. He pulled a lever and one of the opaque glass cylinders slid out of its rack and into space. Another and another and another followed it in obedience to each pull of the lever until a dozen had hurtled downward.

A few seconds later a blinding light flared up from below. We watched the conflagration, fascinated. At short intervals of five or ten seconds the other planes successively dropped their death-dealing cylinders.

"Thermite!" yelled Pat above the roar of the engines. "Incendiary bombs!"

I learned later that Sam Hamilton had designed the glass cylinders especially for this secret bombing. The only sound they made was the crash when they struck the earth. This enabled attack planes to deposit their death loads, wrap the city in flames and escape before the source of the attack was accurately determined.

With a great section of London in flames, it was time to get fairly away. Pat turned the nose of her big plane upward and southward. The air grew rarer. We sealed the cabin and turned on the oxygen tanks as we flattened out at fifty thousand feet. The speedometer read 350 miles an hour.

Weary from the exciting events of the evening and not having slept since six o'clock the previous morning, I began to nod and was soon lost in slumber.

Suddenly I fell forward, banging my head against the shatterproof glass window. I woke up with a start, gazing wildly about me, fear clutching at my throat as I saw that we were descending at great speed and at a precarious angle in the midst of a heavy rainstorm that shook the ship with its intensity.

18

▲▲▲▲▲▲▲▲▲▲▲▲▲▲▲▲▲▲▲▲▲▲

Black Empire's Squadron Lands at Fez
Only to Hear That French Air Fleet Is Attacking;
Two Planes Lost in Air Raid; Pat's Ship Pursued

Visibility was nil as we hurtled straight down. The altimeter needle moved steadily from 50,000 feet to 40,000 to 30,000 to 20,000. Then at last we faintly observed the great airfield at Fez. Only a few pilot lights were on this time instead of the bright illuminations with which the field had been previously flooded. At 2,000 feet Pat straightened out and gave landing orders. One by one we descended through the driving rain to the muddy field, Pat talking to the ground all the time.

As we landed, switched off the motor and lifted the cowling, Commander Sandu hurried up in a motorcycle sidecar, with several big gasoline and oil trucks in his wake. The first streaks of dawn were showing in the East.

Sandu ran up, saluted Patricia and greeted the rest of us with his usual unfailing courtesy.

"I have the honor to report," he told her, "that the squadron is to leave as soon as the ships are refueled, by order of Dr. Belsidus. The other ships left here two hours ago for Kakata. I have brought breakfast for all of you. It will be wise to leave before daylight."

I noticed the haste with which the ground crews were going over the engines and refueling the planes. Every so often one of the subalterns would look anxiously at the sky. One man was seated at a huge, wheeled sound detector nearby. There was an air of suppressed excitement hovering over the place. Around the airport headquarters I noticed, as the dawn came, a battery of formidable anti-aircraft guns pointing menacingly into the still-dark skies. Ever and anon a huge searchlight tore a column of light through the driving rain.

"Are you expecting an attack?" I asked Commander Sandu.

"Yes, if it clears. They may even bomb us in this weather."

"Who?"

"The French. Four days ago they occupied Casablanca, and day before yesterday they bombed us, but we drove them off after quite a dog fight. We got two of their bombers but they got one of our pursuit planes. We're expecting them to attack again at any time. That's why you must leave as quickly as you can. We had more planes than they had yesterday, so they didn't get a chance to bomb us, but our spies in Algiers and Tunis report the entire North African French air fleet will visit us either today or tomorrow. It won't be safe here after sunrise."

"Suppose they destroy the field, what then?"

"We'll put up the best fight we can, of course. But if they are too strong for us, we'll go underground."

"Underground? You mean you have an underground hangar like the one at Ziggeta?"

"Exactly. We can put every plane underground in five minutes. That will save a lot of ships but it won't give us mastery of the air."

"And without controlling the air," Pat added, "we can't control anything, and it will be only a matter of time before we'll be driven back into the jungle like the pygmies."

We fell silent, reflecting gloomily upon this possibility. To have accomplished so much and then have to accept defeat was maddening.

A black non-commissioned officer strode up to Sandu and saluted.

"All ready, sir," he said, and retired.

Sandu looked at the rapidly lightening sky and pulled nervously at his cigarette. The rain had lessened considerably and seemed about to stop altogether. Already the motors of the three other stratosphere planes were thundering. We shook hands with Sandu and went inside to start the last leg of our journey to Kakata, the Imperial capital.

The first plane raced across the field and after a run of half the length took to the air. The other two planes followed. We were just starting our run when all hell broke loose.

Out of the north swooped squadron after squadron of big French bombers at 2,000 feet. Above them raced a cloud of fast little pursuit planes. Sirens screamed. Anti-aircraft guns crashed.

Boom! A geyser of earth shot up in the center of the field and instantaneously a great chasm loomed. Another and another and another.

The airdrome collapsed like a house of cards, a great sheet of flame shooting out as gasoline tanks exploded.

I was proud of Pat in that critical moment. The yawning holes across the airfield made it impossible for us to complete our run. Taking in the situation at a glance, she turned the big plane completely around and ran back the other way. I wondered at the manoeuver because it seemed that any place on that field was dangerous. But there I was wrong.

As we sped along, a strip of earth much wider than our plane opened up as if by command, revealing a wide ramp. Down we went, deeper, deeper, ever deeper into the earth. The earth closed behind us. We finally came to a level, cemented subterranean field about 100 feet underground. Here there were several large and small planes.

Pat came to a halt, cut off the motor, and we all piled out. Far above us we could hear ever so faintly the detonation of the big aerial bombs far overhead.

"My!" exclaimed Martha. "That was close."

"Aye," said big Sam Wilbern, "and that it was."

It was a new experience for him and Jake Stradford, for Della Crambull and little Ezekiel, but the black giant K'bamgi had gone through worse during the world war.

While we were discussing what we should do, a telephone bell rang somewhere. After running around a bit in the dimly lighted cellar, we found the instrument over near the wall. Pat answered it. "Yes, we're safe, Sandu, but what of the others? Did they get away? . . . Oh! Too bad." She turned away from the telephone to speak to us: "They downed two of our ships. The other, being the first off the ground, was able to reach the safety of the stratosphere, I hope." Turning again to the mouthpiece, she said: "Tell us as soon as they are gone."

From a nearby periscope I got a view of the field above. The French had certainly made a thorough job of bombing. Every building was razed and the airfield was pitted with shell holes. It was deserted except for the anti-aircraft guns and their crews.

But now an unusual thing happened. Nearby, great motorized snow shovels came crawling up ramps out of the earth. There were a half dozen in all, followed by two steam rollers. The shovels quickly pushed the dirt back into the shell holes and the rollers followed to level it all down. In less than fifteen minutes there was a straight runway down the field.

We received the signal to come out. Our ramp was lowered. Our engine hummed and we ran up to the field. Sandu, standing on the sideline, waved as we passed.

After a good half-mile run we took the air and promptly curved southward, gaining altitude momentarily. Pat had no intention of being caught as the other ships had. Up we went. At 2,000 feet we broke through the cloud belt into the sunny sky. We all felt considerably easier. Pat telephoned Sandu that we were safe and on our way. Hudginson checked our direction.

We had climbed 5,000 feet and were going higher when Hudginson came forward and, touching Pat on the shoulder, pointed to our left rear. There, less than a mile away, were six pursuit planes bearing down rapidly upon us. Probably they had lain in wait above the clouds for just such an opportunity as this.

K'bamgi ran to one of the two machine guns, and Jake Stradford rushed to the other. Hudginson worked like mad radioing Fez, Kakata and nearby airfields of our predicament. No ship of our size could possibly hold out against these mosquito-like pursuit planes, which made as much speed at low levels as we did in the stratosphere.

On they came. Up we went. They could only follow us to a certain height, but would they get to us before we attained that height? Already they were eating up the space between us. Soon their machine guns would be strafing us fore and aft. One such plane we might fight. To drive off six was out of the question.

I looked over at Pat. She was grim as I had ever seen her. The others watched in terrible fascination as destruction approached.

19

Black Internationale Plane Shot Down in Flames
Following Cat and Dog Fight over Fez; Pat and
Carl Forced to "Bail Out" in Parachutes

Now we could hear the rattle of the machine guns as K'bamgi and Stradford bent to their work. The giant black was in his element. Cap off and sleeves rolled up, he leaned over, squinting along the barrel of the machine gun, pouring a steady stream of bullets behind us. On the other side of the plane Stradford was doing the same.

The pursuers came on. A minute before they had been mere pin-heads, but now they were quite close. Pat sent the nose of our ship upward at a steeper angle. The altimeter read 10,900 feet. The super-charger was put to work to aid our climb.

I went back to help with the ammunition. The two machine guns were eating it up. But how long could we last? What would happen when we had to change guns when the present barrels were worn out?

On came the pursuers, slower now as they struggled to make the altitude. Big, raw-boned Sam Wilbern, grim as an executioner, got out a sub-machine gun and took my seat next to Pat in order to deal with anything that attacked us from in front.

The pursuers were less than 400 yards behind now but on a considerably lower level. They came up shooting. A row of neat bullet holes appeared in the door. One of the African dancers slumped forward with the blood gushing out of his mouth. One of the mulatto secret agents fell into the aisle, a neat hole drilled in his head.

"Parachutes," yelled Tom Hudginson, hitching his own on his back. The others followed his example. There were a score of holes that had appeared in the floor and the walls of the plane.

The gnat-like pursuit planes were circling us now. K'bamgi swung his gun in a wide arc, spraying death as the weapon turned. The leading plane burst into flames and with a sickening lurch to one side slipped down, down, down below the cloud belt to certain death below.

We were climbing higher and higher. The little planes followed relentlessly. K'bamgi and Jake swept the sky in unison. Another plane went down, over and over, its pilot fortunate enough to get loose with his parachute.

The other four planes closed in desperately. It was now or never and they knew it. We were up over 15,000 feet and already the air was becoming difficult to breathe. They wouldn't be able to follow us much longer. Wary now of the devastating fire from the tail of our ship, the four pursuers divided their forces, two attacking on each side.

Bullet holes appeared like magic in the walls, in the floor, in the wings. We gave as good as we received, but four of our crew were dead or mortally wounded.

Pat seemed to bear a charmed life. The windows around her had been struck several times but the gas tanks, oil lines and engines were so far intact.

Hudginson handed around oxygen helmets as the numerous bullet holes made our big oxygen tank ineffective despite the fact that the plane was sealed.

Now the pursuing planes were falling behind as we surpassed them in our ability to climb. Converging in formation, they made one final effort to down us. Through a glass I could see that their pilots had also donned oxygen helmets. That was discouraging, even though it was obvious that they could not follow us much longer. We were up at 19,000 feet.

Suddenly, dropping far below us, the four converged their fire from underneath. Sam Wilbern, who was leaning far out the front window firing at them, dropped his gun and pitched forward. In the rear Jake Stradford's little rat-like face was grim in death. Handsome Della, now grotesque in oxygen mask, grabbed his gun to carry on. K'bamgi, shooting through the trap door in the floor, clasped his stomach, his weapon hurtled to earth and he toppled out behind it.

Grimly, Tom Hudginson dragged the other bodies to the trap door and cast them out. Considerably lightened, the plane climbed inexorably upward.

Della and I poured our last belt of cartridges into the machine guns and sprayed our pursuers with one last desperate volley. Coming up head-on, they made a very small target.

Then, one of them stalled, fell backward, and slipped far, far, down into the sea of clouds, to the earth below.

Only three left now. Della and I grinned at each other. There was some hope perhaps.

Then another burst from the converged machine guns below perforated the plane at all angles.

The big ship lurched sickeningly. The blood was streaming from underneath Pat's helmet. Hudginson, rushing forward, caught her as she swayed to one side. I was right behind him. He handed her to me and took the controls.

"Jump!" he screamed. "I'll follow!"

Della fired the last of her cartridges. I signalled to her to go first. With great courage she dived out of the trap door and fell like a plummet.

But her courage was matched by Pat's. She tried to smile as I stuffed a piece of gauze under her helmet. Hudginson was shouting for us to jump. But the problem was not easy. I wasn't sure that Pat could remain conscious long enough to pull the cord of her parachute. No, I couldn't chance that.

There was no time to ponder. Another burst from the planes below might finish all of us. They were falling behind us but not far enough to enable us to escape. Besides, the bullets had perforated our tanks.

I held Pat firmly in my arms and closing my eyes jumped with her into emptiness.

We shot down, turning over and over. As we passed our relentless pursuers, a bullet tore through my shirt sleeve.

Down we went, with me clutching desperately to my beloved and her holding to me as best she could.

I had wanted to pull our cords as soon as we were free of the ship but that would have made us a clear target. How long should I wait? One's brain works with amazing clarity and speed when one is dropping like a meteor toward the earth.

At last the clouds! Holding on tight with my left hand, I managed to reach over and pull Pat's cord. My heart sank for a breathless second. The pilot parachute checked our fall. I let loose my embrace and prayed that God would protect her—my first prayer in a long time, perhaps my first since I had joined the Black Internationale.

I shot down past her as her big parachute bellied out and she floated gently through the mist. Then I pulled my own cord, and in a moment

I, too, was meandering through the ozone, descending like a wraith or feather through the clouds to the earth below. Above me several hundred feet I could faintly see Pat. She reassured me with a feeble wave.

Safe, at least for the moment, I wondered about Hudginson and the ship. Even as I speculated as to his fate, there was a roar above. I glanced up apprehensively. There, hurtling down in a mass of flames, came the ship falling directly toward Pat and me.

There was no time to do anything. There was nothing we could do. I closed my eyes in agonizing suspense.

20

▲▲▲▲▲▲▲▲▲▲▲▲▲▲▲▲▲▲▲▲▲▲▲▲

Pat, Carl and Tom Hudginson Land on Desert and Learn They Are on the Direct Air Route Between Fez and Kakata

Roaring like a meteor, the great machine came down, swirled past so closely that the flames almost scorched my clothing, then disappeared. I certainly heaved a grateful sigh when that peril was past.

And yet, had not our troubles just begun? Where were we? Where would we land? It had been impossible to follow any direction except upward during the battle. We had gone this way and that trying to shake off our pursuers. Suppose we were over the Mediterranean or over the Atlantic? Supposed we landed in the Sahara, the most desolate spot in the world? Without means of transportation or communication, we would die of privation.

I looked upward, partly to take my mind off those unpleasant thoughts. Pat was floating about a quarter mile above me. I wondered about Tom. Had he been in that plane or had he jumped in time? Even then, had he escaped the machine guns of the French pursuit planes?

Well, it was now time to consider other things. I was through the clouds and could see the earth below. I tore off my gas mask and threw it away. I wouldn't need that any more. As I came closer to earth my worst fears were confirmed. To be sure, I was landing on terra firma instead of on sea, but far as I could see, which was not very far, there was nothing but a barren waste of sand.

I struck ground easily and was only dragged a little way before I pulled in my parachute and came to a halt. Yes, there was no doubt about it, it WAS the desert, and neither food nor water in sight. About a half mile away were the smoking embers of the stratosphere plane that was to have borne us safely to Kakata. I made a mental reservation to rummage through the ruins and see what could be found of any value to us.

But now I had to think of Pat. I looked up. There she was, coming down easily. I got loose from my chute and, going as rapidly as I could through the shifting sand, followed her course.

When at last she struck the ground, I was there to aid her, so that she was not dragged more than ten or fifteen feet. It was lucky I was there, too. I tore off her mask. Her green helmet underneath was drenched with blood from her head wound. She was quite unconscious.

Frantically I felt her pulse, tore loose her collar and massaged her hands and arms like someone possessed. This vigorous treatment brought a little steadier pulse and a flicker to her eye lashes.

Somewhat reassured now, I cut strips from her parachute, bound up the nasty scalp wound and made a pillow out of the rest of the chute.

After what seemed an eternity her eyes flickered open. She looked up, recognized me and smiled faintly.

"Oh, Pat!" I cried. "Darling, I was so frightened. Speak to me, dear. How do you feel?"

After several seconds she slowly murmured, "I . . . I'm . . . all . . . right . . . Just . . . dizzy . . . sweetheart . . . Where . . . are we?"

"I don't know. I can't see anything but sand in all directions."

"Della . . . Tom . . . where are . . . they?"

"I don't know. I haven't seen Della. Tom may have been able to bail out but I haven't seen him yet either. The plane's not far off. You rest easy and I'll run over and see if there's anything worth salvaging."

"Yes," she replied. "I'll wait right here." She smiled grimly at her jest.

Distances in the desert are deceiving. It took me 15 minutes to reach the wreckage of the ship. It was a mass of bent and twisted wreckage, half buried in the sand, but the rear part of the cabin could be used to protect us from the elements.

I looked for traces of Tom Hudginson but there were none. For one or two things I was extremely grateful. The compass was uninjured and Tom's instruments were intact. Best of all, the metal box of emergency rations was almost as we had left it except for considerable buffeting. In it was tomato juice, grapefruit juice, chocolate bars, crackers and several cans of sardines. Nearby was Jake Stradford's automatic, loaded.

Taking a can of tomato juice for Pat, I hastened to return to her. I felt it would be better for us to stay near the plane, where we could be more easily seen by possible rescuers. So after having her drink the tomato juice, I planned to carry her to the wreck if she was unable to walk. The gun I shoved in my belt.

As I topped a small sand hill from which I could see where she was lying, I noticed to my amazement that someone was standing over her. My heart jumped and I redoubled my pace. I had heard of wild desert marauders that lay in wait for hapless travelers, robbing and murdering them. I pulled out the silencer-equipped automatic and hurried through the loose sand to her side.

The man standing over her turned as I hailed him from behind and then my surprise was ten times greater than it had been before. It was Tom Hudginson!

We both grinned and Pat smiled through her pain.

"By George!" the big fellow exclaimed. "I thought I was going to be all alone on this man's desert, and here I find you two as snug as a bug in a rug."

"It's certainly good to see you, Tom. I thought you were a goner. You should have seen me search the plane for you just now."

"Well, I thought I WAS a goner. After you and Pat bailed out I saw the old ship couldn't last much longer. Just as I got ready to jump they set the crate on fire and then I knew I had to go, or else. I landed about two miles from here."

"All right. Now let's carry Pat over to the plane. There's room enough for the three of us in what's left of the cabin. Besides, I found the compass and your instruments okeh. Maybe you can find out where we are."

"Okeh," he laughed, "but a whole lot of good it will do us. I'm sure we're a month's walk from anywhere."

"Well," I jested, "at least we'll have the satisfaction of knowing where we starved to death."

We made a crude swing out of Pat's parachute and as gently as we could carried her over to the wreck. While I went back after my parachute, Tom got out his instruments and tried to ascertain our location. With rare presence of mind he had shoved his maps in his blouse just before taking over the stick from Pat.

Fortunately the sun was quite high now. By the time we had eaten and smoked a cigarette, it was much higher and calculations were easier.

Pat lay quietly, breathing easily. I felt sanguine about her recovery. After all, the machine gun had just grazed her skull, and while she had lost considerable blood, I felt that she would pull through all right even without proper medical attention. She was young and healthy.

An exclamation from Tom aroused me from my thoughts.

"What is it? You're not going to tell me we're only five minutes from the coast, are you?" I jeered.

"Oh, nothing that good," he replied, evidently pleased, "but not much worse. We never got off our course. We're about 400 miles south of Fez on the direct route to Kakata."

"Yes," I sneered, "and right in the heart of the desert."

"Of course," he agreed, "but we're right on the course and that means it will be easier for the others to find us."

"But how do they even know we're down?"

"I told them. I called them as soon as we were attacked. They may be here before night."

"Very comforting, Tom. But suppose they DON'T find us. What then?"

"Oh, well," he said, laughingly, "the chocolate bars and tomato juice will keep us going for a while."

We both laughed with nervous heartiness. I looked over at Pat sleeping peacefully. Suppose, indeed, that they didn't find us?

21

⩗⩗⩗⩗⩗⩗⩗⩗⩗⩗⩗⩗⩗⩗⩗⩗⩗⩗⩗⩗⩗⩗⩗

*Della Crambull Appears Out of the Night at Desert
Camp of Stranded Fliers; Has Two Frenchmen
in Tow; Tom, Carl Inspect Plane*

It was in mid-afternoon before anything happened to brighten
our ill-concealed gloom. A swift plane passed overhead flying very
high. Being without glasses, we were unable to tell whether it was one
of our ships or not, but it certainly lifted our hopes.

"You know, Carl," Tom suggested, "I think we ought to spread out
that chute of yours on the ground. Maybe they'll see us better."

It was a good idea but I improved on it by suggesting we tear it into
strips and make letters on the land. The result was that in about an
hour we had a big "B.I." spread out, the strips weighted down by pieces
of wreckage.

But no more planes passed over. The sun sank lower in the west,
sunset became twilight and twilight sank into darkness. As it got darker
the temperature fell. By 9 o'clock it was real chilly.

Tom I rummaged around through the wreckage and collected a few
odds and ends of wood, paper and cloth. With some difficulty we managed to get this refuse to smouldering and finally burning. We knew it
couldn't last very long, but it was better than lying there almost freezing in Stygian darkness.

Pat was coming around rather nicely, getting over her loss of blood.
We made her eat a rather hearty dinner, according to our meagre standards, and she was now sleeping peacefully.

Tom and I sat silently gazing into the little fire, each to his own
thoughts.

Then we were both startled by a wail out of the darkness!

I thought immediately of those desert marauders who by crying like
a woman lure travelers away from their campfires to robbery and
death. I got out my automatic. Tom took his pistol out of its holster.

"Shall I answer?"

"No!" I commanded sharply. "How do we know who or what it is? Let's just keep quiet and—"

Again came the wail. It was nearer now, definitely a human voice. For certainly there could be no other life in this desert waste.

"Suppose we get away from this fire?" said Tom. "We can move a bit into the dark and when whoever it is approaches the fire we can see them better."

"And leave Pat?"

"We'll not go far. Just a few yards, enough to get out of the light," he explained.

I threw onto the fire a thick magazine I'd fished out of the wreckage and we withdrew into the shadows beyond the ring of light. As the fire flared up on its new fare, there came again that cry out of the darkness.

It was eery, mysterious, bloodcurdling, coming out of the blackness of the night in this desolate place. Was it someone in distress calling for aid? Or was it some devilish trap set by merciless thieves of the desert?

Again came the cry. It was much nearer, much plainer.

"We ought to answer," Tom argued. "Whether friend or enemy, they can't see us, but they can certainly see the fire and they know there is somebody here. I think we ought to answer. Suppose somebody really needs us?"

"All right, all right. Go ahead. Maybe you're right. But if they can see the fire and are undoubtedly coming toward it, I can't see any use in announcing our presence until we find out who they are."

"You win," said Tom, "we'll wait."

We did wait. Five minutes, ten minutes passed. The cry did not come again. We put our ears to the ground.

"I hear somebody coming," Tom whispered.

"Me, too."

The footsteps, whooshing in the sand, came closer and closer. We froze to the ground in the outer darkness and waited, pistols ready.

It was nerve-tingling suspense, lying there under the starless black vault of heaven, awaiting we knew not what.

Finally we heard voices approaching with the footsteps. We drew further into the shadows. Here was no one person approaching but apparently several. We steeled ourselves for the ordeal.

At last figures loomed out of the darkness into the circle of light.

There were two white men in French uniforms, each loaded down with a big white bundle. There was another or others behind them in the darkness.

A voice out of the night shouted a sharp command in French. The two men put down their bundles. We waited breathlessly for the third person, evidently the one in command, to put in an appearance before we played our hand. We didn't have long to wait.

Out of the darkness behind the two Frenchmen came, of all people, Della Crambull, bareheaded, a pistol held firmly in her hand.

"Hello, Della!" called Tom. She whirled as the big fellow approached with me close behind him.

"Hello, boys. My, but it's good to see you. I just figured this was your fire. Came over here on a hunch." Her voice sounded tired.

"Where did you get these fellows? And what's that they're carrying? Where did they come from?"

"Now wait a minute," she laughed. "Not all at once."

She sat down close to us and opposite the two Frenchmen. She gratefully emptied a can of grapefruit juice, and then, lighting one of our few remaining cigarettes, she blew out a column of smoke and began.

"These two fellows are from that last plane we downed before we had to bail out. One of our bullets broke their feed line. They had to come down in a hurry but their plane was intact when it landed.

"Well, I floated down not far away. They didn't see me because they were busy trying to mend the break. I had my pistol. I sneaked up and surprised them. When they saw I was a woman, they tried to rush me and I had to part one fellow's hair. Ever since then they've done just what I told them.

"I saw our plane when it fell and I figured out you couldn't be so far away from it. So I made these fellows bring their parachutes along. I figured we could use the cords to tie them up and use the cloth for covering. It's mighty cold out here even if it is Africa.

"I think there is a chance to use their plane if we can repair that feed line. They've got quite a lot of gasoline."

She paused. The two young Frenchmen kept watching her and us.

"Let's tie those two frogs up," Tom proposed, "before they go lamming out on us."

"Where to?" asked Della. "This place seems to be about the center of nowhere. They'd pass out before they got 50 miles. Their best bet is to

226

stick with us, but we've got to fix them so they can't start anything."

Following her advice, we tied up the Frenchmen securely but not painfully, covered ourselves with sections of their parachutes, and taking regular turns at watching, we all managed to get considerable sleep before daylight.

Pat was certainly pleased when she woke up and found Della at her side. The two talked animatedly while Tom and I parcelled out the rations, giving the two French pilots a chocolate bar apiece, which they ate without being untied.

Then, leaving Della and Pat to watch the prisoners, Tom and I trudged off the five or six miles to the French plane, carrying only a roll of bicycle tape he had salvaged from our wreckage.

After what seemed an interminable walk, we came upon the little snub-nosed fighter in a level place between two sand ridges. It was indeed in good condition but the feed line was cleanly severed, with one of the broken ends stuffed to prevent the loss of gasoline. Nevertheless, it was apparent that a lot had escaped.

"Think we can do anything with it, Tom?"

"It's a gamble, Carl," he said, emerging from his inspection, "but it's the only chance we've got unless one of our planes sees our signal."

"What's a gamble? What are you talking about?"

"This!" He held up the roll of bicycle tape. My heart sank.

"You must be crazy," I growled.

"Yes," he came back, "and I may be smart."

22

⩗⩗⩗⩗⩗⩗⩗⩗⩗⩗⩗⩗⩗⩗⩗⩗⩗⩗⩗⩗⩗⩗⩗⩗

*Carl and Tom Repair Plane, Return to Desert Camp
and Take Off with Pat, Della; But Gas Gives Out
and Party Is Captured by Cannibals*

In less than ten minutes Tom had repaired the broken feed line as good as possible with bicycle tape. He admiringly surveyed his handiwork.

"Now, let's get out of here," he suggested, quite needlessly.

Soon the engine was roaring. We let it run for several minutes to see how our repair work held. It seemed to be doing very well. But I wondered what we would do if something happened while we were aloft, especially since we now had no parachutes. And yet, anything was better than dying in that barren place.

Tom taxied the little plane around until we found a fairly level place, then he took it off the ground and in about two minutes sat it down close to our little camp of the night before.

Even the two Frenchmen were pleased. But they soon realized that there was little reason for them to rejoice. The plane was much too small to accommodate all of us. A two-seater, it would be a tight fit to get four of us into it. To carry six persons was out of the question.

"Why not leave them here?" Della inquired, harshly. "This is war, and our first duty is to ourselves. They can make it to the coast, and if they can't, it's just too bad."

"Couldn't we come back after them?" suggested Tom. I could see his sense of humanity was greater than Della's.

"What? Risk our ships to rescue a couple of punks?" Della's lip curled disdainfully. "Don't you know the French are controlling the air in this section? No, let's leave them here with what little food we've got and let them shift for themselves. They wouldn't do as much for us."

Brutal as it was, Della's suggestion was best. We certainly could not carry the Frenchmen and, as she pointed out, it would be dangerous to return for them with the Moroccan skies dominated by French planes. Pat voiced a mild protest, but she could see that we had no other alternative.

So we untied the two pilots and turned over our little camp to them. Of course, they excitedly demanded that we take them along, but quickly subsided when they saw the futility of their appeals.

Once more Tom started the plane's engine. We were wedged in like sardines. Pat was strapped in the rear seat. Della and I managed somehow to wedge ourselves into the pilot's cabin with Tom.

We were off the ground and flashing southward in a few seconds. I took one last glance below where the two Frenchmen stood forlornly watching us amid the wreckage that had been our camp. The day before our plight had seemed helpless. Now we were winging our way straight south to safety.

It was with a sigh of relief that we saw the sinister desert disappear behind us as we winged over Senegal and then approached the savannahs and the virgin forests of French Guinea. In three hours the speedy little fighter was carrying us over the sluggish Niger.

We were making close to 300 miles an hour, but we were worried as we watched the gasoline slowly disappear. We had had 160 gallons when we started, and now, with only a little more than half our journey behind us, the tanks were rapidly emptying. We began looking for suitable landing places in the wilderness of primeval forest.

Tom shouted his position into his mouthpiece in the hope that some of our planes or stations would pick up the message.

Our map told us we were now approaching Northern Sierra Leone, only a few hundred miles from Kakata. And yet how far that would be if we landed in the trackless jungle!

We were now down to twenty gallons. Tom dropped down to 500 feet so that we might better see any possible landing place. There was none in sight. We rose to a thousand feet and circled about.

We were down to eleven gallons. To land was imperative, but there was no place to land.

In desperation Tom opened the throttle wide. We shot ahead while the gas gauge shot down to zero.

I looked back at Pat. Her face told me that she was aware of our plight, but she smiled reassuringly.

229

Suddenly the motor went dead! The gasoline was gone. We were coasting at 700 feet, gliding down to what?

"There!" shouted Della, pointing excitedly to our right. Sure enough, there WAS a break in the carpet of forest, revealing a tiny village of not more than 50 huts grouped around the usual square.

Tom quickly steered the little ship toward the opening between two huge cotton trees. Our wings brushed through the branches as we shot through.

The square was wide enough for the plane, but it was scarcely a hundred yards long. We all held our breath as the ground leaped up to meet us. We owed our lives that day to Tom Hudginson's great skill.

The little ship was equipped with retractable landing gear. Instead of letting the wheels down for the landing, Tom plumped down and skidded on the belly of the plane. With chickens, goats and naked children running and screaming with terror, we sledded down the little square, rapidly losing speed, to our great relief.

But we couldn't lose enough speed. At the end of the square stood the palaver kitchen, a large, thatched, bandstand-like structure, the pride of the village.

We demolished the front of it and bent our propeller, but we came to a halt with all aboard safe and sound.

We piled out and stretched our cramped legs. The village was still as death, but we could feel eyes watching us. We stood there, just a little ridiculous and somewhat ashamed for having damaged these humble folks' palaver kitchen.

I was about to help Pat out of her seat when the maniacal screams issued from the forest in all directions. We were soon surrounded by angry brown men, naked except for breech cloths, and brandishing bush knives, spears and old rusty rifles. Their teeth were filed to sharp points and their cruel eyes regarded us appraisingly.

A horrible suspicion chilled me. Della removed any doubts I might have had. "Good God!" she cried, "Cannibals!"

Rough hands quickly secured us. It would have been futile to resist. There were too many against us. We were shoved into a dark hut and the door fastened.

I shuddered at the thought of what might happen.

Had we escaped from the desert only to be eaten?

23

∧∧∧∧∧∧∧∧∧∧∧∧∧∧∧∧∧∧∧∧

Black Internationale Group, Captured by Cannibals,
Fail to Convince Chief That They Are Not French;
Prepare to Be Sacrificed

The heat was oppressive; the air was stifling. Hour after hour we waited, alternately fearful and hopeful. I was terribly afraid for Patricia. Her head wound badly needed dressing and she was slightly feverish.

Outside was the drone of voices as the life of the little black village went the even tenor of its way. Several times I beat on the heavy wooden door but no one seemed to pay any attention to it.

"We're in a spot, all right," said Tom, striding around the circular hut, his hands thrust deep in his pockets. "This is a cannibal tribe as sure as you're born. I can tell by their teeth. They'll probably tear us to pieces before morning, especially if it's a moonlit night."

"What's the moon got to do with it?"

"Plenty. Their orgies usually take place on moonlight nights. If you hear a drum in about three hours, just prepare for the worst."

"If there was just some way of making them know who we are . . ." mused Della, who sat holding Patricia's hand. "They must have heard of the Black Internationale. Bishop Binks once told me that there was a Church of Love in every district in Africa, so there must be one in this district. And if there is, they must know about the Black Internationale. I wish we could see the chief."

"You'll probably see him soon enough," I remarked, "but don't forget that we came down in a French plane, and that every native in this part knows and hates the tri-color."

"But they can see we're not white," Tom objected.

"Well, don't you know that most of the French soldiers and aviators in these parts are black men? Oh no, color can't save us now. We've got to dope out something else."

"And we'd better be quick about it, too," Della added.

But minutes slipped into hours, the temperature gradually lowered and the crickets started their evening chorus, and yet we had thought of no scheme to cope with our dangerous situation.

Boom! Boom! Boom! Boom-bup-bup-bup! Boom-bup-bup-bup! Boom-Boom! The initial flourish of the drums froze the words in our throats. I felt a chill creeping over my body. It was a moonlight night. There WOULD be a dance. The worst MIGHT happen.

It was maddening to wait like rats in a trap in this stinking hut, hundreds of miles from succor while men like beasts paced outside, ready to deal out horrible death. I had heard of these terrible orgies in districts deep in the primeval forests, far from any authority.

The naked victims were crucified, head down, while flames leaped about them. And when their pitiful screams had been mercifully stilled by death, they were set upon by these hordes of demons and literally rended limb from limb with those horrible teeth.

Even in one's sitting room in Harlem one shuddered at the thought of such a fate. Here in the heart of the jungle, imprisoned in a hut with the booming of the drums deafening one, the sense of terror was almost paralyzing.

We sought relief in talking airily of many things and once or twice Tom or I tried to manage a witticism, but it just wouldn't come off. We were all deucedly scared and that's all there was to it.

The tempo of the drums now grew steadily faster and louder. Soon we heard wild music of harps and pipes interspersed with savage choruses. The pandemonium grew until it was almost ear-splitting. Then, suddenly, all was quiet. It was a creepy quietness, like a cemetery.

We heard low voices outside the hut. A hand fumbled with the bar. The heavy wooden door was flung wide open revealing a semi-circle of giant, almost-nude warriors bearing streaming torches.

Two of them entered the hut authoritatively and indicated that we were to follow them. The savage sternness of their caste-marked faces brooked no refusal.

With Pat leaning heavily on my arm and Tom and Della following, we marched out into the clean, fresh air, grateful to escape from the evil-smelling hut but by no means sanguine over the immediate future.

The golden moon hung low over the conical huts like a great disc of burnished copper, shedding its effulgent light upon a mighty concourse of native men, women, and children packed around the central square. It looked like every native for twenty miles around had showed up for the feast.

In the exact center of the square stood four freshly hewn crosses describing a rough square, their cross-bars close to the ground. Around them were several piles of kindling wood and logs and two or three gourds evidently filled with palm oil.

"I guess we're in for it, all right," muttered Tom.

As we marched up the square we were greeted with shouts and jeers. At the far end, just in front of our plane, we were ordered to halt.

Before us, in a low carved chair inlaid with gold and ivory, sat an old wrinkled black man, swathed in an elaborate blue and gray striped gown, his bony feet in colored leather sandals, his gray hair braided and tied with tiny red ribbons. On top of his old head sat a yellow fez. The entire assemblage had grown quiet.

He sat motionless, except for his right hand, which toyed with a leather fly switch. His old eyes studied us closely but his ancient face betrayed no emotion. When he was satisfied with his inspection, he suddenly shouted a command.

A little man detached himself from the small group standing behind the chief. Approaching him, he bowed low and, grabbing the old fellow's foot, held it affectionately in his hand.

The old chief was expressionless. The man nodded his head several times in assent. Then he rose, backed respectfully away from the old man and then, when almost upon us, he turned, straightened up and addressed us in miserable French of which I could make neither head nor tail. Fortunately, Della understood him.

"He says the chief wants to know why the French have visited him?"

"Tell him," I said, "that we are not French, that we had a great battle in the sky and that when one of the French planes landed we sneaked up on the French, captured it and made our escape. Tell him that we want to go home to Kakata, to the great black chief whose brave armies have run the white men into the seas."

Della told the interpreter in French and he translated it into the language of the chief. The old man's eyebrows went up in surprise. Stroking his chin slowly, he looked at first one and then the other of us. Then he spoke animatedly to the interpreter who turned and disappeared into the darkness.

The old chief was expressionless once more. He waved his bony left hand. There was a crash of drums in response.

Out from the shadows now moved grotesque masked figures garbed in rice straw, their bare arms streaked with clay. Numbering a dozen or more, they moved to each side of us, swaying rhythmically with the barbaric music.

Then a huge figure bounded out from behind the palaver kitchen: a man with a hideous mask, with necklaces of bones and teeth rattling around his neck and with bracelets of the same gruesome objects gracing his wrists and ankles. Above each knee was a circlet of straw. On his fingers were fastened cruel iron claws. His naked black body was striped with white ashes or clay. His teeth were sharpened to a point like a leopard's.

Around and around us he danced wildly, grotesquely, obscenely, while his chorus of straw-clad figures formed a circle and gyrated in perfect time. More and more the populace joined in as the drums and pipes rumbled and screamed their savage hymns of hate.

It was evident the old chief had not believed us. We prepared for the worst, though whispering reassuringly to each other. It certainly couldn't last much longer. The grotesque figures were moving closer and closer, sniffing, groaning and screaming. I took Pat's hand and awaited the inevitable.

234

24

*Squadron of Black Empire Airplanes Rescues
Quartet Led by Carl Slater, Just as Natives
Prepare to Light Fire and Roast Them*

Tom and Della stood bravely and unmoved as the devil men danced closer. The giant witch doctor whirled before us, brushing our faces rhythmically with a horse's tail and screaming imprecations. It was certainly our end.

"Look at me, Carl," whispered Pat, squeezing my hand.

There, in the shadow of death, we silently pledged our undying love anew. What irony, what bitter irony that we, who had risked so much for the liberation of black people, should come to our death at the hands of black people!

The sweating dancers were now almost touching us. I knew our horrible death could only be a few seconds off.

Sure enough, in another moment eager hands seized us and bore us to the upside-down crucifixes. We were tied securely while volunteers began stacking the faggots around our heads.

Then developments followed each other in such speedy order that it is difficult to give the right impression in writing.

Palm oil had been poured over the faggots and a native woman was running up with a blazing torch. Suddenly overhead there was a drone of many motors. Now from the sky came a dozen vari-colored flares. We could see easily from our position that the low-lying planes silhouetted against the bright moon were the familiar black and gold fighters of the Black Empire. Sixteen in all.

As the red, green, blue and white lights fell into the square and flared brightly, the savage audience fell back in panic, screaming and pushing. The wrinkled old chief forgot his dignity and ran.

The squadron circled back and dropped a shower of tear gas bombs which splattered around us like hail. In a half minute what had been, a few moments before, a cheering, singing, shouting assemblage was turned into a crying, coughing, gesticulating mob running in circles, screaming in strange gibberish. We also were in tears, but our heads being so low, our suffering was not so intense, as the gas rose quickly.

The planes flew over again. This time from each came two parachutes puffing out in the breeze. With uncanny accuracy that attested to long training, the men brought their chutes down in the village square, detached themselves and, clutching their automatic rifles, rushed to our rescue.

In a few seconds we were on our feet again, surrounded by our men. The lieutenant commanding them explained everything.

"We received your last message, sir," he said, "but atmospheric conditions prevented us from getting your positions clearly. Dr. Belsidus immediately sent up several squadrons and we have been combing the entire district between Kakata and Senegal. The country is so thickly forested that we despaired of finding you. Then, a few minutes ago, we saw the big gathering of natives in this square and knew something extraordinary was going on. So we took a chance, dropped a few flares and gas bombs to frighten them off and came down to investigate."

"You came just in time. They were about to light the fire under us."

"This is rather out-of-the-way country, sir," the lieutenant went on. Then he added, "Cannibal country, sir."

"Don't we control this district?"

"Yes, after a fashion. You see, this is a long way from the nearest Temple of Love. Besides, as in days of old, each chief controls his own district. They probably mistook you for French and wouldn't believe you belonged to the Black Empire. Thousands of French and British officials were killed by the natives in similar manner during the conquest."

The soldiers rounded up all the villagers they could, including the chief, and explained who we were. The old chief was terror stricken and would have prostrated himself at our feet if we had not restrained him.

We were given two big guest huts, one for Tom and me and one for Pat and Della. After an excellent native meal, we turned in for the night. The soldiers talked to headquarters over their field radio set, which had been parachuted from the skies when they dropped.

At daybreak next morning the lieutenant came to my hut and

announced that everything was in readiness for our forty-mile trek to the nearest road through the jungle. The old chief willingly supplied hammocks and carriers, and naked porters laden with palm oil, live chickens and turtles, rice, cassava roots, yams, plantains, limes, palm wine and honey. With the 24 soldiers, this made quite a sizeable company.

We made twenty miles the first day, stopping at a much larger village named Kanda. The following day, about one o'clock in the afternoon, we reached the junction of the forest trail with the motor road. We "dashed" the carriers and sent them back home.

Four big Black Empire trucks commanded by a sergeant were waiting for us. The soldiers piled into two of the trucks. In the other two trucks, which were covered, were two army cots each for our comfort during the rough journey over the bumpy roads to Falaba, which we reached about 3 o'clock.

At the airfield outside that large town were three big black and gold transport planes awaiting our arrival. After a good meal at the airfield headquarters with the officers on duty, we boarded the big planes and were soon winging our way southward on the last leg of our journey. The 24 soldiers and the lieutenant were in two of the planes while Pat, Della, Tom and I were in the third.

An hour and a half later we landed at the big airfield at Kakata. As the wheels of the big ships touched the ground a great opening yawned ahead of us, disclosing a ramp leading down into the bowels of the earth. One by one the big planes approached the ramp, throttled down to about 30 miles an hour and disappeared into the ground. I noticed that big anti-aircraft guns bristled around the field. At the far end of the field a gang of laborers was busy filling up a couple of craters.

A staff car was awaiting us. We were whisked to our bungalow. It was now about 6 o'clock. Everything seemed about the same as when we had left Kakata several days before on our mission of destruction, and yet there was a difference.

Where before at night the capital had been brilliantly lighted, it was now in darkness except for an occasional searchlight sweeping the African sky. No light showed even in the capitol building itself. I noticed that our servants kept the shades carefully drawn. There was a tenseness, an air of sinister expectancy pervading everything.

237

"What's been going on, Pameta?" I asked the maid as she served dinner about 8 o'clock.

"Boom Boom from sky," she explained. "Kill many peoples yesterday. Big house go 'squawah.' Airplane come from ship by Monrovia. Maybe come back pretty soon. Maybe tonight. Maybe tomorrow." She rolled her eyes in terror and almost dropped her tray.

Pat was in her room resting after having her wound dressed by one of the surgeons. It proved less dangerous than it had seemed and he prophesied that she would be able to return to duty in a few days. I left her to get a good night's rest and went over to my office.

The capitol building was shrouded in darkness. At the entrance, a sentry hailed me and then with a salute permitted me to enter the great doorway. Inside, the place was brightly lighted. As I started to enter my office, a uniformed page hurried down the corridor.

"Pardon, sir. Dr. Belsidus wishes to see you at once in his apartment. It is very important."

I followed him down the hallway until we went to the Doctor's door. The flunky spoke into the mouthpiece announcing me.

"Have him come right in," said the all-too-familiar voice.

The man swung the door open and I entered the regal chamber where, as I expected, Dr. Belsidus was not alone.

25

▲▲▲▲▲▲▲▲▲▲▲▲▲▲▲▲▲▲▲▲▲▲▲▲

Dr. Belsidus Calls Council of War and Informs Cabinet of Invention of New Device That Will Revolutionize World

It was a resplendently regal place, this apartment of Dr. Belsidus, done in black, red and gold. The Doctor himself, in his purple and white pajamas, was sitting propped up in bed, surrounded by members of the Supreme Council reclining in the fragile-looking gilded chairs with red satin upholstered seats. Sitting on the side of the bed in a sea-green satin hostess gown was pretty Martha Gaskin, head of our espionage service. Her blue eyes were bright and full of love as she glanced periodically at Dr. Belsidus. Her spun-gold hair was caught up behind in the Grecian manner, like some goddess just descended from Olympus.

The Doctor was far more nonchalant than I had expected to find him with his capital just bombed, enemy ships riding outside of Monrovia 50 miles away and another raid imminent. He nodded not unkindly to me as I entered.

"Glad to see you back, Slater. How is Pat?" he asked considerately.

I explained our whole adventure and the superficial nature of Pat's wound. The others congratulated us on our escape while a servant brought me a chair and a slender, cooling drink. When I was settled, Dr. Belsidus began speaking.

"Gentlemen," he said, "I have received and digested the very detailed reports you submitted upon my order. I don't suppose you have anything new to add, have you?"

The others nodded negatively. It was certainly a brilliant group of men. There was Sam Hamilton, the studious brownskin chemist who had developed the revolutionary aquiculture; Alton Fortune, the great engineer who had developed our sun-power machines; Gustave Linke, the black metallurgist who headed our armament works; Dr. Andrew Matson, head of our medical service; Bishop Samson Binks, head of our Church of Love with its temples in every part of the world where Negroes lived; Ransom Just, the short, fat, yellow man who had done wonders in radio and television; Juan Torlier, the airplane designer and builder; Bennie Simpson, Director of Public Works; Alex Fletcher, shrewd financial expert who handled the Black Empire's money; Sanford Mates, the architect; General Barton McNeel, head of the African Armies; and finally Prof. Vincente Portabla, the tall, lean, awkward black scholar who had once headed the department of physics at the University of Rio de Janeiro. Only the absence of Pat, head of the Air Force, prevented us from having a full attendance.

"Well, then," proceeded Dr. Belsidus, "we shall have summation and critique. Briefly, here is the situation at the moment. The Italians have taken the Libyan coast cities and are sending troops to Eritrea. They have already bombed Massawa. The Australian fleet is moving a large body of troops toward South Africa. The British, under cover of their vessels, have occupied Bathurst, Freetown, Accra and other cities along the West Coast. The French have taken the coast towns of Algeria, Morocco, Senegal, French Guinea and the Ivory Coast.

"The white air fleets dominate the skies above Northern Africa and our ships have had to stay on the ground, or under the ground, for the past two or three days. The British, based on Aden, have raided our centers in East Africa, and these raids will increase. We are still in control of the air in central and western Africa, but this cannot apparently last long." He paused, sipped his drink and glanced at the circle of grave faces surrounding him.

It certainly didn't look good for the Black Empire. With control of the air and the sea, Europe would soon again control Africa. We had neither the arms nor the munitions nor the men to hold back trained hordes of Europeans.

"However," he went on, "I do not regard the situation as seriously as you probably do. We are going to win, gentlemen, no matter how dark the future may seem at the moment. And we are going to win because black brains are as good or better than white brains. We have proved this before and we are going to prove it again."

Gray-haired General McNeel asked, "How?"

"By a new product of our scientific knowledge that is far ahead of anything the white man has so far invented," Dr. Belsidus quietly replied. "For this remarkable machine we have to thank Prof. Portabla and our old comrade, Ransom Just. But equally important in the equation is the effect of what we have accomplished in Europe itself."

A diabolical smile came over his dark face. He toyed with Martha's golden hair as he proceeded, as if that action symbolized his subjugation of the white race. Then he spoke again.

"Even if I did think of it myself," he went on jestingly, "the 'bombing' of the European centers with plague-ridden rats was a stroke of genius. In less than two weeks of this activity we have completely terrorized the population of Western Europe. Death creeps over the continent. The medical services have bogged down. White people are dying like flies in the great cities and the survivors are fleeing to the isolated countryside. It is just like the Black Plague of the Middle Ages. This is a new kind of warfare, my friends, and we are practically immune. It is unlikely that the plague will cross the Mediterranean. And if it does, the Sahara will stop it as it did the last one.

240

"This situation, coupled with the destruction of hundreds of key factories by incendiarism, makes it exceedingly unlikely that we shall long be bothered with the white people. It will take them many years to recover to the place where they can again invade Africa."

"But, Chief," objected Alton Fortune, "what about the enemy right here literally at our gates? Those battleships and troop-laden transports are not in Europe. They are right here. How are we going to stop them? And if we don't stop them, isn't it a cinch that we're goners?"

Dr. Belsidus turned slightly on his pillows and pressed a button.

"Look!" he commanded, pointing to the wall directly in front of him. "I am now going to show you the machine which will change the history of warfare and of mankind. All right, Sanders!"

There was a loud mixture of whirrs and hisses, a light appeared on the wall and a blurred figure began to take form. Finally it stood out distinctly. At first it looked like a champagne bottle on wheels, two huge wheels. Then one could see that it had a great network of wires strung all over its surface, stretched on slender steel spines. At the back a great cable descended, disappearing off the screen.

"Move it up and down, Sanders," he ordered into the microphone.

The nozzle lifted slowly until it was in a vertical position. Then the great machine moved backward and forward by itself, turned around and the nozzle went down to horizontal position.

"That machine is right nearby, gentlemen," said the Chief, enjoying our astonishment. "We shall use it when we have to use it, and when we do warfare will be changed. We have several others at strategic points. We are now as far ahead of the white man in armaments as he was ahead of black men in the past when we fought his cannon with spears. I shall not explain how this machine works until you see it in action. That will probably be tomorrow morning. In the meantime, we haven't as much to worry about as you thought. I am sure . . . "

A shrill siren cut his sentence short. Whistles and bells outside sounded stridently. We all jumped up, grim-faced. It was an air raid! "Sit down!" boomed Dr. Belsidus. He had never shifted his position. His capable black hand still fondled the golden hair of Martha Gaskin. We shamefacedly resumed our seats, but with misgivings in our hearts.

"All right, Sanders," the Chief commanded. "Let us have a look outside."

In a flash we were shown on the screen the action outside the build-

241

ing. A great battery of flashlights searched the skies. Dimly, we could see the crews around the anti-aircraft batteries.

Then, far above, there was the drone of motors. The guns began to bark and puffs of light dotted the blackness of night. Now the sky seemed filled with hostile planes, scores of them. Great bombs fell and resoundingly burst. It looked like the end of Kakata, the Black Empire and us.

26

▲▲▲▲▲▲▲▲▲▲▲▲▲▲▲▲▲▲▲▲▲▲▲▲

War Council Sits in Stunned and Awed Amazement
as "Infernal Machine" Wipes Out Air Fleets
of British and French Navy

Awkward, lean Prof. Vincente Portabla galvanized into activity. Excitement made his smouldering eyes blaze behind the gold-rimmed spectacles. His bony black hand grasped the microphone near Dr. Belsidus.

"All right," he shouted. "Stand by, everyone. One million volts. Open the hatch! . . . Sixty degrees . . . Two million volts . . . Move forward. Quickly now!"

We saw a square of light appear in the center of the airfield. It grew larger and larger. Then out of it slowly moved the giant contraption whose workings we had just seen demonstrated on the screen a few moments before.

"Very well," continued the Professor. "Breeng eet up! . . . Quick!"

The drone of oncoming ships was plain now, plainer than before. The sky to the south, now moonlit, saw hundreds of glistening bodies thundering toward Kakata.

Now we could see the great infernal machine of Prof. Portabla rolling up the ramp onto the airfield. It was glowing with some unearthly light. The spines of steel and copper were radiant and sparkling.

"Three million volts!" cried the Brazilian. "Now get your direction."

The nozzle of the great machine swung around slowly as the wheels turned, apparently by remote control.

"Four million volts!" yelled the Professor, growing more and more excited.

This infernal machine was glowing now to a dull red color.

We watched intently, hardly a breath escaping us as we waited to see what this machine, which was not much larger than a bombing plane or a Pullman car, would be able to do against the combined air fleets of the British and French navy.

A deafening roar shook the capitol building as the first of the great serial bombs streaked to earth. We were thrown to the floor. We scrambled up again, dazed by the force of the explosion.

Dr. Portabla shouted into the microphone which he still clutched in his bony black hands. But there was a diabolical tone to his voice now. Gone was the excitement.

"Very well," he ordered. "Go to work. Act quickly. Swing across the southern sky between 45 and 60. Proceed."

We watched the machine with bated breath. As it swung slowly without the touch of human hand, bombs were falling all about us with resounding crashes that split the eardrums.

Dr. Belsidus was quite calm. Dr. Portabla had become almost Teutonically stolid.

Now the nozzle of the machine, pointed upward toward the onrushing planes, waved slowly back and forth like an iridescent finger. Our numerous searchlights lit up the night sky, revealing every plane.

Suddenly, an incredibly amazing thing happened, something I would have never in the world believed if I had not seen it with my own eyes.

One by one the propellers of the swarm of planes fell silent, and one by one the great ships plunged like flaming plummets to the earth, crashing resoundingly.

The huge nozzle waved slowly back and forth, a giant orange ray darting out on its message of death into the blue.

Squadron after squadron crashed to the earth. Panic-stricken, the remaining planes, many of which had already dropped their cargoes of bombs, turned to flee back to the coast from whence they had come.

"Thirty-five to forty-five!" yelled Portabla, grimly stroking his chin. "Five million volts!"

243

The infernal machine glowed to a bright orange. The nozzle lowered. One by one the fleeing bombers and pursuit planes fell like stricken flies.

Soon the southern sky was empty of everything except the moon and stars.

We looked at each other for a full minute before anybody spoke. Then the first one to speak was the Brazilian physicist giving orders to his unseen men.

"Breeng eet down to zero," he commanded, "and put eet away. That ees all."

The machine gradually turned from a bright orange to a red, then from red to black. Slowly a square of light appeared near it again. Uncannily, the great thing moved down the ramp and into the ground. The square of light grew smaller and disappeared as the bomb-proof cover closed over the entrance to the underground chamber.

Dr. Belsidus was as pleased as a boy with a new bag of marbles. The grim smile was gone. In its place was a broad grin.

"Well, Portabla," he said, extending his well-manicured hand to grasp that of the Brazilian. "It worked. You and Just did a swell job. Couldn't have been better. How many of these machines have we ready?"

"There ees ten now," Portabla replied. "Each day Senhor Linke turns out one."

"How many can we use at once?"

"Ze meenimum powar ees four million volts for each. Eef we suspend many othar acteevities, we can use all ze machines at once."

"Do we generate that much power here?" Dr. Belsidus continued.

"Not here, but in many other places. We send ze powar by wire."

General McNeel interrupted at this point. "This is a life saver, all right," he conceded enthusiastically. "It gives us air control again, and with air control we can hold off invasion for a long time."

"Eet also geeves us other control," insisted the Brazilian.

"I don't understand," said the General.

"Seet down, all of you. I wael explain wiz ze 'elp of Senhor Just."

The others took their seats while Professor Portabla paced back and forth, giving us a course in physics applied to modern warfare.

"Ze machine which you see ees in reality two machines in one. Eet

244

ees first of all an atom smasher, a huge cyclotron, which generates an atomic or proton beam which can disintegrate any metal. Secondly, it ees a developer of a radio beam which possesses the faculty of stopping the propellers of machines and rendering batteries and connections useless.

"Ze machine, as you noticed, was not moved by ze human hand. No, gentlemen, no human could approach zees machine. Eet ees moved by radio remote control. Ze beeg cable you see in ze rear furnishes ze electric power. When zees beams turn on any machine, he perish."

"You mean it will stop ANY machine?" cried McNeel, thoroughly excited.

"Certainement, Senhor McNeel," the Brazilian assured him. "Ze machine is ze machine no matter what you call heem. Eeef eet iss metal, eet mus' go. First we stop heem, zen we destroy heem. Come, we shall go out. I weel show you."

Even Dr. Belsidus went with us as soon as he had thrown on some clothes. We did little talking, too awed by the awful potentialities of this machine to say much.

Preceded by an armed guard front and rear, our little party got into automobiles and proceeded to go about Kakata to see what damage had been done by the planes and to them.

One giant bomber had come to grief in the very center of the airfield. We drove close and examined it. It was almost unrecognizable. It had been scorched and melted like slag, its parts fused together as if it had been dipped into a volcano filled with molten lava.

All over the countryside were scattered these blobs of slag which had once been death-destroying bombers piloted by white men who believed themselves all-conquering.

There had been considerable damage done by the bombs. Several buildings were razed and there were a dozen huge craters about the town. Over a hundred persons had been killed and several hundred wounded when one bomb hit a big barracks filled with soldiers. But considering the number of machines participating in the raid, we got off lightly, much lighter than did the attacking fleet. It was reported to Dr. Belsidus that of the 300 planes participating in the raid, only twelve had escaped and returned to the plane carriers off Monrovia.

"Tomorrow," mused Dr. Belsidus, lowering his eyelids and smiling grimly, "we shall move our machines to Monrovia."

27

⩗⩗⩗⩗⩗⩗⩗⩗⩗⩗⩗⩗⩗⩗⩗⩗⩗⩗⩗⩗⩗⩗⩗⩗

Dr. Belsidus and His Huge Cyclotrons Roll into Monrovia and Destroy Navies of France and England in Uncanny Manner

I hurried back to the bungalow. Pat, who should have been asleep, was sitting up bright-eyed when I entered the room.

"Oh, it was wonderful!" she cried. "I wouldn't have believed it possible. I really wouldn't. It's . . . well, it's unbelievable!"

"It's certainly uncanny, all right," I agreed. "That fellow Portabla was a find, wasn't he?"

"Well, Carl, it just shows that we've got enough brains in the colored race to beat the white race doing anything if we can only assemble those brains. Dr. Belsidus realized this and acted upon it. Therein lies his greatness. Other Negroes were merely concerned in protesting that they were not inferior, that they were capable of doing anything that the white man did, and that therefore black men should be given the same chance as white men in a white man's world. But there was one thing plainer than any other and that was that if in truth black men were the equals of white men in all things, white men who controlled the world were not going to willingly give black men the opportunity to demonstrate their equality or superiority. It just doesn't fit in with the laws of survival.

"The first thing that was necessary," she continued, her face a deeper reddish brown with her excitement, "was to find out what we had in the way of brains and achievement. Dr. Belsidus did that. The next thing was to get these men and women catalogued and card-filed. Then came the job of getting them into one secret world-wide organization. After that it was only a matter of time before we had money, and from thence we conquered. I knew from the beginning, darling, that we couldn't fail."

"Well, you'll fail if you don't get back into bed," I warned laughingly.

246

"And if you don't, I'm going to put a pillow over my ears because I've got to get up early."

"What for? You need rest after all that's happened."

"I know, I know, but we've got to start out early tomorrow morning, before daylight. We're attacking the fleet off Monrovia!"

It seemed as though I had scarcely touched the pillow when the telephone rang insistently, again and again. I reached over and grabbed it, cursing sleepily.

"It is three-forty-five," announced the operator. "The chief commands that you report at the capitol at once."

I hurriedly performed my morning ablutions, threw on my uniform, swallowed a glass of orange juice and, kissing Pat goodbye, dashed out of the house and over to the capitol building.

Dr. Belsidus was dressed as usual in his immaculate tropicals and sitting at his low flat-top desk watching the giant map of Africa on the wall, where tiny red and green lights showed where enemy forces and ours were located, which ports were still in the hands of the whites, etc. On the opposite wall was a giant television mirror which brought at intervals pictures of the situation in different parts of the continent.

He looked up as I entered. There was a deadly calm and assurance about him that I don't believe I had seen since the white Powers moved to the attack. He sipped a tall glass of chilled orange juice. I waited respectfully until he had finished.

"All right, Slater," he said finally. "We'll be going."

I telephoned that the Chief was ready to go. As we stepped into the corridor, a guard of four heavily armed, handsome black giants in black and gold uniforms fell in behind us. Downstairs, the Doctor's familiar bullet-proof black limousine awaited with the gigantic Jim, his mute chauffeur, at the wheel.

I followed the Doctor inside. It brought back to me the first night I had ridden in that big car through the streets of Harlem to the Chief's headquarters in the East Seventies. We had certainly gone a long way since those days.

We were driven rapidly to the airfield, our bodyguard standing on the running boards.

Already the huge cyclotrons, ten in all, were lined up, swathed in dun-colored cloth, their huge wheels rising ten feet in the air. Prof.

247

Portabla and Ransom Just were ordering about a swarm of mechanics and electricians as searchlights illumined the scene.

Soon they reported to General McNeel that all was ready. One after the other the cyclotrons wheeled down the paved road that led to Monrovia less than 50 miles away. Behind each of the machines were several truckloads of machinists, electricians and equipment, and a battery of multiple anti-aircraft guns with a giant searchlight.

It was five o'clock when we arrived on the outskirts of Monrovia. Dead and dying men were lying everywhere and the cries of the wounded were a strange accompaniment to the rumble of our giant machines as they passed through the narrow streets like great ghosts of dinosaurs seeking prey in the darkness. Many buildings along the way had been destroyed and several were still smouldering. An orderly explained that the defense forces had beaten off a landing force from the fleet just two hours before. Later General McNeel drove up and told how his men had regained control of the city, after the air fleet had been destroyed over Kakata, only to be attacked two hours later.

"We're expecting another attack in a few minutes," he said, "just as soon as it gets light enough. That barrage they laid down the last time almost wiped out the town."

As he was speaking, Prof. Portabla hurried up and reported that the cyclotrons were in position and cables supplying them with juice would soon be attached.

Dawn was coming up out of the jungle. The fog was heavy over the miasmic swamps and lowlands. We could not see the long lines of enemy ships two miles away. Then, with the typical dramatic suddenness of the tropics, the sun came up, dispelling the fog as if by magic, and there, just a bit off shore, stood the long lines of gray battleships, cruisers and destroyers.

The covers were off the cyclotrons now. Lined up at intervals of about 500 yards, they looked like huge prehistoric monsters. At a wave of Dr. Belsidus's hand, Prof. Portabla shouted his orders into his radio telephone.

There was a low hum all along the line. It grew louder and louder. The crews retreated a couple of hundred feet from the machines. Gradually they grew red, then orange, and the voltage was stepped up. The myriad spines that made them resemble some sort of futuristic porcupines were like livid hairs. The proton rays darted out of the nozzles toward the lines of ships a scarce two miles away.

"We are taking the first line," announced Ransom Just.

For a minute nothing happened except the low hum as the great machines ate up all the electric power which the ingenuity of the electricians had brought down from the interior.

Another minute passed. We all waited, watching intently through our field glasses. Sailors were running frantically about the decks of the proud battleships of the white Powers.

Suddenly explosion followed explosion in uncanny procession. Before our eyes we were seeing the national pride of England and France going sky high and dropping back in fragments into the water. Most of the white men never had a chance to escape, although we did see a few floundering in the heavy sea.

The rumble of the cyclotrons continued. Raising their nozzles a bit, they attacked the second line of ships. In two minutes and ten seconds after Prof. Portabla gave the command, there was a second series of deafening explosions.

Inexorably, the great machines sent their devastating proton rays seaward. It was an ignominious death the whites' fleet died, for not a single shot was sent in reply.

Prof. Portable explained that "Ze radio beam he stop all batteries and dynamos. Zay cannot operate ze beeg guns. Zay cannot operate ze ammunition conveyors. Zay cannot signal because zay cannot use telephone or radio. We blot zem out completely. Zay can only lay zere an' be destroyed."

At seven o'clock the Brazilian gave the command to cut off the power. The great combined navy that had threatened the very existence of the Black Empire was scattered over the bottom of the sea.

28

▲△▲△▲△▲△▲△▲△▲△▲△▲△▲△▲△▲△▲

Battle of Monrovia Stuns Europe; Dr. Belsidus
Prepares to Wipe Out Foreign Armies in Africa
by Use of Latest Electric Ray Machines

News of the great victory was promptly broadcast to the world. It was a greater sensation than the fall of the Roman Empire, the defeat of Russia by Japan or the Bolshevist revolution.

The reaction of the white world was one of profound fear, but great exultation filled the air wherever men and women of color gathered. Throughout Africa, black people danced and sang with joy. In America and the West Indies and Malaysia, colored folk shouted the glad tidings.

We ordered a celebration in every one of the three thousand districts into which Dr. Belsidus had divided Africa.

At high noon the black air fleet took off for Dakar, where four cruisers, remnants of the French fleet, were at anchor. With the loss of only one plane, we sent the craft to the bottom of the harbor.

The entire air fleet, preceded by stratosphere planes, left the following morning for Fez to clear the North African air of enemies.

The outlook seemed more promising now than ever, but victory had by no means been achieved. While a considerable number of units of the British and French fleets had been sunk at the Battle of Monrovia, there were still a number of ships to be reckoned with. Powerful squadrons were at Cape Town, Alexandria, Tunis and Tripoli. As long as they remained, the Black Empire would not be safe because we had no battleships at all, and it is an axiom of warfare that he who controls the sea controls the situation.

That evening Dr. Belsidus called me into the office, along with General McNeel, Prof. Portabla, Juan Torlier and Gustave Linke. Attendants brought chairs and we seated ourselves. The doctor lost no time in getting down to business. A few seconds later, Martha Gaskin and Della Crambull came in. Both bore piles of papers.

"Miss Gaskin," the Doctor began when she was seated, "let us have the reports from Europe."

The white girl remained seated and swiftly read the reports from our various agents in England, France and elsewhere.

"The plague is sweeping Europe with unprecedented virulence. Millions are sick or dying. The situation in this respect is worse in the congested cities than elsewhere. All who can leave are fleeing the towns for the countryside. In the highly industrial areas like Manchester, Birmingham, the Ruhr Valley, the manufacturing areas of Belgium and Northern France, production is virtually at a standstill."

Dr. Belsidus's eyes twinkled at the news. "Go on," he commanded.

"Agents report that typhus is sweeping all central Europe and the Balkans, while smallpox has gripped Italy. Everywhere there is a great increase in the number of influenza cases."

"What is the prospect of them supplying fleets and armies abroad?" asked the Chief, leaning forward slightly, his brow wrinkled in concentration.

Now Della Crambull, the beautiful dark girl, spoke up. "I have been checking the reports from the seaports," she began. "Most of them are doing very little. Passenger service seems to have taken precedence. The rich and influential are getting away as soon as possible, because it is now obvious to everyone that the medical services have broken down. The troops sent on African service will probably not be ordered back home because of the plague, according to our latest information."

"Then they'll be virtually isolated," said the Chief. "Now is our time to annihilate them. McNeel, what is the total strength of the white invaders and where are they located in force?"

The gray-haired soldier reached into his inside pocket and brought out a small card covered with figures.

"There is a large British garrison at Cairo numbering about 15,000 men. The French have a total of about 25,000 men in Tunis and Algeria, while the Italian army in Libya reached 20,000 yesterday. The other garrisons do not count. These troops are mostly infantry, artillery, anti-aircraft batteries and cavalry. There are about a thousand planes in all. It is still a formidable force, sir."

"Yes, I know," said the Chief, scowling darkly. Then, turning to Prof. Portabla, he asked, "I suppose taking the cyclotrons up there would be out of the question?"

"It would take weeks," replied the Brazilian, "in the state of African roads, and even then there is the question of power. Mr. Fortune says most of the sun-power stations near the north coast have been bombed."

The Chief pondered this for a moment. Then he turned to Juan Torlier, Gustave Linke and Ransom Just, who had come in while Portabla was talking.

"The cyclotrons are our best bet," he said, more to himself than to them, "but they weigh 10 tons. It is impossible to use them to drive these white armies out of Northern Africa. We shall have to use our troops and that will take a long time. Is there anything you gentlemen can suggest? The quicker we finish the job the better."

"We still have the electric radio ray," suggested Just. "We have been using it in conjunction with the proton ray. The former will halt all airplane and automobile engines; in fact, it will halt all electric transmissions and batteries, but only the proton ray will destroy."

"But have you any way to project this electric ray except through the cyclotron?" asked Dr. Belsidus.

"Not now," Just admitted. "You see, Linke and Portabla have been so busy getting the cyclotrons into shape that we haven't been able to give much time to developing a machine to carry the other equipment."

"Why couldn't we mount it in one of our stratosphere planes?" asked Torlier. "The machine probably wouldn't weigh over 500 pounds. And even if it weighed a ton we could carry it."

General McNeel, who had been listening carefully, now spoke up. "If we can get something like that we'll have the advantage. They'll have nothing to stop us. It will be a decisive weapon."

Dr. Belsidus straightened with sudden decision. "All right, boys, we'll try that. Just, you get together with Linke, Torlier and Portabla and work out something as soon as you possibly can. Victory must be complete."

Orders were given to have the air fleet return immediately. The following morning, the black and gold ships flew in early and swarms of mechanics began preparing the bombers and stratosphere planes for the new equipment. Pursuit planes stood ready for protection.

Over at the great fabricating steel plant there was great noise and bustle as machinery hammered out the new equipment. At the electric equipment plant, Ransom Just was busy with the powerful cells, bulbs and other accessories for the new infernal machines.

At the order of Dr. Belsidus, my wife remained in the house, but she nevertheless directed the preparation of the Black Empire Air Corps for the final battle and selected the pilots for the planes.

Summaries of news stories appearing in the world press were sent in daily by our representatives. To say that the white world was stunned by our great victory would be putting it mildly. As the decisiveness of the conflict dawned upon them, the white countries became panic stricken. Gone was the old haughty sureness that had come with long possession of superior arms. Black men had the superior arms now, and Europeans knew that black men had good cause for vengeance.

The exodus from the great European industrial centers continued in panicky haste as the plague grew in intensity. Dissatisfied with the speed of the plague, Dr. Belsidus sent at least one great bomber loaded with germ-laden rats nightly to be dumped over some big city. This continued for a week. Meantime, the three principal white armies remaining on African soil held their positions, perhaps wondering what to do. Their numbers were increased during the week as more units were sent out from home countries to save them from the ravages of disease. But our spies informed us that food and equipment and ammunition were scarce because the working classes at home ports and industrial centers were the hardest hit by the plague.

Seven days after the Battle of Monrovia, our factories had turned out 16 of the electric ray machines, sufficient to equip nearly all our stratosphere planes.

On the morning of the eighth day, with Tommy Hudginson in command, the huge squadron took off in the early morning mist, surrounded by a swarm of pursuit planes. A fleet of big bombers followed later in the day, each loaded with huge incendiary and contact bombs.

All that day and far into the night Pat sat up getting reports and issuing instructions.

29

▲▲▲▲▲▲▲▲▲▲▲▲▲▲▲▲▲▲▲▲▲▲▲▲▲▲

Italy, France, England Beaten in Final Battle as "Black Empire" Takes Its Place among Leading Nations of the World to Remain Forever Free

I was torn between two desires. I wanted to stay behind with Pat and I wanted to go along and see this last decisive battle for the Dark Continent. Dr. Belsidus decided the question for me. Shortly after the stratosphere planes left with their infernal cargo, my telephone rang. It was the Chief.

"Get ready to go with me, Carl," he commanded. "I guess we might as well be in at the kill. We'll leave at noon. If Patricia's well enough to go with us she can come along."

So that's how it happened that Dr. Belsidus, Martha Gaskin, Pat and I found ourselves winging northward in the Chief's speedy private plane which Jim, his giant bodyguard and chauffeur, had learned so well how to pilot.

We flew immediately to our secret air base near Murzuk in southern Libya, where the entire air fleet was gathered, arriving there about twilight. Like the airport at Fez, the hangars were underground. There was room enough for the stratosphere ships and bombers, but the pursuit planes had to remain outside.

We went to the rest rooms while the planes were refueling and enjoyed an excellent dinner. After dinner Pat and Tom Hudginson and General McNeel held a conference of war with the pilots, while Dr. Belsidus, Martha Gaskin and I took a stroll on the desert sands under the bright moonlight. Then we all took a bit of a nap in preparation for the ordeal to come.

An orderly awakened us at 2 o'clock. We hurriedly performed our ablutions and after a swallow of orange juice all around we went to our plane. We ran up the ramp to the field above and parked nearby the entrance. In a few moments, four of the huge stratosphere planes in

254

rapid succession rolled out of the ground and took to the air for the 1,000-mile trip to Alexandria. Close behind them came eight big bombers and a dozen pursuit planes.

When they had disappeared to the northeast, a similar fleet left on the 600-mile journey to Benghazi, the great Italian air base near the Libya-Egypt border. We followed closely in the wake of this contingent, leaving the other planes to go on the 450-mile trip to Tripoli and the 700-mile journey to Tunis.

At about 4:30 we were thirty miles from Benghazi, where we knew the bulk of Mussolini's air fleet to be stationed. The stratosphere planes landed with about a mile interval between them. We came down just behind them. The bombers and pursuit planes proceeded to their goal. Dr. Belsidus ordered Jim to take to the air again, as he wanted to see the attack. In about six minutes we were high over the air base. The eight bombers scattered and dived down upon the hangars and barracks. At 1,000 feet they released their messengers of death. There was a terrific roar. The buildings' planes, machinery, everything disintegrated into a million pieces. The bombers wheeled, dived and released their remaining bombs. Gasoline tanks burst into flames. Terrified men ran wildly in all directions. Now the little pursuit planes dived to within a few feet of the ground, their machine guns spitting death pellets at the frantically fleeing Italians. In a few moments the place was a shambles, a field of bloody desolation. Not an Italian plane remained.

A few minutes later a similar report came from Tripoli, to be followed by as favorable news from Tunis. At both places several Italian and French warships and transports had been sunk. And finally, about 6:30, the fleet that had gone to Alexandria reported the destruction of the British base and the sinking of a cruiser and a destroyer.

But now was to come the test. We knew that in a few hours, British planes from Baghdad and Quetta would be seeking revenge, and that Italian planes from Sicily and French planes from Marseilles would be on similar missions. We had only to wait. The bombers returned to Murzuk for more bombs. We and the pursuit planes remained a couple of miles behind the parked stratosphere planes, while a couple of the little wasps patrolled the seashore on the lookout for the enemy.

Just before 8 o'clock, the patrols radioed the approach of the avenging Italian air fleet. In a few moments we could hear the drone of hundreds of motors, like a swarm of gigantic bees.

Jim shot our plane into the air and sped a few miles to the rear, just for safety's sake. The dozen pursuit planes followed us. The motors of the stratosphere planes hummed but they did not leave the ground. Instead, their roofs were shoved back, revealing the glistening, infernal radio machines inside, with short ugly aluminum snouts pointed toward the enemy.

The sky was soon blackened by the great fleet, twice as numerous as that which had bombed Kakata. I admit that I had considerable misgivings. Suppose our radio machines didn't work! Jim must have had the same thought because he went so high that we had to turn on the oxygen.

On came the Italian air fleet. But now an amazing thing happened. On plane after plane, the propellers suddenly went dead and the machines glided to the earth. Several crashed out of control. Again and again this happened, until the earth was covered with grounded ships. A score that were too far back to be affected turned and scooted for Sicily.

Now, at a signal from Pat, our dozen pursuit planes dived out of the skies, strafing the helpless grounded planes with incendiary bullets and small thermite bombs. In a few moments the whole plain seemed to be ablaze. Relentlessly, the little black and gold ships passed back and forth over the helpless Italian planes, reducing them and their pilots to cinders. And what happened at Benghazi was repeated at Tunis, Tripoli and Alexandria. Our bombers later blew up the remaining Italian planes.

After a leisurely reconnaissance flight over the field of victory, stratosphere planes and the rest followed in our wake to Murzuk. There we rested during the heat of the day. At five o'clock we speeded back to Kakata.

Three days passed, three days in which the world marveled at the rise of a new world power, in which black people everywhere rejoiced, in which delegates in their colorful uniforms arrived by plane from outlying districts of the Black Empire, from America, from Malaysia and from India. They flooded the streets of Kakata and taxed the capacity of our two skyscraper hotels.

On the evening of the fourth day the delegates assembled in the great conference hall hung with black and gold streamers. Gorgeous music came from the Imperial Band in the sunken garden below the open windows. Microphones were banked in front of the Doctor's lectern to carry his every word to the ends of the earth. At 9 o'clock the music died. Then a flourish of trumpets brought the vast assemblage to attention. Suddenly the Doctor, in immaculate tropical whites, stepped from behind his high-backed chair and, saluting the audience, seated himself.

After the customary preliminaries he rose to speak. Only a few words they were, but I have preserved them for posterity.

"My dear friends and comrades and colleagues," he said, "we are gathered here this evening to celebrate the liberation of Africa and the emancipation of the black race. We who were once the lowest are now the highest. We who were once despised and slandered are now honored and feared. We who were said to have no future except to hew and haul for the white race have created a future more glorious than the white man ever imagined.

"It was no easy task. We had been miseducated. We had been kept ignorant. We had been kept poor. We were in the main awkward and unskilled. It seemed that only a miracle could save us. But the days of miracles, if they ever existed, are now passed. A few of us realized that no one would or could help the Negro except himself, that no brain except his own could devise a means of extricating him from his dilemma. All we had was our brains, my comrades, and all too often they were twisted by the white man's education.

"But there were a few of us who had hopes and dreams, a few of us who tossed aside the white man's morals and scruples which we had been taught, along with his religion, and made a new philosophy for ourselves, a philosophy of courage, singleness of purpose, of loyalty, of intelligence. We imbued the black people of the world with a new ideal, a new vision, a dream of conquest and nobility. We used every instrument in our power to achieve success, and we have achieved success.

"And now, a word of warning to the black people of the world. You have a great empire created out of black brains and strength. You can only keep it intact by continuing to work and think and plan. You must not make the mistake of the white man and try to enslave others, for that is the beginning of every people's fall. You must banish race hatred from your hearts, now that you have your own land, but you must remain ever vigilant to defend this continent which is rightfully ours.

257

"I have led you to victory, with your cooperation. Now I shall lead you to a higher civilization than Europe has ever seen, with your consent. The glory that was once Egypt's and Ethiopia's and Benin's and Timbuctoo's and Songhoy's and Morocco's shall again make Africa first in the family of nations.

"Through your brains, your labors and your sacrifices, Africa has been redeemed. The shackles have been struck off. We are free and our children shall be free forever. Go forth, my comrades, and imbue your followers with the determination to remain forever free!"

He sat back, looking somewhat weary, I thought, and passed his slender hand over his face and sighed. A storm of applause swept the conference hall.

Pat gently squeezed my hand, communicating some of her intense feeling.

I looked down the front row to where Martha Gaskin sat, her blonde hair looking odd among those Negroes. She was twisting her tiny handkerchief in her hands, while a pair of tears coursed unnoticed down her cheeks.

Afterword

As *Black Empire* opens, its narrator, Carl Slater, witnesses a shocking murder in Harlem. He is then drugged and spirited away to a mansion downtown, where the sinister yet captivating Dr. Henry Belsidus invites him to join a revolutionary black movement known as the Black Internationale. At breakfast the next morning, Slater's awe at the opulence surrounding him moves the suave Belsidus to explain:

> Doubtless you wonder at all this. Perhaps it seems rather garish and unnecessary, something like the extravagances of the newly rich. But I am no Trimalchio, my lad. There is method in what you might call my madness. (p. 12)

Belsidus here alludes to Petronius's first-century *Satyricon*, in which Trimalchio, a wealthy former slave, hosts an ostentatious banquet that occasions grotesque and vastly comical lapses from good taste. However, Belsidus's sumptuous home is no debauched gathering place; on the contrary, it is the deadly serious secret headquarters of a revolutionary organization dedicated to overthrowing white supremacy throughout the world and restoring black rule to Africa.

Through this allusion to Trimalchio, Belsidus—and, by extension, his creator, George S. Schuyler—implies that more is happening here than meets the eye.[1] Indeed, this single piece of dialogue might be taken as emblematic of *Black Empire*: at first glance, the story appears shallow, capricious, even somewhat mad, but as it unfolds, it resonates with ever greater depths and complexities.

The same holds true for Schuyler's popular fiction as a whole. "The Black Internationale" and "Black Empire"—the stories constituting the present volume—were written under the pseudonym Samuel I. Brooks and published in sixty-two weekly installments in the *Pittsburgh Courier* between November 1936 and April 1938. They are among more than

259

four hundred pieces of fiction that Schuyler wrote for the black weekly during the 1930s under his own name and several pen names.

Schuyler's attitude toward his serial fiction seems to have ranged between enjoyment and downright disdain. In April 1937—at the moment in the story that the fictional Dr. Belsidus launches his conquest of Africa (p. 87)—Schuyler wrote to *Courier* staffer P. L. Prattis:

> I have been greatly amused by the public enthusiasm for "The Black Internationale," which is hokum and hack work of the purest vein. I deliberately set out to crowd as much race chauvinism and sheer improbability into it as my fertile imagination could conjure. The result vindicates my low opinion of the human race.[2]

The *Black Empire* stories may indeed have been a cynical joke that Schuyler played on his readers, or a whimsical fantasy written for his private amusement. In any case, Schuyler's amused if cynical disdain has been echoed—and its dominant theme reinforced—by several of his critics. One, apparently unaware of Schuyler's serial fiction, asserted that after 1931 "Schuyler wrote no further fiction."[3] In general, scholars have paid no attention to Schuyler's newspaper serials.

Yet Schuyler's vast serial output should not be relegated to a second-class "jim crow" status, using an arbitrary hierarchy of genres to exclude the "pulp" writings from his legitimate canon. The *Black Empire* stories and some half-dozen of Schuyler's other 1930s pulp serials, as we shall see, possess profound thematic affinities with his contemporary "serious" essays, affinities that transcend the "genre gap" and suggest—Schuyler's own comments notwithstanding—an overarching commonality of literary purpose and concern.

In his illuminating foreword to the 1989 edition of Schuyler's brilliant satirical novel *Black No More,* James A. Miller points out that "it is difficult, if not impossible, to separate George Schuyler's literary artistry from his journalism, or his journalism from his life and his beliefs."[4] We would go further. Even allowing for the view that Schuyler's serial fiction of the thirties might not fit traditional definitions of *belles lettres,* it constitutes an extraordinary literary achievement and supplies an important key to a fuller understanding of his creative versatility. Thus, although some "hokum" clearly exists in *Black Empire,* several important factors suggest that the work—and its relationship to the rest of Schuyler's writings—is far more complex than Schuyler admits. In any case,

260

such comments by a writer about his own work often tell us as much about the writer as about the work itself.

Like his intellectual relationship to the character of Dr. Belsidus, Schuyler's literary relationship to his popular fiction is a problematic and ambivalent one, governed by a broad range of historical, social, literary, and autobiographical influences. Once freed from the imperatives of "high seriousness," it appears that Schuyler gave vent to another side of his literary identity, an aspect that he seemed less than proud to reveal and consequently wished to disguise. Indeed, *Black Empire* contains a wealth of personal, political, and literary allusions, testifying to Schuyler's evolution as a thinker and writer, and, as a historical document, reflecting the turbulence of the crisis-ridden decade during which it was written. Into this highly imaginary story of the liberation of Africa and the elevation of the African-American Schuyler crowded just about everything that he knew or felt about race, psychology, pedagogy, international politics, history, war, technology, health, and modern science. *Black Empire* thus affords us a self-portrait of the author and his times, seen through the medium of melodramatic fiction: a portrait into which Schuyler poured so much of himself that, in our view, the very act of disclosure made him uncomfortable.

Publication of *Black Empire* in book form, then, not only opens a new window onto the little-studied field of black newspaper fiction; it also enables a fuller understanding of several critical areas of Schuyler's life and thought, particularly his activities during the thirties, which have heretofore been almost entirely overlooked.[5] From a literary standpoint, while Schuyler's renown was achieved through satire, it should be noted that the dominant mode of his serial fiction was melodrama. Ideologically, while he is principally remembered today as a militant anti-communist, during the thirties he was staunchly anti-capitalist. Schuyler evolved into a conservative after World War II, but during the thirties he was definitely a radical. If he ended up as a critic and opponent of the civil rights movement in the sixties, he was in the thirties both an activist and a militant advocate of civil rights. And if later he became an apologist for continued imperialist rule in Africa, in the prewar years he was an articulate critic of imperialism. Likewise, while he has been thought of, and with good reason, as anti-Garvey, he was in the thirties a committed Pan-Africanist. Finally, although he prided himself on being a hard-nosed realist, he was also a racial idealist and scientific utopian. *Black Empire* reveals Schuyler as a complex and radical thinker, whose ideological journey toward conservatism was more labyrinthine and problematical than has been appreciated. As a writer and thinker, he defies easy classification and denies us the superficial pleasure of pigeonholing either him or his writing.

Journalist, Essayist, Novelist

George S. Schuyler (1895–1977) is now widely considered to have been America's finest and most prominent black journalist and essayist of the first half of the twentieth century. During the twenties and thirties, he wrote the *Pittsburgh Courier's* lead editorials, his own weekly columns, and several major investigative series, including the influential "Aframerican Today," which reported on race relations in Mississippi in 1925–1926. There were also frequent essays and stories for other publications. Perhaps most influential was a series of articles he did in 1931 for the *New York Evening Post,* following a trip to West Africa to assess Liberia's slave labor controversy. It was, he noted, "the first time anything like this had happened to a Negro newspaperman. . . . So far as I know a colored writer had never before served as a foreign correspondent for an important metropolitan newspaper."[6] After running as a six-part series in the *Post*, the articles appeared in the *Washington Post, Philadelphia Ledger,* and several other major newspapers.[7] The series prompted Hampton College's James W. Ivy to tell Schuyler, "You have no peer among practicing Negro journalists and few equals among your pale-faced contemporaries."[8]

Schuyler's journalistic reputation also owed a great deal to his biting weekly commentary in his "Views and Reviews" column, which he began writing for the *Courier* in 1924. After a short interval during which he managed and edited Harlem's *National News* in 1932, he resumed "Views and Reviews," to the delight of readers who warmly greeted his return. "Many people who do not agree with Mr. Schuyler's outlook on life will nevertheless read him with delight," remarked his *Courier* colleague and friendly critic, Floyd Calvin.[9] The *Courier* also published a letter by Ivy asserting that what Schuyler "now writes has the wit and the brilliance of the writings of the late Anatole France, one of the wittiest commentators on the human scene."[10] Freeman H. Hubbard, a white journalist, praised the column's "frankness, its common-sense, its freedom from platitudes, bunk and mush," and called it "the best newspaper column in America."[11]

At the height of the post–World War I New Negro movement, Schuyler began writing his "Shafts and Darts" column for the black socialist *Messenger* magazine of A. Philip Randolph and Chandler Owen. Aptly subtitled "A Page of Calumny and Satire," the column captured H. L. Mencken's attention and led to Schuyler's publishing "Our White Folks" in Mencken's *American Mercury* in 1927.[12] This essay argued that "the Negro" was "a sort of black Gulliver chained by white Lilliputians."[13] Calling it a "capital article," Mencken made it the lead item.[14] This event proved the turning point in Schuyler's career as an essayist. His reputation thereafter grew in leaps and bounds, in large measure because of his nine essays that Mencken published between 1927 and 1933 in *American Mercury*. Through his pungent, controlled writing style and large literary output, Schuyler "distinguished himself as the titan of published contributors of any race in the *Mercury*, and in turn garnered a reputation as the Negro's Mencken."[15]

Schuyler's serious fiction, like his journalism, was rooted in a strong sense of contemporary social issues. *Black No More* (1931) provided a searing satire on the pathology of racism in America, a satirical slant on America's preoccupation with race-crossing and the consequent corrupting influence of race on the moral claims of American society and institutions. The novel *Slaves Today: A Story of Liberia*, published the same year, exposed forced labor practices in Liberia.[16] At the same time, there was a Rabelaisian coarseness in Schuyler's temperament that along with his general misanthropy not only fit his rebellious character but also came to characterize his literary persona.[17] Schuyler, in fact, might fairly be described as black America's leading misanthrope. In late 1935 he wrote to his wife from Mississippi, confessing, "I find one must not expect too much from the human race. I once did but I have since seen the light and shall sin no more."[18]

Schuyler also garnered ample experience in "pulp" journalism. In August 1928 the *Messenger*, where Schuyler had been assistant and managing editor since 1923, closed. He made his way the following month to Chicago, to assume the editorship of William B. Ziff's *Illustrated Feature Section (IFS)*, a magazine insert appearing in forty Negro weeklies that Schuyler later described as "moron fodder."[19] He got the job through the personal intervention of the *Courier's* owner and publisher, Robert L. Vann. Ironically, Vann himself eventually soured on the supplement, which he regarded as "filled with salacious and sexual matter, entirely obnoxious to our readers."[20] Schuyler also wrote for *IFS*; a former colleague called his stories "servant girl fiction," accusing him of "skim[ming] off the cream of the mass of pulp readers who may be capable of appreciating literature of a higher order."[21] Schuyler declared that he quit the magazine the following January "in order to save what intelligence I possess."[22]

Even after resigning as editor, Schuyler continued to write for the *IFS*. He later recalled a contribution that "was ridiculed as far-fetched sensationalism because I predicted that Negroes would some day rule Manhattan Island."[23] Published under the pen name Danton Smith, "Will Negroes Rule Manhattan in 1940?" anticipated the theme that would dominate Schuyler's *Black Empire* serials. The 1929 article concluded that "black folk will never be sufficiently powerful numerically to control Greater New York, but on Manhattan Island, the wealthiest, most up-to-date, most picturesque and most stimulating part of the world's greatest city, Negroes are very likely to rule in the next ten years."[24]

It was while editing the *IFS* that Schuyler began writing as "Samuel I. Brooks." The name seems to have first appeared in print in an October 1928 advertisement for the supplement's inaugural issue that introduced him as "a Newly Discovered Race Writer," the author of the serial story "Chocolate Baby (A Story of Ambition, Deception, and Success)."[25] The pseudonym was doubtlessly employed to convey the impression that the weekly supplement would foster new literary talent, while disguising the fact that Schuyler doubled as editor and short-story writer. The Brooks name gave Schuyler a literary alter ego that he was to use frequently over the next decade, notably in a six-part analysis of Marcus Garvey published in the *Interstate Tattler* in 1929[26] and in the two stories that make up *Black Empire*.

Grinding It Out

Schuyler's *American Mercury* contributions tapered off after Mencken's retirement as editor in 1933, at the same time that his writing for other white journals virtually came to an end. The transition inaugurated a new phase in his literary career. In addition to his regular journalistic work, he published at least one serial installment or short story every week in the *Courier* from early 1933 through 1939, using at various times his own name as well as numerous pseudonyms, including "Samuel I. Brooks." While the *Black Empire* stories were his longest-running multipart serials, they represent only about one sixth of the output of weekly fiction that can confidently be identified as his during this period.[27] But in contrast to the audience for his satirical essays and *Black No More*, the readership of his serials was almost exclusively black.

From September through November 1935, Schuyler was in Mississippi on assignment to increase the *Courier's* circulation in the Deep South. He roamed widely throughout the state, recruiting newspaper agents and gathering local human interest stories for a Mississippi edition of the *Courier*.[28] Though underpaid and overworked, Schuyler managed, by the time Thanksgiving arrived, to increase the *Courier's* Mississippi circulation from a low of two thousand to the ten thousand copies that he had promised management.[29] He carried out this grueling task while fulfilling his regular journalistic duties as columnist and chief editorial writer for the *Courier*, all the time continuing to dash off weekly short fiction pieces.

It is now clear that Schuyler worked as hard as he did because he desired security. This was also the primary reason that he gave for choosing to write fiction for newspapers instead of book-length novels. "My name is made and I crave no more publicity as such," he told the *Courier*, "but I most certainly *can* use more money than I am presently receiving." Amazing as it must seem by present-day standards, Schuyler then earned less than sixty dollars a week for his weekly columns, editorials, promotional work, and fiction combined.[30] "I am grinding out material by the yard and the pound," he wrote his wife, Josephine, in November 1935. He also confided about his future literary career. "As you know, my primary interest [is] in having sufficient income flowing in to enable us to live properly." He added:

> That is more important than a book, of which the presses pour forth legions. I am not disdaining the advantages that come from authorship but the remuneration is very little unless you write a best seller. For one thing, I know my contacts throughout the South are going to be very helpful when I *do* write another book. You would be amazed at the number of people I meet who talk about *Black No More*. It is in almost every important school library, and literary students groups and others are eager to discuss writing, etc., with me. You would be

surprised to know that hardly any other Negro is so well known throughout this section. I mean Negroes who write. . . . I am preparing the way so that when I do get published again there will be a large sale here and elsewhere in the South.[31]

At the moment that Schuyler wrote to his wife, it had been four years since he published *Black No More* and *Slaves Today*. He would not publish another book until his autobiography in 1966. It was at this point that he began to concentrate on writing serial fiction.

"Nothing Like It in the History of Negro Fiction"

By the mid-1930s, *Courier* circulation had increased dramatically from the depths to which it had fallen a few years earlier. A dramatic upswing followed the paper's extensive coverage of Joe Louis's rise as a heavyweight boxer[32] and the Italo-Ethiopian crisis of 1935–1936. Coverage of Ethiopia alone boosted circulation by about twenty-five thousand copies; another twenty-five thousand copies were gained when the paper published J. A. Rogers's interview with the embattled Emperor Haile Selassie.[33] Freeman H. Hubbard called Rogers's war coverage "the finest thing of its kind I have ever seen," and thought it worthy of a Pulitzer prize.[34]

Soon after Ethiopia's capital, Addis Ababa, fell to Italy and Germany's Max Schmeling knocked out Joe Louis, Schuyler proposed writing a series on the West Indies—an idea that he claimed would boost circulation, though the same idea had not generated any interest when Schuyler had pitched it two years earlier.[35] "The Ethiopian war is over. The news value of Joe Louis is certainly not going to be what it was, at least not for a long time," Schuyler argued. "So, what have you? Is there anything in prospect or on the horizon that will bring in fifteen or twenty-five thousand circulation? If there is I don't see it. Do you?"[36] The answer to his question would not be long in coming.

Schuyler thought a West Indies series would boost sales, especially among West Indians living on the Atlantic coast, but the proposal again fell flat. Four months later, when he proposed an adventure story, the *Courier* responded enthusiastically. No stranger to the world of syndicated supplements, after his years writing for the Chicago-based *IFS*, Schuyler urged that his new story "be illustrated and presented to the public in good old 'American Weekly' fashion"[37]—the same racy techniques used by the immensely successful and sensationalist *American*

Weekly, the Hearst newspapers' Sunday magazine supplement. Under the editorship of Morrill Goddard, it used a formula combining bizarre and shocking stories with abundant illustrations.[38]

"The Black Internationale" debuted on November 21, 1936. A week earlier, a front-page *Courier* banner headline boldly announced:

THE BLACK INTERNATIONALE
Action . . . Intrigue . . . Thrills
an amazing story of black genius against the world[39]

The *Courier* sent agents twenty-five thousand inserts and three thousand placards with screaming headlines:

Thrills—Punch—Mystery—Sales!! . . . Nothing Like It In The History of **Negro Fiction**—a Heart-gripping Breathtaker, Packing Plenty of Punches in Every Paragraph—One of Those "Must" Stories That Send The Fiction Fans Rushing To The Newsstands. It "Sends" Them Like Nobody's Business, And They Come Back Each Week for More.

The placard further "guaranteed" that " 'The Black Internationale' would break all sales records for serial fiction with its fantastic, blood-chilling, heart-stopping plot and action." It gave the following summary, which Schuyler himself may well have written:

It is not a story exclusively about American Negroes, but a story about Negroes everywhere, united by a common bond of hatred of white exploitation, persecution and ostracism.

One determined black man, educated, suave, immaculate, cruel (at times) and unmoral, gathers around him the genius of the Negro world, and using every device imaginable, organizes the greatest conspiracy in history against White Supremacy![40]

Schuyler had an uncanny psychological ability to plumb the desires and fantasies of his black audience. The placard featured an illustration by *Courier* artist Wilbert L. Holloway, with whom Schuyler had collaborated on *Messenger* covers in 1926, depicting a demonic-looking man holding the world aloft in his outstretched hand.[41] As sensational as these promotions were, Schuyler's story itself was to be even more startling. "Readers want to be entertained and instructed, and I know how to do it," he later reminded the *Courier* management.[42]

Aside from several cluttered sheets of handwritten story notes (see Appendix A), Schuyler left no record of exactly *how* he composed "The Black Internationale." Two months into the serial, however, the *Courier*'s managing editor, W. G. Nunn, with a studied nonchalance, conditioned no doubt by a touch of publisher's parsimony, reported to Schuyler, "Incidentally, your story 'The Black Internationale' is going over mighty big. If you will just go along now and inject the woman angle, I think it will be one of the best serials we have ever run."[43] A week later, lovely aviatrix Patricia Givens made her debut.

The appearance of Givens immediately after Nunn's letter strongly suggests that Schuyler was writing only a week ahead of publication, perhaps making up the story as he went. On January 11, 1937, Nunn again wrote Schuyler; but this time his letter was even more effusive. By then, the story's narrator, Carl Slater, was clearly falling in love with Givens. "Your story 'The Black Internationale' should be the answer to a circulation man's prayers," Nunn gushed. "It is getting better and better and everyone in the office makes a grand rush when it comes in."[44]

Some idea of the powerful impact that the extraordinary tale had upon readers can be gleaned from an inquiry addressed to the newspaper by a Chicago woman: "I want to understand about this Dr. Henry Belsidus. Is his conquest going on now, at the present time, in Africa?" The newspaper was obliged to respond, "No, the Black Internationale, which describes the exploits of Dr. Belsidus, is fiction, not truth."[45]

Making the Grade

Financial need was certainly one of Schuyler's primary motivations in writing the *Black Empire* stories. The Depression had hit the white journals hard and they could no longer provide him the income that he had earlier enjoyed for his essays. Aside from a brief autobiographical allusion, he seems never to have admitted publicly that he wrote these stories, though many appeared under his real name.[46] His autobiography's sole allusion to writing serial fiction comes in his recollection of returning to New York from Chicago, when he moved into a new apartment in Harlem's fashionable Sugar Hill in 1929. "My income was not nearly as high as it had been recently," he explained, "but with speaking engagements and freelance writing and writing fiction for the *Courier* under various *noms de plume,* I was making the grade."

Schuyler undoubtedly resented playing the role of a hack cranking out formulaic adventure stories, syrupy romances, and other melodramatic fantasies. "I know a man who has the temperament of a great objective scholar," he wrote in a thinly disguised self-description. "He was made for [the] professor's platform, drawing rooms, salons and intricate research in musty tomes of a forgotten age. Circumstances shunted him into the field of partisan writing, where, it is true, he has achieved international renown. Yet he detests the mere mention of most of the subjects on which he has written voluminously. . . . He would chuck the whole thing tomorrow if circumstances permitted."[47]

Schuyler's newspaper fiction, which lacks the droll humor characteristic of *Black No More*, his signed columns, and his *American Mercury* essays, clearly belongs to the "pulp" fiction genre, with all its attendant limitations: clumsy melodramatic plotting, stereotyped characters, stilted dialogue, and so on—all of which contrasts with the seeming care that he invested in his books and essays. Most of his serial fiction concerns the standard topics of the genre. We find flights of fantasy that might have been inspired by *The Arabian Nights*—one of his favorite literary works: stories about lost cities, hidden treasures, forbidden love, witchcraft, murder, kidnapping, strange science, blackmail, espionage, and power lust. It abounds with depictions of hate, greed, insincerity, hypocrisy, double-dealing, infidelity, rape, physical cruelty, dismemberment, prejudice, ignorance, superstition, and fear. Characters generally succeed less because of mutual trust, altruism, and kindness, than because of superior intelligence and ruthlessness.

In some eight serials, however, including the two *Black Empire* stories, Schuyler dealt with rather more serious issues, exploring such themes as African witchcraft—a fascination he inherited from his grandmother[48]—cannibalism, genetics, scientific experimentation, miscegenation, intra-black color conflict, and interracial cooperation against white oppression. His settings in these pieces ranged from the heart of Harlem and the Mississippi Delta to the African bush. In addition to the *Black Empire* stories (1936–1938), these eight serials include "Devil Town" (1933), "Golden Gods" (1933–1934), "The Beast of Bradhurst Avenue" (1934), "Strange Valley" (1934), "The Ethiopian Murder Mystery" (1935–1936), and "Revolt in Ethiopia" (1938–1939)—all of which have a Pan-African political focus. Indulgence in melodrama for allegorical purpose was the "hokum" or excessive side of Schuyler's

269

creative genius, a side that was no less serious because of it, even though his satirical nature regarded it pejoratively.[49] In fact, the stories about Africa and Africans make use of all the melodramatic elements of intrigue, love, and adventure that characterized the 1930s pulp genre; as used by Schuyler, however, the stories formulate a coherent allegory of African resistance to white domination.

Schuyler's own silence regarding this phase of his literary output has doubtlessly helped blind students of his career to the many revealing expressions of his thinking that it contains. The failure of scholars to notice Schuyler's newspaper fiction is made all the more curious by the fact that fully half of his African-related serials—forty-five separate pieces—appeared with prominent "George S. Schuyler" bylines. In our view, Schuyler's move into serial fiction afforded him broad opportunities to use popular melodrama and allegory to engage—albeit in a different voice and from a different literary identity—issues similar to those that occupied his satirical writing of the same period.[50]

Friend of Ethiopia

In truth, the mid-1930s was hardly a time for irreverent wit. Japan had occupied Mongolia and was threatening China. Italy had avenged its humiliating defeat at Adowa in 1896 by brutally occupying Ethiopia—the only black-ruled country devoid of white connections. Nazi Germany was arming for conquest, and civil war was raging in Spain, where another fascist victory seemed imminent. It is within this context of a world torn by militarism and rival internationalisms—fascist and communist and capitalist—that *Black Empire* must be viewed, for the stories provide a critical commentary on contemporary events, while symbolizing an alternative ideal of black allegiance. In this latter regard, Ethiopia and Liberia play central roles.

As the black world waited through the anxious summer of 1935, watching the military and diplomatic maneuvering that every day tightened Italy's noose around the neck of Ethiopia, Schuyler initially adopted a skeptical attitude toward "the clamor of Aframericans" to come to the aid of "dear, old Ethiopia."[51] While such ventures appeared to him quite impractical, his criticism was directed far more against "big imperialist powers" and their official impediments to western blacks' attempts to fight in Ethiopia. Ethiopia's bravery in the face of such bullying inspired him nonetheless to a sort of reverie of racial solidarity.

"As an old soldier, I would certainly like to participate in such an adventure and press a machine-gun trigger on the Italian hordes as they toiled over the Ethiopian terrain," he mused. "It is one of the few wars in which I could participate with enthusiasm.[52]

Schuyler's dominant concern was the hypocritical diplomacy underway throughout Europe that professed to forestall Italian aggression. Schuyler scorned the motives behind this maneuvering. "It is my fervent hope that this war will get going soon," he declared, reasoning that "the Ethiopian-Italian embroglio will very likely be the match that will touch off the world powder keg again, and I am frankly tickled at the prospect." He predicted that "another great war is inevitable, and it is likely to be the last big one for a long time. It will be the signal for the fretful millions of Africa to arise and massacre the handful of whites left there, once it is definitely known that the Powers are occupied butchering each other at home."[53]

Violent revenge fantasies suffused Schuyler's weekly columns during this crisis period, forming a thematic basis for the international race war that underlies *Black Empire*. "As an avowed militarist," he wrote, "I look forward with pleasant anticipation to the results of the Italo-Ethiopian embroglio. If I were a Christian, I might even fall down on my knees and pray for a general conflagration."[54] Schuyler reminded black readers that "what the white nations say solemnly about honor, justice, love of mankind, Christianity and peace is to be taken with a shovel of salt."[55] As the war finally approached, he asked the *Baltimore Sun* to make him its Ethiopian correspondent.[56] In the end, he had to be content with the *Courier*'s proudly billing him and J. A. Rogers as the "Two Best Informed Men on Ethiopia in the U.S.A.!"[57]

Shortly after Italy invaded Ethiopia, however, Schuyler sounded a dire warning: "It would be a major catastrophe for the darker peoples of the world if Ethiopia should be defeated and subjugated by the Italians." He enquired: "We have an opportunity to give quick and effective aid. What are we going to do about it?"[58] Schuyler opted to support the fund-raising efforts of the Friends of Ethiopia in America, a group organized by amateur Africanist historian Dr. Willis N. Huggins. "For, make no mistake about it, if Ethiopia loses and is enslaved," he argued, "the cause of white imperialism will be immeasurably advanced and the cause of black liberation will be hopelessly retarded. The last of free Africa must remain free."[59] He fantasized that "it would be a magnificent spectacle if all over the United States colored people would swell the ranks of [Huggins's] organization promptly and start a stream of currency toward New York."[60]

Following the first major Italian successes in early 1936, Schuyler renewed his appeal to black Americans to "rally to the cause of Ethiopia in a concrete financial way. . . . I am convinced that the defeat of Ethiopia and its consequent dismemberment will be a very damaging blow to the prestige and aspirations of colored people everywhere."[61] A week later he added that "We all ought to know what the defeat and dismemberment of Ethiopia will mean not only to all of Africa, but also to darker America. It is one of the few remaining exceptions to imperialist rule. It stands as a living disproof of the assertions of our detractors that Negroes have always been slaves and are incapable of self-government."[62]

Freeing Liberia

This pervasive climate of aggressive militarism emboldened Schuyler to advance his own agenda based on the ideal of force in regard to Liberia as well. Unlike most black nationalists who doted on the country as a symbol of modern black independence, Schuyler, who had visited it in 1931, viewed international pressure on Liberia primarily "as a question of freeing the two million natives . . . from murder, rapine and robbery at the hands of a shiftless and ruthless oligarchy."[63] His column actually outlined a plan for the overthrow of the Liberian regime. "Methinks it is high time for an expeditionary force of about 500 Aframericans, liberally supplied with rifles, machine guns and ammunition, to set sail for the West African republic," he wrote, adding that such an invasion might begin with a landing at the capital of Monrovia.[64]

The starting point of the Black Internationale's conquest of Africa is Monrovia—the symbolic target of the grand Garveyist design. The vanquishing of Liberia's corrupt regime vindicates Schuyler's real-life campaign to rid the country of "the tyranny of the Barclay regime."[65] Significantly, the first act of Belsidus's invading forces is to topple President Barclay—whom Schuyler personally met during his 1931 trip to the country. Belsidus then relocates Liberia's—and later the Black Empire's—capital from Monrovia to a town forty-five miles inland, Kakata, which Schuyler actually visited in 1931.[66] In a clear allusion to the Liberian slavery issue, Belsidus warns Black Internationale delegates, "You must not make the mistake of the white man and try to enslave

272

others, for that is the beginning of every people's fall. You must banish race hatred from your hearts, now that you have your own land, but you must remain ever vigilant to defend this continent which is rightfully ours" (p. 257).

The character Ralph Farley, the Black Internationale's "Liberian cell" commander (p. 92) and intermediary between Belsidus and the hinterland chiefs, may have been modeled by Schuyler on the historical figure of George Padmore. This black Trinidadian ex-communist, with whom Schuyler corresponded in the early thirties, broke from the Red International of Labor Unions (Profintern) after eight years of membership when the Communist International decided to liquidate the International Trade Union Committee of Negro Workers (ITUC-NW), of which he had been secretary and chief organizer since its creation by the Profintern in 1928.[67] Padmore sent Schuyler copies of his February 3, 1934, letter of resignation, as well as his open letter to the black press affirming that "one thing is certain: the Negroes of the world will continue their struggles and build their liberation movements—with or without the Comintern."

Communist leaders had charged Padmore with being "a flunky of Firestone and the American State Department."[68] Ironically, exactly the same charge was leveled against Schuyler for his reporting on Liberian conditions. Padmore was the first, as he claimed, to "draw the attention of the International Labour Movement" to Liberia's problems, in his 1931 essay "American Imperialism Enslaves Liberia," published in the *Communist,* the American Communist party's theoretical organ. He followed this with "Hands Off Liberia" in the December 1931 issue of the *Negro Worker,* the official organ of the ITUC-NW.

Although Padmore's articles attracted sympathy for the tiny republic that Schuyler detested for exploiting its indigenous people, Schuyler nonetheless championed Padmore's struggle against calumnies leveled by black Communist party functionaries. He generously supported Padmore in his unequal battle against powerful Communist International propaganda.[69] In June 1934, an unsigned Schuyler editorial in the *Courier* lauded Padmore, explaining that "this militant Negro . . . was successful in doing what Du Bois with his Pan-African Congresses and Garvey with his ridiculous U.N.I.A. failed to do: actually scare the imperialist powers with colonies in Africa and organise groups of black workers there."[70]

During his leadership of the ITUC-NW, Padmore claimed to have organized over four thousand workers internationally.[71] He told Schuyler about his underground political organizing in Liberia—work similar to Schuyler's own mission. "I am the first outsider who went into Liberia and started to form a trade union," Padmore claimed in 1934, "because this is the only way the Kroo 'boys' on the ships can ever hope of getting a few more cents—same applies to Firestone labourers. I even brought out 2 boys—products of Liberia College—in 1932 and trained them in Hamburg in the principle of the labour movement & sent them back to help their folks."[72] Padmore's successful Liberian recruitment and training scheme may well have supplied Schuyler with the prototype for the Black Internationale's clandestine organization of West African revolutionary cells.

Marcus Garvey's Comic Opera Movement

When Schuyler first moved to New York City in 1919, Marcus Garvey and his back-to-Africa movement were just starting their political ascendency as the vanguard of post–World War I New Negro radicalism. For a time in late 1921 Schuyler rented a room in the Phyllis Wheatley Hotel, which was operated by Garvey's Universal Negro Improvement Association.[73] The UNIA grew spectacularly, peaking in numbers by the mid-1920s, only to decline almost as rapidly.

As a member of the Friends of Negro Freedom, an anti-Garvey group formed by black socialists Randolph and Owen and their *Messenger* magazine, Schuyler became a keen if critical observer of Garvey and the UNIA. In 1937 he recalled "the halcyon days of race racketeering, when the Hon. Marcus Garvey rode through Harlem's yokel-banked canyons arrayed like an Oxford don." He reminded readers of "Garvey's comic opera movement," which had " 'sold' Africa to the sable brethren." In sum, Schuyler dubbed Garvey "the best-known of all the Negro hustlers."[74] But if Garvey became a major stock character in Schuyler's satirical repertoire, a nostalgia also crept into the portrayal. "Marcus has his value," Schuyler wrote in 1931. "He furnishes a note of humor and ridiculousness in a world that is worried and blue. And on the other hand his weird and grandiose schemes and pronouncements are as an island of glamour in a sea of practicality."[75] "Personally I regret the passing of Marcus," he added in 1933. "He gave me material for many a paragraph and added much to the mirth of nations."[76] At

274

less sentimental moments, however, Schuyler could still write with a pen dipped in vitriol, as when he described Garvey as a "Master Megalomaniac, [who] was able to cash in on the despair of a few score thousand Negroes until merited imprisonment put an end to his chiseling,"[77] or when he noted acerbically that "all Garvey ever freed Negroes from was their hard-earned cash."[78]

While Schuyler was often outspokenly anti-Garvey, he was by no means a confirmed anti-Garvey*ist*. Belsidus's practical methods may have been the antithesis of Garvey's, but Belsidus embodies Garveyist ideals, and, of course, he succeeds where Garvey fails. The last of Schuyler's 1929 articles appraising Garvey was, in fact, generally favorable:

> Marcus Garvey has a vision. He sees plainly that everywhere in the Western and Eastern hemispheres the Negro, regardless of his religion or nationality, is being crushed under the heel of white imperialism and exploitation. Rapidly the population of the world is being aligned in two rival camps: white and black. The whites have arms, power, organization, wealth; the blacks have only their intelligence and their potential power. If they are to be saved, they must be organized so they can present united opposition to those who seek to continue their enslavement.[79]

The key concepts here are intelligence, organization, and unity. Schuyler endorsed Garvey's strategic vision, particularly as it related to UNIA plans for black Americans to develop Liberia. What infuriated Schuyler was Garvey's serious tactical failings, which he put down to Garvey's penchant for ballyhoo. Schuyler's *Black No More* burlesqued Garvey as the charlatan black nationalist leader, Santop Licorice. *Santop* enhances the satirical impact of *Licorice* (blackness) by recalling black baseball star Louis Santop, renowned for calling home runs in the manner of Babe Ruth—in other words, a "ballyhoo" figure.[80] "Had Garvey been more diplomatic and less mouthy," he wrote, "he might have attained his objective in Liberia. As it was, he bragged about what he was going to do in Liberia and then squawked when the canny Liberians barred him and his movement."[81] Schuyler himself had carefully disguised his true mission to avoid raising suspicion in the government,[82] and capitalized on his resulting freedom of movement to travel widely. "Where others have confined their observations to the 'civilized' coast section of Liberia, I visited fifty native towns and interviewed the chiefs and inhabitants thereof," he declared, defending his findings.[83] The very week that "Black Empire" began in the *Courier,* Schuyler admitted his respect for Garveyist principles. "Without running the risk of being called Garveyistic," he announced, "it can be truthfully said that the colored people all over the world have something in common in these days of white military, economic and financial domination."[84] Such a conviction could hardly have been held by someone who was preparing to satirize Garveyist concepts of black sovereignty or internationalism as a response to the common oppression of blacks. A month earlier, W. P. Bayless, the *Courier's* subscription manager, told Schuyler: "The Black Empire should grip the minds, imagination of all blacks throughout the whole domain."[85]

Schuyler's serials are also influenced by Garveyistic notions of African freedom. Although Schuyler explicitly disavows Garvey's methods, Garveyist symbolism abounds in his fiction, from the moment that *Black No More's* Dr. Junius Crookman is introduced while he is staying in Garvey's Phyllis Wheatley Hotel.[86] The most overt reference to Garvey occurs early in *Black Empire.* Outlining his plans to reconquer Africa, Belsidus notes Slater's amusement and asks, "It sounds mad, doesn't it?" "Yes, rather Garveyistic," Slater replies (p. 10).

Belsidus himself more than once declares that he opposes anything that would draw attention to him or his plans to reconquer Africa. While the Black Internationale's expeditionary force secretly heads to Texas, Belsidus explains to Slater that "one of the great mistakes made by minority leaders in the past has been ballyhoo. Therefore we have established no newspapers or magazines, given no talks over the radio, staged no parades or demonstrations. . . . If we had a newspaper and boasted in it about our far-flung efforts, white people would know all about it and crush us before we were ready" (p. 88).[87] Belsidus's comment here becomes a shrewd, implicit criticism of Garvey's penchant for publicity.

More subtle Garveyist associations resonate throughout the story. Zero hour for the launching of the military expedition to conquer Africa is set for August 1st—the traditional date for the mammoth Harlem parades that opened Garvey's annual UNIA conventions. The fleet carrying Belsidus's expeditionary force to Africa not only mimics the racial patriotism of Garvey's Black Star Line (BSL) with such ship names as *Nat Turner, Bessie Coleman, Samory, Kelly Miller,* and *Sojourner Truth,* it duplicates the name of an actual BSL ship, the *Frederick Douglass,* as well as a planned BSL ship, the *Phyllis Wheatley*.[88] After conquering Liberia, Belsidus assumes the title of "Provisional President" (p. 114), mimicking Garvey's own title, "Provisional President of Africa." The movement paraphrases Garvey's UNIA motto, "One God, One Aim, One Destiny," by declaring, "Mother Africa a great united land—one people, one soul, one destiny" (p. 166). Belsidus even goes one up on Garvey—who had dangled unfulfilled promises of large loans to Liberia—by paying off the country's $2,500,000 debt to the Firestone company in full.

"The Rise of the Black Internationale"

Schuyler's lecture topic list from his 1936 cross-country speaking tour reveals how he viewed relations between black internationalism and white imperialism, as well as domestic social and political concerns. His topics included "The Twilight of White Imperialism," "Next Steps in Negro Advancement," "Appreciating Africa, Its History and Civilization," and "Negro Students, What Now?"[89] Several weeks into the tour we find Schuyler writing about the African-American response to the Ethiopian crisis: "If only we loved our own as fervently as some of us hate the white man! What wonders we could accomplish! What prodigies of cooperation and accumulation of power we could perform!"[90]

These concerns culminated in a major essay that Schuyler wrote during the heightening political and military crisis of 1938, a few months after finishing *Black Empire*. In his autobiography, Schuyler called it his "most significant article" from the period.[91] This seminal essay, written for the NAACP's *Crisis*, was entitled "The Rise of the Black Internationale"; as Schuyler later wrote, it "predicted much that has happened in the developing color conflict, including the worldwide liberation of the colored peoples from white rule, which I referred to as the White Internationale."[92] The essay also encapsulates the political worldview underlying *Black Empire*.

Despite its Garveyist tinge, Schuyler may well have derived some of the ideas and inspiration for the Black Internationale concept from his colleague and close personal friend, J. A. Rogers, whose 1935 pamphlet *The Real Facts About Ethiopia* explores how an African conflict might lead to a global race war. Schuyler praised the booklet in his *Courier* column, as he did all of Rogers's self-published works.[93] Rogers foresaw how "growing resentment of the darker races against white supremacy" might eventually turn into "a conflict and even a war between the races," in the same way that Carl Slater describes Belsidus's "fanatical plans for an international race war" (p. 51). When Slater and Givens must land their plane while returning from a raid on Meridian, Mississippi, Slater's greatest fear is that if they are caught, a "race war would result before the organization was ready" (p. 71).

Rogers saw Italy's invasion of Ethiopia as a potential trigger that might awaken the slumbering historic animosity of nonwhites to whites and provide "a unifying consciousness." In language anticipating the apocalyptic sentiments of the fictional Belsidus, Rogers warned: "The avalanche is on its way and it will not stop until the last vestiges of the brutal and debasing color-line imposed on the world by the white race shall have been shattered into irretrievable fragments."[94]

In February 1936, the *Courier* recalled Rogers from Ethiopia to conduct a national lecture tour that would capitalize on his popularity. The paper also asked Schuyler to manage the proposed tour, whose profits were to be divided equally among it, Rogers, and Schuyler. Schuyler declined, however, since he was about to make his own annual lecture tour—which, since 1928, had given him "a *very needed source of revenue*" (emphasis in original). He also reminded the *Courier* that Rogers was his personal friend, and that it was he who had started Rogers writing the *Courier*'s black history features.[95]

In "The Rise of the Black Internationale," Schuyler discussed the history of white domination of black Africa and heralded the arrival of the New Negro, who is rightly suspicious of the world's white power structure, capitalist and communist alike: "No longer blindly worshipful of his rulers, he yet has learned to respect and study the intelligence and accumulation of power that has put them where they are." The New Negro believes that to combat the "White Internationale of oppression a Black Internationale of liberation is necessary. . . . No longer ignorant, terrorized or lacking confidence, he waits, and schemes, and plans. He is the Damoclean sword dangling over the white world. Everywhere he is on the march, he cannot be stopped, and he knows it."

Black Empire—A Historical Critique

"A Damoclean sword dangling over the white world": Dr. Henry Belsidus would certainly have appreciated the classical allusion; indeed, he would have been hard put to formulate a more accurate description of the promise and program of his revolutionary organization.

"The Black Internationale" serial, like the essay of the same name, embodies profound criticisms of the white power monopoly that, in Schuyler's view, oppressed people of color the world over. Indeed, when taken together, the two, one highly "serious" and the other the purest "pulp," written within months or perhaps weeks of each other, read like ideological companion pieces, each explicating and elucidating the other. The essay addresses the intractable wrongs of the world; the serial, freed by the melodramatic imagination from the imperatives of realism, provides a vision of swift, if symbolic, retribution and invincibility.

How seriously did Schuyler mean for anyone to take *Black Empire's* black utopian vision? To what extent is the story a political allegory, a prophetic hint of the coming black struggle in America and the drive toward African decolonization after the next world war? As wild and improbable as the notion of a powerful worldwide organization of blacks may have seemed in the 1930s, *Black Empire* possesses a radical vindicationist air that gives it a structural and ideological coherence. This framework confers an ironic depth and intellectual complexity that could easily be overlooked were the story to be read merely as pulp entertainment. As the story begins, for example, Belsidus says:

> We must get used to bloodshed, Slater. We must be hard. We must be cruel. We must be unrelenting, neither giving nor asking quarter, until either we or the white race is definitely subjugated, or even exterminated. There is no other way. Softness is weakness. Compromise is disastrous. Tolerance is fatal. (p. 14)

These harsh words echo those of Schuyler himself. In mid-1937, when "The Black Internationale" was nearing its conclusion, he wrote that "the world seems just about ripe for another World War. Every nation is preparing for it. When it comes, which I hope will be soon, I am anxious that it be long, bloody and exhausting. Therein lies hope for the oppressed millions of Africa, India, China and the islands of the sea."[96] "I haven't the slightest interest in Europe nor its institutions erected upon the bruised and bleeding bodies of colored people in Asia, Africa and America," Schuyler wrote just before this, in April 1937. "The quicker they destroy themselves the better it will please me. As long as they remain up, we must remain down. Hence my inability to fathom Negroes who favor world peace."[97]

279

During this time of conflicting militarisms, Schuyler was fascinated by Japan and by the meaning to blacks worldwide of its great military expansion. At the invitation of the *Courier* he wrote a series of articles on the subject that the publisher found too pro-Japan to be printed. "Here is no Abdel Krim, Fuzzy Wuzzy or Haile Salassi to be strafed into submission after a short period of terror," Schuyler commented, calling his readers' attention to the reality of Japanese might. "Here is a great Power with matchless technological equipment, superb training and discipline, and disconcerting disdain of white pretensions. Here is modern Japan, on the march and refusing to be halted."[98] At an early meeting of the Black Internationale organization in *Black Empire,* a delegate concerned about white superiority in military technology uses almost identical words to ask, "Have you forgotten Abdel Krim, Haile Selassie and numerous other chieftains . . . who threw themselves against the machines of white civilization and failed?" (p. 36). While Schuyler saw Japan as an example of a nonwhite nation successfully taking on the white world on its own terms, he was quick to point out that the Japanese—who did nothing to help Ethiopia against Italy—showed no interest in liberating Africa. Japan's chief use, therefore, was as an inspirational model for the organization of black strength.

The European war that Belsidus's Black Internationale foments fulfills Schuyler's fondest hope. *Black Empire* expresses a fictional act of revenge against the white establishment and the social and historical conditions of the time, echoing several issues that concerned Schuyler in his serious writings. Most telling, perhaps, are the issues of racial oppression and the freedom of Africa.

Symbolic Retributions

The mid-thirties' Ethiopian crisis invited a revaluation of African civilization. Italy's conquest of Ethiopia had thrown the black world into crisis and, in particular, starkly posed anew the question that dominated the agenda of black nationalism between the two world wars, namely, whether Africa would remain slave or free. *Black Empire*'s solution is to make "all Africa once more the possession of black men" (p. 133).

Indeed, the many references to Ethiopia and Italy that permeate *Black Empire* reveal that Schuyler himself shared in the general black desire to avenge "the Italian rape of Ethiopia" (p. 127). Significantly, the first serial climaxes with Ethiopia's liberation from Italian oppression. The pent-up anger of blacks everywhere finds expression in Belsidus's jubilant description of his success: "It was a massacre. . . . Those that we didn't kill in their beds, the Ethiopians did. With the arms and ammunition they've got, the Italians will never reconquer them" (p. 132). The second serial climaxes with crushing defeats of Italy. In view of the tremendous sense of violation and outrage that the Italo-Ethiopian war unleashed among blacks worldwide, including the frustration of those who had attempted to volunteer to fight in Ethiopia but were prevented from doing so by the U.S. and other western governments, the serials provided a sense of epic revenge.

A war with Italy over Ethiopia, Schuyler wrote, was not the only engagement that he would welcome. "The others would be a war against England and another conflict between the North and the South. What a joy it would be to drop a two-ton air torpedo on Picadilly Circus or to strafe a stream of cracker refugees leaving Jessup, Ga.!"[99] Schuyler's fantasy of bombing London's busy Picadilly Circus may have been inspired by Padmore's book, *How Britain Rules Africa*, which Schuyler hailed in July 1936 as "a tour de force, a masterpiece of research . . . a perfectly devastating indictment of British misrule, a painstaking panorama of an entire continent where the treatment of blacks by whites makes Hitlerism seem like child's play."[100] Was it mere coincidence that at this very moment Schuyler was beginning to write "The Black Internationale"? It may also have had a more personal meaning, relating to the humiliating treatment that he suffered in 1931 when several London hotels had turned him away.[101]

Interracial Love and Female Revenge

The thirst for revenge that pervades *Black Empire* is expressed early, in the terrible retribution visited upon the whites of Newton, Mississippi, for lynching an innocent black man.[102] When Belsidus orders the elimination of the two white men who witness the crash landing of the Black Internationale plane in Intercourse, Alabama, on its return from Newton, Slater objects that it "seems like useless murder," only to have Belsidus tell him, "Come, let's not worry about two cracker farmers in Alabama who have probably helped in many a lynching" (p. 77).[103]

The sexual connotation of the town named Intercourse touches on the theme of revenge, this time for the sexual violence suffered by blacks at the hand of whites. Schuyler strongly believed "what every person on the street knows," namely, that Negrophobia and fears of race mixing derived their intensity from "the connection between blackness and virility." "The darker peoples *are* more virile than the whites," he asserted; more importantly, however, it was *belief* in black virility that mattered: "It is this widespread belief in the physical superiority of the Negro that accounts for much, if not most of the restrictions surrounding him. Let some dictator sterilize all of America's male Negroes and the race problem would be solved post haste."[104] Just such a solution, albeit a chemical one, is the subject of satire in *Black No More.*

The sexual revenge theme seems to be woven into the character of Martha Gaskin, "the beautiful white girl" devoted to Belsidus, whom "she would never possess" (p. 142). One scene explicitly describes how Belsidus "toyed with Martha's golden hair . . . as if that action symbolized his subjugation of the white race" (p. 240). But Gaskin's role becomes much more than sexual, reflecting Schuyler's fascination with interracial cooperation between the sexes as a metaphor for the destruction of the established racial order. "I believe miscegenation is the way—perhaps the only way—the race problem is going to be solved in these United States," he argued.[105] "The ultimate solution . . . is amalgamation of the two so-called races to form a new one, more handsome, more healthy, more cultured, more secure, more civilized than either the present day whites or blacks."[106]

When Gaskin first appears, she seems to be little more than another slavishly devoted and easily dispensable white lover whom Belsidus is using to enrich his movement. After an embarrassing scene in which Belsidus turns her away when she drunkenly begs for his attentions, he tells Slater, "Inevitably she will find out that I care nothing for her except to get this information. Then, Slater, she will be dangerous. And, of course, she will have to be removed." Slater is "amazed by his callousness." Belsidus adds that "Miss Gaskin knows nothing about the Black Internationale nor our other activities" (p. 81).

Just four chapters later, however, Gaskin's role shifts dramatically. She is now on her way to becoming Belsidus's head of European espionage. By the second serial, she is virtually Belsidus's alter ego and is largely responsible for precipitating Europe's devastating war. She oversees the destruction of Britain's technological brain trust in the great massacre at Delphane Hall. When the getaway of the Black

Internationale assassins is threatened by a policeman at a road block outside London, Gaskin herself saves the day by shooting him (p. 207).

Ultimately, despite the recognition of this white woman's commitment to the cause of black freedom, the barrier of race proves insurmountable. In the final scenes of both serials, we sense what amounts to a silent plea in the slightly despondent voice of the author as Gaskin sits listening to Belsidus deliver his victory speech:

> There were wet eyes and damp cheeks when Dr. Belsidus ended. I saw Martha Gaskin look longingly at him. She realized she would never possess this black man for whom she had risked so much, and I felt sorry for her. (p. 142)

The conclusions of both serials suggest that Belsidus's relationship with Gaskin will never be emotionally consummated. Martha Gaskin is permitted to sacrifice everything in order to serve Belsidus, but as a symbol of the white race, she is punished by being denied a full relationship with him. Love across racial lines in America was something that Schuyler experienced personally in his own marriage. It is another reason that he might have written these stories not as satire but as melodrama, disguising a profound criticism of the oppressiveness of race.

Black Empire's only other major female character complements Martha Gaskin. Patricia Givens, Belsidus's beautiful black air force commander, represents a nod toward the principle of equality for women. Givens, in addition to being an important narrative device—the "woman angle" that Schuyler drops into the story in the ninth week in order to give Slater a love interest—is the other side of Schuyler's erotic fantasy. She is described approvingly as having "the color of a pale Indian with the softness of feature of the Negro" (p. 40). Her position as air force commander makes her central to the Black Internationale organization, giving Slater another excuse to get close to the action. As a pilot, she has mobility—the freedom to transport Slater and the story almost anywhere. Referring to the near mystical strength of the partnership of Belsidus and Givens, at the moment that the Fascist powers in Europe appear ready to "patch up some sort of truce," the narrator notes that "all their efforts were in vain against the clever scheming of a black man and the bravery and skill of a black woman" (p. 128).

Several real-life women may have inspired the Givens character.[107] Shortly after launching "The Black Internationale," Schuyler was calling attention to the late Bessie Coleman, who, he proclaimed, "started us out in the air. . . . Some day when the transportation of the world is largely aloft, some group of Negroes will think of erecting a suitable monument to her memory."[108] Significantly, Schuyler not only memorialized the name of Bessie Coleman in the naming of a Black Internationale ship; it was also the very ship on which Belsidus, Slater, and Givens herself meet with the captains of the fleet before it sets sail for Liberia. [109]

Another influence may have been beautiful Chicago aviatrix Willa B. Brown, described as the first black woman to hold a commercial pilot's license. Left jobless as a schoolteacher as a result of the Depression, Brown moved to Chicago, where she met two outstanding black aviators, Cornelius Coffey and John Robinson, who encouraged her to learn to fly in the early thirties.[110] In 1936, the same year that Schuyler wrote "The Black Internationale," the *Courier* carried two stunning front-page photographs of Brown stylishly decked out in flying outfit, headlined, "Wants to Fight Italian Bombers." The picture caption read:

> Horrified by the attacks of Italian aviators on undefended Ethiopian cities and towns, Miss Willa B. Brown, Chicago aviatrix, is ready to answer the call to Ethiopia.[111]

Another intriguing possibility is the famous aviator Amelia Earhart, the wife of Schuyler's publisher, George Putnam. Schuyler met Earhart at least once and gave her an "elephant-toe bracelet" that he brought back from Liberia.[112] Though Earhart was not black, she fits much of Schuyler's physical description of the lovely, demure Givens.

The Paradigm of the Black Liberator

Although strikingly innovative in many ways, Schuyler's utopian fantasy had precursors in the Afro-American literary tradition of conspirational novels in which blacks quest for sovereign states in order to protect their freedom. One of the earliest extant Afro-American novels, *Blake; or the Huts of America* (1859–62) by well-known black nationalist Martin R. Delany, dramatizes a black militant uprising against Western racist oppression—in this case, chattel slavery.[113] This novel, originally serialized, concerns a growing rebellion based on the subversive activities of a brilliant, courageous black leader, Blake, who is aided by blacks from diverse countries and classes.

284

Perhaps even more relevant is Sutton E. Griggs's *Imperium in Imperio* (1899), which is set against the backdrop of the intense, brutal racism that characterized the United States in the late nineteenth century. The novel creates a secret all-black organization, *Imperium in Imperio,*[114] complete with national congress, army, state legislatures, and constitution. Dedicated to securing full civil rights for Afro-Americans, this group ultimately concludes that outright war is the only option open to blacks in the face of the violence perpetrated upon them by white Americans.

The black liberator is a recurrent figure in Schuyler's work. His 1934 "Strange Valley" serial, a clear precursor to *Black Empire,* contains yet another black American physician, Dr. Augustus Cranfield, who, supported by a team of black American war veterans, rules an African kingdom from within a naturally fortified valley in a remote region of West Africa. Cranfield's people work ancient mines for gold with which to buy modern weapons to liberate Africa. In a revealing scene, Cranfield speaks to Stella, a young black maid whom he has taken prisoner:

> "We have a regiment of trained soldiers here, fully armed. With the gold from these hills, we shall arm more; thousands, tens of thousands, hundreds of thousands. Then we shall strike. And when we do strike we shall drive the white man into the ocean." The King's eyes glowed with intense excitement that belied the calmness of his exterior.
>
> Stella said nothing. She only leaned forward to catch his next words.
>
> "I guess you're thinking of Garvey, aren't you?" he challenged. Then, before she could answer, he plunged on. "Well, he was a fool. Like most Negroes, he told his business to the white folks. I am a smarter man than Garvey. I, too, want to free Africa, but I didn't tell the whole world about it."[115]

As a transitional incarnation of Schuyler's recurring black liberator figure, Cranfield follows Dr. Junius Crookman, inventor of the "black-no-more" process that "liberates" blacks by turning them into whites, and he anticipates Belsidus as a would-be conqueror of Africa. All three doctors are described as tall, dark-skinned, and physically imposing. The Cranfield character is the least demonic of the three; his harsher side is embodied in his ruthless partner, Sam Morgan. While Cranfield becomes romantically involved with Stella, the black American, his alter ego Morgan becomes involved with a white woman, Virginia, who like Belsidus's devoted Martha Gaskin elects to join in the struggle to liberate Africa. This evolving pattern suggests that none of Schuyler's black liberator figures is complete by himself. However, if we regard all three doctor characters as a parts of a single evolving persona, Belsidus emerges as the key to Schuyler's worldview.[116]

While the magnetic, symbolic center to *Black Empire* is the figure of Dr. Belsidus, the all-powerful leader of the Black Internationale, Schuyler reveals almost nothing about Belsidus's own background. This contrasts sharply with Carl Slater, whose entire curriculum vitae is spelled out at the beginning of the story. Belsidus remains a man without a past until the next-to-last chapter of the "Black Internationale," when he finally discloses to Slater, "Years ago I married myself to the ideal of a free Africa" (p. 134). In the serial's final chapter, a few pages later, Belsidus adds, "For twenty years I have struggled and striven to free Africa, and I am tired, very tired. But I am not going to quit now" (p. 141). We know nothing, however, of how Belsidus developed these convictions; it is, indeed, the convictions themselves that take center stage. By not providing Belsidus with the accoutrements of a personal history, Schuyler ensures that the doctor will remain a mythical figure.

The relationship between Slater and Belsidus might be illuminated by a brief consideration of classic theories of the "doppelgänger," or "double." These theories focus on literary works in which different characters mirror each other, works in which the "missing part of a given character is . . . represented by a completely different person in the story."[117] In works of narrative prose, "the first self is the one who tends to be in the foreground of the reader's attention, usually the one whose viewpoint the reader shares; he is the relatively naive self. . . . The second self is the intruder from the background of shadows, and however prominent he may become he always tends to remain half-shadowed; he is much more likely to have knowledge of his foreground counterpart than the latter of him, but the exact extent and source of his knowledge . . . are always left in relative obscurity."[118]

When applied to *Black Empire*, this paradigm suggests that Slater and Belsidus represent different aspects of Schuyler's ideological weltanschauung, particularly regarding such contemporary issues as revolutionary ideology, black liberation, and black power. The story unfolds through Slater's eyes; even as his fascination with Belsidus's ruthlessness grows, he embodies a viewpoint of moral restraint. He repeatedly describes Belsidus as "diabolic," "satanic," and "demoniacal"; such allusions evoke images of the phonologically similar Beelzebub. We also know that in Schuyler's rough notes, he called his central character "Dr. Beast." And Belsidus's organization, according to Slater, accomplishes "every fiendish scheme for the overthrow of white supremacy . . . with devilish cunning." Belsidus incarnates a radical, revolutionary ideology; he becomes both demon and savior—a committed revolutionary, a cruel yet, perhaps, necessary corrective to Slater's naive humanism.

The Demonic and African Magic

Despite Schuyler's claim to being "a rather thoroughgoing skeptic" about religious belief, he was deeply drawn to ideas of the demonic and the occult as embodied in the black folk tradition of African magic. He once wrote a poignant autobiographical essay recalling his grandmother, who had "a great respect for the Devil." She married a West African "well versed in the voodoo ritual, a clever fellow who knew how to make the souls of dead folk do all sorts of queer things." Schuyler's grandmother, "a sage, crusty, and industrious matriarch, the repository of all knowledge, it seemed, and a mine of folklore," was clearly the major influence upon Schuyler's youth, especially after the early death of his father and his mother's remarriage.[119] Her death had a powerful impact on him, which he recorded in an unpublished autobiographical story.[120]

Schuyler's published reminiscence of his grandmother, suitably entitled "Black Art," celebrates her African-based folk beliefs, which required "one to keep a weather eye on Satan, and to know how to circumvent the machinations of his numerous disciples: the conjurers, witches, necromancers and whatnot."[121] He contrasted how "she never grew sleepy when reading or talking about the Forces of Evil" with her customarily dozing off while reading the Bible. "The Scriptures were, after all, only hearsay, a sort of second-hand information, though indubitably God's Word, but she knew from first hand about the doings of the Devil and his assistants, the conjurers." [122]

From childhood, Schuyler's psyche was imprinted with respect for the magical power subsumed by his grandmother's frequent "talk about conjuring, magic roots and the power of lodestones," which sprang from within the African-American folk belief in the spirit-world. It was "the prospect of hearing more about black art from her," Schuyler later recalled, that "impell[ed] me to hurry through my chores." He added:

> My respect for Satan grew apace, and secretly I held him to be more powerful than the Master Himself. It struck me that he was a most industrious fellow, working twenty-four hours a day and with remarkable success. I wondered that he had time to look after all of the people he had frying in Hell, what with so many conjurers to direct on earth, but Grandma very satisfactorily explained that he could be everywhere at once.[123]

Schuyler's five months in the West African bush in 1931 reminded him of his familial inheritance and left him more amazed than ever. "I came to the conclusion after my observations in Africa," he humbly confessed, "that the people there are masters of psychology and have perhaps delved more deeply into the strange, obscure corners of the human mind than the people anywhere else in the world."[124] The theme of African magic triumphing over western missionary Christianity recurs in several of his short stories and serials during the thirties.

The African-American tradition of storytelling and folk spiritual beliefs thus imparted a culturally idiosyncratic and compelling quality to Schuyler's mode of fabulation. From this perspective, the literary re-creation of the Devil figure in Schuyler's fiction and the demonic quality of his male characters are rooted in African-American folk magical belief, especially in its traditional, performative, oral tradition. Schuyler's preoccupation with the demonic should not, therefore, be confused with pejorative Christian presuppositions about the Devil. In contrast to the Christian belief system, the African-American folk worldview sees the Devil connected not so much with sin as with the qualities of a powerfully creative, charismatic anti-hero, a trickster-magician, a beguiling genius of fathomless prowess—scientific, sexual, psychological—and, beyond all this, the animating source of folktales and the victor in many of these tales of contestation.[125]

Viewed through the prism of black folklore and mythology, therefore, Schuyler's Belsidus is not a deranged personality. He is, rather, simultaneously a hero and an authentic anti-hero who, like the African trickster, turns weakness into strength, upsets the machinery of domination, deals out retribution, commands absolute fealty, and, ultimately, vindicates the concept of magical dread as the source of power.

Three books that engaged Schuyler's interest between the moment he assumed the pen name "Samuel I. Brooks" and the time he wrote *Black Empire* further illuminate Belsidus's character. W. E. B. Du Bois's 1928 novel *Dark Princess*[126] impressed Schuyler greatly. "Although I have only reached Page 127, I couldn't resist the temptation to write and tell you what a masterful piece of work it is," he wrote Du Bois. "Beside you other contemporary writers hailed as 'great' pale into insignificance. Not only do I think 'Dark Princess' is a fine work from a literature standpoint, but it is also great as a portrayal of the soul of our people."[127]

Dark Princess is the story of a young black American, Matthew Towns, who quits medical school because its racially discriminatory system makes it impossible for him to complete his studies satisfactorily. He goes to Berlin—where Du Bois himself had studied—and meets the beautiful, dark-skinned princess, Kautilya, from Bwodpur, India. Kautilya heads an incipient international movement, the "Great Council of the Darker Peoples," dedicated to overturning white rule throughout the world. Like Belsidus's Black Internationale, Kautilya's movement believes in the superiority of nonwhite brains and culture. Kautilya's underground council, however, has no black American representation. Its largely Asian and North African members do not believe black Americans are politically and psychologically ready to join them.[128] Initially motivated by his attraction to the princess, Towns returns home to contact a black resistance movement on her behalf. The princess also travels to America to learn about black people. Both characters experience painful transformations on the way to the enlightenment that reunites them and gives black America its rightful place on the Council of the Darker Peoples.

In addition to the model of a great international antiwhite organization, Schuyler would have found much in Du Bois's book to inspire him—the character of a frustrated black would-be doctor, the notion that the center of world power has shifted to Africa and Asia,[129] and powerful strains of Hindu mysticism and religion.[130]

Another book rekindled Schuyler's interest in African witchcraft: D. Manners-Sutton's *Black God: A Story of the Congo*,[131] which Schuyler read in 1934 and called "one of the best-written novels about contemporary life in Africa." *Black God*'s dominant theme is the power of African magic, described as "the last stronghold" of Africans in the face of

European colonial hegemony. Schuyler's plot summary in his review reveals the focus of his interest:

> Here is the timelessness of Africa—its wonder, patience, mystery, cruelty . . . and stupidity. It is a weird, amazing, incredible country, this region of the Little River in the center of the Belgian Congo, where M'Kato, the handless Zulu, sits twenty years on the bank of the stream ["like some black god intent upon creation"] awaiting the coming of [the] planter who had his hands severed at the wrists, and silently surveys the society growing up about him. A pall of witchcraft, terrifying yet fascinating, hangs over this land. It holds the blacks in its grip; the whites cannot escape its influence.[132]

One of the novel's principal figures is the "Black Master," a European-educated Gold Coast African who comes to the trading post of Chembi, near the Little River, where the main character sits out his fate. The Black Master sells charms and exerts great power over women, black and white. He openly ridicules whites and speaks of becoming governor of the province. "The man was frankly black, and his name, the Black Master, seemed to indicate power, leadership, and things perhaps even less savoury."[133] Eventually, the man becomes intimate with the administrator's wife; when her husband is found with his throat slit, he moves in with her. Her brother-in-law takes her away but the Black Master remains in the residency by himself; no one can get him out.

The Black Master wishes to restore all Africa to black rule. Deflowering vestal virgins without completing the sexual act is the key to his power. Lafontaine, the local magistrate's white clerk, recognizes that the Black Master threatens the entire white settlement and embarks on a study of African magic which he believes is the only way to get rid of him. He devises a charm that breaks the Black Master's spell and leads to his being torn limb from limb by his own followers. "There would never be his black rule upon the Little River, white civilisation would go on, progress as it had always done." [134] Lafontaine writes in his diary, "The Black Master . . . was a man of unbounded ambition, and possibly saw in himself a potential ruler of all Africa. It was his open boast that he wished to break white civilisation and white domination in Africa. It fell upon me, as a white man interested in seeing civilisation built up in this savage land, to break this negro's sway, and remove his dangerous presence from the Little River for ever."[135]

Schuyler's unrestrained praise for this haunting work may well have been stimulated by the character of the Black Master. Interestingly, in December 1931 the *Courier* had carried a brief front-page news item from Brussels headlined, "Find 'Black Messiah' In Congo Belt." The item reported that "one of the reasons ascribed for the (native) uprisings (in various parts of the Belgium Congo) is that reports have come to the Congo district that a 'Negro Messiah' from the United States is coming to take over the administration of the colony from foreign whites."[136]

Schuyler seems to have been particularly fascinated by the Congo. He uses it in his sketch for "The Last White Man," where the Congo supplies the fictional capital for "a Communistic Confederacy of Negro States." *Black Empire* evokes Congolese images in the African music played in the Temple of Love rites (p. 62), and it is a "Congo Ballet" that is performed for the doomed British technicians in the Delphane Hall (p. 202). During the Black Internationale's conquest of Africa, the Congolese people rise up and massacre all the whites in the colony to retaliate for the years of atrocities endured under Belgian rule (p. 129).[137]

A third novel that fascinated Schuyler was *The Man Inside; Being the Record of the Strange Adventures of Allen Steele Among the Xulus* by the independent white Marxist literary critic and polymath, V. F. Calverton.[138] Published just weeks before the first installment of "The Black Internationale" appeared, Calverton's novel of ideas struck Schuyler with its use of "hypnotism and its possibilities as an instrument for shaping human conduct. . . . All in all, it is a thought-provoking book."[139]

Schuyler had a close relationship with the like-minded Calverton, whose "intellectual and social relationship to the Negro," according to one authority, "was a remarkable phenomenon that deserves close examination." Indeed, the relationship between Calverton and blacks reflects an important phase in the link between radicalism and race that obtained in the United States in the interwar period. Haim Genizi notes:

> Unlike Communist or literary critics who attacked him bitterly, his [Calverton's] black friends remained enthusiastic supporters. When, during the thirties, his radical and later his liberal friends deserted him one by one, the heartfelt response of black companions eased the pain of this disappointment. It would not be an exaggeration, therefore, to consider Calverton's affiliation with blacks as one of the brightest phases of his short life.[140]

291

Calverton expressed great sensitivity to African-American history and literature. He included a chapter on slave revolts in his revisionist *The Awakening of America* (1939), written "to reread American history . . . in terms of the ruled instead of the rulers, the underdogs instead of the top dogs" (p. vii). He also contributed the "Negro" entry to Harold E. Stearns's *America Now: An Inquiry into Civilization in the United States by Thirty-Six Americans* (1938).[141] Earlier, he included Schuyler's essay "Our Greatest Gift to America" in his *Anthology of American Negro Literature* (1929); he published that same year in his *Modern Quarterly* Schuyler's essay "Emancipated Women and the Negro," in which Schuyler considered "what effect the emancipation of women will have on the future of race relations in the alleged Land of the Free."[142] Schuyler examined this topic further in his partly autobiographical essay "When Black Weds White," in Calverton's February 1934 issue of *Modern Monthly*.[143] Most importantly, Schuyler credited Calverton with encouraging him to write *Black No More* and helping to get it published.[144] There is no question that Schuyler's relationship with Calverton was important to both men—a point that Schuyler acknowledged when invited to contribute to *Modern Quarterly*'s special memorial issue, following Calverton's death in 1940.

Stripped of its plot complexities, Calverton's *The Man Inside* is the story of a white man, Joli Coeur (French for "pretty heart"), who conducts experiments in hypnosis in the African jungle, exploring the power of the human mind. This leads him to the view that society is a highly developed result of "social hypnosis," which controls people through mental suggestion, in the form of such institutions as churches, schools, and the media.[145] Revolutionaries' failure to win followings, Coeur believes, derives from their failure to acknowledge the overriding power of humanity's irrational impulses. Western civilization, by seeking to understand the world through science and rationalism, ignores the fact that people are not rational.

According to Coeur, people are confined by their narrow prejudices and are therefore unable to see what they have in common with other national, ethnic, or racial groups. Like the myth of rationality, the myth of individuality propagated by western civilization is especially insidious; it keeps people from recognizing their collective identity as part of a single human race. This individuality is based on the fear of death, and it is this deeply rooted fear that Coeur attempts to eliminate in his experiments with hypnosis on the Xulus. Coeur is finally killed by a revolt when his failure to control a plague costs him his legitimacy as a spiritual leader. Similarly, in *Black Empire*'s Temple of Love, the audience "stared hypnotically" at the gigantic God of Love, whose luminous eyes "looked down in hypnotic scrutiny"(p. 63).

White Terror and the Psychology of Revolt

The depiction of Belsidus's uncanny, demonic power in *Black Empire* definitely resonates with Joli Coeur's experiments in hypnosis. When Belsidus tells the assembled Liberian chiefs, "I do not know fear because I am the great leopard. . . . Today you have nothing to fear, for today, I, the King of Kings, rule" (p. 111), he is attempting nothing less than the elimination of fear in the African *à la* Joli Coeur. Several years earlier, Schuyler had held that such fear was so pervasive among blacks that it was presumed to be a basic psychological characteristic. He wrote:

> The majority of Negroes have been so conditioned by this long wave of terrorism that now lynching is no longer necessary on a large scale to keep them in their supposed place as the mudsill of society. This "adult education" of the Negro by the White Terror has reached the point where it is not only automatic but also reproductive. That is to say, a certain type has been developed among Negroes that advocates and insists upon all those things that will perpetuate white supremacy. Thus, we find the advocates of racial separation, the 49th Staters, the professional Negrophiles, the ballyhoers of the boycott, the diligent defenders of jim crowism, and their ilk, doing effectively the work which the White Terror once had to do with bullet, rope and torch. The Negro of the Grant-McKinley era had to be beaten into submission. The Negro of today yells like the African serf, "Massa, I hold your foot," and camouflages it with amazing rationalism into a pragmatic raceology.[146]

Belsidus's final, triumphant speech sums up the vindicationist message of the story: "We who were once despised and slandered are now honored and feared" (p. 257). *Black Empire* thus seems to argue that the conquest of fear is necessary to overcome white supremacy; it is fear, Schuyler suggests, that has conditioned blacks not to recognize their true collective strength. *Black Empire* figuratively turns the tables. "White world supremacy must be destroyed, my lad, and it will be destroyed," Belsidus tells Slater near the outset of the story. "I have dedicated my life, Slater, to destroying white world supremacy" (p. 10). At the triumphant climax of the story, we are told that "the reaction of the white world was one of profound fear, but great exultation filled the air wherever men and women of color gathered" (p. 250).

Black Empire might thus be read as an allegory of the conquest of fear or "the man inside" in the form of—in Schuyler's words—the "White Terror." "It took fifty years for the savage White Terror of the K.K.K., the police, the courts and the chain gangs to kill the militancy of the Negroes, but it has been done," he observed during the February 1935 congressional hearings on the Costigan-Wagner anti-lynching bill. He attributed the decline in the number of lynchings mainly to "the crushing of Southern Negro militancy by the White Terror." "Make no mistake about it," he declared, "the purpose of lynching is not now and never has been to stop Negroes from raping white women. Its purpose has been to keep the Negro in 'his place,' i.e., out of politics and economic competition on the higher levels, by periodically terrorizing him with a burning or a hanging."[147] From the perspective of psychological reconditioning, *Black Empire*, with its fictional narrative describing "the overthrow of white supremacy," is an exercise in ideological suggestion. It answers the clarion call, issued by Schuyler in his 1938 essay "The Rise of the Black Internationale," for the "new Negro" who is "no longer . . . terrorized."

Perhaps for this reason Schuyler ardently believed in the methods of John B. Watson's school of behavioristic psychology. *Black Empire*'s Patricia Givens reflects these beliefs when she states that "we will recondition the Negro masses in accordance with the most approved behavioristic methods" (p. 47). In a weekly column, Schuyler detailed the "revolutionary character" of Watson's discoveries, explaining how "Watson demonstrated that the child is born . . . possessed of only two tendencies which might be called instincts: fear of falling and fear of loud noise; that man's whole complicated equipment of responses is the result of conditioning based on those two primary fears." Accepting this premise of conditioned responses, Schuyler was convinced that "we can recondition humanity and we can recondition the individual. The first is the duty or the job of the revolutionary and leader, whether for better or worse. The second is the job of the parents."[148] Thus, although Belsidus is portrayed as possessed of satanic features, he is also a revolutionary in the theoretical, behavioristic sense. He is absolutely not a mountebank. In the words of Schuyler's narrator, "the genius of Dr. Belsidus had freed our race" (p. 190).

294

In a further exploration of this theme, in September 1937 Schuyler chided the black intelligentsia: "The cynic derives a certain grim amusement from observing how effectively 'education' prevents us from thinking intelligently about our forbears and contemporaries in Africa." Then, following a detailed examination of the biases behind concepts of superiority and inferiority, Schuyler attacked the "triumph of that Nordic propaganda which we misname education."[149] In *Black Empire*, "miseducated Negroes"—those "who still favored the rule of white men to the rule of black men," and "who now tried to help them by stirring counter-revolution"—are "ruthlessly purged and executed" (p. 138).

Communism and Fascism

In addition to the twin themes of Africa and race, *Black Empire* resonates with many of Schuyler's other contemporary concerns. Beginning with the title of the first serial itself, it makes ironic use of communism as an international phenomenon. "Black Internationale," the name of Belsidus's conspiratorial organization, invites comparison with the parallel socialist, communist, and anarchist internationales.[150]

Essentially, Schuyler saw the activities of the Communist or Third Internationale more as reflections of the "rampant and raging nationalism"—which he called "the greatest single characteristic of the postwar period"—than as expressions of class conflict. "Nationalism is the dominant force in every modern country," he warned, pitying those "black segregationists who mouth nonsense about 'group economy' and 'voluntary segregation' as 'a way out.' " The ultimate choice before minorities was a stark one, governed by this modern-day Leviathan:

> Whether it be called Communism as in Russia, Fascism as in Italy, Nazism as in Germany, or Americanism as in the United States, minority groups will be well advised if they seek to merge with it at once. The quicker they ditch their identity as minority groups the surer they will be of individual security.[151]

In an especially penetrating analysis, published in June 1937, Schuyler attempted to explain "the rising tide of tribalism" in the world.[152] It was "the fire [that] now encircles the earth," he claimed. If the phenomenon was atavistic, however, it was also very modern. "It is merely the old tribalism of paleolithic and neolithic ages parading in modern dress and made more ruthless and totalitarian," he argued, "by harnessing science to its chariot." This modern mixture of nationalism and science was what Schuyler worked into *Black Empire*.

The revolutionizing impact of the modern state carried over to the economic sphere. Under this reorganization, Schuyler confidently believed, America would become collectivized. In an unpublished 1934 essay, "The Negro Turns to Fascism," Schuyler was optimistic about the prospects of what the new, collectivized dispensation might hold for blacks. "Intelligent Negro radicals believe," he declared, "that in the Collective State, which they think will soon be here, racial antagonism will die with the assurance of economic security for all, Black Belts will become anachronisms and amalgamation will closely follow social integration." It was out of character for Schuyler to believe in radical dreams, but his belief in the inevitability of economic collectivism as a necessary step of social organization was certainly one such instance.[153]

Thus, while Schuyler harshly criticized "the infantile paralysis of communism" in the United States, he nonetheless saw the Soviet model, though flawed, as a prototype of both revolutionary politics and technological transformation.[154] Schuyler's description of the Black Internationale's scientific accomplishments in *Black Empire* makes the link explicit. " 'This is our farm,' announced Sam, a little proudly. 'Only one of its kind in this country on a big scale. I understand there are some in Russia and Germany, though' " (pp. 48–49). A further explicit reference comes when Belsidus snaps: "We mustn't make the mistake of Russia and try to work without brains and skill" (p. 79).

The Black Internationale comprises a network of "cells" similar to that in classic Bolshevik organization, and its leader, Belsidus, is called a "bloodthirsty, fanatical revolutionist" (p. 18). "I have the responsibility of directing this revolution," he says early in the story. Two hundred Black Internationale cells are reported in the U.S., with another "half hundred national cells in Europe, Asia, Africa, South America and the West Indies" (p. 82). The cells teach literacy, erect temples as Black Internationale centers, combat lynching, propagandize, foment strife among whites, prepare Africa for conquest, and, finally, represent black workers at conferences. The Black Internationale's final victory is "a greater sensation than the fall of the Roman Empire, the defeat of Russia by Japan or the Bolshevist revolution" (p. 250).

Concerned throughout the 1930s with "fighting the forces of Fascism," Schuyler would attempt to correct what he claimed was the misconceived tactics of the Communist party. As a result, he became embroiled in running controversies with an assortment of black and white Communist spokesmen throughout what could aptly be termed the "red decade" in African-American history by virtue of the unprecedented level of black recruitment into the ranks of the Communist party.[155] "No group in this country has been more assiduously proselytized by the Red brethren than the Sons of Ham," Schuyler declared with characteristic satire, "albeit the bulk of Senegambians were too cynical to succumb to the raucous rabble-rousing even during the Scottsboro hysteria, on which the Reds ate for years."[156]

In a less provocative, though hardly less critical, assessment, Schuyler took stock of the peak years of Communist party organizing among blacks. "The Communist party has for the past three or four years concentrated on the Negro group to the exclusion of every other section of the American working class in an effort to win the Aframericans over to a working class viewpoint," he declared. "The goal is a commendable one," he asserted, but he doubted the wisdom of the party's tactics. The party's concentration on organization among blacks, he believed, "to the virtual neglect of the white majority," would likely strengthen "the rising Fascist movement," result in the "extermination of thousands of Negro workers," and ultimately "divide rather than unite the black and white workers for the coming struggle for power."[157]

Thus was Schuyler embroiled in a prolonged polemic with the Communist party over its recruiting of blacks, even as he simultaneously attacked the spreading appeal of black nationalist and separatist sentiment during the decade of fascist ascendancy. The result of these divergent intellectual engagements left a definite mark, as seen in the fantastical mixture of competing, contradictory ideologies subsumed within *Black Empire*, which at the same time gave full vent to Schuyler's idiosyncratic vision of a revolutionary utopia.

The Rising Tide of Race Chauvinism

Intellectually, Schuyler held out for a distinctly non-racialist view of the world: "Personally, I am opposed to worship of things Nordic as I am of things Negroid."[158] It was a view that placed him at odds with a significant segment of black and white opinion during the late twenties and thirties, which held that the emergence of a truly black art and literature was a necessary condition of cultural and intellectual autonomy. "So accustomed have we become to thinking of Negroes in terms of a stereotype or caricature manufactured and foisted upon us, that our minds have become muddled by wrestling with this ghost of reality, and we fail to see ourselves as we are," he complained, adding caustically:

> We are submerged under a tidal wave of claptrap: Negro wealth, Negro art, Negro statistics on everything under the sun, Negro education, Negro religion, Negro psychology, Negro civilization, Negro literature, Negro history, Negro housing, Negro mortality, Negro morality, Negro athletics, Negro business, Negro medicine, Negro this, that and the other, ad infinitum, ad nauseum. And as if prejudiced and well-meaning, if ignorant, white people were not doing sufficient injury to clear thinking by this flubdubbery, colored folk themselves have taken to baying the same nonsense.[159]

Schuyler enjoined blacks to forswear separatism. "Again, the rising tide of race chauvinism among Negroes (to counteract that of the white folks) is becoming more and more forbidding with the passage of time," he warned. He went so far as to declare that "the Negro segregationists are to be feared more than the white segregationists."[160] He also said it was his "unshakable opinion that Negro segregation in any form is a menace to the colored folk in this country whether that segregation be brought about by external pressure or international urgings."[161] Here he was attacking the "new school of 'thought' [that] has sprung up in our midst emphasizing the so-called cultural value of voluntary segregation"—a reference to W. E. B. Du Bois's espousal during the Depression of a black group economy. In addition, Schuyler variously denounced the Communist party's program that advocated "self-determination" for the Black Belt of the South; the Chicago-based "National Movement for the Establishment of a 49th State"; the Harlem store boycott movement; and assorted African emigration groups.

Schuyler himself was intimately involved with the Manhattan Medical Society, which from its inception in May 1930 was opposed to those in the medical profession who accepted segregated facilities. He called it a group of "unselfish Negro physicians and surgeons" who deserved to be "hailed up and down the land as public benefactors"—not the "crackpots and visionaries" that they were said to be. In his opinion, the society was distinguished for "militancy and intelligence rare for groups of colored physicians and surgeons."[162] By his account, the group's major achievements were "scotch[ing] the efforts of the Rosenwald Fund to perpetuate discrimination and segregation in New York by establishing a 'Negro' hospital," and fighting "the establishment of a jim crow Veterans Hospital in Pennsylvania or anywhere else in the North."

Against the general backdrop of Schuyler's opposition to all forms of racial self-segregation during the thirties, particularly in the case of his bitter polemics against the "many Negro physicians [who] have joined the ranks of the Race racketeers,"[163] the fictional Belsidus symbolizes a triumph over segregation. Significantly, his medical practice consists of "fashionable white patients [who] saw only the well-appointed office of a wealthy physician" (p. 22). Similarly, Belsidus lives "downtown," in "a large private residence in the Seventies between Park and Madison Avenues," like white Manhattan physicians. When, at the conclusion of the story, Belsidus tells his followers, "You have a great empire created out of black brains and strength" (p. 257), the conquest of Africa and end of white supremacy stand as a parable of competence and capacity. "We have the natural resources, the will and the ability to create the greatest civilization the world has seen," Belsidus tells delegates to his second world conference at the end of the first serial, and he concludes, "This conquest proves that white men are not our superiors" (p. 140).

Despite the clearly racial nature of Belsidus's Black Internationale, Schuyler was also intent on distancing himself from a line of racial argument he did not really believe. Rather than provide the simplistic ontological racial reductionism current among contemporary fascist thinkers, *Black Empire* embodies a critical understanding and use of race as a facilitating part of a broader revolutionary strategy. For Schuyler, racism was a reality that necessitated serious analysis. Race by itself, however, could not provide a self-sufficient explanation either for racism or its overthrow. In any case, Schuyler always put nation over race.

Black Belles Lettres

The theories of race and revolution that Schuyler presents in *Black Empire* illuminate his concerns about the professions of the arts and the sciences. His "Advice to Budding Literati," written during the movement later known as the Harlem Renaissance, had complained vociferously about the limitations placed on black writing by the white power structure, which demanded that black writing had to be "bizarre, fantastical and outlandish, with a suggestion of the jungle, the plantation or the slum. Otherwise it will not be *Negro* literature, and hence not acceptable."[164] Its "predominant characteristic," he noted bitterly, "should be naivete as befits simple children just a century or two removed from the so-called uncivilized expanses of the Dark Continent." His essay "The Negro-Art Hokum" ridiculed the notion of a distinctively African-American art aesthetic popularized during the Harlem Renaissance.[165]

By early 1936, however, Schuyler could rejoice that the "Cult of the Negro" and the "day of a white and Negro standard of literary appraisal" were "happily past." Recalling the twenties' vogue of black culture, he announced: "The Sambo Era has gone. The Coon Age is no more. Only a few of the white literati who once boasted of their kennels of Negro 'artists' are any longer interested. . . . Eroticism is no longer a 'natural.' "[166]

Later that same year, Schuyler announced an appeal to launch a "publication exclusively devoted to belles lettres, to the encouragement and development of Negro writers and a medium for publishing their wares," targeting black newspapers in particular. "It is not without significance that not a single Negro newspaper has a literary page or makes any effort to stimulate belles lettres," he declared, while "no Negro newspaper is without a sports page or two and certainly never without a society page." "It seems to me that there are enough civilized people in Aframerica to support at least one real literary publication that would serve to stimulate our young writers and offer them a critical medium of expression," Schuyler wrote.[167] Rather than be imposed by white patrons, this "genuine literary renaissance . . . must come from within. Our writers must write what they want to write, as well as they can write it, for an audience sympathetic to the themes on which they write."[168] Pulp readers paid the bills, but it was committed "Negro literati" that Schuyler desired most to cultivate.

Schuyler's literary organ never materialized, but his resultant disappointment curiously did not translate into a questioning of a new black literature as an elite preoccupation. Paradoxically, he seems to have directed his resentment at the mass readership that supported his serial stories. It was probably his black readers' ready acceptance of the sensationalism and race pride of "The Black Internationale" that seemed to revolt him. He associated such easy acceptance with traits of the same so-called "true Negro psychology" that he believed whites expected from black writers. The very story that he belittled as "hokum," however, not only presents "the American Negro as a product of machine civilization"; it also depicts him as a *master* of "machine civilization,"—one who even exceeds the level attained by supposedly superior whites.[169]

Black Genius Against the World

In the summer of 1935 Schuyler had written, "far from being the benighted, ignorant savage, a notch above the gorilla, which white folk love to depict, the African today is quite alert and informed. More, he is rapidly becoming industrialized and is now quite familiar with the white man's tools. He is using them today. He will be manufacturing them himself tomorrow." He listed Africa's natural resources and predicted that "some time in the near future, native Africans will not only be inhabiting it and doing the work, but will be governing it as well."[170]

Schuyler's fascination with scientific and technological progress had been sparked at an early age and remained a lifelong preoccupation. Indeed, it may have been his personal search for a rational, scientifically ordered universe that caused him to reject the notion of a distinctively African-American art aesthetic during the time of the Harlem Renaissance. It was not so much his disagreement with the basic concept as his difficulty in interesting himself in questions of art and aesthetics as a way to comprehend the world around him.

Schuyler consistently connected applied science with youthful ambition. "Science offers a wonderfully thrilling field for the young man and woman in this day and time," he exclaimed in a 1931 column that reads like a piece of career counseling. "Here are always new worlds to conquer, new vistas to open and set society marveling. It has always seemed to me that more Negroes should be active in the exact sciences such as engineering, chemistry, physics, geology, etc. We have Prof. Carver and his remarkable discoveries but to how many others can we point?"[171] In a 1936 essay, published as the "Black Internationale" serial was first appearing, Schuyler criticized the fact that "86 per cent of our college and vocational graduates in the past quarter century" were in the traditional occupations of teaching, medicine, dentistry, preaching, and law, with "73 per cent of this number having taken up teaching and preaching."[172]

Against this professional myopia among the black elite, Schuyler offered a radical alternative. "This is the age of technics and the key man is the technical scientist. Without him we should promptly return to a seventeenth century economy," he declared. "We may do without teachers, preachers, doctors and dentists . . . but our civilization is bogged down without electricians, engineers, chemists, metallurgists and their like." He recognized the political consequences that such a reorientation implied: "It is desirable that our future Negro leadership consists of scientists rather than teachers and preachers, not only because we are living in an age dominated by science but because the psychology of the engineer is more likely to incline to Negro integration in American life and less toward tacitly accepting and promoting segregation." Schuyler concluded with an almost utopian appeal:

> A new world is unfolding compared to which the scientific wonders of the present will be as the radio to the tom tom. Let young Negroes prepare themselves for new places and new responsibilities in this new world, and let old Negroes, parents, friends and well-wishers, furnish the scholarships and backing which even genius requires.[173]

Black Empire's Patricia Givens articulates a similar sentiment when she and Carl Slater tour Black Internationale installations:

> It is the skilled technician, the scientist, who wins modern wars, and we are mobilizing the black scientists of the world. Our professors, our orators, our politicians have failed us. Our technicians will not. Every day sees another trained young colored man or woman . . . added to our group. (p. 46)

Schuyler's emphasis on science is symbolically expressed in the name "Ransom Just"—Belsidus's radio engineer—whose surname reflects Schuyler's identification with the brilliant black biologist of the time, Ernest Everett Just.[174] Schuyler may have intended to convey a truth beyond race or revenge. "White people haven't got all the brains," Belsidus tells Slater, assuring him that "young Negroes like yourself: intellectuals, scientists, engineers . . . are mentally the equal of the whites. . . . All they need is money, instruments, new weapons of science." Once these have been provided, "you will see in your time a great Negro nation in Africa, all-powerful, dictating to the white world" (p. 15). The application of scientific empowerment to political ends is conveyed in the subtitle, "Black Genius Against the World."

302

Cooperation and the Critique of Religion

Belsidus's assertion that "we can build here on this, the second largest continent, an empire of black men and women working toward a cooperative civilization unexcelled in this world" (p. 142) vindicates the principle of consumer and producer cooperation underlying the Young Negroes' Co-operative League of America (YNCL), which Schuyler organized in 1930.[175] Schuyler describes how he became involved in the cooperative movement and eventually launched the YNCL:

> Back in 1921 I became a member of a cooperative bakery and have helped to launch two colored cooperatives. In December 1930, in association with a score of individuals in various parts of the country, I organized the Young Negroes Cooperative League after I discovered that not a single national Negro organization was interested in launching such a progressive program. Probably their lack of interest was due to the fact that white funds and foundations and "leading" white people had not endorsed it.[176]

The nationalistic edge to the criticism is unmistakable, especially when set in the context of the plan of development sketched in *Black Empire*. A month later, Schuyler added that "consumers' co-operation is more revolutionary than communism" and that "a revolution just as fundamental and far-reaching (as the Socialist or Communist Utopia) can be brought about through consumers' co-operatives."[177]

Schuyler's emphasis on rational cooperation also elucidates his hostility toward religion. He was particularly critical of what he took to be the betrayal by the black church of its role as an instrument of social change: "In the Negro church there are a few ministers who sound off about lynchings, segregation, etc., but few, if any, are opposed to the present social order which grinds down the poor and dooms millions of Negroes to perpetual serfdom."[178] In a 1935 essay, Schuyler argued that the black church arose out of the black revolt against segregated churches and "supplied the race's first leaders." Gradually, however, the black church lost its historical function, until it merely supplied "the race's worst bleeders." He called religion "the black man's burden," that which "keeps him in ignorance, poverty and degradation."[179]

Schuyler's disgust with the organized church's failure to fulfill its early emancipatory promise made him attempt to win it over to the principles of his consumer cooperative program. "As for giving the churches a

303

chance, I have personally been urging church congregations for years to form themselves into cooperative societies and have a Negro butcher, groceryman, coal man, etc., as well as a Negro clergyman," he wrote in 1931. Although the response was disappointing, to say the least, he did not give up hope. "If church people can support schools, colleges and hospitals for education and medical attention," Schuyler argued, "they should not find it difficult to support their democratically owned stores for the sustenance of the people."[180]

Schuyler's critique of the institutional black church became the rationale for the *Black Empire*'s "Temple of Love"—a neo-pagan, quasi-Egyptian religion that gave the revolutionary Black Internationale both a spiritual and material framework. Significantly, the only time that *Black Empire* actually employs the pejorative term "hokum" occurs when Carl Slater reacts to the giant animated idol in the Temple of Love. Although Slater knows *how* he is being manipulated by the machine, he succumbs psychologically, as modern technology and emotional atavism meld. This primitive-modern linkage comes across even more forcefully later, when Belsidus's organization lures fifteen thousand British "Master Technicians" to an African dance recital in London. After enjoying the *Congo Ballet* for an hour, the entire assemblage returns from the intermission to be cold-bloodedly gassed to death. What exquisite irony that a product of superior black chemistry should be used to wipe out England's finest technicians as they savor a tranquil African ballet!

Autobiography of Ambition

Allusions to Schuyler's formative experiences and youthful aspirations appear throughout *Black Empire*. To appreciate their significance, it is useful to go back to a column that he wrote in 1934, replying to Kelly Miller's characterization of Schuyler as "the most cynical and caustic" of the so-called self-educated group of Negro radicals.[181] Schuyler used his "historical background" to explain his views:

> Aside from attending first class public schools in a far Northern city for over ten years, I knew about Crispus Attucks, Toussaint L'Ouverture, Hannibal, Alexander Dumas, Bishop Alexander Crummel, Sojourner Truth, Aunt Harriet Tubman and some of the part Negroes played in the development of American civilization before I entered the first grade. Six years in the Regular Army in the days before it became a Y.M.C.A. camp taught me order and a sense of reality. Time spent as

stevedore, porter, building laborer, dishwasher and gandy dancer, while educational in the extreme, can hardly be termed self-education. Nor can my twelve years in journalism be so labeled. Nor can the time spent under the voice of John B. Watson and Alfred Adler be so termed. If one is self-educated who has never attended or graduated from a college or university, then of course, I am self-educated.[182]

If we go back to 1931, when Schuyler was on his way to Africa, we find a column in which he recounts the hurt he had suffered when his youthful ambition was crushed. "I often shudder," he said, "when I think of the thousands of colored youngsters who each year are being turned out to face the world with little real preparation and no opportunities in these two 'greatest empires on earth,' the United States and Great Britain. I can so clearly recall my own first adventure in the workaday world, and remembering I cannot but feel a sinking of the heart whenever I see bright-faced Negro boys and girls leaving high school and college to take their places in the world." He went on to recount his own painful awakening after graduating at the top of his high school class:

> I had daily hobnobbed with the boys in the best white families. . . . I felt fully equipped to hold my own anywhere. I planned to work just long enough to procure money to take me through college where *I intended to learn how to build great bridges and handsome edifices. I already drew sketches of them. They would stand for centuries and perpetuate the grandeur of this age!* But what a jar my youthful pride and aspirations received when I applied for work at the very offices and factories owned by the men whose sons had been my intimates. They were polite, even apologetic, but very, very definite. No office, nor even decent factory work, was open to "colored"—but I might sweep out in the mornings, and oh yes, there was trucking. . . . In disgust I joined the army and left the country. (italics added)[183]

Allusions to building and engineering reverberate in the names of several of *Black Empire*'s characters. The Black Internationale's chief architect, Sanford Mates, for example, echoes the name of Stanford White, whose elegantly built homes along Harlem's 138th Street are still landmarks.[184] Similarly, Gustave Linke, "the black French metallurgist" in charge of armament factories, suggests the surveying term for a unit of length, "Gunter's link."[185] Schuyler actually acquired firsthand knowledge of the building trade when he worked as a hod carrier in

Syracuse in the early 1920s.[186] Significant parts of *Black Empire* deal with the construction of industrial bases and such complexes as an airplane factory, cement mill, hydroponic farm, sun-powered steam engines and electrical generating plants, temples, radio stations, medical clinics, and armament factories. Schuyler's enthusiasm for such engineering feats clearly expressed his boyhood fantasy.

Shortly after Belsidus's conquest of Africa is accomplished, Carl Slater exclaims, " 'What installations!' " Schuyler himself had been similarly excited in 1931, when he reported that Georges Claude, the French inventor of the neon light, had "invented a method of utilizing the differences in temperature of tropical waters to generate electricity." This invention suggested astonishing possibilities to Schuyler. "Think how a chain of power plants like that, getting power free of charge, will revolutionize our civilization!" he remarked enthusiastically. He went on to speculate about the long-term social and environmental consequences of the discovery of oceanothermic energy:

> Millions and millions of people will leave the northern countries and settle in the tropics. Perhaps the centers of civilization will move to the equator where life will be made more bearable by the introduction of refrigerated houses. Neither politics nor war can cause such a shift of population, and yet a French scientist, once obscure and unknown, is on the way to do it.[187]

Claude's invention anticipates Al Fortune's "famous sun engine" that generates energy for the Black Internationale's hydroponic farm. " 'We are way past white science already,' " Sam Hamilton tells an astonished Slater. " 'Wait until you see our steam and electric plant tomorrow. We'll soon be able to turn every wheel in America' " (p. 50).

Science Fiction of the Thirties

As a writer and would-be black savant, Schuyler found in science fiction an emancipatory vision of science that he used to work out his frustrated youthful ambitions. He used science fiction as a literary device for both satirical and allegorical purposes. He was, for example, intrigued by the idea of "electrical nutrition," which he borrowed from an electric engineer named Bela Gati.[188] He developed the idea to postulate a process for transforming black people into white people in his first novel, *Black No More*, a work even today regarded as superior science fiction.[189]

Black Empire is filled with an abundance of the science fiction motifs of what has been dubbed "that amazing decade," 1926–1936, which gave rise to such pulp magazines as *Science Wonder Stories, Astounding Stories,* and *Amazing Stories.*[190] The start of modern science fiction in America, begun by Hugo Gernsback's *Amazing Stories* in 1926, continued the serial tradition of pulp magazines of earlier years.[191]

This was also a period during which the movies—many serialized—began to entrance mass audiences with mad scientists bent on world-conquest, super warfare in the air, then-futuristic devices such as television, fabulous death rays and powerful gasses, and a host of other machines, many of which figure prominently in Schuyler's *Black Empire.* Popular horror and fantasy films such as *Dracula* (1930), *Frankenstein* (1931), *Dr. Jekyll and Mr. Hyde* (1932), *King Kong* (1933), and *The Invisible Man* (1933) shocked audiences, stretched their imaginations, and helped to prepare them for science fiction concepts by exposing them to alternative realities.

Well before the serials based on "Flash Gordon" and "Buck Rogers" made space opera popular, science-fiction themes and devices were finding their way onto the screen. In 1930, for example, the low-budget feature *The Last Hour* used a "death ray" to force airplanes down, while a ten-chapter serial, *Voice from the Sky,* concerned a mad scientist bent on world conquest.[192] In 1932 Boris Karloff starred in *The Mask of Fu Manchu,* in which Sax Rohmer's evil Chinese scientist tried to unite Asia against white rule, employing a death ray in his cause. Death rays that brought down planes reappeared in *Air Hawks* (1935) and several of Schuyler's favorite themes figured in *The Lost City* (1935). In that twelve-part serial William Boyd (the future Hopalong Cassidy) played Zolok, a mad scientist plotting to conquer the world from his subterranean African city; Zolok not only possessed the obligatory death ray, he had a machine that made black men white and vice versa.

The extent to which Schuyler kept up with science fiction magazines and films is not known; however, his fiction employs many themes common to the era's genres. *Black Empire* alone explores such classic science fiction themes as "far traveling," the wonders of science, man and the machine, progress, man and the future, war, genetics, cataclysm, man and his environment, superpowers, genius, and man and religion.[193] Furthermore, Schuyler assigns prominent roles to such science fiction favorites as "huge cyclotrons" (the cyclotron was invented only in 1930) and "electric ray machines." Along the way he introduces such revolutionary devices as television, shortwave radio, and facsimile machines. We are also made aware of the political uses to which Belsidus puts the conditioned-response theory developed by Pavlov exactly ten years earlier and amplified by John B. Watson.

Three of Schuyler's unpublished story sketches indicate his great interest in science fiction. The first, "The Land Under the Sea," is about "a country where civilization has existed for millions of years; where black men have conquered telepathy, [and] atomic energy." The second is "The Insect War," a "sensational 'terror' novel about a scientist who in experimentation creates a gigantic species of insect that is able to procreate its kind." Schuyler's third story idea, "The Last White Man," is "a satire dealing with the results of birth control, abortion, late marriages, etc. Yellow and Black races take [control of] earth. Last White Man born in remote Arkansas hills—his adventures in mulatto America. United States becomes a monarcho-communistic State ruled by a few remaining black Negroes with general population mulatto."[194]

Schuyler's sketch of "The Last White Man" echoes the title of Olaf Stapledon's popular and influential scientific romance, *Last and First Men: A Story of the Near and Far Future* (1931), as well as its sequel, *Last Men in London* (1932). One of the most sweeping epics ever attempted, *Last and First Men* covers two billion years of future human history, beginning with the downfall of the "First Men" in the aftermath of the First World War. A series of debilitating wars weakens Europe, allowing America to administer the final blow.[195] Stapledon's influence is reflected not only in Schuyler's title, but also in the manner in which his outline applies to the racial struggle Stapledon's notions about the progressive disappearance of the human species.

Schuyler also parallels Stapledon's story in at least one conspicuous detail. Stapledon's chapter on Europe's downfall centers on a Chinese physicist who presents a subatomic ray gun to a meeting of world scientists in the belief that his invention will be welcomed as a peaceful boon to mankind.[196] After the awesome destructive power of the device is demonstrated, the scientists unanimously vote for its obliteration. A moment later, an enemy American airfleet appears in the sky. At the scientists' urging, the Chinese uses his gun to destroy the fleet. "The young man . . . took careful aim at each black dot in turn. One by one, each became a blinding star, then vanished."[197]

In *Black Empire* the Brazilian physicist Vincente Portabla creates a similar invention. Portabla's "infernal machine," a combined atomic cyclotron and remote-controlled electronic radio transmitter, annihilates first the "combined air fleets of the British and French navy" and later the Italian air fleet, saving the day for the empire.[198] In the final showdown, as in Stapledon's story, enemy planes are shot out of the sky: "One by one the propellers of the swarm of planes fell silent, and one by one the great ships plunged like flaming plummets to the earth" (p. 243).

Belsidus as General and Genius

It seems just possible that Schuyler's coining of the name Belsidus alludes to two distinct names: *Belisarius,* the sixth century Byzantine general who reconquered Africa and Rome for the Emperor Justinian,[199] and *Sidis,* the surname of the great early twentieth-century child prodigy, William James Sidis, often dubbed "America's greatest brain."[200] Invoking the name Belisarius, the reconqueror of Africa and the vanquisher of Rome, would undoubtedly have provided an ironic pleasure to any black author writing in the immediate aftermath of Italy's conquest of Ethiopia. Schuyler must have been well aware also of Sidis, since his own daughter, Philippa, was herself renowned as a child prodigy during the thirties, when she was featured in *Time* magazine.[201]

Schuyler's awareness of the Belisarius legend might have come to him by way of the writings of Procopius, the secretary who accompanied Belisarius on his campaigns and became the major chronicler of Justinian's reign. While Procopius's *History of the Wars of Justinian* and *Secret History* constitute the major historical sources for the political and military career of Belisarius, he also wrote *Buildings,* a work commissioned by Justinian to extol the emperor's extraordinary construction program. In view of Schuyler's expressed interest in building, the writings of Procopius might well have served as an important source of information not only on Justinian's edifices, but also regarding the legend of the famed Byzantine general, Belisarius. Indeed, Slater's role as Belsidus's secretary and chronicler exactly mirrors Procopius's relationship with Belisarius.

Race, Reason, and Revolution

Black Empire creates a fictional alliance of black youth, trained and guided by scientific genius and principles. For such an alliance actually to occur in 1930s America would have required the cooperation of the Talented Tenth, which Schuyler tried valiantly to rally from its dispirited state. He also tried to point out the interdependent fates of the Talented Tenth and the black masses. "The Negro writer, artist, professional person—all of the Talented Tenth, the intelligentsia, owe it to the masses upon whom they live, as does the flea upon the hound, to take the leadership and not permit the masses of Negroes to wander aimlessly and hopelessly in the mire of poverty and degradation; to become literally an untouchable class," he declared. "For unless the Negro masses are able to organize their economic power effectively and intelligently, there will be no berths for the Negroes of education and culture."[202]

This summons might well have been the last invocation addressed to the Talented Tenth as a historical class prior to the great changes that would be wrought by the modern civil rights movement. With its model of international black cooperation, Schuyler's clarion call for black mobilization to fight discrimination would go unanswered until after World War II, by which time, ironically, he himself had soured on the goal of radical political action. His later conservatism may account for how little his prewar radicalism is appreciated today. In 1937, however, his popular fiction urged blacks to undertake their own liberation. As Belsidus tells Slater, "You can do much to aid the cause of Negro liberation, not only in America, but throughout the world" (p. 10).

The Depression-era struggle for economic survival was linked in Schuyler's mind with the movement of international black solidarity impelled by the Italian invasion of Ethiopia. In the face of this dual crisis of black survival, Schuyler intervened with both pen and practical program in order to pierce the hide of black passivity.

First published as pulp, then dismissed as hokum by Schuyler himself, *Black Empire* today recreates an important moment in the history of African-American thought. Like Shakespeare's Hamlet, who feigned madness to mask his vengeful intentions, Belsidus adopts a mask of opulent respectability to disguise his true revolutionary goal. And so, too, does Schuyler use melodrama in *Black Empire* to mask a radical vision. We can, indeed, say of Schuyler and Belsidus, as Polonius says of Hamlet, "Though this be madness, yet there is method in it."[203]

Robert A. Hill & R. Kent Rasmussen

Notes

1. Philip B. Corbett, *Petronius* (New York: Twayne, 1970), pp. 52–75; *The Satyricon of Petronius*, trans. William Arrowsmith (Ann Arbor: University of Michigan Press, 1959), pp. 25–80. Another possible *Satyricon* allusion occurs in Schuyler's novel *Black No More* (1931), whose fictional Dr. Shakespeare Agamemnon Beard is a thinly disguised parody of W. E. B. Du Bois. The *Satyricon's* Agamemnon is a teacher who invites students to attend Trimalchio's banquets. Schuyler's manuscript essay, "Bolshevism and the Blacks," has yet another allusion: "[The Aframerican] doubts that he will secure a squarer deal under the Redneck dictatorship than he has from the regnant Trimalchios . . ." (George S. Schuyler Papers, Schomburg Center for Research in Black Culture, New York Public Library [cited hereafter as GSSP/Sc]). This essay was revised as "Negroes Reject Communism," *American Mercury* (June 1939): 176–81.

2. Schuyler to Prattis, Apr. 4, 1937, P. L. Prattis Papers, Moreland-Spingarn Research Center, Howard University Library, Washington, D.C. (cited hereafter as PLPP).

3. Norma R. Jones, "George Samuel Schuyler," *Dictionary of Literary Biography*, vol. 51: *Afro-American Writers from the Harlem Renaissance to 1940* (Detroit: Gale, 1987), p. 250.

4. George S. Schuyler, *Black No More, Being an Account of the Strange and Wonderful Workings of Science in the Land of the Free, A.D. 1933–1940* (1931; reprint, Boston: Northeastern University Press, 1989), pp. 1–2.

5. Cf. Nickieann Fleener, "George S. Schuyler," *Dictionary of Literary Biography*, vol. 29: *American Newspaper Journalists, 1926–1950* (Detroit: Gale, 1984), pp. 313–22; Michael W. Peplow, *George S. Schuyler* (Boston: Twayne, 1980); Harry McKinley Williams, Jr., "When Black is Right: The Life and Writings of George S. Schuyler" (Ph.D. diss., Brown University, 1988).

6. *Black and Conservative: The Autobiography of George S. Schuyler* (New Rochelle, N.Y.: Arlington House, 1966) (cited hereafter as *B&C*), p. 186.

7. "Is Liberia a Slave State?" *New York Evening Post*, June 29–July 6, 1931.

8. James W. Ivy to Schuyler, July 16, 1931, George S. Schuyler Papers, George Arents Research Library for Special Collections, Syracuse University Library, Syracuse, N.Y. (cited hereafter as GSSP/SU).

9. Floyd Calvin, "Welcome," *Pittsburgh Courier*, Oct. 1, 1932.

10. "He's Back, I'm Back," letter to the editor, *Pittsburgh Courier*, Sept. 24 1932. Schuyler told Peplow that Anatole France's *Penguin Island* "had a pro found influence on him" (*George Schuyler*, p. 22).

11. Freeman H. Hubbard to the editor, *Pittsburgh Courier*, April 4, 1936. Hub bard had been on the editorial staffs of the *Philadelphia Evening Ledger*, *Philadel phia Inquirer*, and *New York Evening Journal* (*Contemporary Authors* [Detroit: Gale Research Co., 1963], pp. 568–69).

12. Williams, "When Black Is Right," pp. 247–49.

13. Schuyler, "Our White Folks," *American Mercury* (Dec. 1927): 390–91.

14. Mencken to Schuyler, Sept. 15, 1927, quoted in Williams, "When Black is Right," p. 249; Schuyler, "Our White Folks," pp. 385–92.

15. Williams, "When Black is Right," pp. 245–46. See also Fenwick Ander son, "Black Perspectives in Mencken's *Mercury*," *Menckeniana: A Quarterly Review* 70 (1979). Mencken followed Schuyler's career for two decades, trying, unsuc cessfully, to interest other newspapers and magazines in "the most competent Negro journalist" he knew (*Diary of H. L. Mencken*, ed. Charles A. Fecher [New York: Knopf, 1989], p. 383). The same year Mencken added, "I am more and more convinced that [Schuyler] is the most competent editorial writer now in practice in this great free Republic" (quoted in Williams, "When Black Is Right," p. 240). Mencken's first supplement to *The American Language* (1945) calls Schuyler America's "most competent" black journalist, adding, that "few white columnists . . . can match him for information, intelligence, indepen dence and courage" (quoted in *Diary*, p. 382). See editorials, "Out-Menckening Mencken," *New York Age*, Dec. 10, 1927, and "A New Kind of Writer," *Chicago Whip*, Dec. 10, 1927. For Schuyler on Mencken, see *B&C*, pp. 233–35.

16. New York: Brewer, Warren & Putnam, 1931.

17. *Pittsburgh Courier*, June 29, 1935, Oct. 24, 1936. Along with the Bible and *The Arabian Nights*, Schuyler ranked the works of French satirist François Rabe lais among the greatest achievements of mankind. In "Revolt in Ethiopia"—a serial Schuyler later published under the name Rachel Call—protagonist Dick Welland hears his valet "booming out some Rabelaisian stanzas of that under world Negro classic, 'Bud' " (*Pittsburgh Courier*, July 16, 1938).

18. Schuyler to Josephine Schuyler, Oct. 6, 1935, GSSP/SU.

19. "George S. Schuyler," autobiographical preface to "Some Unsweet Truths about Race Prejudice," in Samuel D. Schmalhausen, ed., *Behold America!* (New York: Farrar & Rinehart, 1931), p. 88.

20. Quoted in Andrew Buni, *Robert L. Vann of the Pittsburgh Courier: Politics and Black Journalism* (Pittsburgh: University of Pittsburgh Press, 1974), p. 223. For Schuyler's account of the *Illustrated Feature Section*, see *B&C*, pp. 165–67. The supplement commenced on November 3, 1928.

21. Theophilus Lewis, "Negro Literature," *Amsterdam News*, July 13, 1935; *B&C*, p. 142. During the 1920s Lewis and Schuyler worked together on the

Messenger. In 1925 they coauthored "Shafts and Darts: A Page of Calumny and Satire." See Theodore Kornweibel, Jr., *No Crystal Stair: Black Life and the Messenger, 1917–1928* (Westport, Conn.: Greenwood, 1975).

22. "Some Unsweet Truths about Race Prejudice," p. 88. Schuyler later said that he resigned because he was fed up with frequent cost overruns resulting from Ziff's failure to uphold advertising deadlines (*B&C*, p. 166).

23. *B&C*, p. 167.

24. *IFS*, Oct. 5, 1929.

25. *Pittsburgh Courier*, Oct. 13, 1928. The serial commenced on Nov. 3, 1928.

26. "Marcus Garvey, an Analysis," *Interstate Tattler* (July 5–Aug. 9, 1929). It seems likely that Schuyler consciously used his middle name, Samuel, in "Samuel I. Brooks." (It is possible that the initial "I" was also a sly reference to himself.) In addition to his pen name, Schuyler used his middle name for such fictional characters as the chemist Sam Hamilton and the chemist/strongman Sam Morgan in the story "Strange Valley." *Black No More* has a music group called Sammy Snort's Bogalusa Babies (p. 147) and a racist statistician, Dr. Samuel Buggerie (p. 155).

27. An annotated bibliography appears at the end of this volume.

28. This was his second such *Courier* assignment; ten years earlier the paper had sent him south to raise circulation and to report on black conditions. His earlier series, "Aframerica Today," which ran from November 1925 through July 1926, remains an important document of Depression-era race relations in the South (*B&C*, pp. 153–57). Schuyler revisited Mississippi in December 1932, investigating labor conditions on the Mississippi Flood Control Project for the NAACP. He traveled with NAACP assistant secretary Roy Wilkins and was arrested as a holdup suspect by the Mississippi state police (ibid., pp. 198–205).

29. Nickieann Fleener, " 'Breaking Down Buyer Resistance': Marketing the 1935 Pittsburgh *Courier* to Mississippi Blacks," *Journalism History* (autumn–winter 1986): 78–85; *B&C*, pp. 228–29.

30. Schuyler to Ira F. Lewis, Jan. 8, 1937, GSSP/SU.

31. Schuyler to Josephine Schuyler, Nov. 9, 1935, GSSP/SU.

32. Joe Louis (1914–1981) made his pro boxing debut in 1934 and won a string of bouts before losing to Max Schmeling. After taking the world heavyweight championship from Jim Braddock on June 22, 1937, he met Schmeling in a rematch and knocked him out in the first round.

33. Buni, *Robert L. Vann*, pp. 246–47, 254–56. A more complete account of the *Courier*'s role in shaping African-American opinion during this crisis is William R. Scott, *The Sons of Sheba's Race: Black Americans and the Italo-Ethiopian War, 1935–1941* (Bloomington: Indiana University Press, forthcoming). The war climaxed on May 5, 1936, when Italian forces took the Ethiopian capital.

34. Hubbard, letter to the editor, *Pittsburgh Courier*, Apr. 4, 1936.

35. Schuyler proposed the idea in the memo that he submitted for the 1935

Mississippi promotional trip; a third proposal was to create of a Harlem edition of the *Courier* (Fleener, " 'Breaking Down Buyer Resistance,' " p. 79).

36. Schuyler to Lewis, June 25, 1936, GSSP/SU.

37. Schuyler to P. L. Prattis, Dec. 5, 1936, PLPP.

38. John Arberry Haney, "A History of the Nationally Syndicated Sunday Magazine Supplement" (Ph.D. diss., University of Missouri, 1953), p. 98. See Morrill Goddard, *What Interests People and Why: Modern Miracles Underneath the Veneer of Civilized Man, The Sixteen Elements of Universal Interest* (New York: American Weekly, 1935).

39. *Pittsburgh Courier*, Nov. 14, 1936.

40. Enclosed in Chester L. Washington to Schuyler, Jan. 28, 1937, GSSP/SU.

41. *B&C*, p. 159.

42. Schuyler to Lewis, Jan. 20, 1939, GSSP/SU.

43. Nunn to Schuyler, Jan. 6, 1937, GSSP/SU.

44. Nunn to Schuyler, Jan. 11, 1937, GSSP/SU.

45. P. L. Prattis, "Questions and Answers," *Pittsburgh Courier*, May 15, 1937, replying to a letter from Louise E. Kelly.

46. *B&C*, p. 167.

47. Schuyler, "Views and Reviews," *Pittsburgh Courier* (cited hereafter as V&R), Feb. 6, 1937.

48. "My mother denounced all this talk of witchcraft as nonsense, the product of ignorance and superstition, saying that one had to actually believe in such things in order to be affected. My grandmother held stubbornly to her beliefs and cited an impressive list of apt anecdotes in support of them. . . . Actually, Grandma had plenty of company then in her belief in the occult, and would have plenty now" (*B&C*, pp. 20–23). Earlier, Schuyler wrote, "I have been amazed by it [African magic] myself"(V&R, Mar. 9, 1935).

49. This concept of a satirical/melodramatic duality illuminates the stylistically jarring last chapter of *Black No More*. What until the story is almost over has been a good-natured, albeit ferocious, satire suddenly becomes a violent and mean-spirited orgy of revenge. Two white racist politicians, Buggerie and Snobbcraft, fleeing to escape retribution for their actions, disguise themselves as blacks to avoid recognition. In a final irony, they are mistaken for blacks and brutally lynched by adherents of the True Faith Christ Lovers Church (*Black No More*, pp. 197–218). What previous commentators have called an abrupt stylistic shift from satire to grotesquerie actually is a reflection of the mix of satire and melodrama that characterized Schuyler's serial fiction.

50. In this sense, *Black Empire* fits the literary genre of melodrama that Peter Brooks calls "heightened dramatization inextricably bound up with the modern novel's effort to signify . . . an important and abiding mode in the modern imagination" (*The Melodramatic Imagination: Balzac, Henry James, Melodrama, and the Mode of Excess* [New York: Columbia University Press, 1985], p. ix).

51. V&R, July 27, 1935; "Helping Ethiopia," unsigned editorial, *Pittsburgh Courier,* July 27, 1935; cf., "God Help Africa!" *Time* (July 29, 1935): 14–15. For accounts of the worldwide black mobilization to defend Ethiopia, see Scott, *The Sons of Sheba's Race;* Robert G. Weisbord, "Black America and the Italian-Ethiopian Crisis: An Episode in Pan-Negroism," *Historian* (Feb. 1972): 230–41, and "British West Indian Reaction to the Italian-Ethiopian War: An Episode in Pan-Africanism," *Caribbean Studies* (Apr. 1970): 34–41; S. K. B. Asante, *Pan-African Protest: West Africa and the Italo-Ethiopian Crisis, 1934–1941* (London: Longmans, 1977); and Cedric Robinson, "The African Diaspora and the Italo-Ethiopian Crisis," *Race & Class* 27, no. 2 (1985): 51–65.

52. V&R, July 27, 1935.

53. Ibid.

54. V&R, Aug. 17, 1935.

55. Unsigned editorial, *Pittsburgh Courier,* July 13, 1935.

56. Wm. E. Moore to Schuyler, July 5, 1935, GSSP/SU.

57. *Pittsburgh Courier,* July 27, 1935.

58. *Pittsburgh Courier,* Nov. 23, 1935.

59. *Pittsburgh Courier,* Dec. 7, 1935.

60. V&R, Nov. 23, 1935.

61. V&R, Feb. 29, 1936.

62. V&R, Mar. 7, 1936.

63. V&R, Nov. 28, 1936.

64. V&R, Jan. 26, 1930.

65. *Pittsburgh Courier,* Oct. 17, 1931.

66. V&R, Jan. 6, 1934; "Liberian Congressmen Get 'Autosick' on Rough Roads," *Pittsburgh Courier,* Nov. 1934; *B&C,* p. 80.

67. James Hooker, *Black Revolutionary: George Padmore's Path from Communism to Pan-Africanism* (London: Pall Mall, 1967); idem, "The Negro American Press and Africa in the Nineteen Thirties," *Canadian Journal of African Studies* (Mar. 1967): 43–50. On the Profintern, see E. H. Carr, *Twilight of the Comintern, 1930–1935* (New York: Pantheon Books, 1982).

68. V&R, Aug. 25, 1934, Jan. 12, 1935.

69. George Padmore, "Why I Left the Communist International: Padmore Refutes Lies and Slanders of Communists," Apr. 16, 1934, manuscript copy, GSSP/SU; cf. J. R. Hooker, "Africa for Afro-Americans: Padmore and the Black Press," *Radical America* (July–Aug. 1968): 14–19; Padmore, "A Negro Looks at British Imperialism," *Crisis,* Dec. 1938.

70. "The Communist Jonah," *Pittsburgh Courier,* June 23, 1934.

71. Padmore, open letter to Earl Browder, secretary of the American Communist party, Oct. 7, 1934, GSSP/SU.

72. Padmore to Schuyler, July 23, 1934, GSSP/SU; cf. "Padmore Answers to Heywood's Slanders," *Pittsburgh Courier,* Sept. 22, 1934.

73. *B&C*, p. 119; *Pittsburgh Courier*, July 24, 1937. Both Garvey and Schuyle misspelled Phillis Wheatley's name.

74. *Pittsburgh Courier*, Jan. 27, 1934, Dec. 25, 1937, June 27, 1936. Garve responded to Schuyler in his own newspaper, the *Black Man;* see issues of Dec 1933, Feb. 1934, and Mar.–Apr. 1934.

75. V&R, Oct. 10, 1931.

76. V&R, Oct. 28, 1933. Garvey had been deported from the U.S. in 1927

77. V&R, Mar. 3, 1934.

78. V&R, Dec. 9, 1933.

79. *Interstate Tattler*, Aug. 23, 1929.

80. Robert Peterson, *Only the Ball Was White: A History of Legendary Black Play ers and All-black Professional Teams* [New York: McGraw-Hill, 1984], p. 224. Not also the phonetic similarity of *Licorice* and *Louis*.

81. *Pittsburgh Courier*, Nov. 18, 1933.

82. *B&C*, pp. 175ff.

83. V&R, Dec. 9, 1933.

84. V&R, Oct. 9, 1937.

85. Bayless to Schuyler, Sept. 11, 1937, GSSP/SU.

86. *Black No More*, p. 25. This is the hotel in which Schuyler stayed in 1921

87. See Silas Bent, *Ballyhoo: The Voice of the Press* (New York: Boni & Liver ight, 1927).

88. Samory Touré was a West African ruler who resisted French conquest Miller was an educator at Howard University. Coleman is discussed below.

89. "Schuyler on Coast-to-Coast Tour," *Pittsburgh Courier*, Feb. 29, 1936.

90. V&R, Mar. 7, 1936.

91. *Crisis*, Aug. 1938; for the complete text of the article, see Appendix B.

92. *B&C*, p. 248.

93. V&R, May 17, 1930, Sept. 29, 1934, Feb. 16, 1935, Oct. 12, 1935, Oct. 9, 1937. Schuyler wrote, "A million of his [Rogers's] books in the Black Bel would work wonders on the Aframerican mentality." For his moving obituary of Rogers, see "Nation Mourns Top Negro Historian," *Pittsburgh Courier*, Apr. 9, 1966; cf. W. B. Turner, "J. A. Rogers: Portrait of an Afro-American Historian," *Black Scholar* (Jan.–Feb. 1975): 32–39; and Valerie Sandoval, "The Bran of History: An Historiographic Account of the Work of J. A. Rogers," *The Schomburg Center for Research in Black Culture* (spring 1978): 5–7, 16–19.

94. Rogers, *The Real Facts about Ethiopia* (1935; reprint, Baltimore, Md.: Black Classic Press, 1982), pp. 2–3. Originally issued in October 1935, the pamphlet went through three editions and a revision in the next year.

95. Ira F. Lewis to Schuyler, Feb. 11, 1936; Schuyler to Lewis, Feb. 16, 1936, GSSP/SU; cf. "J. A. Rogers Explains Just How He Checked Up on All the Facts about Race," *Pittsburgh Courier*, Nov. 21, 1936. Rogers wrote features for the *Messenger* during the early 1920s while Schuyler edited the magazine. Schuyler

declared that Rogers "has done as much as any other person to acquaint the masses of literate Negroes with their glorious past" (V&R, Feb. 16, 1935).

96. V&R, June 12, 1937.

97. V&R, Apr. 24, 1937.

98. "Japan and the Negro," GSSP/Sc.

99. V&R, July 27, 1935. Earlier, in an unsigned editorial, Schuyler wrote, "Georgia has for years retained the pennant in the Lynching League and in many respects is more backward than the Belgian Congo" ("Hitlerism in Georgia," *Pittsburgh Courier*, Sept. 29, 1934). See also, "Some Unsweet Truths about Race Prejudice," pp. 94–95. A report on a session of the 1922 UNIA convention contained the following: "Coming from near Jessup, Ga., where she said they lynch Negroes for the fun of it, a woman delegate declared that Georgia is known as the 'lynching State' " ("Lynching and How to Prevent It," *New York World*, Aug. 18, 1922, quoted in *The Marcus Garvey and Universal Negro Improvement Association Papers*, ed. Robert A. Hill [Berkeley and Los Angeles: University of California Press, 1985], 4: 917). Schuyler recommended what should be done with the "genus Cracker" in V&R, Aug. 7, 1937.

100. V&R, July 18, 1936; cf. Schuyler, "Hitlerism Without Hitler," review of *The Colour Bar in East Africa* by Norman Leys in *Crisis* (Dec. 1941): 384, 389.

101. V&R, Mar. 14, 1931. In June 1935, "the Four Mills Brothers, unable to find a hotel [in London] to take them, had to sleep in a railway station" (unsigned Schuyler editorial, "America Not So Bad," *Pittsburgh Courier*, June 15, 1935). Marcus Garvey, Paul Robeson, and Robert Abbott were other prominent blacks refused places in London hotels during the thirties. Schuyler blamed American tourists for introducing race prejudice "wherever they have gone" ("Some Unsweet Truths about Race Prejudice," p. 94).

102. Schuyler apparently forgot his lynching victim's name: in the first reference he is Lester Peters (p. 68); he is Ed Lovett a chapter later (p. 74).

103. Two American towns are named Intercourse: one in Pennsylvania, the other in Alabama. The Alabama town took its name because it "was at a road junction which made communication easy" (George R. Stewart, *American Place-Names: A Concise and Selective Dictionary for the Continental United States of America* [New York: Oxford University Press, 1970], p. 221).

104. "A Treatise on Mulattoes," *Crisis*, Oct. 1937. The essay was a flattering review of Cedric Dover's *Half Caste* (London: Secker & Warburg, 1937).

105. V&R, Mar. 16, 1935.

106. V&R, Sept. 15, 1934.

107. Curiously, Givens is also the name of the Southern white family into which the black-turned-white Max Disher marries in *Black No More*.

108. V&R, Jan. 30, 1937. In April Schuyler wrote: "Although aviation is the real coming field, there are all too few of our youngsters interested in it. If all the young Negroes who are eager to emulate Bill Robinson, Joe Louis and Cab

Calloway were only as anxious to follow in the footsteps of Bessie Coleman and Charles Lindbergh, we might get somewhere" (V&R, Apr. 24, 1937).

109. Schuyler discussed Coleman's career in a letter rebutting the claim that "Negroes cannot fly" (*American Mercury* [Dec. 1936]: xxviii, xxx).

110. *A Journey into 365 Days of Black History 1990 Calendar* (Petaluma, Calif.: Pomegranate Calendars & Books, 1989). Brown became the first black member of the Civil Air Patrol in Illinois and was responsible for directing a flight training school in Chicago under the Civil Pilot Training Program.

111. *Pittsburgh Courier,* Jan. 18, 1936.

112. *B&C,* p. 174. Earhart was often photographed wearing the bracelet that Schuyler gave her, and he later wondered if she had it when her plane disappeared over the South Pacific in July 1937. We are indebted to Earhart's flying companion, Fay Gillis Wells, for confirming that Earhart did indeed wear the bracelet during the first part of her journey; however, she sent it home from New Guinea in an effort to shed every possible ounce of weight in order to take on more fuel (Wells to Marcus Garvey Papers, Mar. 26, 1991).

113. Reprint, Boston: Beacon Press, 1970.

114. Reprint, Miami, Florida: Mnemosyne Publications, 1969.

115. "Strange Valley," chap. 5, *Pittsburgh Courier,* Sept. 22, 1934.

116. The diabolical aspect of all three men is made explicit in a Schuyler short-story sketch about a "Sinister Physician who decides to avenge treatment of Negroes by blowing up public buildings, setting one faction against another [and] starts civil war"—which sounds much like the civil strife among whites that Belsidus provokes in *Black Empire* ("The Sinister Physician," GSSP/Sc). We also find the satanic motif in *Black No More*'s description of Crookman as a "scientific black Beelzebub" (p. 65). Even that novel's picaresque character Max Disher, before being made white by Crookman, is described as possessing a "slightly satanic cast" (p. 17). See also Michael Peplow, "The Black 'Picaro' in Schuyler's *Black No More,* " *Crisis,* Jan. 1976, p. 8.

117. Clifford Hallam, "The Double as Incomplete Self: Toward a Definition of Doppelgänger," in *Fearful Symmetry: Doubles and Doubling in Literature and Film* (Tallahassee: University Presses of Florida, 1981), p. 4.

118. C. F. Keppler, *The Literature of the Second Self* (Tucson: University of Arizona Press, 1972), p. 3.

119. *B&C,* pp. 3–8.

120. "Escape," GSSP/Sc.

121. "Black Art," p. 335. This was the essay that Schuyler proposed making the lead story in a composite portrayal, "Ladies of Color," to be made up of thirteen stories dedicated to individual black women. The first story, as Schuyler sketched it, was to be "Grandma 'Black Art' Helen" (GSSP/Sc).

122. "Black Art," p. 336.

123. Ibid., pp. 336, 337, 340, 341.

124. V&R, Nov. 14, 1936, Mar. 9, 1935.

125. Robert D. Pelton, *The Trickster in West Africa: A Study of Mythic Irony and Sacred Delight* (Berkeley and Los Angeles: University of California Press, 1980); Henry Louis Gates, Jr., *The Signifying Monkey: A Theory of African-American Literary Criticism* (New York: Oxford University Press, 1988).

126. New York: Harcourt, Brace, 1928.

127. *The Correspondence of W. E. B. Du Bois,* ed. Herbert Aptheker (Amherst: University of Massachusetts Press, 1973), 1: 382. Schuyler's brief review appeared in *Illustrated Feature Section* (Nov. 1928).

128. Late in the story, a Japanese character is described as the "prime minister of the Darker World" (*Dark Princess,* p. 261).

129. Ibid., p. 285.

130. See ibid., especially p. 220.

131. New York: Longmans, 1934.

132. V&R, Sept. 29, 1934.

133. Manners-Sutton, *Black God,* p. 221.

134. Ibid., pp. 233–34.

135. Ibid., p. 241.

136. *Pittsburgh Courier,* Dec. 10, 1931. Rumors of foreign agitators were common among colonial administrators, particularly in the Congo. In 1931, its Equateur and Congo-Kasai provinces experienced revolts that administrators blamed on Americans agitating for creation of a black-ruled state (Jean-Luc Vellut, "Résistances et espaces de liberté dans l'histoire coloniale du Zaïre: avant la marche à l'indépendance," in *Rébellions-Révolution au Zaïre,* ed. Catherine Coquery-Vidrovitch et al. [Paris: L'Harmattan, 1987], 1: 41).

137. *Black Empire* recalls a particularly grotesque incident in Manners-Sutton's novel, when the decrepit servant Cheteba reveals "that he had no tongue; his mouth was just a red, mutilated gap." In *Black Empire,* when Slater asks Belsidus's chauffeur Jim why he cannot speak, Jim opens his mouth: "There was nothing but a great, red cavity surrounded by fine white teeth. His tongue was gone!" (p. 8). In the next chapter, Belsidus explains "they burned off his tongue with a poker one day in Georgia about eight years ago" (p. 16).

138. New York: Charles Scribner's Sons, 1936. See Haim Genizi, "V. F. Calverton: Independent Radical" (Ph.D. diss., City University of New York, 1968); Leonard I. Wilcox, "V. F. Calverton: A Critical Biography" (Ph.D. diss., University of California, Irvine, 1977).

139. V&R, Dec. 19, 1936.

140. "V. F. Calverton, A Radical Magazinist for Black Intellectuals, 1920–1940," *Journal of Negro History* (Jan. 1972): 241.

141. *B&C,* pp. 255–56; *Modern Quarterly* (fall 1940): 84–87.

142. *Modern Quarterly* [1929]: 361–63.

143. Schuyler's essay "Some Unsweet Truths About Race Prejudice" was

published by Calverton's colleague, Samuel D. Schmalhausen, in the anthology *Behold America!* (1931); *B&C*, p. 190.

144. *B&C*, p. 170.

145. Cf. Leonard I. Wilcox, "Marxism, Death, and Social Hypnosis: V. F. Calverton and the Old Left's 'Crisis of Reason,' " *History of Political Thought* (spring 1984): 129–47; according to Wilcox, "*The Man Inside* is a bizarre novel, particularly to have been written by a radical" (ibid., p. 140).

146. V&R, Feb. 9, 1935.

147. Ibid.

148. V&R, Mar. 14, 1936; see also Schuyler's reference to Watson in *B&C*, p. 125. It is noteworthy that in Schuyler's bibliography for a 1938 in-service course for teachers, his book list is headed by this entry: "*Behaviorism* by John B. Watson. See conditioned reflexes" (GSSP/SU).

149. V&R, Sept. 25, 1937; James Hooker, "The Negro American Press and Africa in the Nineteen-Thirties," *Canadian Journal of African Studies* (Mar. 1967): 43–50, and "The Impact of African History on Afro-Americans, 1930–1945," *Black Academy Review* (spring–summer 1972): 39–62.

150. Schuyler also used "Munitions Internationale" to describe the international armaments trade (V&R, Sept. 8, 1934). The latter term was used in commenting upon F. C. Hanighen's and H. C. Engelbrecht's lead article, "Don't Blame the Munitions Makers," in *American Mercury* (Sept. 1934): 1–10.

151. V&R, June 5, 1957.

152. Note the ironic wordplay on Lothrop Stoddard's unabashedly racist book, *The Rising Tide of Color Against White World-Supremacy* (1920).

153. "The Negro Turns to Fascism," GSSP/Sc. A year later Schuyler wrote: "That Americans are ready for the change to collectivism with its planned economy that will insure economic security to the greatest number is evidenced by the pathetic scrambling after the straws of the New Deal, Coughlinism and Share-the-Wealth" (V&R, June 15, 1935).

154. V&R, Mar. 27, 1937.

155. Cf. Harvey Klehr, *The Heyday of American Communism: The Depression Decade* (New York: Basic Books, 1984), pp. 324–48; Robin D. G. Kelley, *Hammer and Hoe: Alabama Communists During the Great Depression* (Chapel Hill and London: University of North Carolina Press, 1990), pp. 92–116.

156. V&R, Apr. 10, 1937. In a further contribution, Schuyler argued that "one of the chief reasons for the failure of the Communists to snare more black bucks has been the poor quality of the female bait used" (cited in Orrick Johns, "Review and Comment: *American Spectator*—A Nazi Sheet," *New Masses* [Oct. 16, 1934], p. 23). *Senegambian*, a term combining *Senegal* and *Gambia*, is a word that Schuyler frequently applied to black Americans.

157. "Revolution and the Aframerican," GSSP/Sc.

158. V&R, May 15, 1937.

159. V&R, June 23, 1934.

160. V&R, Jan. 25, 1936.

161. V&R, Mar. 17, 1934.

162. Ibid. Schuyler called the fight to make Harlem Hospital a black-only hospital "one of the most shameful chapters in the history of Aframerica. As an exhibition of Negro lying, venality and skullduggery I am sure it cannot be surpassed, not even by some of the worst Negrophobes, or even by the suave and shifty apologists for Liberian and Haitian class snobbery and ignorant misrule" (*Pittsburgh Courier*, Feb. 24, 1934). The Manhattan Medical Society issued a series of pamphlets that Schuyler probably wrote, as is evidenced by the style of a press release, dated Aug. 15, 1932, that Schuyler quotes extensively in his unpublished essay, "The Race Racket" (GSSP/Sc).

163. "The Race Racket," pp. 11–14.

164. Schuyler, "Shafts and Darts," *Messenger*, Jan. 1926.

165. Schuyler, "The Negro-Art Hokum," *Nation* (June 16, 1926): 662–63; *B&C*, pp. 157–58. Langston Hughes's response is regarded by his biographer as his finest essay ("The Negro Artist and the Racial Mountain," *Nation* [June 23, 1926]: 692–94; Arnold Rampersad, *The Life of Langston Hughes* [New York: Oxford University Press, 1986], 1: 130; cf. "J. A. Rogers Discusses the Schuyler and Hughes Articles," *Amsterdam News*, June 30, 1926).

166. V&R, Jan. 4, 1936. In an obvious allusion to the title of Langston Hughes's famous rejoinder, Schuyler declared: "As the mountain labored and brought forth a mouse, so all of this hullabaloo about the Negro Renaissance in art and literature did stimulate the writing of some literature of importance which will live. The amount, however, is very small, but such as it is, it is meritorious because it is literature and not Negro literature. It is judged by literary and not by racial standards, which is as it should be."

167. V&R, Apr. 17, Mar. 6, 1937.

168. V&R, Mar. 27, 1937. Several months later, Schuyler wrote, "I am beginning to doubt that the interest in belles lettres in Aframerica is very great" (V&R, June 12, 1937).

169. Schuyler, "Shafts and Darts," *Messenger*, Jan. 1926.

170. V&R, Aug. 17, 1935.

171. Ibid.

172. "New Job Frontiers for Negro Youth," *Crisis*, Nov. 1936. Among the topics of Schuyler's annual lecture tour in 1936 was "Youth and Fields for Which they should Be Prepared" (*Illinois State Journal*, Mar. 6, 1936).

173. "New Job Frontiers for Negro Youth."

174. Kenneth R. Manning, *Black Apollo of Science: The Life of Ernest Everett Just* (New York: Oxford University Press, 1983). *Ransom* suggests a symbolic political link with the surname of the militant African Methodist Episcopal bishop Reverdy C. Ransom (1861–1959), a founding member of the Niagara

movement that was a forerunner to the NAACP, and later a sympathizer with the Garvey movement. See R. C. Ransom, "Back to Africa: A Militant Call," *AME Church Review* 37 (1920): 88–89; "The Horizon," *Crisis*, Sept. 1924; *Dictionary of American Negro Biography* (New York: Norton, 1982).

175. Schuyler, "Consumers' Co-operation," *Messenger*, Dec. 1925; "The Young Negro Co-operative League," *Crisis*, Jan. 1932; "Consumers' Cooperation, the American Negro's Salvation," *Cooperation*, Aug. 1931; "Some Impressions of England," *Wheatsheaf*, May 1931; "Co-operation among American Negroes: A Summary of Accomplishments and Efforts before and since the Founding of the Young Negroes Co-operative League," GSSP/Sc.

176. V&R, Sept. 5, 1936.

177. Ibid.

178. V&R, Dec. 19, 1931.

179. Schuyler, "The Black Man's Burden—Religion," *The Rationalist Annual*, ed. E. Haldeman–Julius (Girard, Kans.: Haldeman–Julius, 1935), pp. 52, 56.

180. V&R, Nov. 7, 1931.

181. Schuyler quotes Miller in his own column (V&R, Sept. 22, 1934). This was the moment when Miller defined a Negro radical "as an over-educated West Indian without a job."

182. Ibid.

183. V&R, Mar. 21, 1931. Schuyler drew pictures he labeled "Some Liberian Impressions from Memory for My Josephine" while sailing home from Africa; these offer proof of his draftsmanship (GSSP/SU).

184. Paul R. Baker, *Stanny: The Gilded Life of Stanford White* (New York: Free Press, 1991).

185. Named after a seventeenth-century English mathematician, a Gunter's chain is a sixty-six foot surveying measure comprising one hundred links.

186. B&C, pp. 116–18. As late as the 1960s, Schuyler still kept his International Hod Carriers Building and Common Laborers Union card.

187. V&R, Feb. 7, 1931.

188. Schuyler later acknowledged Gati in his column (V&R, Dec. 28, 1935).

189. Neil Barron, *Anatomy of Wonder: Science Fiction* (New York: Bowker, 1976), p. 110.

190. James Gunn, *Alternate Worlds: The Illustrated History of Science Fiction* (Englewood Cliffs, N.J.: Prentice–Hall, 1975), p. 117.

191. Ibid., p. 121.

192. These film synopses and those that follow are taken from Phil Hardy's excellent and exhaustive *Encyclopedia of Science Fiction Movies* (New York: Woodbury Press, 1986), pp. 82–100.

193. Ibid., "Science Fiction Themes," pp. 242–43.

194. Box of Ideas, file 16/1, GSSP/Sc.

195. Interestingly, the first war is touched off by an event involving an

African. A false accusation that a Senegalese soldier has raped an English-woman escalates into an incident that leads England and France to war (*Last and First Men* [New York: Jonathan Cape and Harrison Smith, 1931], p. 10).

196. The meeting at which the Chinese physicist presents his invention is chaired by the president of the scientific society, a West African biologist, "famous for his interbreeding of man and ape" (ibid., p. 36). Another unpublished Schuyler story summary is about a character, simply named Ape, the offspring of the union between an African gorilla and an Englishwoman. Ape uses his superior intelligence and strength as a successful criminal until he falls in love with a woman. He tries to win her by abandoning crime for politics and leads a fascist movement that carries him to the presidency of the United States. Under his administration, American scientists "invent the most deadly weapons ever conceived" and his air force conquers the world (GSSP/Sc).

197. Stapledon, *Last and First Men*, p. 41.

198. The Brazilian physicist occasions a typically Schuyleresque piece of satire, as the name *Portabla* appears to caricature the Italian natural philosopher and scientist Giambattista della Porta (1535?–1615). In addition to being one of the great comic writers of his age, Porta was the first to recognize the heating effects of light rays, and his camera obscura work made him a pioneer in lenses; he is also said to have anticipated the steam engine (*Encyclopedia Britannica*). *Portabla,* which is not a Portuguese word, also suggests "portable," perhaps an unconscious allusion to the portability of Portabla's cyclotron weapons.

199. *Dictionary of the Middle Ages,* ed. Joseph R. Strayer (New York: Scribner, 1983), 2: 165; C. W. Previte-Orton, *The Shorter Cambridge Medieval History* (Cambridge: Cambridge University Press, 1971), 1: 189. The Belisarius legend is celebrated in Dante's *Paradiso* (VI.10ff); the legend was also perpetuated through "innumerable poems, plays, romances and novels about Belisarius and [his wife] Theodora from the sixteenth century to the present day" (Averil Cameron, *Procopius and the Sixth Century* [Berkeley and Los Angeles: University of California Press, 1985], p. 261).

200. Amy Wallace, *The Prodigy* (New York: Dutton, 1986). We thank Dr. Joseph N. Natterson for calling Sidis and Wallace's biography to our attention.

201. "Harlem Prodigy," *Time* (June 22, 1936): 40. See also, "Prodigious Crop," *Time* (Aug. 26, 1935): 27; "The Schuylers' Secret Has Been Revealed at Last; Twenty-nine Month Old Philippa Is Prodigy!" *Pittsburgh Courier,* Jan. 27, 1934; "Philippa Schuyler Rated as 'Superior' Pianist by Guild," *Pittsburgh Courier,* June 12, 1937. Philippa mastered her mathematical tables at three (Schuyler to Josephine Schuyler, Oct. 16, 1935, GSSP/SU). A year later, Schuyler mentioned in a flight of imaginative fantasy a four-year old girl "interested in interstellar mathematics" in an essay exploring suspended animation.

202. V&R, Feb. 14, 1931.

203. *Hamlet*, 2.2.203–4.

▲▲▲▲▲▲▲▲▲▲▲▲▲▲▲▲▲▲▲▲▲▲

Appendix A: Schuyler's story notes (ca. 1936–1937)

(i)

Suggested Names

1. Dr. Beast of Harlem	6. Eternal Love
2. Black Saviour	7. Sweet Papa Love
3. Black Belt Millenium	8. Daddy Love
4. Black Utopia	9. Black and Tan Heavens
5. Black Temples	10.

PLOT:

—Beginning in a humble side street store front church, Eternal Love, gradually gathers a following from among the poor and degraded of Harlem. (a) He feeds all who come, (b) takes no collections, (c) Bans the flesh, (d) preaches eternal love of all by all, (e) wants to use whatever power he has to combat sin and evil, all that is contrary to the Ten Commandments and the Sermon on the Mount.

—In his Heavens his angels sing all day and praise him.

—Whites join him in increasing numbers. A beautiful white girl gives up everything to follow him, becoming his secretary and adviser, Sister Marietta.

—It is all beautifully naive and strangely successful. All is to be accomplished through love.

—A sheetless Negro editor who has failed at politics persuades Eternal Love that he needs an organ—a world newspaper to propagate his message. This is done and the paper "News of Love" flourishes.

—A former theological student and ex-minister steeped in religious lore of the ancient world comes into the movement and with his radical atheist friend introduces beauty and ritual

325

There are

1. Temples with black glass and chromium exteriors, following Egyptian designs.
2. Great shining black nude statue of Eternal Love, 25 feet high behind the alter, indirectly lighted. Is Robot. Talks. moves eyes and arms.
3. Great gilt throne where Eternal Love or his disciples sit and speak to the multitude.
4. People sit on cushions. There are no chairs.
5. Lighted from the top, air-conditioned, great murals of unity of man, of love and peace on the great walls.
6. Offerings are placed at the feet of the image.
7. Robed virgins with breasts exposed.
8. "Heavens" where men and women angels live separately.
9. "Green Pastures" [where] children are kept.
10. Great sealed library where all strange lore of past religions is kept. Private preserve of theologian.
11. Giant priests in gold loin cloths with nude, chalked bodies who shout "He is the Saviour" & "He is Arisen" & "Love One Another"
12. Long, narrow black staircase leads up to great gold door of his quarters which are simply but richly furnished. Leopard guards at head of bed.
13. [*remaining notes are illegible*]

(ii)

Dr. Beast of Harlem
Black Saviour
Millenium in the Black Belt
Black Utopia
The Black Temple (Each Temple black and silver outside)

—Two black leopards. Chained with long chain at head of bed.
—Harlem pageant with elephants—enormous statues
—Great shining nude black statue 3 times life size on pedestal in temple. Illuminated indirectly.

326

—Milk & fruit & blood for all the sacred. Will live forever

—Okeh until goes political. Great success at first. Gets masses. Halts criticism of classes. Awes them. Finally wins adherence.

—~~Long black staircase leading to giant iron door of his quarters (use description of Becton [*illegible word*])~~

—Will conquer "world's soul"

—~~"He is arisen" chant of giant priests with nude chalked bodies. "He is the Saviour."~~[″]

—~~Robed virgins with breasts exposed.~~

—~~"Heavens" where men and women live separately~~

—~~"Green Pastures" where children are kept.~~

—~~Great sealed library~~

—Has clever, ambitious lawyer-editor who wants him to try for world domination through religion. Flatters his ego. Introduces racial angle up[on] which movement finally wrecks.

—Sister Marietta

—The Confessional—Stand nude before priest or priestess

—Combination of Garvey-Christ-Gandhi

—~~The devoted white woman~~

—The bitter Negrophile like Du Bois with visions of destroying white imperialism. General Manager

—The radical atheist artist who stages things.

—The editor-propagandist who carries on publicity. Owes his rejuvenation to "Eternal Love"

—The ex-minister, theological student, who knows all the religious lore of the ancient world, a voluptuary

—The Cherubim—the Children

—The Lambs—the Men

—The Doves—the Women

—Sacred Hearts—the Aged

—The Fugitives (from Sin)—Novitiates

—Joy Praise, Truth Delight, Sympathetic Heart, Blessed Virgin

SOURCE: George S. Schuyler Papers, file 16/1. Schomburg Center for Research in Black Culture, New York Public Library

Appendix B: "The Rise of the Black Internationale" (1938)

The three generations since Lincoln signed the Emancipation Proclamation (which a quarter million black Union soldiers rescued from oblivion as a mere scrap of paper) have been the most momentous in the history of the world. They have seen unprecedented shifts and incredible alignments. They have seen miraculous inventions fantastic in their potentialities. They have seen such cruelty, such conquests, such persecution and oppression, such exploitation as humanity never dreamed before.

More important to colored people, these 75 years have seen the steady decline in the power and prestige of people of color the world over, thanks to the improvement in European firearms, the amazing technological advance of the West and the shattering of distance and isolation by modern transportation and communication. And most important of all, these years have seen the resultant rise of the White Internationale and the gradual rise of the Black Internationale in opposition; not powerful opposition as yet, perhaps, but containing vast potentialities of which the white world is all too painfully cognizant.

So far as the colored world is concerned, one might refer to these three generations as the period of fluctuating inferiority complexes. The decline in the fortunes of the darker races was quickly reflected in the attitude of the white world toward them and the colored people's attitude toward themselves. An important factor in the racial equation, this self-opinion, for there is a human tendency to become what we *think* we are. Status largely determines hope or hopelessness. Coupled with white control of colored education through control of government and missionary schools, the colored races were put on the defensive psychologically and so remained until the World War. It is important to trace the politico-economic changes that altered the world *without* and so altered the world *within*.

In 1863 Africa with the exception of South Africa, Sierra Leone, Senegal, the Boer Republics, various stations and forts on the West Coast and the Barbary States on the fringes of the South Mediterranean was virtually unknown territory to Europeans. Europe had not yet been sufficiently prodded by circumstances or implemented by armaments to effect the conquest of Africa.

In the 7th century the dusky Moslems had conquered all northern Africa. They had planted colonies at Mombasa, Malindi and Sofala which developed into powerful commercial states. They had swept into Spain and Portugal, ruled the former for 700 years and threatened the freedom of white Europe. In 1453 the Turks had conquered Constantinople. From 1517 to 1551 they extended their rule over Egypt, Algeria, Tunisia and Tripoli, and at one time rolled up to the gates of Vienna. Beginning with the European "Age of Discovery" in the 15th Century the fortunes of the darker races began to decline, but the trend was slow until 1875. As late as the beginning of the 19th century the dusky Barbary States held tens of thousands of whites captive and flaunted their banners in the faces of Europe's navies.

While the slave trade had undermined the excellent, monarcho-communistic economy of Africa, black men still ruled it (and often profited from the traffic). Europe had first to defeat the "Infidel," to end its disastrous nationalistic wars, to down Napoleon and to start the age of steam before it could know Africa. Prior to that it was only interested in slaves and tall stories from the Dark Continent.

Interest in Africa revived with the explorations beginning in 1788. Interestingly enough this was also the age of Watt and Eli Whitney, of the Declaration of Independence and the Rights of Man. France occupied Egypt in 1793–1803 and Britain followed her. But an almost independent state was formed there under Mehemet Ali which extended its rule deep into the Sudan from 1820 onward. The first recorded crossing of Africa was accomplished between the years 1802 and 1811 by two Portuguese Negro traders, Pedro Baptista and A. Jose, who passed from Angola eastward to Zambezi. In 1814 England formally annexed Cape Colony, over 150 years after the first permanent white settlement by the Dutch on April 6, 1652.

Waterloo in Europe spelled Waterloo for Africa. But the end was still a long way off. There was still the ages old struggle between Christianity and Mohammedanism for trade rights and political supremacy disguised as Holy War and suppression of slavery. The Moslems were accused of continuing the slave trade and stripping Africa of man-power. The Christians with their developing power economy needed raw materials furnished by enslaved black workers at the source of supply. So the rush of "Christian" explorers, traders and missionaries descended upon Africa.

In 1863 Livingstone was exploring the Zambezi and Lake Nyasa, and making mulattoes the while. Speke was "solving the riddle of the Nile," Baker was "discovering" Lake Albert Nyanza, Stanley was yet to "find" Livingstone and solve the "mysteries" of Victoria Nyanza, Tanganyika and the Congo River. It was the age of Schweinfurth and du Chaillu, of stirring tales of rich and powerful black kingdoms with swarms of stalwart black warriors, of mysterious cities like Timbuktu, of strange religious rites deep in the heart of steaming jungles.

As late as 1875 Great Britain controlled but 250,000 square miles, France 170,000 square miles, Portugal 40,000 square miles, Spain 1,000 square miles and the Dutch Republics of Transvaal and Orange Free but 150,000 square miles of Africa. Turkey held sway very loosely over Egypt; the Egyptian Sudan, Tripoli and Tunis, Morocco, Abyssinia, Zanzibar and Liberia were independent. The great kingdoms of Ashanti, Dahomey, Benin, Uganda, Cazembe, Musta Yanvo and countless other Mohammedan sultanates and pagan countries still enjoyed their freedom. The Boers paid yearly tribute to the warlike Zulus and it was not until England's successful campaign against the Ethiopians in 1867–1868 that that mountain kingdom learned what to expect from the white world.

In 1869 the richest diamond fields on earth were discovered in the Vaal River valley and the Suez Canal was opened to traffic: two events that focused added attention on Africa. Two years later England completed acquisition of the Gold Coast littoral. Already France had grabbed Senegal (1854) and Obok (1862) at the entrance to the Red Sea. In 1873 England worsted the Ashantis and two years later lifted the Union Jack over Delagoa Bay. Events were happening faster than anyone imagined, and yet on the eve of the biggest land-grab in history a House of Commons committee considering West Africa affairs could recommend "that all further extension of territory or assumption of government, or new treaty offering any protection to native tribes, would be inexpedient." Thick-witted Britons!

Now economic rivalry, political necessity and rapid flow of invention were forcing the issue. The South beaten, the U.S. government forced withdrawal of France from Mexico and compelled other European powers to relinquish hopes of snatching territory in South America. Prussia defeated France in 1870 and the land-hungry German Empire was born late on the colonial scene. Italy became a nation instead of a conglomeration of Caribbean-like dukedoms and baronies and began looking for real estate abroad to add to her prestige.

Defeated France perforce switched her ambitions from Europe to Africa. The ambitions of young Germany and the grasping Leopold of Belgium set the pace for the imperialistic-minded world. These two countries had only Africa and the South Seas in which to seek exploitable territory. England, France, the Netherlands, Spain and Portugal had grabbed everything else. Leopold's 1876 conference grew into the International African Association which afterward snatched the rich Congo "Free" State, with the United States the first to recognize the robbery. In 1879 the Zulu military power was broken. The Germans called the 1884–1885 imperialistic conference for the "proper" regulation of all stolen lands in Africa, but even while the criminals were conferring German agents planted the Kaiser's emblem in Southwest Africa, Togoland, Cameroons and Southeast Africa. Alarmed by these precipitous and typically Teutonic methods, the British, French and Portuguese redoubled their efforts. By means of bullets, chicanery, gin and Christianity the white nations by 1900 had conquered or annexed all the rest of Africa and native kings who opposed them were either in exile or gathered to their fathers.

The Americas

The period from 1863 to 1876 which saw the African kingdoms drop into the European sack, also saw the emancipated Americans rise to the full promise of Appomatox, the 13th, 14th and 15th Amendments and the political power inaugurated by Reconstruction. There was hope in their breasts that the darkest era was behind them; that they were on the threshold of full citizenship rights and privileges in the Union, and destined to march arm in arm with their white fellow men to the creation of a truly great civilization.

Southward in Mexico chaos reigned. In Spanish America dictator followed dictator and black men played their part in nation-building. In Brazil and Cuba slavery still obtained. Unhappy Haiti was torn with the usual strife and tyranny. In the Orient Britain had just emerged from a serious Indian rebellion. The Malay peninsula, Indo-China and the spice islands, asleep in the azure seas, were still under their native rulers. China was still powerful, despite the aggressions of Britain, Russia and France, and lording it over Korea, Manchuria, Mongolia, Tibet, Formosa and adjacent lands. Little Japan, forced out of her voluntary isolation by Admiral Perry, was hastening to make up for lost time with the classic policy stated by one of her diplomats as "We adopt, we adapt and so we become adept."

Railroads and steamships were in their infancy. Electric lights, telephones, bicycles, automobiles, the airplane, motion pictures, vulcanizing rubber, the phonograph, the radio, television and countless other inventions and processes that have revolutionized industry and commerce and are now taken for granted were still in the future. The use of oil was confined to kerosene lamps and lubrication. Production and distribution of foodstuffs was yet to be revolutionized. Neither the repeating rifle, the machine gun or the submarine had made its appearance. The new world economy that, by a combination of purely fortuitous circumstances, was already making the white nations the world rulers of colored nations was still in its infancy and the needs of national industry could still be served by the nation.

The scramble for colonies was not only a scramble for robber prestige but also a scramble for raw materials (or war materials) necessary to meet the essential demands of the new power economy without which no nation could or can become or remain a great power. The astounding technological mutation in the West in the century preceding and the years following 1875 also firmly established the international color line which until recently was only challenged by the sturdy and canny Nipponese. Black, brown and yellow alike were maligned and jim-crowed on every side and in every place. Everywhere white people took precedence over darker people. "Science" justified the stealing, exploitation and oppression by "proving" to white satisfaction the "inferiority" of colored folk. History was rewritten in the light of the Aryan race theory. The so-called social sciences were yoked to the chariot of imperialism. The whole thing was blessed by the Church which undermined the psychology of colored peoples under the guise of teaching "morality."

American Negroes Groping

Betrayed by the Great Compromise of 1876 when Northern Republicans blessed their virtual re-enslavement in exchange for white southern recognition of the crooked Hayes election, the colored freemen progressively lost power and prestige in the face of the Ku Klux Klan persecution and public indifference. By 1900 only one Negro's voice was heard in the halls of Congress and he was soon gone. The loudly hailed rapprochement between the white South and the white North was well under way.

Nevertheless there was a tremendous store of hopefulness, optimism and naivete in colored America. All you needed was education, religion and thrift to succeed. You must pioneer and build something. Let down your bucket where you are. The Republican Party is the ship, all else the sea. The name of Lincoln made hearts leap under dusky hides and whatever white folks said was gospel.

Perhaps there was something to what they said about our having no history! Perhaps, after all, colored folks were inferior. Where, pray, was our background? What had our forefathers done except hew wood and haul water for Marse John? Mightn't it be true that we had never built a civilization? Wasn't that what our "education" taught us? Was there anything for us to be proud of—even our smooth dark skins and soft krinkly hair? Wasn't there some logic to the white contention that the lighter we were, the better we were? Didn't that put us nearer to perfection? So let's ridicule anything and everything Negro and eulogise everything white per se. Let's insist that black be comic and yellow refined but of course not as refined as no color at all! Let's make wall flowers out of our dusky-hued maidens and yell "Did you order any coal?" when a black man appeared. True, Negroes had ruled under Reconstruction, but weren't they corrupt like white folks said and too ignorant to be entrusted with responsibility of office?

Thus some of the gropings of the Aframerican mind: fearful, uncertain, ignorant and yet hopeful withal. Elsewhere in India, China, Malaya and Africa the products of mission training were similarly groping.

Then something else happened. World population, especially in Europe, was taking a tremendous spurt as forecast by Malthus. World area had not expanded an inch. Indeed, excessive and ignorant cultivation had contracted the arable surface. As competition in international trade grew, capitalism turned to more intensive exploitation of home lands and there also competition grew more fierce. Panics came, unemployment grew, talk of a workers' revolution grew. There were insufficient markets for the goods produced in an ever endless stream. Fewer markets means fewer jobs. Fewer jobs made emigration imperative. The United States became the great labor market for white alien workers. The lower middle class of the white colonial powers sent their sons to Africa and Asia as clerks, army officers and petty administrators. In America the growing emigration pushed Negroes farther and farther out to the economic fringes.

The period of 1900–1920 saw the social consequences of the politico-economic imperialism. Color discrimination and segregation grew apace as job competition intensified and imperialism became solidified. The lynching wave reached its peak. The Grandfather Clauses and the Springfield Race Riot were straws in the wind. Then the triumph of Japan over Russia in 1904 roused hope among colored people that the balance of power might again shift to their side. The Pan-African Conference in Paris in 1899, the Niagara Movement in 1904 and the organization of the National Association for the Advancement of Colored People in 1909 marked a turning point in the mentality of the Negro. Elsewhere, brown, black and yellow men were coldly appraising this enforced white ideology and inaugurating a renaissance in opinion of self.

Beginning of Revolt

The World War came. The migration of black southerners to the industrial North, the transportation of millions of brown and yellow and black workers and soldiers to the docks and battlefields of Europe gave new impetus to Negro thought; brought up new ideas of solidarity in

334

the world of color. A quarter million dusky Americans in uniform went to France to be insulted and maligned and returned to be shot down. The Wilsonian slogans stirred the hearts and minds of the oppressed Africa and Asia. Dark colonial emigres schemed and planned in the salons and cellars of London, New York, Paris, Bombay, Batavia, Singapore and Cairo. Mahatma Gandhi electrified the world with Noncooperation. White people were not united, the colored world learned, and there were flaws in the armor of imperialism. Spengler and Stoddard wrote gloomily of the decline of the West and the rising tide of color. Soviet Russia, emerging from the slime of Czarism, tossed her bloodstained cap into the international arena professing love for all the oppressed the better to win concessions from their oppressors. Race riots swept over America and occurred elsewhere. American Negroes fought back with the white man's weapons in Chicago, Washington, Longview and Tulsa. Thousands of Indians defied the British Raj and went to jail. In South Africa Clements Kadalie threw down the challenge of organized black workers to the brutal Boers. Four Pan-African Congresses under DuBois brought together many bright minds of the Negro world.

Black scholars turned to piecing together the Negro's background. Negro newspapers, once mere pamphlets, challenged the best in America and unified the thinking of their people as never before. Black magazines seriously discussed the Negro's place in the world and his relation to other colored peoples. Black lawyers thundered at the bar of white justice. Marcus Garvey stirred the imagination of the ignorant and romantic; fostered pride of color where before there had too often been shame. Dusky surgeons headed hospitals. Businesses sprang up throughout Aframerica attesting to Negroes increasing belief in themselves if nothing more. Again men of color sat in a dozen State legislatures and even returned to the halls of Congress. Black agitators spouted the jargon of socialism and communism and openly plotted the overthrow of the capitalist system.

In America, in Asia, in the islands of the sea the darker men became critical and condemnatory of white civilization where once they had been worshipful and almost grateful for shoddy castoffs. Today the colored worker strikes in Trinidad and Jamaica, in Bathurst and Cape Town, in Nigeria and the Gold Coast. He sits down in Detroit and Chicago and pickets in New York and Pittsburgh. He sees whites relinquishing extraterritoriality in China and Egypt and giving Burmah and India self-government. He sees erstwhile haughty whites cowering in the shell-holes of Shanghai, a British ambassador machine gunned on the road to Nanking and an American gunboat bombed to the bottom of the Yangtse River without reprisal from a Caucasia become panic-stricken and paralyzed.

The New Negro Arrives

The New Negro is here. Perhaps no more courageous than the Old Negro who dropped his shackles in 1863, and fought against ignorance, propaganda, lethargy and persecution, but better informed, privy to his past, understanding of the present, unafraid of the future. No longer blindly worshipful of his rulers, he yet has learned to respect and study the intelligence and accumulation of power that has put them where they are. He has less illusions about his world.

He is aware that the balance of power is shifting in the world and so are his cousins in Africa, in India, in Malaysia, the Caribbean and China. He is rightly suspicious of white labor even when it is sincere. He has seen white labor forget the Marxist divisions of proletariat and bourgeoisie and join the White Internationale with the capitalists. He has seen both the 2nd and 3rd Internationales abandon the colored peoples to the mercies of their masters in order to perpetuate the industrial system of Europe which is based on colonial slave labor. He sees Russia abandon its revolutionary role and with French and British workingmen back Deladier and Chamberlain. And, as crowning infamy, he has seen the ruthless rape of defenseless Ethiopia with the Pope applauding on the sidelines.

He knows that the fear of losing the colonial peoples and their resources is all that prevents another World War. He believes that to combat this White Internationale of oppression a Black Internationale of liberation is necessary. He sees and welcomes a community of interest of all colored peoples. No longer ignorant, terrorized or lacking confidence, he waits, and schemes and plans. He is the Damoclean sword dangling over the white world. Everywhere he is on the march, he cannot be stopped, and he knows it.

SOURCE: *Crisis*, August 1938.

Bibliography: George S. Schuyler's Pittsburgh Courier fiction, 1933–1939

Items are arranged by date of publication; bylines are in italics

"Sugar Hill: A Powerful Story of Harlem Life Today," *Samuel I. Brooks*, 12 chapters, Mar. 25, 1933–June 10, 1933
> A black doorman, working in Harlem's exclusive Sugar Hill, spurns his dark-skinned girlfriend for the lighter-complexioned mistress of an Italian gangster, whose murder is blamed on him.

"Between Bells," *Rachel Call*, Mar. 25, 1933
> Two men mustering out of the army are returning home from Hawaii on a ship. The shiftless mulatto who has blown all his money on women and partying resents his hardworking black buddy—who has sent his pay home to his sick mother and aunt—and contemplates killing him for the $400 the latter earned doing odd jobs.

"Pullman Car Episode," *Edgecombe Wright*, May 20, 1933
> A white woman riding in the coach section of a train to Des Moines envies a prosperous black lawyer who can afford a Pullman car. She tries unsuccessfully to beguile his money out of him with her color.

"Broadway Brown's Masterpiece," *Edgecombe Wright*, May 27, 1933
> Two black men plan the perfect bank heist.

"The Shoemaker Murder," *William Stockton*, June 3, 1933
> A black detective solves the baffling murder of a shoemaker.

"Remaking Minnie," *Rachel Call*, June 10, 1933
> A black coed sensitive about her color meets a man who helps her get over her complex and they become engaged.

"Devil Town: An Enthralling Story of Tropical Africa," *George S. Schuyler*, 3 chapters, June 17, 1933–July 1, 1933
> A white missionary couple ignore a witch doctor's warnings and enter mysterious "Devil Town" in Liberia's "Ganda" country. Their reception is hostile and they barely escape with their lives.

"Special Delivery," *Rachel Call*, June 17, 1933

When an old boyfriend with evil intentions re-enters a woman's life, she learns how to stay true to her husband.

"Elusive Edith," *Rachel Call,* June 24, 1933

A streetwise man uses charm and money in a futile attempt to win the classiest woman in the neighborhood.

"Woman Against Woman," *Rachel Call,* July 1, 1933

When a party-loving mulatto woman attempts to steal a wealthy man away from his darker and more sincere girlfriend, her rival fights back successfully, using intelligence against beauty and feminine wiles.

"Georgia Terror: Those Who Live by the Sword Shall Die by the Sword," *George S. Schuyler,* 12 chapters, July 8, 1933–Sept. 23, 1933

A young black pharmacist, Charlie Morgan, leads the "Merciless Avengers," a group committed to ending oppression and injustice. When a member organizing black Georgia sharecroppers is lynched, the Avengers seek vengeance and Morgan uses his drug expertise to poison lynch mob members. A Northern white artist playing amateur detective discovers that the lynched man's girlfriend is the daughter of the lynch mob leader and that she is a member of this avenging group.

"Reefers," *Rachel Call,* July 15, 1933

A family man worn down by making ends meet risks everything on a "surefire" numbers tip, only to lose everything.

"One Grand," *Rachel Call,* July 22, 1933

A man with a weakness for married women asks a friend to lend him a thousand dollars to invest in a pool hall; eventually he admits to wanting the money to seduce his friend's wife.

"Sophisticate," *Rachel Call,* July 29, 1933

A man convinced that his wife is having an affair wins her back through sophisticated attentiveness.

"Feminist," *Rachel Call,* Aug. 12, 1933

An advocate of equal rights for women changes her tune when her boyfriend actually starts treating her as an "equal."

"Depression," *Rachel Call,* Aug. 19, 1933

A young man unable to find work during the Depression suspects his beautiful wife of infidelity—despite her kindness and support—when she turns up with money.

"Perfect Murder," *Rachel Call,* Aug. 26, 1933

An idler seeking money to keep his girl tries to steal an old woman's savings, and gets involved in a murder in the process.

"Necromancy," *Rachel Call,* Sept. 2, 1933

A young man uses a rival's witchcraft beliefs to win the attention of the woman for whom they are competing.

"Chicken Dumplings," *Rachel Call,* Sept. 9, 1933

Depression conditions force a white couple to split up and let their faithful black cook go, but mutual affection and the servant's great cooking eventually bring everyone back together.

"Innocent Harlem," *Rachel Call,* Sept. 16, 1933

A woman working for a numbers runner is so taken by the power of money that she hesitates to marry her impoverished journalist boyfriend, until he saves her from her boss's advances.

"Smart Guy," *Rachel Call,* Sept. 23, 1933

A bright young man takes over his future father-in-law's family business and reverses its steady decline.

"Mississippi Mud: A Seething Story of Life on the Levee," *George S. Schuyler,* 10 chapters, Sept. 30, 1933–Dec. 2, 1933

Fordney, a white engineer, and Bill, a black handyman, both fall for Clementine, a young black woman who prefers Bill. Mabelle, a white woman, likes Fordney, but is repulsed by his attraction to Clementine. Fordney and Bill fight for the attention of Clementine and Bill wins. When Fordney organizes a white mob to seek a violent revenge, Clementine finally admits her love to Bill, with whom she elopes.

"Southern Road," *Rachel Call,* Sept. 30, 1933

An old man tells a poor young suitor that he will not permit his daughter to marry until plans for a major roadway going past his store are changed.

"Wife on Vacation," *Samuel I. Brooks,* Oct. 7, 1933

A man planning to party with a young woman while his wife is away has the tables turned when she returns early.

"Jim-Crow Car," *Samuel I. Brooks,* Oct. 14, 1933

An upper-class woman chooses between a wealthy man and a penniless man who loves her, when each reacts differently to the racism they encounter on a street car.

"Blackmail," *Rachel Call,* Oct. 21, 1933

A black maid uses her wits to save her white mistress from a blackmailing lover.

"The Family Friend," *Samuel I. Brooks,* Oct. 28, 1933

A woman helps a male friend win a divorce from his cheating wife and discovers that she loves him herself.

"Wheat Triangle," *Samuel I. Brooks,* Nov. 4, 1933

A young woman married to a wealthy sixty-year-old farmer confides her desperate loneliness to a young farmhand, who tries to seduce her. She resists, realizing that she loves her husband.

"Southern Episode," *Samuel I. Brooks,* Nov. 11, 1933

Whenever a wealthy white woman's husband is away, she takes up with her black servant—until he and his girlfriend, the black maid, use blackmail to end her unwelcome advances.

"Porter Wanted," *Samuel I. Brooks,* Nov. 18, 1933

339

When an unemployed black man applies for the lone job not advertised "white only," he finds himself thirty-eighth in line, but uses his head to get to the head of the line and win the job.

"Lucky Number: 742," *Verne Caldwell,* Nov. 25, 1933

A young woman is forbidden by her father from seeing the man she loves because he plays the numbers. She is instead encouraged to see a good Christian man—but he, too, proves to be a numbers player. Eventually, her original suitor abandons gambling, becomes a physician, and wins permission to marry her.

"Thanksgiving Dinner," *Rachel Call,* Dec. 2, 1933

When both parents cannot work, a black family is about to lose its home—until their young son steps forward to save the day.

"Kidnaped," *Rachel Call,* Dec. 9, 1933

A black nanny, kidnapped along with the child of a white banker, is rewarded for thwarting the abductors.

"Golden Gods: A Story of Love, Intrigue and Adventure in African Jungles," *George S. Schuyler,* 12 chapters, Dec. 9, 1933–Feb. 24, 1934

A dying African gives Gail Reddick, a black American man, a map to a secret city and two golden statues worth $100,000. En route to Liberia, Reddick is joined by a beautiful black missionary, with whom he bests both Africans and a German trader.

"The Sap," *Verne Caldwell,* Dec. 16, 1933

A college graduate who sells stock to black businessmen and a fifth-grade dropout who does business in unconventional ways compete for the same woman. The woman's parents favor the college graduate over the school dropout, but when the Depression hits, everyone's feelings change.

"Suburban Christmas," *Rachel Call,* Dec. 23, 1933

A black couple buy a suburban house in order to raise their children in a prejudice-free environment. They encounter an angry white mob that trashes their house, but the kindness of a few white people persuades them to stay.

"No More Liquor," *Samuel I. Brooks,* Dec. 30, 1933

A terrible hangover persuades a man never to drink again. His steadfast sobriety drives his girlfriend to another man. When she grows drunk and out of control, he reasserts his control.

"First Love," *Rachel Love,* Jan. 6, 1934

A fifteen-year-old boy comes to recognize the importance of girls when he meets an attractive sixteen-year-old.

"Homecoming," *Verne Caldwell,* Jan. 13, 1934

After getting rich in the West, a man returns to his Southern home for the girl to whom he had never revealed his love, only to find that she has gone west in search of him.

"Always Count Ten," *Rachel Call,* Jan. 27, 1934

A man convinced that his girlfriend is unfaithful determines to kill his suspected

340

rival. Before doing anything rash, he counts to ten, as he had learned as a child. During this pause, he discovers that his girlfriend has been faithful.

"Slick Hair," *Rachel Call*, Feb. 3, 1934

Carrie, a plump dark woman with "bad" black hair rejects her dark-skinned lover with equally "bad" hair in favor of the light-skinned and slick-haired "man of her dreams," whom she ends up supporting.

"Harlem Holiday," *Rachel Call*, Feb. 10, 1934

A woman convinced that her husband is cheating on her during business trips goes to Harlem to have her own affairs. When she realizes that the single men she is meeting are not as good as her husband, she returns to him.

"The Philanderer," *John Kitchen*, Feb. 17, 1934

A smooth-talking ladies' man meets his match in a good-looking woman who is new in town.

"Ten o'Clock," *Rachel Call*, Feb. 24, 1934

A woman awaiting her lover's ten o'clock call admits her infidelity when her husband does not leave as expected, because—unknown to her—the clock is fifteen minutes fast.

"The Beast of Bradhurst Avenue: A Gripping Tale of Adventure in the Heart of Harlem," *Samuel I. Brooks*, 12 chapters, Mar. 3, 1934– May 19, 1934

After the headless bodies of a princess of a cannibalistic African society and another woman are found, a detective proves that the murderer is a German scientist experimenting on transplanting the brains of black women into dogs.

"The Marriage Hater," *Rachel Call*, Mar. 10, 1934

A man who constantly complains that marriage is like jail learns from a friend that the problem is not marriage but his own inability to treat women properly.

"The Water Cure," *Rachel Call*, Mar. 24, 1934

A young woman frees herself from the spell of a heartless ladies' man—but only after he fails to try to save her from drowning.

"A Hard Job," *D. Johnson*, Mar. 31, 1934

A man about to leave his wife for a mistress discovers that his wife has already left him for another man.

"Revenge Is Not Always Sweet," *Rachel Call*, Apr. 7, 1934

A man planning revenge against a friend who has stolen his wife gives up the idea when he sees how happy they are together.

"The Lady Untouchable," *Rachel Call*, Apr. 14, 1934

A young black man fantasizes about white women but hesitates to take seriously a flirting white co-worker. Eventually, he discovers that this woman is the girlfriend of a buddy.

"A Brown Body," *Rachel Call*, Apr. 21, 1934

A young white widow is attracted to a young black boy who has moved next door. When the boy saves her son from drowning, she thanks him with a kiss and invites him to call on her.

341

"The Worm Turns," *Rachel Call,* Apr. 28, 1934

>A man who keeps his wife "in line" with verbal abuse finally suffers the wrath of her suppressed anger.

"Check Out," *Rachel Call,* May 5, 1934

>A woman deserts her husband for a singer who promises to make her a star in New York. When the man tosses her aside, she has him framed for attempted murder.

"Coincidence," *Rachel Call,* May 12, 1934

>Two white girls stood up by their boyfriends hang out in Harlem, where they have a wonderful time with two black men.

"The Cat Man of Manhattan," *George S. Schuyler,* 12 chapters, May 26, 1934–Aug. 11, 1934

>Donald Martin, leading a double life as a cat burglar, wants to go straight after he meets Esther Van Alstyne, the daughter of a wealthy black realtor. He keeps some gems from his last job, but his boss's girlfriend discovers his crime and blackmails him when he rejects her advances. He tries to escape with Esther, but police kill him.

"A New Young Man," *Rachel Call,* May 26, 1934

>A sophisticated, unfaithful Harlem woman tries to pick up a man at a party she goes to with her husband, only to discover that her pickup is her husband's old college chum.

"The Revolt of Martha," *Rachel Call,* June 9, 1934

>Martha, the sole black child in her school class, rebels against the daily abuse she receives from the other children and her teacher by telling her story to the principal, ready to suffer any consequences which may arise.

"Strange Valley," *George S. Schuyler,* 12 chapters, Aug. 18, 1934– Nov. 10, 1934

>Two white American men, the daughter of one, and a black maid crash-land in the jungles of West Africa. They are taken prisoner by Africans ruled by a black American, Dr. Cranfield, who plans to liberate Africa. When the white daughter Virginia falls in love with Cranfield's assistant, the white men try to escape and are killed. The two American women stay to join the struggle for African freedom.

"Black Mistress: A Thrilling Novel of the Strange Life of Harlem's Half World," *Samuel I. Brooks,* 12 chapters, Nov. 17, 1934–Feb. 2, 1935

>Lucy Brown is the mistress of white millionaire Charles Porter, who sets her up luxuriously. Her material possessions do not make her happy. Her position makes her unpopular in Harlem, so she throws a party to win friends and meets a charming con-man, Alfred Dancer. After Dancer tries to blackmail Lucy, Porter overcomes his own jealousy and offers to marry her.

"The Confessions of a Taxi Driver: The Drama, Romance and Tragedy in the Life of a Harlem Hacker," *anon.,* 14 chapters, Feb. 9, 1935–May 11, 1935

>A series of "true confession" stories that may have been partly inspired by Schuyler's own experiences as a taxi driver in Hawaii after he left the army. The

342

fictional cabbie plays good Samaritan when his passengers are in a jam.

"Down in the Delta: A Thrilling Story of Life and Romance Along the Mississippi," *Samuel I. Brooks*, 20 chapters, May 18, 1935–Sept. 28, 1935

Dan Hughes, a Northern black activist organizing sharecroppers in Mississippi, is opposed by Palmer Mitchell, a wealthy white planter, and Yancey Roberts, Mitchell's mulatto son. When Roberts and Mitchell kill a white store manager, Hughes bands whites together and then bands blacks together when he himself is wrongly accused of the murder and threats are made against him. Eventually, the white mob lynches Mitchell and Roberts.

"The Ethiopian Murder Mystery: A Story of Love and International Intrigue," *George S. Schuyler*, 18 chapters, Oct. 5, 1935–Feb. 1, 1936

An Ethiopian prince in his country's secret service is killed in New York, apparently on suspicion of planning to turn over secret plans of a death ray to the Italians. Roger Bates, a newspaper man, solves the case after the police arrest his love interest. He discovers that the murderers are other Ethiopian secret service men dedicated to fighting the Italians.

"A Forbidden Romance: A Story of Strange Love in Deep Dixie," *Samuel I. Brooks*, 21 chapters, Feb. 8, 1936–July 4, 1936

Home from college, Andrew Richards acts as butler for the white family for which his mother cooks. He and the family's daughter, Carol, fall in love. When he tries to drop his previous lover, she threatens to expose his secret affair. He and Carol flee to New York, where they are married before her family finds them.

"The Black Champion: A Story of Intrigue, Romance and Triumph in the Prize Ring," *George S. Schuyler*, 19 chapters, July 11, 1936–Nov. 14, 1936

Black boxing champ Bill Jackson loses a big fight with a European heavyweight, Castonie, thanks to the double dealing of his girlfriend, Erleen, and her secret lover, Tony. When the traitors are not paid off, Erleen tries to sell Bill's managers letters Bill wrote that would ruin his career. Bill falls in love with a Harlem debutante, Millie, while training for a rematch, in which he reclaims his title. The blackmail plan is exposed and Erleen and Tony go to jail, while Bill and Millie make plans to marry.

"The Black Internationale: Story of Black Genius Against the World," *Samuel I. Brooks*, 33 chapters, Nov. 21, 1936–July 3, 1937

A Harlem newspaper reporter becomes private secretary to Henry Belsidus, a brilliant and ruthless doctor who is building an international organization dedicated to retaking Africa from European colonial powers.

"Midsummer Madness: A Tale of Romance at the Seashore," *Rachel Call*, 10 chapters, July 10, 1937–Sept. 11, 1937

Irma, the bored young wife of a jealous middle-aged man, takes a lover, Roger, and gets him a job at the place where she spends the summer with her husband. Roger is upset to learn he is cuckolding his generous boss, but nevertheless continues the affair. However, when Roger rejects the attentions of a maid, she exposes the affair, forcing Irma and Roger to flee the vengeful husband.

"Black Empire: An Imaginative Story of a Great New Civilization in Modern

Africa," *Samuel I. Brooks,* 29 chapters, Oct. 2, 1937–Apr. 16, 1938
A direct sequel to "The Black Internationale." After the success-ful reconquest of Africa, Belsidus's organization builds up its military strength to resist Europe's attempt at reconquest.

"Murder! on South Parkway," *Rachel Call,* 12 chapters, Apr. 23, 1938–July 9, 1938
When a young black woman is murdered, her white lover is charged with the crime. A retired black detective believes in the man's innocence and proves that one of the woman's many former lovers killed her.

"Revolt in Ethiopia: A Tale of Black Insurrection Against Italian Imperialism," *Rachel Call,* 28 chapters, July 16, 1938–Jan. 21, 1939
A wealthy young black American on a cruise gets involved with a beautiful Ethiopian princess seeking a hidden treasure needed to finance Ethiopia's war against Italian occupation.

"The Cemetery Mystery," *Samuel I. Brooks,* 6 chapters, Jan. 28, 1939–Mar. 4, 1939
A black detective proves that a white man and his black wife were murdered to prevent their receiving an inheritance.

"Sweet Potato Lady: A Story of Harlem Today," *Rachel Call,* 16 chapters, Mar. 11, 1939–June 24, 1939
Madge Wundus leads a secret double life: she sells sweet potatoes on Harlem's streets by day and lives in the suburbs by night. She wants her daughter, Dolores, to have a "decent" life; however, Dolores has her own double life: she is both good girl and bad girl. Madge unwittingly gets financially involved with a drug peddler whom Dolores is dating and a black detective uses their involvement with the man to crack a big drug case.

"Dream Girl," *Samuel I. Brooks,* July 1, 1939
A traveling salesman returns to a town he had passed through fifteen years earli-er to look up a girl he had once loved. She turns out to be a person quite different from the one he remembered and she pretends not to remember him.

"Lucky Day," *George S. Schuyler,* July 8, 1939
A white man rapes and kills his stepdaughter and manages to throw the blame on the town's only black man. He feels lucky when a mob lynches and burns the young man, but his wife figures out that he is the murderer and shoots him.

"Bowery Basement," *Samuel I. Brooks,* July 15, 1939
Stumpy, a peg-legged black man who cooks for cruel hobos, retaliates against their abuse by absconding with all their money.

"The Man Who Ate," *Samuel I. Brooks,* July 22, 1939
A stranger in town ignores the advice of fellow blacks by eating in a "white only" restaurant.

Acknowledgments

The tasks of recovering, transcribing, editing, and researching the serialized texts that make up *Black Empire* have involved many hands over the past two years. Indeed, publication of this edition would have been nearly impossible without the resources and expertise provided by a historical documentary editing project such as the Marcus Garvey Papers. We must therefore first acknowledge the Garvey Papers Project itself, which has received generous support from the National Endowment for the Humanities, the National Historical Publications and Records Commission, and the UCLA Foundation.

Creation of this edition of George S. Schuyler's long-forgotten story began with a vague tip that a Jamaican informant supplied to Robert Hill during his research into the Rastafari movement. This particular phase of Jamaican field research was made possible by a grant from the Ford Foundation–funded Afro-American Studies Program for Interdisciplinary Research (ASPIR) through the UCLA Center for Afro-American Studies, whose extremely generous support is hereby acknowledged. Starting with little more than a rumor that a novel that *might* relate to Marcus Garvey had been serialized in the *Pittsburgh Courier* around the mid-1930s, David Ralston, an undergraduate research assistant, tracked down "The Black Internationale" on a microfilm copy of the newspaper.

Nick Batsdorf did an excellent job of transcribing what in many places was a nearly illegible text. Later, LaDonna Perry of Chicago, at UCLA on an internship with the Summer Research Program for Minority Undergraduate Students, discovered the sequel, "Black Empire," making possible reconstruction of the entire *Black Empire* saga. Her research also opened our eyes to the vast quantity of serial fiction written by "Samuel I. Brooks" and "others" in the newspaper.

Professor Nickieann Fleener, of the University of Utah's Department of Communication, confirmed our growing suspicion that George S. Schuyler was the pseudonymous Brooks. She guided us into Schuyler's journalism of the period, sharing her own discovery that Schuyler used many pen names to write fiction for the *Courier* during the 1930s. She also alerted us to the important collections of Schuyler papers at Syracuse University Library and the Schomburg Center for Research in Black Culture, in New York, as well as the P. L. Prattis Papers at the Moorland-Spingarn Research Center, at Howard University, Washington, D.C. Leila Monaghan, a UCLA graduate student, cheerfully traveled to all three collections and gathered an extraordinary amount of original Schuyler material to add to the Garvey Project's research files.

Supported by an ASPIR grant through UCLA's Center for Afro-American Studies, Adenike Davidson read all of Schuyler's *Courier* fiction and compiled the annotated bibliography. Erika Blum, the project's graduate research assistant, helped with the increasingly extensive bibliographical research and, with Adenike, examined several literary texts that we learned had influenced Schuyler. Tim Seymour of UCLA's Institute of Archaeology realized Schuyler's vision of empire in the excellent map.

Sushma Raman, production assistant with the Marcus Garvey Papers Project, transcribed most of the ''Black Empire'' newspaper serial. In addition, she typeset the entire manuscript of the book, using page composition software donated by Interleaf, Inc., on a workstation donated by Sun Microsystems, Inc. She brought to this task not only impressive computer skills, but also an unusual degree of tolerance for working with the demands of editorial colleagues, complex computer software, and, inevitably, the stresses of book production deadlines. A major share of the credit for successful completion and production of this book is owed to her dedicated efforts, for which we here record our deep appreciation.

A very special debt is owed to our newest editorial colleague, Tevvy Ball. In addition to carefully proofreading the entire text, he lent his exceptional writing skills to enhancing the historical afterword, to which he also contributed the illuminating discussion of doppelgänger theory as applied to the two main characters of the story.

For their research assistance, we must thank the staffs of the Research Library of the University of California at Los Angeles, Fisk University Library Special Collections, Schomburg Center for Research into Black Culture of the New York Public Library, Moorland-Spingarn Research Center of Howard University, and George Arents Research Library for Special Collections of Syracuse University Library.

346

We feel very fortunate to have as our UCLA colleague Professor Richard Yarborough, the general editor of the Northeastern Library of Black Literature. His enthusiasm for publishing *Black Empire* encouraged us to continue our efforts. Furthermore, the Afterword benefited greatly from his close and critical reading; especially valuable was his explication of the literary tradition underpinning the theme of the black liberator in black fiction.

William Frohlich, the director of Northeastern University Press, and Ann Twombly, the press's production director—who designed and copyedited the book—both invested a great deal of thought and effort in the project. We wish to express our deep appreciation for their support throughout and to Northeastern University Press for giving us the opportunity to bring this work to fruition.

Finally, we owe a special debt of gratitude to Mrs. Carolyn Mitchell, literary executrix of George S. Schuyler, for her cooperation and for generously granting permission to republish this important work of imaginative fiction, which, after a hiatus of more than fifty years, is now once again made available.

The Type

The text of this book was set in the Adobe Type Library version of Meri
dien typeface. The book was typeset by Sushma Raman of the Marcu
Garvey and UNIA Papers Project, UCLA, and Inprint Publishing Corp.
Hudson, Mass. The page composition software used was Interleaf TP
4.0, donated to the Garvey Papers Project by Interleaf, Inc., Cambridge
Mass., running on a Sun workstation donated to the project by Su
Microsystems, Inc., Mountain View, Calif.